Business BASICS

A study guide for degree students

ECONOMICS

First edition May 1995
Second edition June 1997

ISBN 0 7517 21204

British Library Cataloguing-in Publication Data

A catalogue record for this book
is available from the British Library

Published by
BPP Publishing Limited
Aldine House, Aldine Place
London W12 8AW

Printed and bound by Progressive Printing (U.K.) Limited, Leigh-on-Sea, Essex.

BPP would like to thank the following:
David Whigham for authorial input and
Genesys Editorial for editorial and
production input.

CONTENTS

PREFACE

BUSINESS BASICS are targeted specifically at the needs of:

- students taking business studies degrees;
- students taking business-related modules of other degrees;
- students on courses at a comparable level;
- others requiring business information at this level.

This *Economics* text has been written with two key goals in mind.

- To present a substantial and useful body of knowledge on economics at degree level. This is not just a set of revision notes – it explains the subject in detail and does not assume prior knowledge.
- To make learning and revision as easy as possible. Each chapter:
  - starts with an introduction and clear objectives;
  - contains numerous activities;
  - includes a chapter roundup summarising the points made;
  - ends with a quick quiz

  and at the back of the book you will find:
  - multiple choice questions and solutions;
  - exam style questions and solutions.

The philosophy of the series is thus to combine techniques which actively promote learning with a no-nonsense, systematic approach to the necessary factual content of the course.

BPP Publishing have for many years been the leading providers of targeted texts for students of professional qualifications. We know that our customers need to study effectively in order to pass their exams, and that they cannot afford to waste time. They expect clear, concise and highly-focused study material. As university and college education becomes more market driven, students rightly demand the same high standards of efficiency in their learning material. The BUSINESS BASICS series meets those demands.

BPP Publishing
June 1997

Titles in this series:

Accounting
Law
Information Technology
Economics
Marketing
Human Resource Management
Quantitative Methods
Organisational Behaviour

You may order other titles in the series using the form at the end of this book. If you would like to send in your comments on this book, please turn to the review form following the order form.

HOW TO USE THIS STUDY GUIDE

This book can simply be read straight through from beginning to end, but you will get far more out of it if you keep a pen and paper to hand. The most effective form of learning is *active learning*, and we have therefore filled the text with exercises for you to try as you go along. We have also provided objectives, a chapter roundup and a quick quiz for each chapter. Here is a suggested approach to enable you to get the most out of this book.

(a) Select a chapter to study, and read the Signpost and objectives in the box at the start of the chapter.

(b) Next read the chapter roundup at the end of the chapter (before the quick quiz and the solutions to exercises). Do not expect this brief summary to mean too much at this stage, but see whether you can relate some of the points made in it to some of the objectives.

(c) Next read the chapter itself. Do attempt each exercise as you come to it. You will derive the greatest benefit from the exercises if you write down your solutions before checking them against the solutions at the end of the chapter.

(d) As you read, make use of the 'notes' column to add your own comments, references to other material and so on. Do try to formulate your own views. In economics, many things are matters of interpretation and there is often scope for alternative views. The more you engage in a dialogue with the book, the more you will get out of your study.

(e) When you reach the end of the chapter, read the chapter roundup again. Then go back to the objectives at the start of the chapter, and ask yourself whether you have achieved them.

(f) Finally, consolidate your knowlege by writing down your answers to the quick quiz. You can check your answers by going back to the text. The very act of going back and searching the text for relevant details will further improve your grasp of the subject.

(g) You can then try the multiple choice questions at the end of the book and the exam style questions to which you are referred at the end of the chapter. Alternatively, you could wait to do these until you have started your revision – it's up to you.

Further reading

While we are confident that the BUSINESS BASICS books offer excellent range and depth of subject coverage, we are aware that you will be encouraged to follow up particular points in books other than your main textbook, in order to get alternative points of view and more detail on key topics. We recommend the following books as a starting point for your further reading on *Economics*.

J Sloman, *Economics*, Third edition 1997, Harvester Wheatsheaf

D Begg, S Fisher and R Dornbusch, *Economics*, fourth edition, 1994, McGraw-Hill

J Beardshaw, *Economics – a student's guide*, third edition 1992, Pitman

A Griffiths and S Walls (eds), *Applied economics*, seventh edition 1997, Longman

P Hardwick, B Khan and J Langmead, *An Introduction to Modern Economics*, fifth edtion, forthcoming, Longman

K Heather, *Understanding Economics*, second edition, 1997, Prentice Hall

M Hirschey, J Pappas and D Whigham, *Managerial Economics*, European edition, 1995, Dryden Press

M Parkin, M Powell and K Matthews, *Economics*, third edition, 1997, Addison Wesley

Chapter 1

THE NATURE AND SCOPE OF ECONOMICS

Introduction

Economists use many special terms, and it is important to be clear about their meaning. As well as introducing some of these special terms and defining them, in this chapter we discuss the basic problems of human society with which economics is concerned.

Your objectives

After completing this chapter you should be aware of:

(a) the problems which the social science of economics attempts to address;

(b) the basic tools of economic analysis;

(c) the alternative systems which have been devised to tackle economic problems;

(d) the assumptions about consumer behaviour which shape the solutions to economic problems.

1 THE SCOPE OF ECONOMICS

A social science deals with some aspect or aspects of human society. Economics is a social science, concerned with the allocation of scarce resources to provide goods and services that meet the needs and wants of consumers.

1.1 Rationality

One of the important assumptions in economics, and one on which much economic theory is based, is the rationality of human behaviour. In order to make predictions about their economic behaviour, economists assume that human behaviour is rational and that consumers and producers act rationally. For example, producers and consumers will make reasoned decisions about how much to produce or buy at any given price.

1.2 The optimum

The assumption of the rationality of human behaviour, and that people will take decisions and actions which are directed towards a rational objective, leads us to the concept in economics of *the optimum*.

Definition

The *optimum* means the best possible given the constraints which apply. The following are underlying assumptions in much economic analysis.

(a) Producers will seek to maximise their profits and returns.
(b) Consumers will seek to maximise the benefits they obtain (their 'utility') from using the income at their disposal.
(c) Governments will seek to maximise the well-being of their population (for example, by maximising the national income per head of the population).

Activity 1

These underlying assumptions of economics may have struck you as far from self-evident. For example, economists must reckon with consumers who spend large amounts of their income on cigarettes (or even addictive drugs) in full knowledge of the health risks. Is this rational? Or what about people who donate part of their income to charity – in what sense are they seeking to maximise their utility?

1.3 Positive and normative economics

You might already have strong personal views about what sort of economic society we should have, eg whether a free market capitalist economy is desirable, or whether a centrally planned command economy is preferable. In the study of economics, it is easy for us to be influenced in our views by our ideas of what ought to be.

Economists also have views on these subjects, and some economic writing is aimed at influencing decision-makers by prescribing actions which, in the opinion of the author, will lead to ends which he or she considers desirable. Other economic research, however, is directed purely to finding out what the consequences will be if certain actions are taken, without expressing any view on the desirability of those consequences. These two different approaches are referred to as *normative economics* and *positive economics*.

(a) *Normative economics* is concerned with the expression of value judgements by economists, of what they would like to happen – eg what sort of economic society they would like to see in operation.

(b) *Positive economics* is concerned with objective statements about what does happen or what will happen. A positive approach is more objective and more scientific, and is the approach we shall try to take in this study of economics.

1.4 Microeconomics and macroeconomics

The study of economics is divided into two halves, microeconomics and macroeconomics.

'Micro' comes from the Greek word meaning small.

Definition

Microeconomics is the study of individual economic units or particular parts of the economy – eg how does an individual household decide to spend its income? How does an individual firm decide what volume of output to produce or what products to make? How is the price of an individual product determined? How are wage levels determined in a particular industry?

'Macro' comes from the Greek word meaning large.

Definition

Macroeconomics is the study of global or collective decisions by individual households or producers. It looks at a national or international economy as a whole – eg total output, income and expenditure, unemployment, inflation, interest rates and the balance of international trade etc, and what economic policies a government can pursue to influence the condition of the national economy.

1.5 The fundamental problem of economics

A fundamental concept in economics is the scarcity of resources. There are not enough resources to meet the needs of consumers and producers.

(a) In the case of consumers, the scarcity of goods and services might seem obvious enough. Everyone would like to have more – another car, a bigger home, more domestic goods, better food and drink, more holidays, more trips to the cinema or theatre, a boat, a private plane, membership of more clubs and societies, more clothes and so on. There simply is not enough to go round to satisfy the potential demand.

(b) In the case of producers, there are four scarce resources:
   (i) natural resources, referred to collectively as 'land';
   (ii) labour;
   (iii) capital – eg equipment and tools;
   (iv) enterprise or entrepreneurship.

Scarce resources mean that producers cannot make unlimited quantities of goods and services.

Since resources for production are scarce and there are not enough goods and services to satisfy the total potential demand, choices must be made. *Choice is only necessary because resources are scarce.*

(a) Consumers must choose what goods and services they will have.

(b) Producers must choose how to use their available resources, what goods and services to produce and in what quantities.

The fundamental problem of economics is the allocation of these scarce resources. What will be produced? What will be consumed? And who will benefit from the consumption?

2 THE TOOLS OF ECONOMIC ANALYSIS

In going about their work economists have to deal with a number of *variables*. To the economist, a variable is anything that influences the basic decisions which are the subject of his science: what will be produced, what will be consumed and who will benefit from the consumption? Economic variables therefore include, among many others:

(a) prices of commodities and of services;

(b) quantities of production resources available;

(c) numbers of skilled and unskilled workers;

(d) consumer attitudes (since these can affect decisions about spending and saving).

To assist them in their analysis of variables, economists need to accumulate *data* about them: price levels, stock counts, employment statistics, consumer surveys and so on.

Often it will be convenient to represent the variables under discussion by means of a model. At its simplest, this process may mean no more than drawing a graph, and indeed you will find that the use of graphs is a very common technique in economics.

But economists also use much more complex models than this. Later in this book, for example, we develop a model that attempts to show the way in which income circulates among the households and firms in an economy.

One point which may already have struck you is that no matter how complex the model becomes, no matter how many variables the economist tries to put in, the end result will never be more than an approximation of the real world. This is true even of the complicated computerised models used by government economists in their attempts to predict economic trends. The complexity of a real-life economy is simply too great to be simulated in a model.

Despite this, economic models (even the simplest graphs and equations) are of great value. The very complexity of a real economy is a barrier to understanding. By using models, economists are able to isolate the variables that appear relevant to any particular problem from the great mass of raw economic activity. Models enable the economist to understand and analyse a situation and, eventually, to make predictions about future economic events.

2.1 The production possibility curve

We will begin our examination of the fundamental problem of economics by using a very simple model: that of a society which can spend its money on two products, guns and butter. The society's resources are limited: therefore there are restrictions on the amount of guns and butter that can be made, which can be shown by a *production possibility curve* or *transformation curve*.

NOTES

Definition

A *production possibility curve* shows the limits of the quantities of two commodities, or groups of commodities, which may be produced given limited resources.

The curve from G_1 round to B_1 in Figure 1 shows the various combinations of guns and butter that a society can make, if it uses its limited resources efficiently.

(a) The firm can choose to make up to:

   (i) G_1 units of guns and no butter;

   (ii) B_1 units of butter and no guns;

   (iii) G_2 units of guns and B_2 of butter (point P on the curve);

   (iv) G_2 units of guns and B_3 of butter (point Q on the curve).

   Points P and Q on the curve are chosen at random. Any other point on the curve would indicate production of another possible combination of guns and butter.

(b) The combination of G_a units of guns and B_a units of butter plotted at point X is within the production possibility curve. More than these quantities can be made of either or both guns and butter. Point X is therefore an inefficient production point for the economy, and if the society were to make only G_a of guns and B_a of butter, it would be under-utilising its resources.

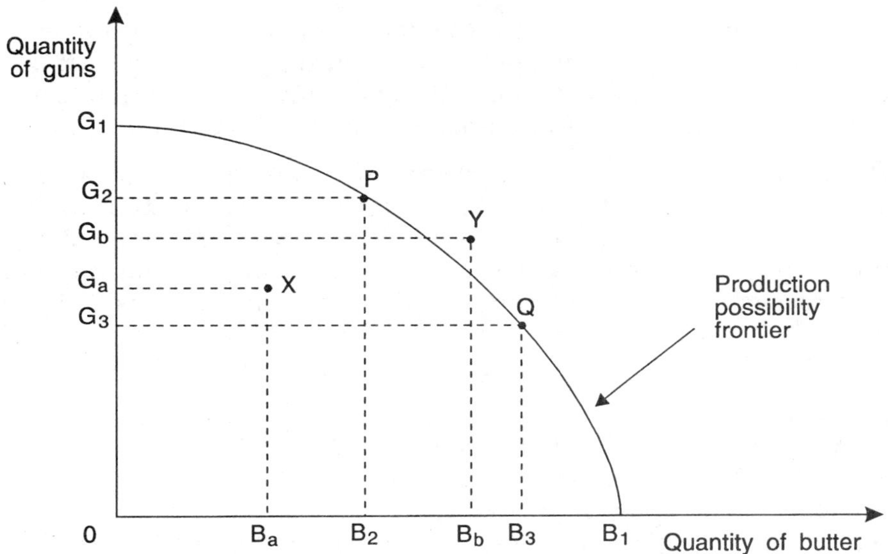

Figure 1 Production possibility curve

The production possibility curve illustrates the need to make a choice about what to produce (or buy) when it is not possible to have everything – ie when there is scarcity. Although we have characterised the products of our hypothetical economy as guns and butter, we can generalise the production possibility curve to show the production possibilities for different types of good, as for 'good X' on one axis and 'all other goods' on the other axis.

Activity 2

What can you say about the combination of guns and butter indicated by point Y in Figure 1?

2.2 Opportunity cost

Choice involves sacrifice. If there is a choice between having guns and having butter, and a country chooses to have guns, it will be giving up butter to have the guns. The cost of having guns can therefore be regarded as the sacrifice of not being able to have butter.

There is a sacrifice involved in the choices of consumers and producers, as well as the choices of governments.

Suppose a consumer has a limited amount of money and chooses to buy some eggs. One measurement of the cost of the eggs is their money price. Another way of looking at the cost is to consider the sacrifice involved in choosing eggs rather than, say, milk. If the consumer has some eggs, he or she is giving up the opportunity to have some milk, and the benefits that the milk would have provided.

Definition

The cost of an item measured in terms of the alternatives done without is called its opportunity cost. The *opportunity cost* of buying six eggs can be measured as the two pints of milk or the one bus ride that could have been bought instead. Similarly, the opportunity cost of a country having a nuclear missile could be measured in terms of the number of schools that could have been built and staffed with the same amount of resources.

Opportunity cost is an important economic concept. A production possibility diagram illustrates opportunity costs. For example, if in Figure 1 it is decided to switch from making G_3 units of guns and B_3 units of butter (point Q) to making G_2 units of guns and B_2 units of butter (point P) the opportunity cost of making $(G_2 - G_3)$ more units of guns would be the lost production of $(B_3 - B_2)$ units of butter.

At the level of the firm, the production possibility curve can be seen as showing the maximum output of different alternative goods which the firm can produce when all of its resources are fully used – for example, a firm might operate production lines capable of producing washing machines *or* refrigerators. Producing more washing machines bears the opportunity cost of a lower level of production of refrigerators.

2.3 Shifts in the production possibility curve

When the availability of resources changes, or there is a development in technology, the production possibility curve may shift. Changes are made possible by developments such as a bigger labour force, more efficient methods of working, more efficient machinery, or a new discovery of natural resources, such as oil, natural gas or minerals.

(a) If the production possibility curve moves outwards, to the right, it means that the economy is capable of producing more goods and services in total than it could before, and there is *economic growth*.

(b) If it moves to the left (inwards) it means that the economy cannot produce as much as before (eg because of a significant decline in population or the exhaustion of a natural resource).

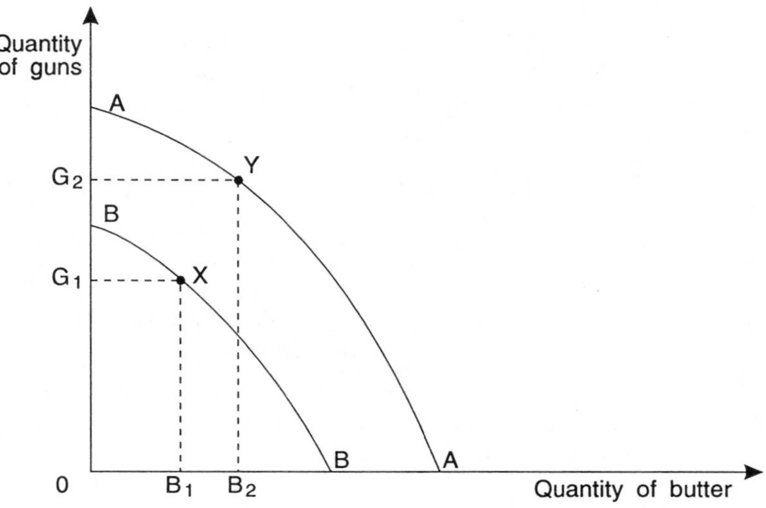

Figure 2

In Figure 2, curve AA represents greater production possibilities than curve BB. If a society's production possibility curve shifts out from BB to AA, there is economic growth. The society could now switch from making G_1 of guns and B_1 of butter (point X) to making G_2 of guns and B_2 of butter (point Y).

2.4 Exchange value

When a resource is scarce (that is, when less of it is available than is needed to satisfy the wants and needs of producers and consumers), it has an economic value or an exchange value. Producers will give something in exchange for the natural resources, labour and equipment that they need to help them to produce goods and services. Consumers will give something in exchange for the goods and services that they can obtain.

In an advanced economy, value is measured in money terms – eg the price of goods, wage levels and the cost of raw materials. But similar principles apply in a primitive barter economy. (A barter economy is one in which goods are traded for other goods, without the use of an exchange medium such as money.) For example, if a potato grower were to ask someone to help him to dig up the potatoes he had grown, he might offer some of the potatoes to the helper in exchange for the labour the helper puts in.

For resources to have an exchange value, it is assumed that exchange can take place. In a market economy, this is what does happen.

(a) Resources are owned, sometimes by society as a whole, and often by individuals, or groups, or organisations. Individuals, for example, own their own labour. Property owners own land and the minerals in it.

(b) Owners of resources will give some of their resources in exchange for others. Individuals, for example, will give their labour in exchange for a wage. In a barter economy, a farmer might give up some land in exchange for some horses or cows.

(c) In an advanced market economy, an important medium of exchange is notes and coin.

2.5 The division of labour

Significant features of all modern economies are *specialisation* and the *division of labour*, both of which increase the need for exchange.

(a) *Specialisation* of labour occurs where a worker makes just one type of product or provides one type of service – eg a farmer, a doctor, an accountant, a butcher, an entertainer, and so on. Individuals are not self-sufficient and do not themselves make all the products and services they require for their personal wants. Instead, individuals specialise in making a particular good or service.

(b) The *division of labour* refers to specialisation within a single industry. The manufacture of one product sometimes calls for the work to be divided up into 'sub-specialities'; for example, in the making of motor cars, there are car body builders, paint sprayers and engine tuners.

The existence of specialisation and division of labour necessitates *exchange* in a modern market economy, because specialists are not self-sufficient; they must exchange what they produce in return for other goods and services they need. In practice, most workers sell their labour to a firm (or to the government) in exchange for money wages. *Money* is the medium of exchange which permits them to buy other goods and services.

Specialisation applies to land, capital and entrepreneurship, as well as to labour. (You may already have a feeling for the meaning of these terms, but their exact meaning in the context of economics is explained later in the chapter on factor markets and factor rewards.) Specialised machinery is a common feature of production; some entrepreneurs specialise in a certain type of industry or market, and land can have a specialised use.

Activity 3

Why do you think that specialisation of labour has become so much a part of modern economies? What benefits does it bring?

3 ALTERNATIVE ECONOMIC SYSTEMS

3.1 Means of allocating resources

Scarcity of resources means that choices must be made about how the resources will be allocated. There are three basic resource allocation decisions.

(a) *What goods and services should be produced?* This will depend on what consumers want to buy, and what they will pay for each product or service. The decisions about what will be produced relate to demand and supply.

   (i) Demand means the demand from customers or consumers, and satisfied demand is actual consumption.

   (ii) Supply of goods and services is referred to as *production*.

(b) *How will these goods and services be produced?* The producers or suppliers of goods and services might be small companies, large companies, monopolies, state-owned enterprises or the government itself.

   The choice about who will produce the goods and services, and what mix of resources the producers will use, will depend on the costs of resources and the efficiencies of resource utilisation.

(c) *To whom will the goods and services be distributed?* Some goods and services are provided free by the state (eg in the UK, some health care and education) but others have to be paid for. The distribution of goods and services will therefore depend on the distribution of income and wealth in society. This in turn will depend on what individuals and organisations earn, and the theory of distribution in economics is concerned with what rewards are earned by the owners of scarce economic resources: land, labour, capital and entrepreneurship.

The way in which these resource decisions are resolved depends on the type of economy we are dealing with. In this context, a number of terms are explained briefly below and will be developed more fully in later chapters.

(a) In a *free market economy*, the decisions and choices about resource allocation are left to market forces of supply and demand, and the workings of the price mechanism. In other words, what producers will make and what consumers will buy are kept in balance by the price that producers will want for their output and the price that consumers are willing to pay.

(b) In a *centrally planned economy* or *command economy*, the decisions and choices about resource allocation are made by the government. Money values are attached to resources and to goods and services, but it is the government that decides what resources should be used, how much should be paid for them, what goods should be made and what their price should be.

(c) In a *mixed economy* the decisions and choices are made partly by free market forces of supply and demand, and partly by government decisions. All national economies are mixed economies, although with differing proportions of free market and centrally planned decision-making from one country to the next.

Activity 4

The failure of command economies in the former Soviet Union and in Eastern Europe has led to well-publicised criticisms of such systems. Jot down what you think are the main disadvantages of a command economy. Try to think also about what the advantages might be.

4 CONSUMER BEHAVIOUR

In this section we look at how consumers make economic choices, so that we can then go on to examine how those choices interact in economic markets.

A key concept in the study of consumer behaviour is *utility*. Utility is the word used to describe the pleasure or satisfaction or benefit derived by a person from the consumption of goods. *Total utility* is then the total satisfaction that a person derives from spending his or her income and consuming goods.

Definition

Marginal utility is the satisfaction gained from consuming one additional unit of a good or the satisfaction forgone by consuming one unit less.

If someone eats six apples and then eats a seventh, total utility refers to the satisfaction she or he derives from all seven apples together, while marginal utility refers to the additional satisfaction from eating the seventh apple, having already eaten six.

Activity 5

Suppose that we are trying to establish the satisfaction that a person gets from a long holiday. Satisfaction is not easy to measure, and so we will assume that an individual is asked to give a total points score out of 100 to show how well the holiday to date matches up to the perfect holiday. The individual is asked to give a total score to date

NOTES

after every day of the holiday and provides the following schedule.

Day (= Total utility)	Total satisfaction score
1	19
2	33
3	45
4	55
5	64
6	72
7	78
8	81
9	82

Calculate the marginal utility derived from each day of the holiday. What do you notice about the pattern of marginal utility?

4.1 Assumptions about rationality

We need to make some additional assumptions about the rational behaviour of the consumer, which was discussed earlier:

(a) Generally the consumer prefers more goods to fewer.

(b) Generally the consumer is willing to substitute one good for another provided its price is right.

(c) Choices are transitive. This means that if at a given time a commodity bundle A is preferred to bundle B, and bundle B is preferred to bundle C, we can conclude that commodity bundle A is preferred to commodity bundle C.

Acting rationally means that the consumer attempts to maximise the total utility attainable with a limited income. When consumers consider whether any unit of a good is worth buying they are deciding whether the marginal utility of buying another unit of the good exceeds the marginal utility that would be yielded by any alternative use of the same amount of money.

If people have maximised their total utility, it follows that they have allocated their expenditure in such a way that the utility gained from spending the last penny on each of the commodities will be equal. This means consumers will spend their income in such a way that they get the same marginal utility from the last penny spent on each commodity.

4.2 Diminishing marginal utility

As a person consumes more of a commodity, the total satisfaction gained will continue to increase, but the marginal utility derived from increasing consumption will fall with each additional unit consumed. The earlier example of an individual on holiday provides an illustration of this. The total satisfaction gained will increase as the holiday gets longer. The individual is unlikely, however, to derive as much utility from the second day as from the first, or the third as much as the second, and so on.

The *law of diminishing marginal utility* states that, all other things being equal, the additional satisfaction derived from consuming additional units of a commodity will diminish with each successive unit consumed. Total utility will continue to rise as each successive unit is consumed, but at a decreasing pace.

NOTES

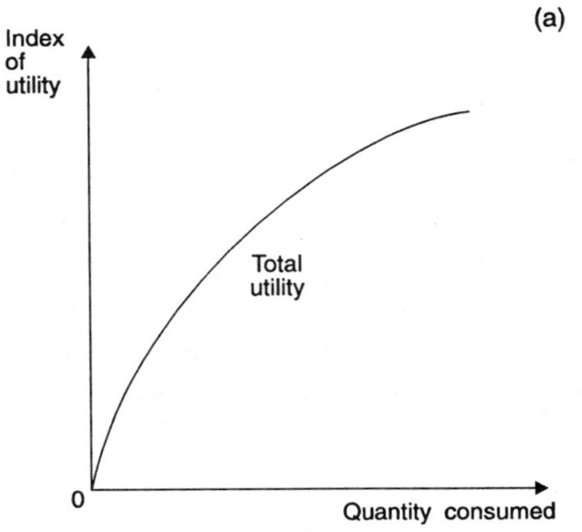

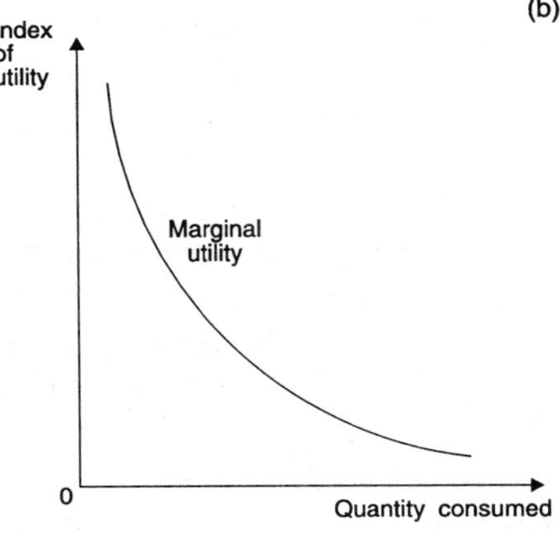

Figure 3

The law applies only if the assumptions of fixed household income and fixed tastes or fashion are valid. If either changes, the law will not apply temporarily until a stable situation is re-established.

(a) *Income:* if income changes, the utility a consumer obtains from a commodity will be affected by the changing consumption of other commodities. For instance, someone may drink instant coffee and switch to buying fresh-ground coffee.

(b) *Tastes:* a change in tastes, fashion or attitudes may occur as more of a commodity is consumed and marginal utility may increase where such a change is taking place. For example, a person may progress from an occasional buyer of pictures into an obsessive art collector.

4.3 Consumer equilibrium, marginal utilities and relative prices

We stated earlier that a consumer will maximise his total utility, with a given income and tastes, at a level of consumption where the marginal utility from the last penny spent is the same for each commodity bought.

The law of diminishing marginal utility implies that when this position has been reached, a person cannot increase his or her total utility. By switching expenditure from one commodity to another, the marginal utility gained from the new purchases will be less than the marginal utility lost by forgoing the other purchases that he or she can no longer afford.

This proposition can be developed into an algebraic formula. Suppose that a household buys two commodities, X and Y.

Let the marginal utility of a unit of X be MU_x

and the marginal utility of a unit of Y be MU_y

Let the price per unit of X (in pence) be P_x

and the price per unit of Y be P_y

The household will attain a utility-maximising equilibrium where the marginal utility from the last penny spent is the same for X and Y, ie where

$$\frac{MU_x}{P_x} = \frac{MU_y}{P_y} \qquad \text{........... (1)}$$

Cross multiplying gives: $$\frac{MU_x}{MU_y} = \frac{P_x}{P_y} \qquad \text{............ (2)}$$

This is true for any pair of commodities bought by the household.

4.4 The law of equi-marginal returns

In order to maximise their total utility, people will distribute their expenditure in such a way that the ratio of marginal utilities for all the goods they consume (MU_x: MU_y: MU_z etc) is equal to the relative price of the goods (ie the ratio of prices P_x: P_y: P_z).

Definition

The law of *equi-marginal returns* is a statement of the principle that a utility-maximising household will allocate its expenditure so that the marginal utility of that last penny spent on each good is equal for each good that it buys.

This is how the household decides what quantities of each good it would want to buy, given the existing prices of all goods.

We can use the concept of equi-marginal returns and the equilibrium relationship expressed in equation (2) above to predict what will happen to consumer spending patterns when there is a change in the price of a commodity.

4.5 Price rises and changes in income

In speaking of a price rise, we mean a rise in the *real price,* as distinct from the *money price* or *nominal price* of a commodity. If all prices rise in the same proportion because of inflation, there would be a rise in the nominal prices, but real prices would remain the same because *relative* values would be unaltered. If the price of a good has risen more than those of other goods and incomes generally, then a real price rise has occurred.

We saw above that the household is in equilibrium when the ratio of marginal utilities of commodities is equal to the ratio of their prices. We can therefore predict that if the price of a commodity rises, the marginal utility of the commodity per penny spent will fall, ie if the price of a commodity X rises while the price of Y remains the same, MU_x/P_x will fall. Therefore $MU_x/P_x < MU_y/P_y$, and so $MU_x/MU_y < P_x/P_y$ (note: < means 'is less than'). The price rise alters the consumer's equilibrium.

Activity 6

Follow the logic of this theory through to its conclusion by analysing what the consumer would now do in order to restore equilibrium.

This analysis leads to a basic prediction of demand theory, which we shall be examining in the next chapter.

(a) If the price of a commodity rises (with income, tastes and all other prices constant), demand by each household for that commodity will fall.

(b) If the price of a commodity falls (with income, tastes and all other prices constant), demand by each household for that commodity will rise.

Chapter roundup

- Economics is a social science concerned with how resources are allocated and how choices are made about resources. Economic decisions are about what gets produced, what gets consumed and who gets what.
- The need to make economic decisions, about what to produce or what to buy, arises because economic resources are scarce. Making decisions involves the sacrifice of benefits that could have been obtained from using resources in an alternative course of action: these sacrificed benefits are called opportunity costs. In economics, costs of production are measured as opportunity costs.
- The relative influence of different types of decision-maker varies according to circumstances in the market and the economic structure of society (ie free market economy, centrally planned economy, mixed economy).
- In a risk-free environment, rational decision-makers are assumed to maximise utility, subject to constraints imposed by their limited income and market prices.
- Marginal utility declines as consumers obtain more and more of a product. A consumer's utility-maximising bundle of purchases made with his or her available income, is where the quantities of each product or service bought are such that the relative marginal utility from the last unit of each is the same as their relative prices.

Quick quiz

1. Why is economic choice necessary?
2. Give examples of how the concept of opportunity cost is relevant to:

   (a) an individual;

   (b) a government;

   (c) a firm.
3. What is division of labour?
4. Contrast the principal features of a command economy and a free market economy.
5. What is the law of diminishing marginal utility?
6. Why is the law of equi-marginal returns important in the analysis of consumer expenditure?

Answers to Activities

1 Economists do indeed reckon with the behaviour of consumers who buy products dangerous to their health. Such behaviour is perfectly rational in the economic sense – the consumers enjoy the products and want to buy more of them. Whether their behaviour is sensible is another question, which goes beyond the scope of purely economic analysis.

The donation to charity is more debatable. Perhaps such an action is not really explicable in economic terms, although the economic concept of utility does recognise that there is more to individual behaviour than merely wanting more and more products in ever increasing quantities. Utility theory is examined in more detail later in this chapter.

2 Point Y lies outside the production possibility curve. Even with efficient use of resources it is impossible to produce this combination of guns and butter. To reach point Y either current resources must be increased or production methods must be improved – perhaps by developments in technology.

3 The main reason is that specialisation of labour leads to greater production efficiency. Workers engaged in just one part of the production process will be able to develop expert skills, and will work more quickly to produce output of higher quality. You might also be aware of the criticisms levelled at specialisation – that it leads to boredom and frustration for the workers involved, and that workers' ignorance of how their own contribution fits into the overall scheme can lead to inefficiencies – but that takes us beyond the point under consideration.

4 There are many disadvantages you might have identified. Some possibilities are given below.

(a) The price of goods is controlled by the state rather than by market forces. This makes it almost impossible to judge the real wants of households. What gets produced might therefore not be what households want.

(b) Planning usually involves large bureaucracies, which are costly and wasteful of labour resources.

(c) The co-ordination and management of large-scale economic plans are difficult in practice because of the enormous scope of the undertaking. Think of the management problems experienced in a large corporation, and then multiply by a thousand!

(d) It is arguable that the lack of private ownership and the profit motive lessens incentives for individuals and so reduces initiative and productivity.

In spite of the collapse of the command economies in Eastern Europe, they still have their advocates, who would claim that command economies are more stable than free market economies, with a greater likelihood of 'public' goods (see later chapter) being produced. There is also an argument – though it is difficult to support it from the empirical evidence – that a command economy will lead to a fairer distribution of wealth among the population.

5

Day	1	2	3	4	5	6	7	8	9	Total
Marginal utility	19	14	12	10	9	8	6	3	1	82

The marginal utility schedule shows a steady decline from day 1 (19 points) to day 9 (1 point). It suggests that by the end of the holiday he or she is just about ready to go home and get back to work.

6 The consumer will:

(a) buy more of product Y. This will reduce the marginal utility of Y;

(b) buy less of product X. This will increase the marginal utility of X.

Eventually MU_x/P_x will come back into line with MU_y/P_y.

It is easy to become confused by the mathematical expression of some economic propositions. Try to cut through the complexities by thinking of them in commonsense terms. What the above analysis is saying, plausibly enough, is that if the price of X rises, the consumer will be less inclined to buy X and more inclined to buy Y.

Further question practice

Now try the following practice questions at the end of this text.

Multiple choice questions **1–12**

Exam style question **1**

Chapter 2

PRICE THEORY – SUPPLY AND DEMAND

Introduction

It is usual for textbooks in economics to cover microeconomics before macroeconomics, and this book is no exception. In this chapter, we begin to look at microeconomics. Many of the concepts here, such as price, demand and supply are in everyday use. It is important to be clear about the precise way in which economists use such concepts. For example, note the difference between an individual household's or consumer's demand and market demand. The establishment of equilibrium in a market is a key idea here.

Your objectives

After completing this chapter you should:

(a) understand that the supply of and demand for commodities is influenced by competitive factors;

(b) be aware of the factors that stimulate or depress supply of and demand for a commodity;

(c) understand how the price of a commodity is determined by the interaction of supply and demand.

1 MARKETS AND COMPETITION

1.1 Introduction

In microeconomics, the theory of consumer behaviour, the theory of the firm and price theory seek to explain how economic decisions are reached.

(a) What makes consumers decide what they are going to buy, and in what quantities?

(b) What makes firms decide what goods and services they are going to produce, and in what quantities?

(c) How are the market prices for buying and selling arrived at?

1.2 The concept of a market

The concept of a market in economics goes beyond the idea of a single geographical place where people meet to buy and sell goods. It is a term used to refer to the buyers and sellers of a good who influence its price. Markets can be worldwide, as in the case of oil, wheat, cotton and copper, for example. Others are more localised, such as the housing market or the market for second-hand cars.

Definition

Markets are situations in which potential buyers and sellers of goods or services come together in order to exchange.

Markets for different goods or commodities are often inter-related. All commodities compete for households' income so that if more is spent in one market, there will be less to spend in other markets. Further, if markets for similar goods are separated geographically, there will be some price differential at which it will be worthwhile for the consumer to buy in the lower price market and pay shipping costs, rather than buy in a geographically nearer market.

Activity 1

This latter phenomenon (exploiting the price differences between different geographical markets) is very common in practice. Can you think of examples?

1.3 Decision-takers in a market

There are two major groups of decision-takers in a market, namely buyers and sellers, or more accurately:

(a) purchasers and would-be purchasers;

(b) suppliers and would-be suppliers.

Suppliers and would-be suppliers are referred to in economics as *firms*. Buyers and would-be buyers are often referred to in economics as *households*. We often refer to households rather than to individual consumers, partly because economic data that is collected refers to household financial transactions rather than individual consumers' spending. We can then ignore all problems of decision-making within the household (ie which member of the household makes the spending decisions) and regard the household as though it were a single individual.

Some markets have buyers who are not households at all, but other firms or government authorities. For example, a manufacturing firm buys raw materials and components to go into the products that it makes. Service industries and government departments must similarly buy in supplies in order to do their own work.

However, the demand for goods from firms and government authorities is a *derived demand.*

Definition

A *derived demand* means that the size of the demand depends on the nature of the demand from households for the goods and services that they in turn produce and provide.

To begin with, we shall concentrate on *product markets*, which are markets in which a good or a service to consumers is bought and sold.

Later, we shall go on to look at *resource markets*, which are the markets in which production resources – especially labour and capital – are bought and sold.

1.4 Price theory

Price theory (or demand theory as it is sometimes called) is concerned with how market prices for goods are arrived at, through the interaction of demand and supply.

The economist distinguishes between perfect and imperfect competition in markets. All markets have some imperfections, but the perfect market provides a useful theoretical benchmark or starting point for assessing the characteristics of a market in the real world.

1.5 Perfect competition

Definition

A perfect market is where there is a large number of buyers and a large number of sellers and no individual buyer or seller can influence the market price.

In a perfect market for a product:

(a) an individual firm must accept the prevailing market price – ie it must be a price taker;

(b) there is perfect communication so that all buyers and sellers have the same information about prices through the market, and buyers and sellers can obtain this information without cost;

(c) the consumer will act rationally and will therefore try to pay the lowest price at which a product is offered. The producer, acting rationally, will try to get the highest possible price for his product in order to maximise his profits;

(d) the product is *homogeneous*, ie it is uniform across the market and there is no *product differentiation*. So one firm cannot sell a product similar to its competitors' products by emphasising or advertising its differences or brand image;

(e) there is freedom of entry into the market by new sellers;

(f) there is an absence of transport costs in travelling between one part of the market and another.

These conditions ensure that price differences within the market are rapidly eliminated and a single price is established throughout the market for all products sold in the market.

NOTES

Activity 2

Think about the market for a particular product – say motor cars. To what extent is this market 'perfect', as defined by the six criteria above?

1.6 Market imperfections

Although organised markets come close to the theoretical model of a perfect market, perfect markets do not exist in the real world, and actual markets are all imperfect to some degree. There are the following reasons for this.

(a) Buyers and sellers usually have incomplete information about prices ruling in all other parts of the market. For instance, a shopper may find it inconvenient to check the price of strawberries in every local shop, and might as a result buy at a price above the lowest obtainable.

(b) Producers can create the impression that their goods are better than those of their competitors, although they are really quite similar. Such *product differentiation* is achieved not only by differences in product design but also by means of advertising and branding.

(c) Customer loyalty or inertia sometimes prevents rational decisions by buyers. Customers might continue to go to a supplier who has given good service in the past rather than try out a new and cheaper competitor.

(d) Many markets are not *perfectly competitive*. Perfect and imperfect competition will be discussed in a later chapter. However, the essence of the distinction is that in an imperfect market there is an imbalance in economic power. A group of suppliers or buyers may be able to influence total market quantities supplied or demanded and the price of the product.

For our immediate purpose, however, a perfect market is assumed to exist. Although this is an over-simplification, it helps to provide useful insights into price determination. The assumption of perfect markets will be related in later chapters.

We shall now look at demand and supply in turn, and then consider how demand and supply interact through the price mechanism.

2 DEMAND

Definition

Demand refers to the quantity of a good that potential purchasers would buy, or attempt to buy, if the price of the good were at a certain level.

It is important that you should appreciate the concept of demand properly. Demand does *not* mean the quantity that potential purchasers wish they could buy. For example, potential purchasers might desire to have one million units of a good, but there might only be actual attempts to buy one hundred units at a given price.

Demand is what would be the actual attempt to buy at a given price. Demand might be satisfied, and so actual quantities bought would equal demand. On the other hand, some demand might be unsatisfied, with more would-be purchasers trying to buy a good that is in insufficient supply, and so there are not enough units of the good to go around.

Several factors influence the total market demand for a good. One of these factors is obviously its price, but there are other factors too, and to help you to appreciate some of these other factors, you need to recognise that households buy not just one good with their money but a whole range of goods and services.

The factors on which the quantity of demand for an individual good is dependent include:

(a) the price of the good;

(b) the price of other goods (products and services);

(c) the size of household income;

(d) tastes and fashion;

(e) expectations;

(f) the distribution of wealth among households – ie how wealth is spread among the population.

Each of these factors is discussed more fully in the paragraphs that follow.

The total quantity demanded is referred to as the *market demand.* Whereas factors (a) to (e) can affect buying decisions by individual households, factor (f) is important because it influences the potential aggregate size of the market as a whole.

Activity 3

Try to think less abstractly, for a moment, about factor (f). What do you think might be the demand for swimming pools among a population of five households enjoying total annual income of £1m, if the distribution of income is as follows:

	Annual income	
	Assumption 1	*Assumption 2*
	£	£
Household 1	950,000	200,000
Household 2	12,500	200,000
Household 3	12,500	200,000
Household 4	12,500	200,000
Household 5	12,500	200,000

2.1 Demand and the price of a good

In the case of most goods, the higher the price, the lower will be the quantity demanded, and the lower the price, the higher will be the quantity demanded. It is common sense that at a higher price, a good does not give the same value for money as it would at a lower price, and so households would not want to buy as many. This dependence of demand on price applies to all goods and services, from bread and salt to houses and space rockets.

2.2 The demand curve

The relationship between demand and price can be shown graphically as a *demand curve.* The demand curve of a single consumer is derived by estimating how much of the good the consumer would demand at various hypothetical market prices over a given period. Suppose a consumer has the following demand schedule for soap powder.

NOTES

Price per kilogram (£)	Quantity demanded (kilos)
1	93
2	8
3	64
4	41
5	23
6	1

We can show this schedule graphically, with:

(a) price on the vertical axis; and

(b) quantity demanded on the horizontal axis.

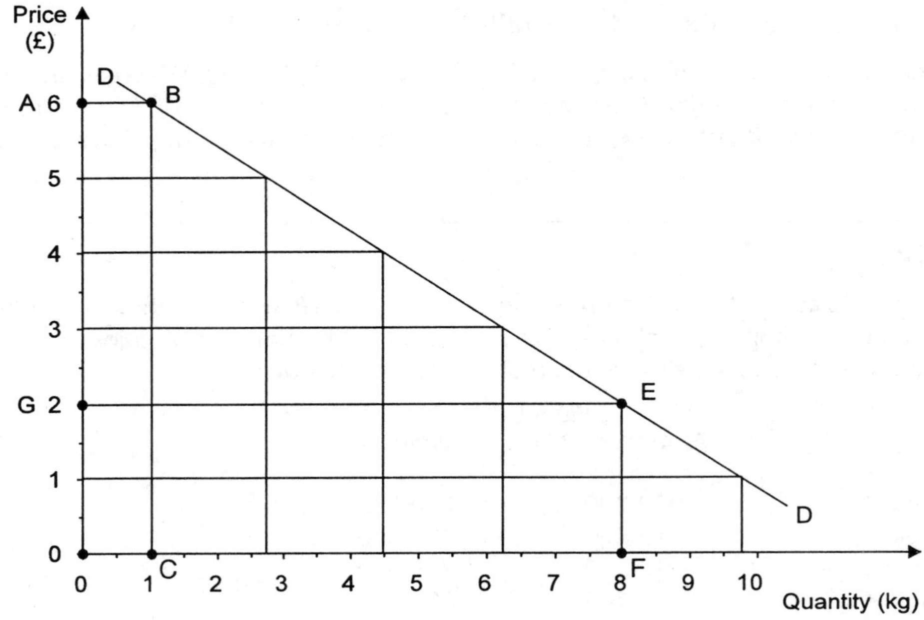

Figure 1 Graph of a demand schedule

The area of each rectangle represents consumers' total money outlay at the price in question. For example, at a price of £6, demand would be 1 kilogram and total spending would be £6, represented by rectangle ABCO. Similarly, at a price of £2, demand would be 8 kilograms and the total spending of £16 is represented by rectangle GEFO.

If we assume that there is complete divisibility, so that price and quantity can both change in infinitely small steps, we can draw a demand curve joining the points as shown in Figure 1 by a continuous line, DD. This is the consumer's demand curve for soap powder in the particular market we are looking at.

Here the demand curve happens to be a straight line. Straight line demand curves are often used as an illustration in economics because it is convenient to draw them this way. In reality, a demand curve is more likely to be a curved line convex to the origin. A convex demand curve will mean that there are progressively larger increases in quantity demanded as price falls.

NOTES

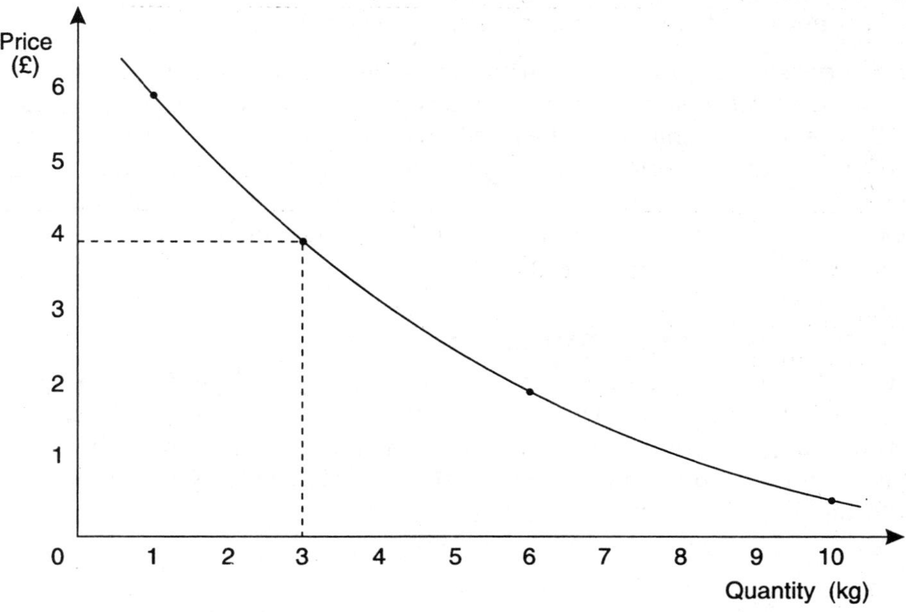

Figure 2 Demand curve convex to the origin

Activity 4

Refer to Figure 2. Suppose the price of the commodity is £3. What would be the (approximate) demand for the commodity? And if the price fell to £2?

Changes in demand caused by changes in price are represented by movements along the demand curve, from one point to another. The price has changed, and the quantity demanded changes, but the demand curve itself remains the same.

In this simple example, we are looking at the demand schedule of a single household. A *market demand curve* is a similar curve, drawn from a demand schedule, expressing the expected total quantity of the good that would be demanded by all consumers together, at any given price.

Market demand refers to the total quantities of a product that *all* households would want to buy at each price level. A market demand schedule and a market demand curve are therefore simply the sum of all the individual demand schedules and demand curves put together. Market demand curves would be similar to those in Figures 1 and 2, but with quantities demanded being higher – ie total market demand.

The market demand curve generally slopes down from left to right because:

(a) for the individual consumer, a fall in the price of the good makes it relatively cheaper compared to other goods and with a limited budget, expenditure will be shifted to the good whose price has fallen. It is the *relative price* of the good that is important. A fall in the relative price of a good increases demand for it. This is referred to as the *substitution effect*;

(b) a fall in the good's price means that people with lower incomes will also be able to afford it. The overall size of the market for the good increases. The converse argument applies to an increase in prices; as a price goes up, consumers with lower incomes will no longer be able to afford the good, or will buy something else whose price is relatively cheaper, and the size of the market will shrink. This is referred to as the *price effect*.

NOTES

This analysis indicates that the relationship between price and quantity demanded is an inverse one: as price rises, demand falls; as price falls, demand increases.

A demand curve shows how the quantity demanded will change in response to a change in price *provided that all other conditions affecting demand are unchanged* – ie provided that there is no change in the prices of other goods, tastes, expectations or the size of household income. (This assumption, that all other variables remain unchanged as we examine changes in the variable that interests us, is often referred to by use of the Latin phrase ceteris paribus – other things being equal.)

2.3 Substitutes and complements

A change in the price of one good will not necessarily change the demand for another good. For example, we would not expect an increase in the price of cocoa to affect the demand for motor cars. However, there are goods for which the market demand is in some way inter-connected. These inter-related goods are referred to as either *substitutes* or *complements*.

Definition

Substitute goods are goods that are alternatives to each other, so that an *increase* in the demand for one is likely to cause a *decrease* in the demand for another.

Switching demand from one good to a rival good is *substitution*. Examples of substitute goods are:

(a) rival brands of the same commodity, eg Coca-Cola and Pepsi-Cola;

(b) tea and coffee;

(c) bus rides and car rides;

(d) different forms of entertainment.

Substitution *takes place* when the price of one good rises or falls relative to a substitute good.

Definition

Complements are goods that tend to be bought and used together, so that an *increase* in the demand for one is likely to cause an *increase* in the demand for the other.

Examples of complements are:

(a) cups and saucers;

(b) bread and butter;

(c) motor cars and motor spares.

Activity 5

Try to work out for yourself a solution to the following problem.

What may be the effect of an increase in the ownership of domestic deep freezers on the price of perishable food products?

2.4 Demand and household income

The amount of income that a household earns will affect the demand for a good. As you might imagine, more income will give households more to spend, and they will want to buy more goods at existing prices. However, a rise in household income will not increase market demand for all goods and services. The effect of a rise in income on demand for an individual good will depend on the nature of the good.

Demand and the level of increase may be related in different ways (see Figure 3).

(a) A rise in household income may increase demand for a good. This is what we might normally expect to happen, and goods for which demand rises as household income gets bigger are called *normal goods*.

(b) Demand may rise with income up to a certain point, but then falls as income rises beyond that point. Goods whose demand eventually falls as income rises are called *inferior goods*, eg tripe, cheap wine. The reason for falling demand is that as incomes rise, demand switches to superior products, eg beef instead of tripe, better quality wines instead of a cheaper variety.

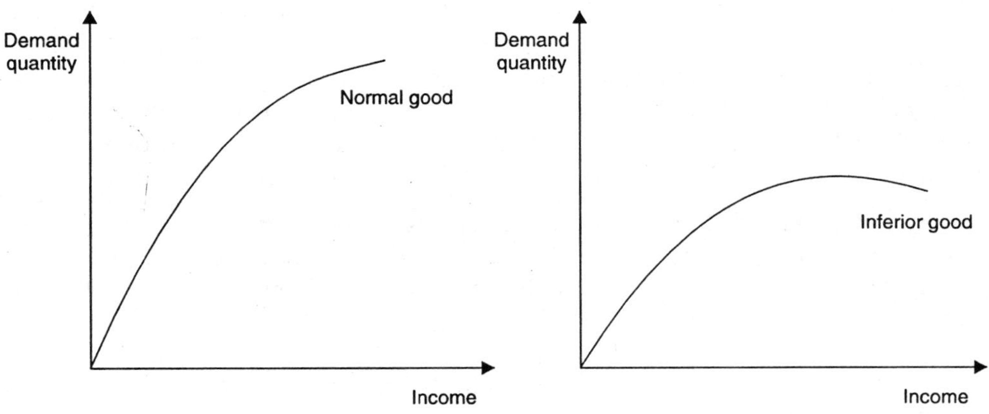

Figure 3

The response of demand for a good to a change in the consumer's income is indicated by the *income elasticity of demand*. This will be discussed further in the next chapter.

2.5 Tastes, fashion and expectations

A change in fashion will alter the demand for a product. For example, if it becomes fashionable for middle class households in the UK to drink wine with their meals, expenditure on wine will increase. There may be passing crazes, such as roller skates or skateboards.

If consumers believe that prices will rise, or that shortages will occur, they may attempt to stock up on the product, thereby creating excess demand in the short term, which will increase prices. This can then lead to panic buying. Examples include fear of war, the budget, the effect of strikes, or a rumour.

2.6 Market demand and the distribution of national income

Market demand for a good is influenced by the way in which the national income is shared between households. Consider the following patterns of income distribution.

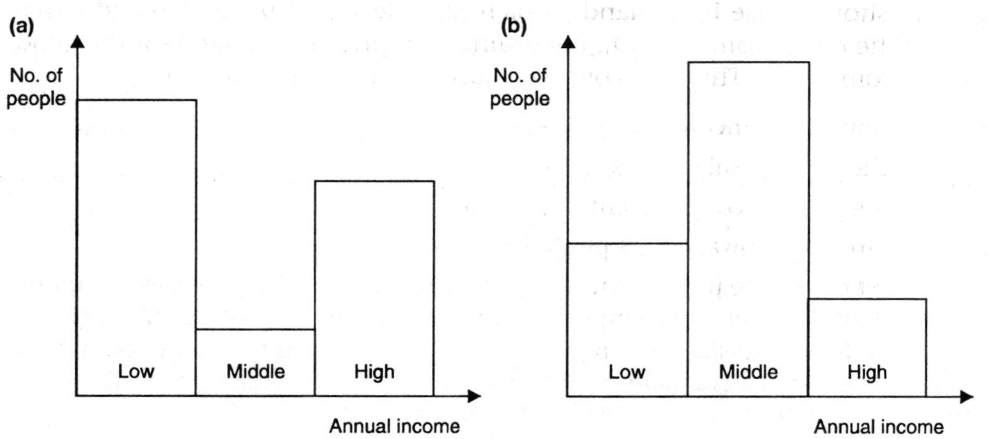

Figure 4

In Figure 4(a), which has many rich and poor households and few middle income ones, there should be a large demand for luxury cars and yachts and also for staple foods such as bread and potatoes. In case (b), there should be high demand for medium-sized cars and TV sets, and other middle income goods.

To summarise, the market demand curve relates the total quantity of a commodity demanded to its own price, on the assumption that all other prices, household incomes, the distribution of total income among households, assets and expectations and other factors are held constant.

2.7 Changes in demand

If the price of a good goes up or down, given no changes in the other factors that directly affect price, then there will be a shift in the quantity demanded along the demand curve.

When there is a change in other factors that affect demand, the relationship between demand quantity and price will also change. Then there will be a different price/quantity demand schedule and so a different demand curve. We refer to these changes as a shift of the demand curve.

This is an important distinction, which bears repetition in a slightly different form to consolidate your understanding of it.

(a) *Movements along a demand curve* for a good are caused by changes in its price.

(b) *Shifts in the demand curve* for a good are caused by any of the other factors which affect demand for a good, other than its price.

2.8 Shifts of the demand curve

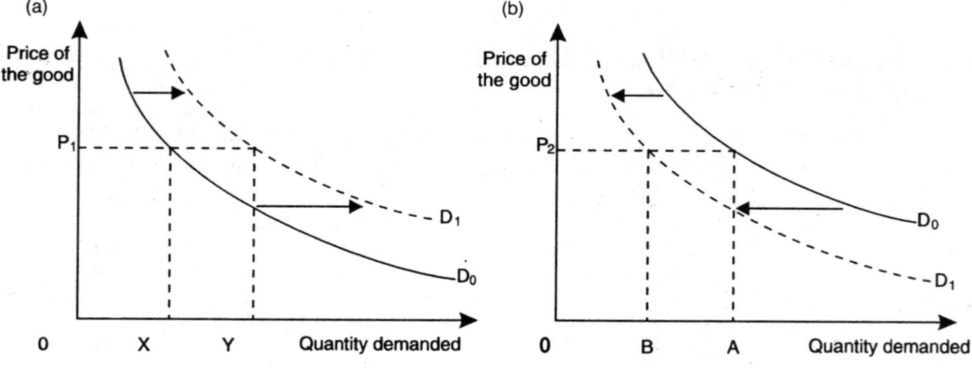

Figure 5

Figure 5(a) shows a rise in demand at each price level, with the demand curve shifting to the right, from D_0 to D_1. For example, at price P_1, demand for the good would rise from X to Y. This shift could be caused by any of the following:

(a) a rise in household income;

(b) a rise in the price of substitutes;

(c) a fall in the price of complements;

(d) a change in tastes towards this product;

(e) an *expected* rise in the price of the product. If the price rise later fails to occur, the shift in demand would be temporary. If the price rise does occur, the demand curve would go back to its previous position, but fewer goods would be demanded because the price is now higher.

Figure 5(b) shows a fall in demand at each price level, which is represented by a shifting to the left of the demand curve, from 'old' curve D_0 to 'new' curve D_1. This shift may be caused by the opposite of the changes described in the previous paragraph.

For example, at price P_2 the demand will fall from A to B.

To summarise:

(a) a shift of the demand curve to the right portrays an increase in the quantity demanded at any given price level;

(b) a shift of the curve to the left portrays a reduction in the quantity demanded at any given price level.

Activity 6

(a) Consider the demand for flower vases. The price of cut flowers goes up sharply. What will happen to the price and demand for vases?

(b) Consider the demand for Channel crossing tickets by ferry. The price of Channel crossings by tunnel goes up. What happens to the price and demand for crossings by ferry?

---

3 SUPPLY

Definition

Supply refers to the quantity of a good that existing suppliers or would-be suppliers would want to produce for the market at a given price. In this context, and usually in economics, the term 'good' includes services as well as tangible products.

The quantity of a good that can be supplied to a market varies up or down, either because:

(a) existing suppliers increase or reduce their output quantities; or

(b) firms stop producing altogether and leave the market, or new firms enter the market and begin producing the good.

If the quantity that firms want to produce at a given price exceeds the quantity that purchasers would demand, there would be an excess of supply, with firms competing to win what sales demand there is. Over-supply and competition would then be expected to result in price-competitiveness and a fall in prices.

As with demand, supply relates to a period of time – eg an annual rate of supply quantities, or a monthly rate.

As with demand, a distinction should be made between:

(a) market supply, which is the total quantity of the good that all firms in the market would want to supply at a given price; and
(b) an individual firm's supply schedule, which is the quantity of the good that the individual firm would want to supply to the market at any given price.

3.1 Factors which influence the supply quantity

The quantity supplied of a good depends on:

(a) the *price* obtainable for the good;
(b) the *prices of other goods*. An increase in the price of other goods would make the supply of a good whose price does not rise less attractive to suppliers;
(c) the *cost of making the good*, which in turn depends on the prices of factors of production – ie wages, interest rates, land rents and profit expectations. A rise in the price of one factor of production (say labour), will cause producers to shift away from supplying goods whose costs and profits are closely related to the price of labour, towards the supply of goods where the cost of labour is less significant;
(d) *changes in technology*. Technological developments which reduce costs of production (and increase productivity) will raise the quantity of supply of a good;
(e) *changes in the weather* may affect the availability of supply (eg agricultural goods).

The factors that affect supply can be summarised briefly as prices and costs, and so profits.

In this chapter, our main interest is with the influence of price on supply and demand. The influence of cost on output decisions by firms, and so on supply to the market, will be discussed more fully in a later chapter.

3.2 Supply and the price of a good

In general, suppliers will want to supply a greater quantity of their output at higher prices.

For example, if the price of product X is £5 per unit, a supplier might be willing to supply 1,000 units of the product to consumers in the market at that price. If the price of product X now goes up to £10, the supplier will be willing to supply more than 1,000 units of the product. Just how many more than 1,000 he would want to supply would depend on circumstances.

Why would a supplier be willing to supply more output at a higher price?

It might seem logical to suppose that higher prices should mean higher profits, and so the firm would be attracted by the prospect of bigger profits into supplying more units of output. This is not the full answer, however. We must also ask why, in our example, the supplier was only willing to supply 1,000 units of product X at a price of £5.

Activity 7

Before reading on, try to work out the answer to this question yourself. As a hint, remember that the supplier is interested in its own profits: not just the amount of revenue earned, but the costs involved in earning it.

The answer must presumably be that it would not be worthwhile, and that the unit cost of making extra output would exceed the sales price of £5 per unit. This might be, for example, because the supplier's capacity is already fully extended, and the costs of increasing capacity (anything from overtime premiums to the cost of a new factory) would not be covered by the £5 per unit sales price. At a higher selling price per unit, the output limit where unit costs begin to exceed unit prices will be at a higher level, and so the supplier would now be willing to produce more at the new higher price.

3.3 The supply curve

A supply schedule and supply curve can be drawn:

(a) for an individual supplier; or

(b) for all firms which produce the good. This total supply curve of all suppliers is the market supply curve.

EXAMPLE: THE SUPPLY CURVE

Suppose that the supply schedule for product Y is as follows.

Price per unit	*Quantity that suppliers would supply at this price*
£	Units
100	10,000
150	20,000
300	30,000
500	40,000

A supply curve is constructed in a similar manner to a demand curve (from a schedule of supply quantities at different prices), but shows the quantity suppliers are willing to produce at different price levels. It is an upward-sloping curve from left to right, because greater quantities will be produced at higher prices.

Contrast the *inverse* relationship between price and quantity demanded, which we examined in our analysis of demand. In the case of supply, the relationship between price and quantity supplied is *positive*: as price rises, so too does the quantity that producers are willing to supply.

The relationship between output and price, using the data in our example, is shown as a *supply curve* in Figure 6.

NOTES

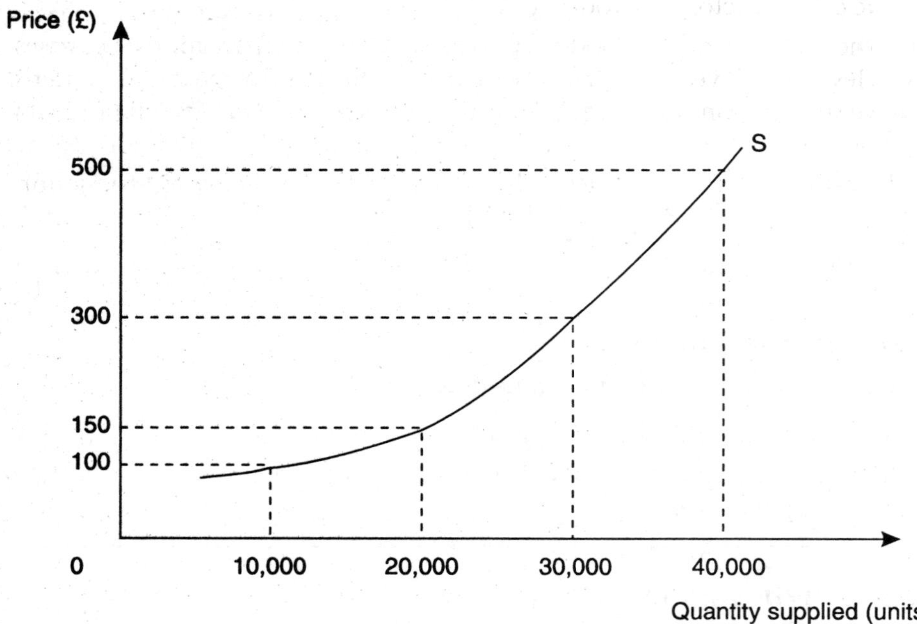

Figure 6

A supply curve shows how the quantity supplied will change in response to a change in price, provided that all other conditions affecting supply remain unchanged (*ceteris paribus*). If supply conditions (the price of other goods, or costs of factors of production, or changes in technology) alter, a different supply curve must be drawn. In other words, a change in price will cause a shift in supply along the supply curve. A change in other supply conditions will cause a shift in the supply curve itself.

This corresponds to the important point made earlier about demand curves, and again bears repetition.

(a) *Movements along a supply curve* represent changes in the total quantity of a good that suppliers would want to supply when there is a change in the price of the good.

(b) *Shifts of the supply curve* represent changes in the total quantity of a good that suppliers would want to supply at all prices, because of a change in the cost of supply – eg technological progress, or a change in the price of other goods.

Activity 8

Imagine that the government of a country decides to impose regulations to ration the supply of product Z to 15,000 units per annum. Sketch the shape of the supply curve for product Z.

3.4 Shifts of the market supply curve

The *market* supply curve is the aggregate of the supply curves of individual firms in the market. A shift of the market supply curve occurs when supply conditions – ie factors influencing supply, other than the price of the good itself – alter (eg the price of factors of production, the prices of other goods, technology etc). Figure 7 shows a shift in the supply curve from S_0 to S_1. A rightwards shift of the curve shows on expansion of supply and may be caused by:

NOTES

(a) a fall in the cost of factors of production;

(b) a fall in the price of other goods. The production of other goods becomes relatively less attractive as their price falls. We therefore expect that (*ceteris paribus*) the *supply* of one good will rise as the prices of other goods fall (and *vice versa*);

(c) technological progress – which reduces unit costs and also increases production capabilities.

In effect, a shift of the supply curve is the result of changes in costs, either in absolute terms or relative to the costs of other goods.

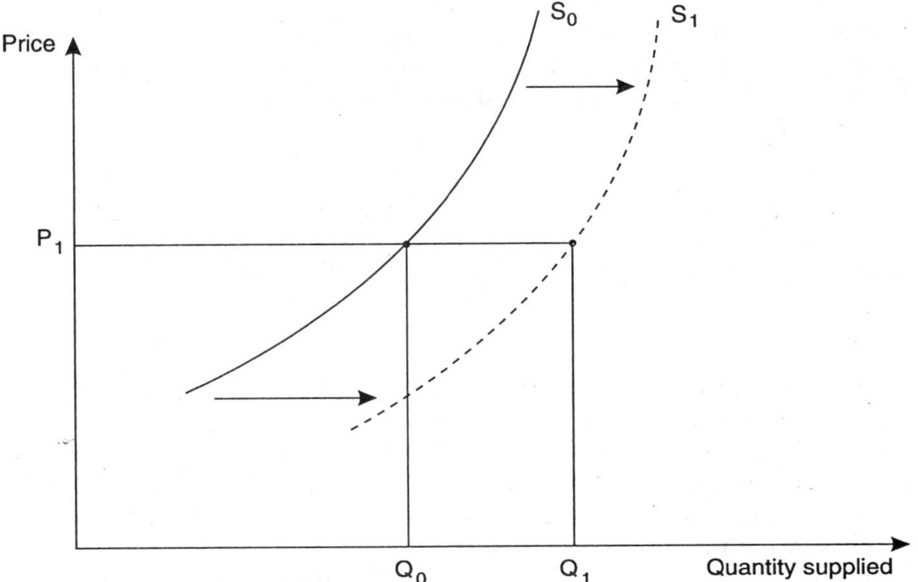

Figure 7

If the price of the good is P_1 (Figure 7), suppliers would be willing to increase supply from Q_0 to Q_1 under the new supply conditions.

Note that we need to distinguish between short-run and long-run responses of both supply and demand. In the short run both supply and demand are relatively unresponsive to changes in price, as compared to the long run.

In the case of supply, changes in the quantity of a good supplied often require the laying off or hiring of new workers, or the installation of new machinery. All of these changes, brought about by management decisions, must take some time to implement.

In the case of demand, it takes time for consumers to adjust their buying patterns, although demand will often respond more rapidly than supply to changes in price or other demand conditions.

In some markets, such as the market for chocolate bars, responses to changes in price are relatively rapid. In others, such as the market for military aircraft, response times are much longer.

Activity 9

On a stock market the 'products' bought and sold include shares in companies. What can you say about the supply of and demand for these 'products', and how quickly does their price change in response to changes in supply and demand factors?

NOTES

4 THE PRICE MECHANISM

If demand for a good exceeds supply, consumers must either stop demanding what they cannot have, or they must be prepared to pay more for the good. At a higher price, firms will be prepared to supply more of the good. On the other hand, if the price of a good is such that firms want to supply more than consumers are willing to buy, production must be cut back in volume or the price must be reduced so as to stimulate demand.

4.1 The equilibrium price

The price mechanism brings demand and supply into equilibrium and the *equilibrium price* for a good is the price at which the volume demanded by consumers and the volume that firms would be willing to supply are the same.

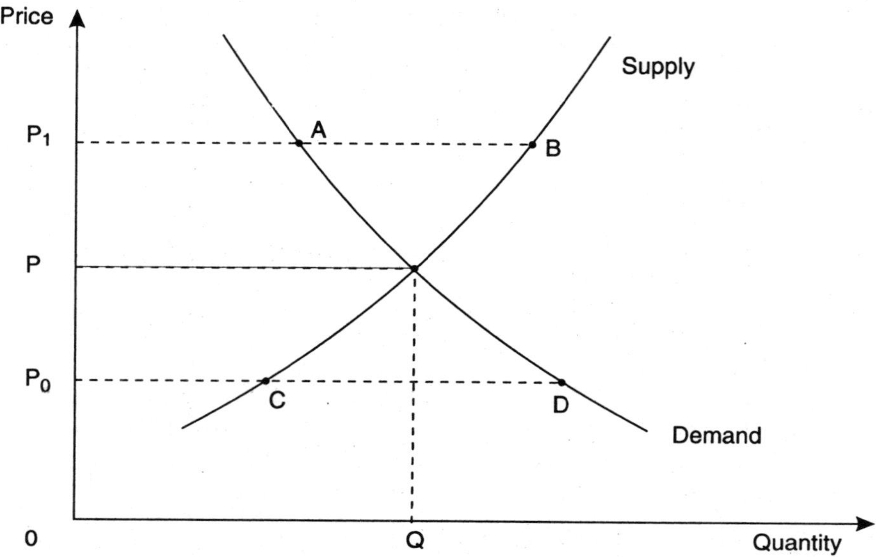

Figure 8

At price P_1 there is an excess of the quantity that suppliers want to produce over the quantity demanded at that price, equal to the distance AB. The reaction of suppliers as unsold stocks accumulate would be:

(a) to cut down the current level of production in order to get rid of unwanted stocks (ie de-stock); and/or

(b) to reduce prices in order to encourage sales.

The opposite will happen at price P_0 where there is an excess of demand over supply shown by the distance CD. Output and price would increase.

At price P the amount that sellers are willing to supply is equal to the amount that customers are willing to buy. There will be no unusual variation in stocks and, unless something else changes, there will be no change in price. P is the *equilibrium price.*

At the equilibrium price P, consumers will be willing to spend a total of $P \times Q$ – ie PQ – on buying Q units of the product, and suppliers will be willing to supply Q units to earn revenue of $P \times Q$.

The forces of supply and demand push a market to its equilibrium price and quantity.

(a) If there is no change in conditions of supply or demand, the equilibrium price will rule the market and will remain stable.

(b) If the equilibrium price does not rule, the market is in disequilibrium, but supply and demand will push prices towards the equilibrium price.

(c) Shifts in the supply curve or demand curve will change the equilibrium price and quantity.

The law of supply and demand is that in a free market, the equilibrium price and output level of a good is the price and output level at which the market demand curve and the market supply curve intersect.

In a free market, price acts as a mechanism which signals demand and supply conditions to producers and consumers. It therefore determines the activities of both producers and consumers, influencing the levels of demand for and the supply of goods.

> ***'The price system was not consciously created. It does not require that anyone consciously foresee and co-ordinate the necessary changes; adjustments occur automatically as a result of the separate decisions taken by a large number of individuals, all seeking their own best interest.'***
>
> ***(R G Lipsey)***

Now try a more detailed activity.

Activity 10

What conditions will decide the price in:

(a) a retail fruit and vegetable market? and

(b) an auction of antiques and paintings?

Chapter roundup

- The demand curve is an indication of what consumers are willing to pay – responsiveness to price.
- The supply curve is an indication of what producers are willing to supply – responsiveness to price.
- Both the demand curve and the supply curve relate to business.

  Demand   revenue

  Supply   cost
- The competitive market process can be summarised briefly with demand and supply curves.
- The competitive market process results in an equilibrium price, which is the price at which market supply and market demand quantities are in balance. In any market, the equilibrium price will change if market demand or supply conditions change.

Quick quiz

1 What is a market?

2 What are the conditions necessary for a perfect market?

3 What factors influence demand for a good?

4 What is market demand?

5 What are (a) substitutes and (b) complements?

NOTES

6 What is the difference between a movement along a demand curve and a shift of the demand curve?

7 Define supply.

8 What factors affect the supply quantity?

9 What is the market supply curve?

10 What is the difference between a movement along a supply curve and a shift of the supply curve?

11 What is equilibrium price?

Answers to Activities

1 Examples are numerous. Close to home, think about a day trip to the Boulogne hypermarkets to stock up with alcoholic drinks. (A similar example is trips across the border between Northern Ireland and the Republic of Ireland.) Another one you may have thought of is the idea of buying a BMW (left-hand drive, unfortunately!) in Germany and driving it back to the UK. More exotically, exporters who sell at differential prices to both Singapore (a high income, high price economy), and Malaysia (a far less wealthy economy) have to reckon with the fact that the two countries are linked by a causeway.

2 (a) There is a huge number of buyers, and many sellers too. For any given model of car, a particular dealer is likely to be a price taker.

(b) Communication is generally good. Product features are well known and list prices are freely available. And discount levels too are widely commented on, in the press and by word of mouth.

(c) Consumers do not always act rationally. A car which appeals to a buyer's self-image, or snobbishness, may command a higher price than another model apparently similar in all material respects.

(d) The product is very far from homogeneous.

(e) Entry to the market is not easy, whether we are talking about manufacturers of motor cars (very high start-up costs), or dealers.

(f) Transport costs are *not* absent. On the contrary, significant geographical price differentiation is possible because of the high transport costs involved.

3 Under assumption 1, the demand for swimming pools will be confined to household 1. Even if this household owns three or four properties, the demand for swimming pools is likely to be less than under assumption 2, where potentially all five households might want one. This point is discussed in more detail later in the chapter.

4 Demand is about 4.5 kilos at a price of £3 per kilo, rising to 6 kilos at the reduced price of £2 per kilo.

5 (a) Domestic deep freezers and perishable food products are complements because people buy deep freezers to store perishable products.

(b) Perishable products are supplied either as fresh produce (fresh meat, fresh vegetables etc); or as frozen produce, which can be kept for a short time in a refrigerator but for longer in a freezer. The prices of both forms of perishable product are likely to be affected by the ownership of deep freezers.

(c) Wider ownership of deep freezers is likely to increase bulk buying of perishable products. Suppliers can save some packaging costs, and can therefore offer lower prices for bulk purchases.

6 (a) Cut flowers and flower vases are likely to be complementary goods. The rise in price of cut flowers will have an adverse effect on demand for flower vases, and the demand curve for flower vases will shift to the left. Given no change in supply conditions for vases, the new equilibrium price for vases will be lower.

(b) Sea ferry tickets and tunnel tickets for Channel crossings are likely to be substitute goods. An increase in the price of tunnel tickets will cause a shift to the right

NOTES

(increase in demand) for sea ferry tickets. Given no change in supply conditions, the consequence will be an increase in the number of sea ferry tickets sold, at a higher price than before.

7 The answer is given in the text.

8

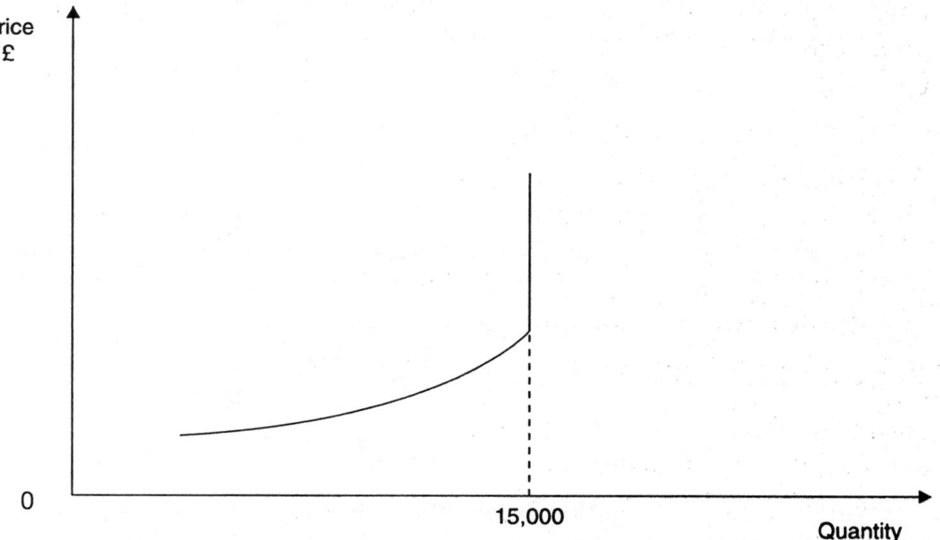

The important point is that the supply curve becomes vertical once output of 15,000 units is reached. No matter what the price of product Z, no more will be produced.

9 The supply of shares in a particular company is relatively static, although new shares will be issued from time to time. Demand for a company's shares will depend largely on how well the company is performing, although broader economic considerations are also influential. The price mechanism responds very rapidly – a share price may fluctuate up and down at very short intervals, sometimes undergoing several changes in the course of a single day.

10 (a) *A retail fruit and vegetable market*

The market will probably consist of many small traders, each with his own stall and competing with each other. The market will possibly be a near-perfect one.

The supply conditions affecting prices are:

(i) *costs:* the main cost to traders will be of their own wholesale supplies; although there will also be costs of renting a stall and of wages/labour. Even so, costs will be lower in a market of this kind than in a shopping centre.

(ii) *the availability of stalls:* the prices that traders can charge will depend to some extent on the number of stalls that there are and the ease with which new traders can acquire a stall and enter the market. Ease of entry into and exit from a market is a characteristic of perfect competition, which is described more fully in a later chapter.

The demand conditions affecting price are:

(i) the price of similar goods in shops;

(ii) shopping habits – ie whether householders are accustomed to buying their food from markets;

(iii) the quality of the goods on the market and how they compare with similar goods in shops;

(iv) how much money shoppers have to spend.

(b) *An auction of antiques and paintings*

The items up for auction will probably have a reserve price. Once the price bid during the auction rises above the reserve price, the seller cannot supply more of the items. He or she can only sell the item at whatever the maximum bid price happens to be. This is an example of perfectly inelastic supply, which is described later.

The supply of items for auction is unlikely to be influenced by cost. The factors relevant to the supply decision are:

(i) the reserve price – ie the minimum price the supplier will accept;

(ii) the expected price – ie the supplier might put an item up for auction in the expectation of receiving a certain price;

(iii) other circumstances (eg personal factors) influencing the supplier's decision to sell.

The price obtained at an auction is mainly determined by demand. Factors influencing demand are:

(i) the number of potential customers at the auction and the amount of money they have to spend. An auction at Sotheby's, for example, is likely to attract a wealthier class of customer than an auction in a small town;

(ii) the investment value of the items;

(iii) the taste of customers and the artistic value they perceive in the items up for sale;

(iv) the price of similar items at recent auctions elsewhere.

Comparison

Broadly speaking, it could be argued that prices in a retail fruit and vegetable market are influenced mainly by costs – ie wholesale prices – and in an auction of paintings the main factor influencing price will be demand. In other words, different conditions have varying degrees of importance between one type of market and the next.

Further question practice

Now try the following practice questions at the end of this text.

Multiple choice questions	**13–24**
Exam style question	**2**

Chapter 3

ELASTICITY OF DEMAND AND SUPPLY

Introduction

The equilibrium between demand and supply in a market, which we explained in Chapter 2, can be looked at initially as a static phenomenon, with demand and supply conditions taken as given. Then, as we saw in Chapter 2, we can consider how demand or supply conditions can change to shift the demand and supply curves. In this chapter, we discuss the concept of elasticities of demand and supply, which shows us the relative effects of *movements* along a demand or supply curve. The most widely used elasticity measure is the price elasticity of demand, which we explain first.

Your objectives

After completing this chapter you should:

(a) understand the concept of elasticity in relation to both demand and supply;

(b) be aware of some of the factors that influence elasticity of supply and demand in the cases of particular products.

NOTES

1 PRICE ELASTICITY OF DEMAND

1.1 The concept of elasticity

So far we have discussed the *direction* of changes in demand and supply when prices change. When price goes up, the quantity demanded will fall, and the quantity suppliers will be willing to produce will go up. But we have not yet considered the *extent* of these changes. For example, if prices went up by 10%, would the quantity demanded fall by 5%, 20%, 50% or what? And would the quantities that suppliers would want to produce go up by 5%, 10%, 15% or what? The extent of these changes is measured by the *price elasticity of demand* and the *elasticity of supply.*

We have also discussed shifts in the demand curve due to changes in the price of substitutes and complements and changes in household income, but we have not yet considered the extent of the shifts in demand arising from shifts in the demand curve. The extent of these changes is measured by:

(a) the *cross elasticity of demand,* in the case of substitutes and complements;

(b) the *income elasticity of demand,* in the case of household income.

Definition

Price elasticity of demand (often denoted by the Greek symbol η, pronounced 'eeta') is a measure of the extent of change in market demand for a good in response to a change in its price.

It is measured as:

$$\eta = \frac{\text{change in quantity demanded, as a percentage of demand}}{\text{change in price, as a percentage of the price}}$$

Since the demand goes up when the price falls, and goes down when the price rises, the elasticity has a negative value, but it is usual to ignore the minus sign.

EXAMPLE: PRICE ELASTICITY OF DEMAND

If the price of X rises from £1 to £1.50 and demand falls from 1,000,000 units to 600,000, calculate the price elasticity of demand between these two points on the demand curve.

Solution

Old demand				1,000,000 units
New demand				600,000 units
% change in demand	$\frac{400,000}{1,000,000}$	× 100%	=	40%
Old price				£1.00
New price				£1.50
% change in price	$\frac{50p}{£1.00}$	× 100%	=	50%
Price elasticity of demand =	$\frac{-40\%}{50\%}$		=	–0.8

Ignoring the minus sign, price elasticity is 0.8.

The price elasticity of demand over this price range would be said to be inelastic because it is less than 1. In other words, the demand for this product is not very responsive to price changes.

Now try this Activity yourself.

Activity 1

If the price of X rises from £1.40 to £1.80 and the demand falls from 220,000 units to 180,000 units, what would be the price elasticity of demand?

1.2 Elastic and inelastic demand

As mentioned already, the elasticity of demand will generally have a negative value since demand curves are normally downward sloping. However, since the minus sign is often ignored, an elasticity of –1 is usually referred to as elasticity of 1, or unity. The value of demand elasticity may be anything from zero to infinity.

Demand is:

(a) *inelastic* if the absolute value is less than 1; and

(b) *elastic* if the absolute value is greater than 1.

Where demand is inelastic, the quantity demanded falls by a smaller percentage than price, and where demand is elastic, demand falls by a larger percentage than the percentage rise in price.

1.3 Price elasticity and the slope of the demand curve

Generally, demand curves slope downwards. Consumers are willing to buy more at lower prices than at higher prices. Except in certain cases (which are referred to later), elasticity will vary in value along the length of a demand curve.

At high prices (the top of the demand curve), small percentage price reductions can bring large percentage increases in quantity demanded. This means that demand is *elastic* over these ranges, and price reductions bring increases in total expenditure by consumers on the commodity in question.

At lower prices (the bottom of the demand curve), large percentage price reductions can bring small percentage increases in quantity. This means that demand is *inelastic* over these price ranges, and price increases result in increases in total expenditure.

Elasticity is rarely the same at all price levels. For example, the price elasticity of demand for a good might be elastic (greater than 1) at some prices and inelastic (less than 1) at other prices.

It is not possible merely by looking at the slopes of any two curves to state their comparative elasticities over other, different price ranges, even if there is the same absolute fall in price. This is because the elasticity of a demand curve is not constant over the entire curve. However, it is possible to say that if a demand curve becomes steeper over a particular range of quantity, then demand is becoming more inelastic. Conversely, a shallower demand curve over a particular range indicates more elastic demand. This is illustrated in Figure 1(a) and 1(b) below.

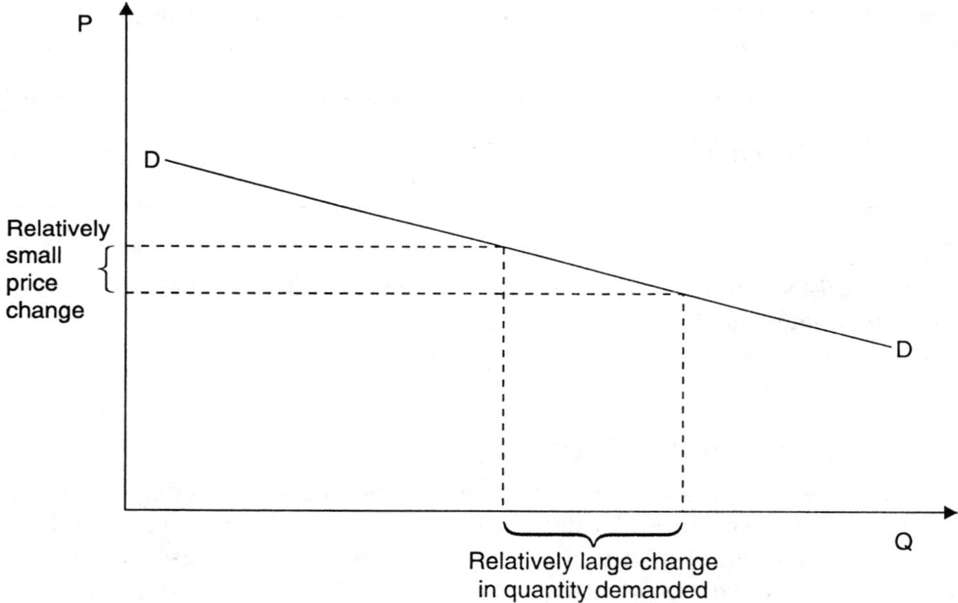

Figure 1(a) Elastic demand

NOTES

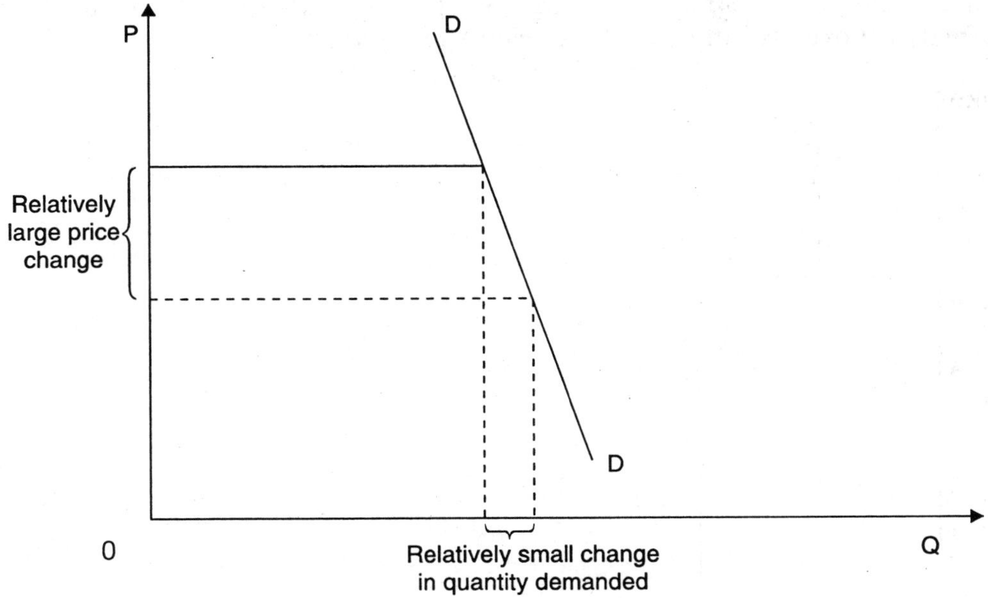

Figure 1(b) Inelastic demand

Activity 2

If price elasticity of demand is greater than 1, a fall in price will result in a fall in total expenditure on the product. True or false?

1.4 Special values of price elasticity

There are three special values of price elasticity of demand: 0, 1 and infinity.

$\eta = 0$. *Demand is perfectly inelastic* (Figure 2(a)). The demand curve is a vertical straight line and there is no change in quantity demanded, regardless of the change in price. A close example to this in real life is the demand for table salt which will be largely unaffected by price changes; we would not expect people to demand more salt if the price halved, nor less salt if the price doubled.

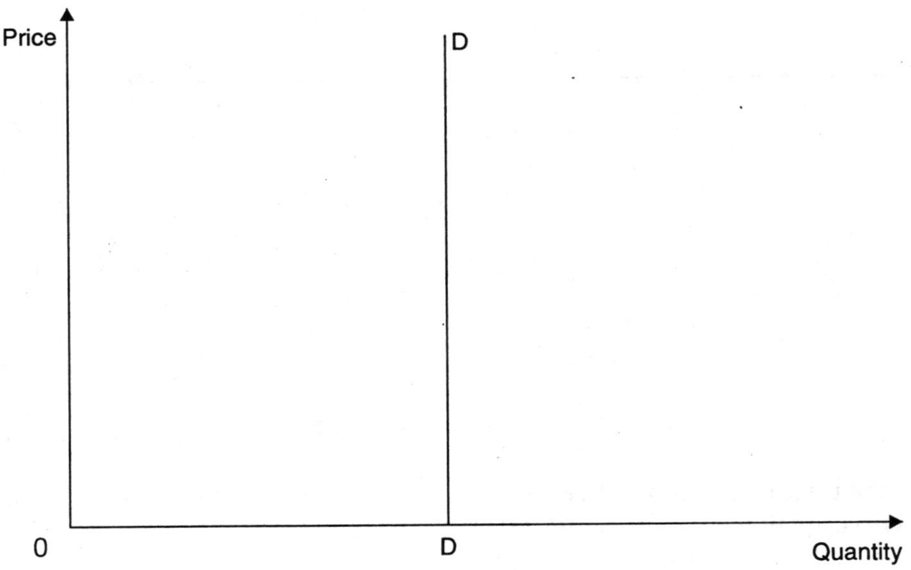

Figure 2(a) Perfectly inelastic demand

Unit elasticity of demand: $\eta = 1$ (Figure 2(b)). The demand curve of a good whose elasticity is 1 over its entire range is a *rectangular hyperbola.*

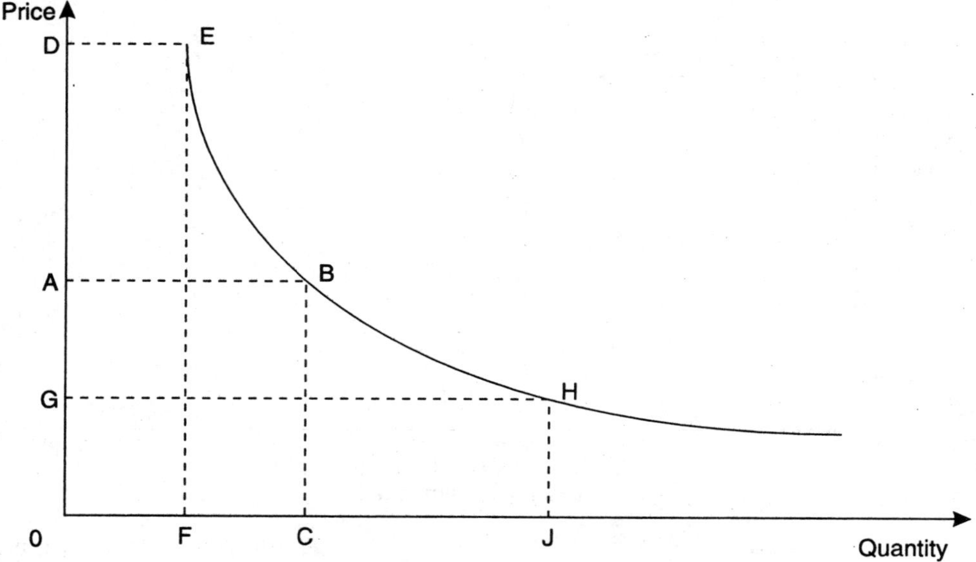

Figure 2(b) Unit elasticity of demand

The significance of this is that the rectangles 0ABC, 0DEF, 0GHJ in Figure 2(b) all have the same area. The area in each case is calculated by multiplying the unit price by the quantity sold: in other words, it represents the total amount of expenditure on the product which, in the case of a product with unit elasticity of demand at all price levels, is the same at all price levels.

Perfectly elastic demand: η = A (infinitely elastic) (Figure 2(c)). The demand curve is a horizontal straight line. Consumers will want to buy an infinite amount, but only up to price level P_0. Any price increase above this level will reduce demand to zero.

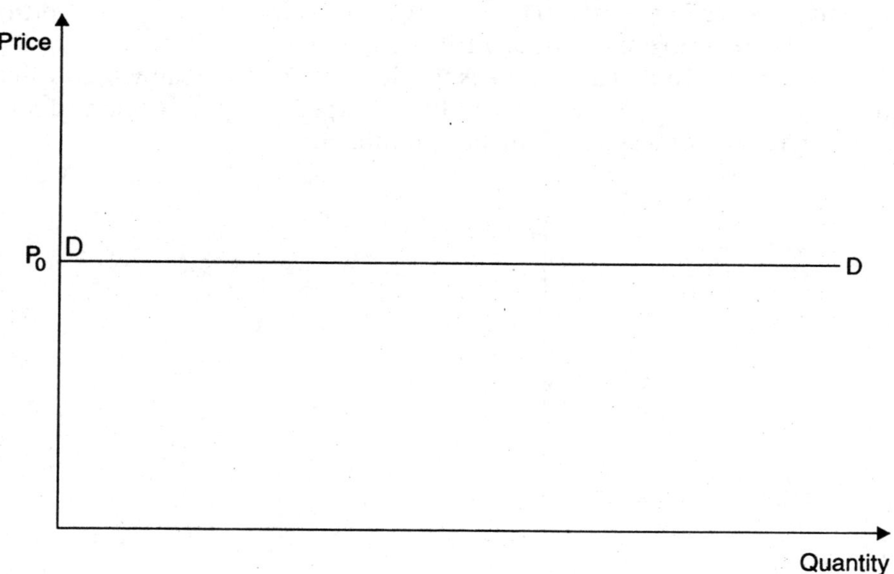

Figure 2(c) Perfectly elastic demand

The ranges of price elasticity at different points on a downward-sloping straight line demand curve are illustrated in Figure 3.

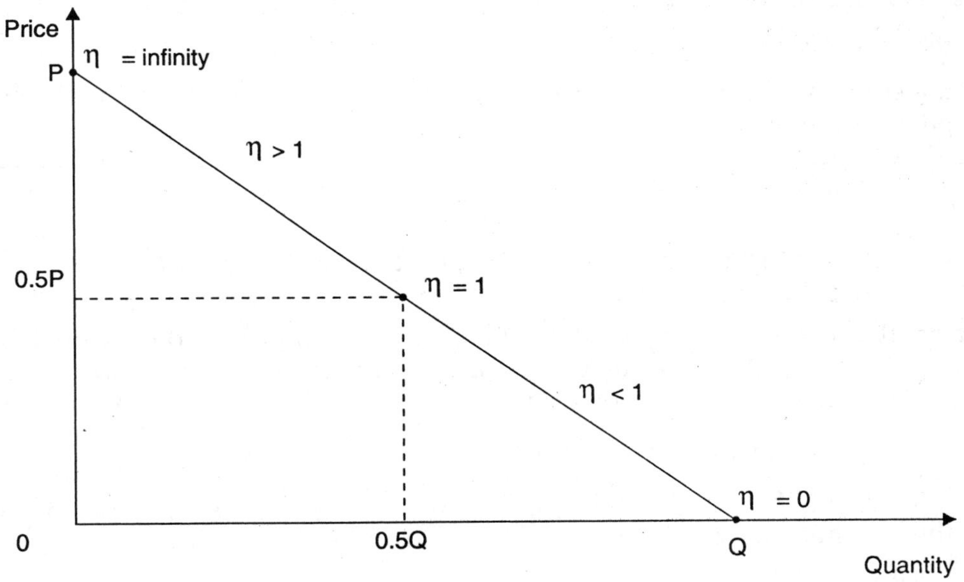

Figure 3 Ranges of price elasticity

By studying Figure 3 you may be able to see the justification for the following important rules.

(a) For a commodity whose price elasticity is greater than 1 over the range of the price change:
   (i) a reduction in price produces an increase in total expenditure on the commodity;
   (ii) a rise in price produces a reduction in total expenditure on the commodity.

(b) For a good whose price elasticity is less than 1 over the range of the price change:
   (i) a reduction in price produces a reduction in total expenditure on the commodity;
   (ii) an increase in price produces an increase in total expenditure on the commodity.

Business people can make use of information on how consumers will react to pricing decisions, not least because of the effect of this on profits. Government policy makers can use information about elasticity when making decisions about indirect taxation. Items with a low price elasticity of demand, such as cigarettes and alcohol, tend to be targets for high taxation since by increasing taxes on these, total revenue can be increased. If cigarettes were price elastic, increases in taxation would be counter-productive, as they would result in lower government revenue.

Activity 3

Suppose that there are two products, A and B.

Product A currently sells for £5, and demand at this price is 1,700 units. If the price fell to £4.60, demand would increase to 2,000 units.

Product B currently sells for £8 and demand at this price is 9,500 units. If the price fell to £7.50, demand would increase to 10,000 units.

NOTES

In each of these cases, calculate:

(a) the price elasticity of demand; and

(b) the effect on total revenue, if demand is met in full at both the old and the new prices, of the change in price.

1.5 Factors influencing price elasticity of demand for a good

Factors that determine price elasticity of demand are similar to the factors other than price that affect the volume of demand. Elasticity is really a measure of the strength of these other factors on demand.

The main factors affecting price elasticity of demand are:

(a) the availability of substitutes;

(b) the time horizon;

(c) the pricing policies of competitors.

Definition

Substitutes are goods which can replace other goods.

The availability of close substitutes. The more substitute goods there are, especially close substitutes, the more elastic will be the price elasticity of demand for a good. For example, in a greengrocer's shop a rise in the price of one vegetable such as carrots or cucumbers is likely to result in a switch of customer demand to other vegetables, as many vegetables are fairly close substitutes for each other. Again, the elasticity of demand for a particular brand of breakfast cereals is much greater than the elasticity of demand for breakfast cereals as a whole, because the former have much closer substitutes. This factor is probably the most important influence on price elasticity of demand.

The time period. Over time, consumers' demand patterns are likely to change. If the price of a good is increased, the initial response might be very little change in demand (inelastic demand), but as consumers adjust their buying habits in response to the price increase, demand might fall substantially. The time horizon influences elasticity largely because the longer the period of time which we consider, the greater the knowledge of substitution possibilities by consumers and the provision of substitutes by producers.

Competitors' policies. If the response of competitors to a price increase by one firm is to keep their prices unchanged, the firm raising its prices is likely to face elastic demand for its goods at higher prices. If the response of competitors to a reduction in price by one firm is to match the price reduction themselves, the firm is likely to face inelastic demand at lower prices. This is a situation which probably faces many large firms with one or two major competitors (ie oligopolies).

Other factors influencing elasticity of demand. Generally speaking, the higher proportion of a consumer's income that a commodity takes up, the greater will be the elasticity of demand. Thus motor vehicle demand can be expected to be more responsive to a 10% price change than, say, the demand for postage stamps or for milk.

Activity 4

What is the significance of a product's price elasticity of demand:

(a) to the Chancellor of the Exchequer; and

(b) to a manufacturer?

2 OTHER ELASTICITIES OF DEMAND

2.1 Income elasticity of demand

The income elasticity of demand for a good indicates the responsiveness of demand to changes in household incomes. It is measured as:

$$\frac{\text{change in quantity demanded, as a percentage of demand}}{\text{change in household income, as a percentage of household income}}$$

(a) A good is *income elastic* if income elasticity is greater than 1 so that quantity demanded rises by a larger percentage than the rise in income. For example, if the demand for compact discs will rise by 10% if household income rises by 7%, we would say that compact discs are income elastic.

(b) A good is *income inelastic* if income elasticity is between 0 and 1 and the quantity demanded rises less than the proportionate increase in income. For example, if the demand for books will rise by 6% if household income rises by 10%, we would say that books are income inelastic.

Both of these categories are said to be *normal goods*, which means that demand for them will rise when household income rises, and so they have a positive income elasticity of demand.

If income elasticity is less than 0, income elasticity is negative and the commodity is said to be an *inferior good* since demand for it falls as income rises.

Definition

Cross elasticity of demand refers to the responsiveness of demand for one good to changes in the price of another good.

Cross elasticity =

$$\frac{\text{change in quantity of good A demanded, as a percentage of quantity demanded*}}{\text{change in the price of good B, as a percentage of price}}$$

*(given no change in the price of A)

(a) *If the two goods are substitutes, cross elasticity will be greater than 0* and a fall in the price of one will reduce the amount demanded of the other.

(b) *If the goods are complements, cross elasticity will be negative* and a fall in the price of one will raise demand for the other.

Definition

Complements. Goods are complementary to each other if changes in the demand for one will have an effect on the demand for the other, eg compact disc players and compact discs; cars and petrol.

NOTES

Cross elasticity involves a comparison between two products. Cross elasticity is significant where the two goods are close substitutes for each other, so that a rise in the price of B is likely to result in an increase in the demand for A.

Cross elasticity of demand between two complementary products can also be significant; a rise in the price of B would result in some fall in demand for A because of the fall in demand for B.

2.2 Demand elasticity and time

Elasticity of demand for any good – price elasticity, income elasticity and cross elasticity – can and does change over time. Generally, there are some substitutes for all goods.

3 ELASTICITY OF SUPPLY

The elasticity of supply indicates the responsiveness of supply to a change in price. It is measured as:

$$\frac{\text{change in quantity supplied, as a percentage of quantity supplied}}{\text{change in price, as a percentage of price}}$$

Activity 5

Consider each of the following statements.

(a) Elasticity of supply is normally negative rather than positive.

(b) Elasticity of supply is normally greater the shorter the time period involved.

(c) Elasticity of supply depends on the alternative uses to which suppliers can put their resources.

Which, if any, of these statements is true?

The elasticity of supply will vary between the three illustrated in Figure 4 (a), (b) and (c).

(a) Perfectly inelastic supply (b) Unit elastic supply (c) Perfectly elastic supply

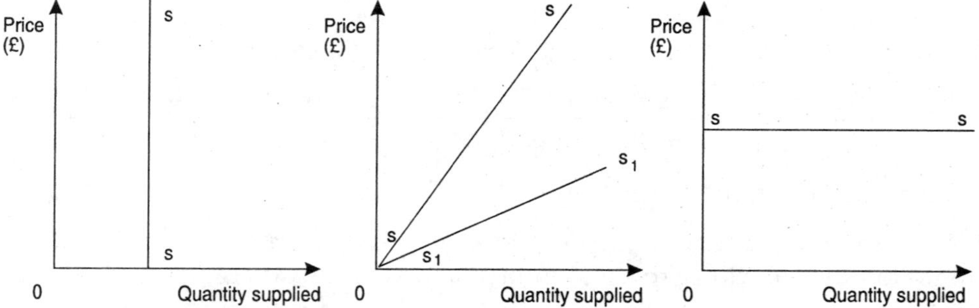

Figure 4

Where the supply of goods is fixed whatever price is offered, eg in the case of antiques, vintage wines and land, supply is *perfectly inelastic*, and the elasticity of supply is 0 (Figure 4(a)).

Where the supply of goods varies proportionately with the price, elasticity of supply equals 1 (Figure 4(b)). Both supply curves in the following diagram have *unit elasticity* because they are straight line curves passing through the origin.

(Note that a demand curve with unit elasticity along all of its length is not a straight line, but a supply curve with unit elasticity *is* a straight line.)

Where the producers will supply any amount at a given price but none at all at a slightly lower price, elasticity of supply is infinite, or *perfectly elastic* (Figure 4(c)).

Supply is *elastic* when the percentage change in the amount producers want to supply exceeds the percentage increase/decrease in price. Supply is *inelastic* when the amount producers want to supply changes by a smaller percentage than the percentage change in price.

Activity 6

Why do the prices of agricultural products fluctuate more than the prices of manufactured goods?

3.1 Elasticity of supply and time

As with elasticity of demand, the elasticity of supply of a product varies according to the time period over which it is measured. For analytical purposes, four lengths of time period may be considered.

(a) *The market period,* which is so short that supplies of the commodity in question are limited to existing stocks. In effect, supply is fixed.

(b) *The short run* is a period long enough for supplies of the commodity to be altered by increases or decreases in current output, but not long enough for the fixed equipment (ie plant, machinery, etc) used in production to be altered. This means that suppliers can produce larger quantities only if they are not already operating at full capacity; they can reduce output fairly quickly by means of lay-offs and redundancies. A common way of referring to this is to say that the short run is a period during which at least one of the factors of production is fixed in supply.

(c) *The long run* is a period sufficiently long to allow firms' fixed equipment to be altered. There is time to build new factories and machines, and time for old ones to be closed down. New firms can enter the industry in the long run.

(d) *The secular period* is so long that underlying economic factors such as population growth, supplies of raw materials (such as oil) and the general conditions of capital supply may alter. ('Secular' is derived from the Latin word '*saecula*' meaning 'centuries'.) The secular period is ignored by economists except in the theory of economic growth.

These types of time period were postulated by Alfred Marshall in his *Principles of economics* (1920).

The price elasticity of supply can be seen as a measure of the readiness with which an industry responds to a change in price following a shift in the demand curve. An example will help to show what this means.

Suppose that there is an increase in the demand for restaurant meals in a city, shown by the rightward shift in the demand curve in Figure 5 below from D_1 to D_2. The capacity of the industry is limited in the short run by the number of restaurants in operation. The restaurants can be used more intensively to a certain extent, and so supply is not perfectly inelastic, but supply is relatively inelastic because of the limit to this process. As a result, in the short run there is a large increase in the price from P_1 to P_2.

NOTES

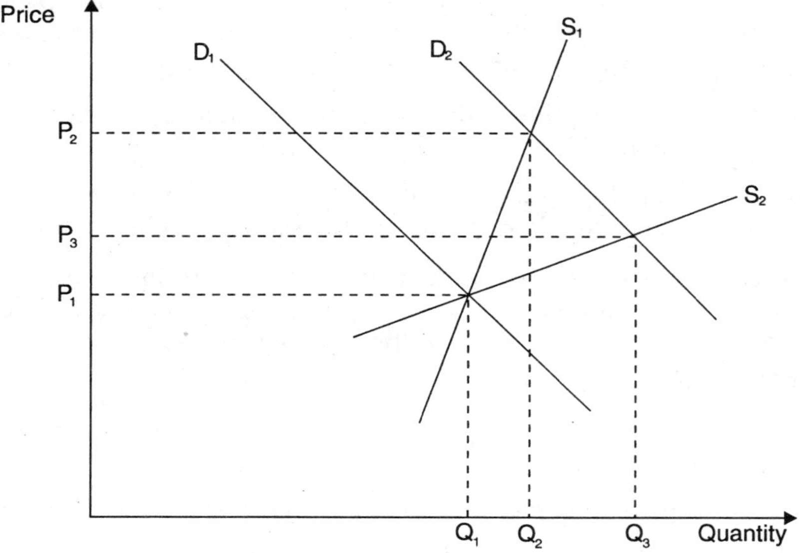

Figure 5

The rise in price in the short run will encourage entrepreneurs to open new restaurants to take advantage of the profits to be earned. In the long run, supply is consequently more elastic and is shown by supply curve S_2. The expanded output in the industry leads to a new equilibrium at a lower price P_3 with the new level of output being Q_3.

3.2 Elasticity of supply and the cost of factors of production

The cost of factors of production will affect the elasticity of supply. If demand increases, the supplier might attract more factors of production. If the cost of attracting new amounts of the factor is high, the supply curve will be more inelastic than if this cost is low. This is because suppliers will need a higher price rise to cover these costs, in order to justify an increase in supply.

Activity 7

What will be the effect on price and quantity demanded and supplied of sailing boats, given a significant reduction in income tax?

Chapter roundup

- Demand for a good depends largely on price, household income and the relative price of substitutes or complementary goods. Changes in any of these will cause either a movement along the demand curve or a shift in the demand curve. Elasticity measures how much of a movement or a shift there will be.
- Price elasticity of demand also measures the responsiveness of sales revenue to price changes.
- Firms with control over prices will always try to operate in an elastic segment of the demand curve for their product.
- If firms can discover a market segment with low price elasticity they can improve their profit margins and revise their prices.
- Cross elasticity is determined by the closeness of substitute (competitors') products.

Quick quiz

1 What is the formula for measuring price elasticity of demand?
2 Price elasticity of demand is higher at relatively high prices than at relatively low prices. True or false?
3 What is the shape of a demand curve for a product with unit price elasticity of demand at all price levels?
4 What is the shape of a supply curve for a product with unit elasticity of supply at all price levels?
5 List three main factors influencing the price elasticity of demand.
6 What is an inferior good?
7 What is the formula for measuring cross elasticity of demand?

Answers to Activities

1

	Old	*New*	*% change*		
Quantity demanded	220,000	180,000	$\frac{40,000}{220,000}$	× 100%	= 18%
Price	£1.40	£1.80	$\frac{40}{140}$	× 100%	= 29%

Price elasticity of demand = $\frac{-18\%}{29\%}$ = –0.62

The minus sign is again ignored, and the price elasticity of demand is 0.62.

The price elasticity of demand over this price range is inelastic, because its value is less than 1.

2 The statement is false. Because demand is elastic, the fall in price will result in a more than proportionate increase in demand. The reduction in unit price will be more than compensated for by the number of units purchased. This point is discussed later in the chapter.

NOTES

3 (a) *Product A*

Price elasticity of demand

$$\frac{300}{1{,}700} = 17.7\%$$

$$\frac{40p}{£5} = 8\%$$

$$\eta = \frac{-17.7\%}{8\%} = -2.2$$

The price elasticity of demand is *elastic* and so a fall in price should result in such a large increase in quantity demanded that total revenue will rise.

	£
Revenue at old price of £5 (× 1,700)	8,500
Revenue at new price of £4.60 (× 2,000)	9,200
Increase in total revenue	700

(b) *Product B*

Price elasticity of demand

$$\frac{500}{9{,}500} = 5.3\%$$

$$\frac{50p}{£8} = 6.25\%$$

$$\eta = \frac{-5.3\%}{6.25\%} = -0.85$$

The price elasticity of demand is *inelastic* and so a fall in price should result in only a relatively small increase in quantity demanded, and total revenue will fall.

	£
Revenue at old price of £8 (× 9,500)	76,000
Revenue at new price of £7.50 (× 10,000)	75,000
Fall in total revenue	1,000

4 A government is interested in elasticity because it should want to know the effects of (an indirect) tax on commodities. For example, do taxes leave prices unchanged or do they cause prices to rise and does the producer or the consumer pay the tax? And so how much tax revenue would be earned? Similarly, if a tax such as VAT is increased from 17½%, say, to 20%, will total tax revenue increase or fall? We shall look at the effects of indirect taxation on a market in some more detail later.

Firms will also be concerned as to the effect on consumer demand, and so on revenue and profits, of a change in the price they charge for their product.

5 Statement (a) is false: supply quantities increase as prices increase and vice versa, so elasticity of supply is normally positive.

Statement (b) is false: elasticity of supply is greater the *longer* the time period.

Statement (c) is correct: elasticity of supply will be greater if suppliers can switch their resources to or from the production of other goods.

6 Demand for agricultural and manufactured goods is likely to be fairly stable, although demand for both may be influenced slightly by seasonal factors. Demand for agricultural produce tends to be more elastic than demand for many manufactured items. On the other hand, *supply* of agricultural goods is likely to be far less stable than manufactured goods. Fluctuations in supply of agricultural goods arise from seasonal factors as well as weather conditions and disease. These seasonal factors can cause major shifts in the supply curves of agricultural goods.

7 The demand curve for sailing boats will shift to the right. Both price and quantity demanded/supplied will go up. The effect of a cut in income tax is to leave households with more to spend. Sailing boats are a luxury good, and the income elasticity of demand is likely to be quite high. The percentage increase in demand for boats is therefore likely to be greater than the percentage increase in after-tax household income.

Case Study 1

'The combination of a downward long-run trend in real prices and large short-term fluctuations around this trend has made LDCs (less developed countries) reluctant to persist with the route of development through exports of primary products. With the exception of petroleum, the trend in real prices of primary products has been downward for two decades. This can be attributed to both increased supply and decreased demand.

A second disadvantage of concentrating on the production of primary products is that their prices tend to be very volatile. In any particular year, LDCs are uncertain how many imports their export revenue is going to finance.

Equilibrium prices for primary products tend to fluctuate a great deal because both supply and demand are price inelastic. A small shift in one curve will lead to a large change in the equilibrium price. In recent years there have been attempts to organise commodity price stabilisation schemes in coffee, cocoa and tin. LDCs argue that the benefits would accrue to industrial nations as well as LDCs that are heavily dependent on exporting these commodities.'

Begg D, Fischer S & Dornbusch R: Economics

Use the extract to answer the following.

(a) Explain the term 'price elasticity'. Why might the demand for primary products be price inelastic?

(b) Why might large price fluctuations result from a combination of price inelastic supply and price inelastic demand?

(c) Explain income elasticity of demand and why the long-run trend in primary product prices is downwards

Answers to Case Study 1

(a) The price elasticity of demand measures the sensitivity of the quantity which will be demanded by consumers of a good to changes in the price at which it is available to them. The price elasticity over a particular range is expressed in the following equation:

$$\text{Price elasticity of demand} = \frac{\text{Percentage change in quantity demanded}}{\text{Percentage change in price}}$$

Since an increase in price will normally lead to a reduction in the quantity demanded and a decrease in price will lead to an increase in demand, the price elasticity of demand will be a negative number. In other words, price and quantity demanded are inversely related. Usually, the minus sign is ignored, and the absolute size of the elasticity is used.

The price elasticity of supply is a measure of the responsiveness of the quantity supplied by firms to changes in price.

$$\text{Price elasticity of supply} = \frac{\text{Percentage change in quantity supplied}}{\text{Percentage change in price}}$$

Where the percentage change of demand or supply is greater than the percentage change in price, then it is said that demand, or supply, respectively, is elastic.

Demand for primary goods, such as food and raw materials, is generally price inelastic. A major reason for this is that such goods have relatively few substitutes to which demand can be switched if price rises. To a certain extent, the price elasticity of demand for food is also attributable to the relatively low proportion of income which is spent on it.

(b) The length of time it takes for agricultural and other primary products to be produced means that supply cannot easily be adjusted when prices change. Therefore, the supply of primary products is likely to be inelastic in the short run. This may be particularly so if stock levels are low, as it will not be possible to run down stocks to meet new conditions.

Extraction of raw materials is a process that usually requires large amounts of capital, and this requirement will act as a barrier to market entry, again making supply price-inelastic.

Cyclical movements in the economies of developed countries may cause changes in the demand schedules for primary products. Given that supply is inelastic, shifts in the demand curve will lead to large fluctuations in the prices of primary products. This is illustrated in Figure 6 below, where the shift in the demand curve from D_1 to D_2 results in a steep rise in price from P_1 to P_2.

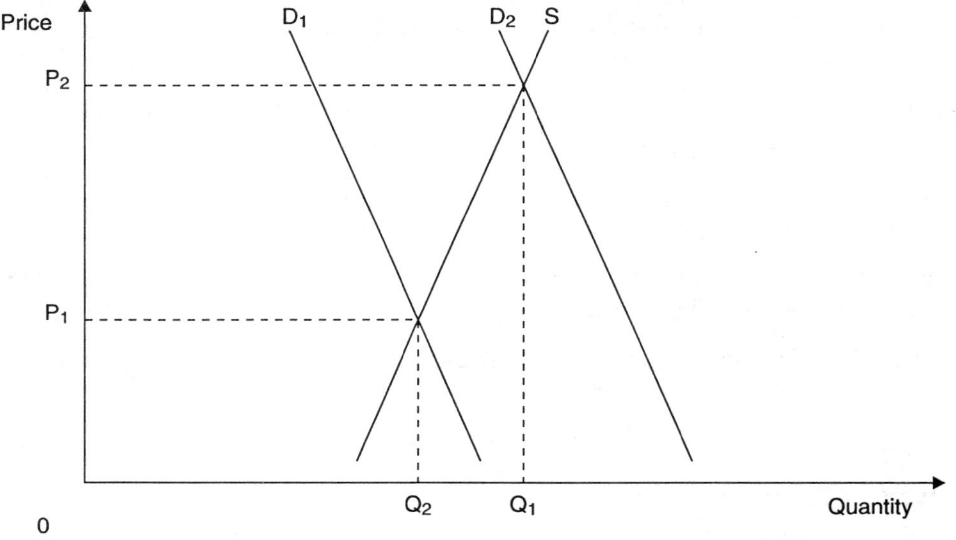

Figure 6

Crop failures can easily change quantities available for supply from the planned levels. Where the demand for primary products is price-inelastic, shifts in the supply curve can result in marked changes in price, as illustrated in Figure 7. In this diagram, a shift in the supply schedule from S_1 to S_2 results in a large rise in price from P_1 to P_2.

NOTES

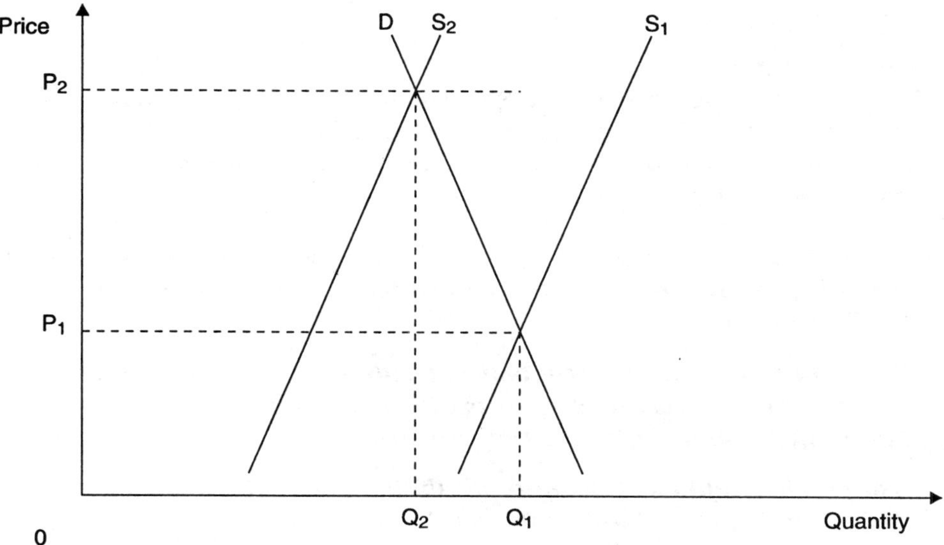

Figure 7

These illustrations show how large price changes can result from changes in demand and supply conditions for products with price-inelastic supply and demand.

(c) Income elasticity of demand measures the sensitivity of demand to changes in income.

$$\text{Income elasticity of demand} = \frac{\text{Percentage change in quantity supplied}}{\text{Percentage change in income}}$$

For most goods, the income elasticity of demand will be positive, so that a rise in income leads to an increase in demand. These are called normal goods. However, there are some goods known as inferior goods where an increase in income leads to a fall in the quantity demanded. Therefore, the income elasticity of demand is negative. Bread is one of the most common examples of an inferior good, being regarded in some countries as a poor quality substitute for staple items such as fish or meat.

The long-term downward trend in prices of primary products can be explained in part by the low income elasticity of demand of primary products in developed countries. As already mentioned, food products can have a low income elasticity if they are seen as necessities, of which consumers will not wish to buy more as their income rises.

A further long-term process is that of technological innovation, which has led to the development of more synthetic raw materials and more efficient productive use of them. The resulting increase in demand for raw materials has not kept pace with the growth in incomes.

The output of many primary products, such as raw materials, has increased as new sources have become available. Rising supply coupled with slow growth in demand have combined to create the conditions for a long-term downward trend in the real prices of many primary products, on which many less developed countries rely.

NOTES

Case Study 2

The following extract concerns the operations of the Eurotunnel company, which runs the rail tunnel link between the United Kingdom and the European continent. Eurotunnel opened for business in 1994, providing new competition for the existing ferry companies.

> *'Eurotunnel is risking bankruptcy by setting its initial prices for travelling through the Channel Tunnel too high', according to a report published today.*
>
> *Dr Stefan Szymanski, economics lecturer at London University's Imperial College, concludes that pricing too high is more of a threat to Eurotunnel's financial future than pricing too low.*
>
> *'Lower prices could double the profitability of the £10 billion project', he says, claiming that Eurotunnel could feasibly halve its prices once the tunnel is running at full capacity.*
>
> *The report sets out various scenarios detailing the impact on revenue of varying levels of consumer enthusiasm and price sensitivity which show that, given Eurotunnel's £8 billion debt burden, 'in most cases failure to implement optimal prices (to maximise profits) significantly reduces revenue and may even lead to bankruptcy.'*
>
> *But more competitive pricing would inevitably kill off ferry services on the key Dover-Calais route. 'Under most plausible scenarios Eurotunnel will find it profitable to offer considerably lower prices and take a dominant share of the market,' Dr Szymanski says. 'In response, the ferry companies will find it hard to offer prices which can compete and still cover their overhead costs.'*
>
> *The Guardian, 19 January 1994*

Use the extract to do the following.

(a) Explain price elasticity of demand. Use it to discuss the conclusions reached by the report, concerning the appropriate pricing policy for Eurotunnel.

(b) Explain cross elasticity of demand, and use it to discuss the possible problems, highlighted in the report, facing the ferry companies.

(c) Assess the possible benefits to consumers of competition between Eurotunnel and the ferry companies in both the short and long run.

Answer to Case Study 2

(a) The price elasticity of demand is a measure of the sensitivity of the quantity which will be demanded by consumers of a good to changes in the price at which it is available to them. The price elasticity over a particular range is expressed in the following equation:

$$\text{Price elasticity of demand} = \frac{\text{Percentage change in quantity supplied}}{\text{Percentage change in price}}$$

Because an increase in price will lead to a reduction in the quantity demanded in normal circumstances, and a decrease in price will lead to an increase in demand, the price elasticity of demand will be a negative number. In other words, price and quantity demanded are inversely related. Normally, the minus sign is ignored, and the absolute size of the elasticity is noted.

The price elasticity of demand indicates the effects that changes in price have on sales. If demand is relatively elastic (more than 1), it may be unwise for a business to raise prices, since demand may fall significantly enough to reduce total revenue and possibly to reduce profits. If, on the other hand, demand is relatively inelastic (less than 1), increasing prices may allow total revenue to be increased.

The price elasticity of demand is affected by the existence of substitute products. In the market for transport across the English Channel, a substitute for the tunnel services is the alternative ferry services. The existence of substitutes will make consumers more sensitive to changes in price of a good, since they have an alternative to switch to if prices are set too high. Therefore, where there are substitutes, the price elasticity of demand will be higher.

In the article extract, Dr Szymanski argues that Eurotunnel could double profitability by lowering its prices, and that it could reasonably halve its prices when the tunnel is running at full capacity. This implies that the price elasticity of demand is more than 1 and that total revenue can be increased by lowering prices. The revenue lost through lowering the prices for all customers is more than compensated for by the additional revenue gained from extra traffic. If it is true that halving prices will increase Eurotunnel's revenue, it must also be true that this action will more than double the volume of customers.

If Eurotunnel sets its prices too high, more customers will choose the substitute services offered by ferry companies and much of Eurotunnel's capacity will remain unused.

It is worth noting that when deciding on its pricing policy, Eurotunnel will consider the current capacity of its services. When it first opened, the capacity of the tunnel was relatively low. Setting prices relatively high at first avoids the risk of demand exceeding capacity, which could result in customers being disappointed by delays. At the same time, this policy tests the market, seeing how much is demanded at the initial price set. As capacity increases, Eurotunnel can reduce its prices in stages to allow more capacity to be taken up. Again, this will test the market at different prices, providing information on the demand curve faced by the firm.

(b) The cross elasticity of demand refers to the responsiveness of demand for one good to changes in the price of another good. Given no change in the price of good A:

$$\text{Cross elasticity of demand} = \frac{\text{\% change in quantity of good A demanded}}{\text{\% change in the price of good B}}$$

If the two goods are substitutes, cross elasticity will be greater than 0 and a fall in the price of one will reduce the amount demanded of the other. If the goods are complements, cross elasticity will be negative and a fall in the price of one will raise demand for the other.

Cross elasticity in this way involves a comparison between two products. Cross elasticity is significant where the two goods are close substitutes for each other, so that a rise in the price of B is likely to result in an increase in the demand for A. The cross elasticity of demand between two complementary products can also be significant, because a rise in the price of B would result in some fall in demand for A. This is because of the fall in demand for B.

Since tunnel and ferry services are very close substitutes for one another, the cross elasticity of demand between them will be significantly positive. If Eurotunnel raises its prices, for example, more people and more freight carriers will switch to ferries and the volume of ferry services demanded will increase.

The article suggests that either Eurotunnel or the ferry companies could face eventual cutting back of services, depending upon the pricing policies Eurotunnel adopts. If Eurotunnel's prices are too high, it will be unable to attract enough custom away from the ferries and may face bankruptcy as a result. If its

NOTES

prices are set low enough, ferry companies will attempt to compete by lowering their prices. However, it will then become difficult for these companies to generate enough traffic to cover their overheads and their services may consequently be killed off.

(c) The addition of Eurotunnel as a competitor to the ferries widens the choice of services available to the cross-channel car traveller and freight carrier. There are some differences between the various services available, for example with respect to the journey time and the susceptibility to cancellation in bad weather.

In the short run, Eurotunnel's strategy is to set prices close to those of the ferries. There is then no cost saving for consumers. The possible consumer benefits are those relating to increased choice and increased capacity. Increased cross channel transport capacity makes it less likely that customers will have to queue for services, and more likely that they will be able to travel when they wish to.

In the longer term, it is likely that there will be price competition. Prices will move closer to the firms' marginal costs and both ferry and tunnel users will benefit from paying lower prices. This will cause more cross-channel trips to be made. If the prices fall to levels at which ferry companies can no longer make a profit, these companies may leave the market. If this process happens on a wide scale, consumers will face a reduction of choice compared with the short-run situation. If Eurotunnel then becomes the dominant firm in the market, it will be a monopolist and might raise its prices again. Consumer choice will then be limited and consumers would have to pay more. The tunnel company, as the monopolist producer, could be protected by high start-up costs, which would form an entry barrier against re-entry of ferry firms into the market.

Further question practice

Now try the following practice questions at the end of this text.

Multiple choice questions **25–36**

Exam style question **3**

Chapter 4

MARKET FAILURE: EXTERNALITIES AND INTERVENTION

Introduction

In this chapter, we shall be concerned with why a free market would result in an allocation of resources that is not optimal. If a free market has certain weaknesses and drawbacks, the question arises of whether there ought to be some regulation of the markets by the authorities (ie a mixed economy), in order to improve the allocation of resources.

Your objectives

After completing this chapter you should:

(a) be aware of the reasons why free markets may not lead to an ideal allocation of resources;

(b) understand the concepts of externalities, public goods and merit goods;

(c) understand why, how and for what purposes a government may intervene in a market in order to improve the allocation of resources.

1 MARKET IMPERFECTIONS AND MARKET FAILURE

1.1 The case for a free market

Advocates of a free market economy argue that the *market forces* of supply and demand will result in an efficient allocation of economic resources.

(a) Consumers will decide what they want to buy by relating the prices of goods to their marginal utilities.

(b) Producers will decide what goods to produce, and in what quantities, by relating their prices to the costs of production (and the costs of the scarce resources needed to produce the goods).

Definition

Market failure refers to a situation in which the market mechanism fails to produce the best (the optimal) allocation of resources.

Market failure is caused by a number of factors, which might be listed as:

(a) imperfections in the market ;

(b) a divergence between private costs and social costs (externalities);

(c) public goods;

(d) the need to consider non-market goals, such as social justice.

Activity 1

In Chapter 2 we examined the features of a perfect market. To remind yourself, try to identify which of the following factors are imperfections in a market.

(a) Consumer brand loyalty to a firm's branded goods, regardless of price.

(b) Lack of complete and accurate information for consumers.

(c) Slow response to price changes and the relatively inelastic supply of a product in the short run.

2 EXTERNALITIES AND PUBLIC GOODS

2.1 Social costs and private costs

In a free market, suppliers and households make their output and buying decisions for their own private benefit, and these decisions determine how the economy's scarce resources will be allocated to production and consumption. Private costs and private benefits, therefore, determine what goods are made and bought in a free market.

It can be argued that a free market mechanism would result in a satisfactory allocation of resources, *provided that* private costs are the same as social costs and private benefits are the same as social benefits.

When private benefit is not the same as social benefit, or when private cost is not the same as social cost, an allocation of resources which reflects private costs and benefits only may not be socially acceptable.

Private cost measures the cost to a firm of the resources it uses to produce a good. (This economic cost, as we shall see in a later chapter, is the opportunity cost of the resources used).

Social cost measures the cost to society as a whole of the resources that a firm uses.

An example where private cost and social cost differ is where a firm produces a good, and during the production process, pollution is discharged into the air. The private cost to the firm is the cost of the resources needed to make the good. The social cost consists of the private cost plus the additional costs incurred by other members of society, who suffer from the pollution.

Private benefit measures the benefit obtained directly by a supplier or by a consumer.

Social benefit measures the total benefit obtained, both directly by a supplier or a consumer, and indirectly, at no extra cost, to other suppliers or consumers.

An example where private benefit and social benefit differ, is where customers at a cafe in a piazza in Italy benefit from the entertainment provided by professional musicians, who are hired by the cafe. The customers of the cafe are paying for the service, in the prices they pay, and they obtain a private benefit from it. At the same time, other people in the piazza, who are not customers of the cafe, might stop and listen to the music. They will obtain a benefit, but at no extra cost to themselves. The social benefit from the musicians' service is greater than the private benefit to the cafe's customers.

Definition

An *externality* may be defined as a difference between the private and the social costs, or benefits, arising from an activity. Less formally, an externality is a cost or benefit which the market mechanism fails to take into account because the market responds to purely private signals.

Activity 2

An industrial company alters its production methods to reduce the amount of waste discharged from its factory into the local river. What will be the effect (increase or decrease) on:

(a) private costs;

(b) external benefits;

(c) social costs?

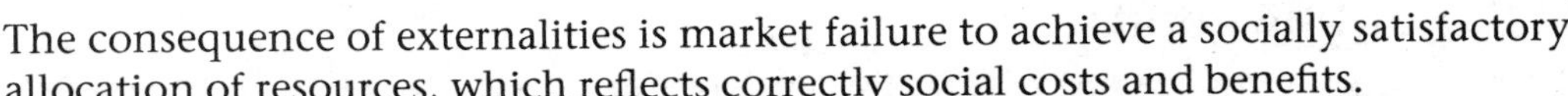

The consequence of externalities is market failure to achieve a socially satisfactory allocation of resources, which reflects correctly social costs and benefits.

We can use demand and supply analysis to illustrate the consequences of externalities. However, you need to accept that if there is an adverse externality, so that the social cost of supplying a good is greater than the private cost to the supplier firm, then:

(a) a supply curve which reflects total social costs will be to the left of the (private cost) market supply curve; and

(b) the vertical distance between the private cost supply curve and the social cost supply curve represents the size of the externalities.

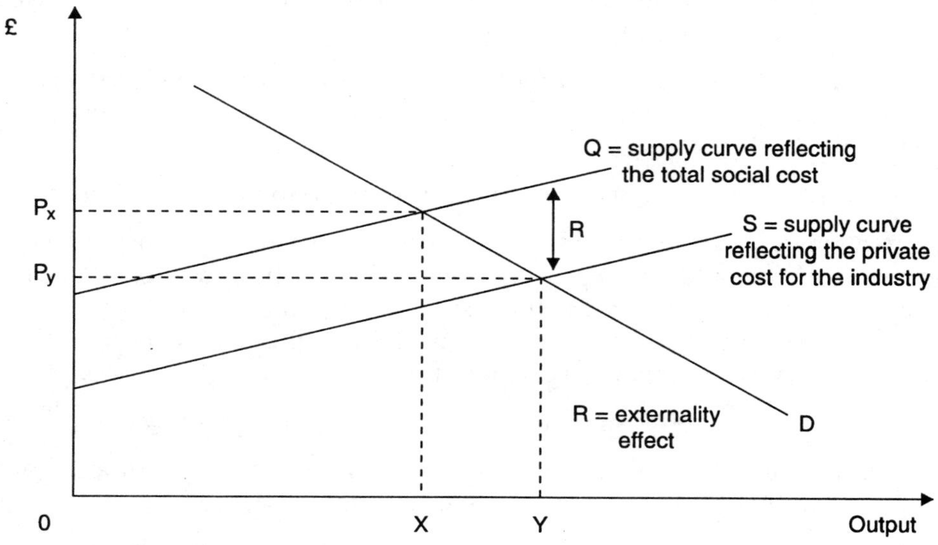

Figure 1

In Figure 1:

(a) if a free market exists, the amount of the good produced will be determined by the interaction of demand (curve D) and supply curve S. Here, output would be Y, at price P_y;

(b) if social costs were taken into account, and the market operated successfully, the amount of the good produced should be just X, at price P_x.

Given a free market, output of the good will exceed what it should be ideally, and so resources will have been over-allocated to production of this particular good.

Activity 3

Much Wapping is a small town where a municipal swimming pool and sports centre have just been built by a private firm. Which of the following is an external benefit of the project?

(a) The increased trade for local shops.

(b) The increased traffic in the neighbourhood.

(c) The increased profits for the sports firm.

(d) The increased building on previously open land.

2.2 Public goods

Some goods, by their very nature, involve so much spillover of externalities that they are difficult to provide, except as public goods whose production is organised by the government.

In the case of such goods, the consumption of the good by one individual or group does not reduce significantly the amount available for others. And if one individual uses the good, it does not reduce the availability of the good and its benefits to other individuals. Also, it is often difficult or impossible to exclude anyone from its benefits, once the good has been provided.

Examples of such goods are:

(a) defence and the armed forces;

(b) the police service;

(c) the fire service;

(d) the Thames flood barrier in England, and the Aswan Dam in Egypt.

Defence and policing are perhaps the most obvious examples of naturally public goods. It is not possible for individuals to buy their own defence systems or policing arrangements.

2.3 Merit goods and demerit goods

There are some types of goods which, without intervention, the market would not supply at all, or would not supply in the right quantities. This is because individuals do not always realise where their best interests lie, and so might fail to buy goods which would benefit them or, alternatively, might buy goods which do not benefit them.

Definition

Merit goods are considered to be desirable in themselves, for instance health and education, and the government supplies them for the public benefit.

(a) The government encourages, or insists upon the purchase of goods (*merit goods*), which it believes consumers should buy. For example, if you use a motorbike you are compelled by law to buy a helmet.

(b) The government discourages, or prohibits the purchase of goods (*demerit goods*) which it believes should not be bought by consumers. For example, children are not allowed to buy cigarettes, and nobody (other than doctors etc) is allowed to buy addictive drugs.

3 PRICE REGULATION

3.1 Market failure and the case for regulation of the market

Market failure, remember, refers to the failure of a free market to result in an optimal allocation of resources.

The existence of market failure and of externalities suggests the need for regulation of the market by the government, in order to improve the allocation of resources.

The main ways in which a government might choose to regulate or control markets are as follows:

(a) control the means of production (ie have state-owned industries);

(b) provide public goods;

(c) provide some goods (eg education, health) in greater quantities than there would be if an entirely free market operated;

(d) influence markets through legislation and regulation (eg regulation of monopolies, bans on dangerous drugs, enforcement of the use of some goods such as car seat belts, laws on pollution control, and so on);

(e) redistribute wealth, perhaps by taxing relatively wealthy members of society and redistributing this tax income to benefit the poorer members;

(f) influence market supply and demand through:

 (i) price legislation;

(ii) indirect taxation – for example, the lower tax on lead-free petrol in the UK compared with leaded petrol is aimed at encouraging greater demand for unleaded petrol to reduce environmental pollution;

(iii) subsidies;

(g) intervene in the market to create a demand for output that is labour-creating. A free price mechanism will result in a total demand for goods and services that would be met by a matching total supply. However, this total supply quantity might be insufficient to create full employment within the economy. Government might therefore wish to intervene to create a demand for output in order to create more jobs.

3.2 Maximum and minimum prices

The government might introduce regulations either:

(a) to set a maximum price for a good, perhaps as part of an anti-inflationary economic policy (eg a prices and incomes policy); or

(b) to set a minimum price for a good. For example, the Organisation of Petroleum Exporting Countries (OPEC) has tried in the past to impose minimum prices for oil on the world markets.

3.3 Maximum price legislation

The government may try to prevent prices of goods rising by establishing a price ceiling. If the price ceiling is higher than the equilibrium price, it will have no effect at all on the operation of market forces.

The price ceiling is above the equilibrium market price and is therefore ineffectual because the equilibrium price and output is reached by the free market interaction of supply and demand.

If the maximum price M is lower than the equilibrium price would be, there will be an excess of demand over supply (Figure 2). The low price attracts customers, but puts off suppliers.

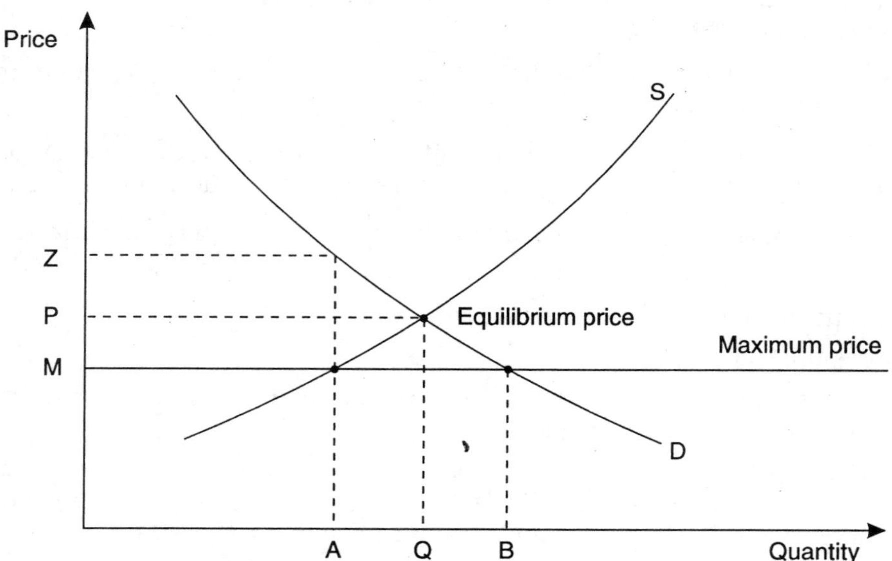

Figure 2

Here the price ceiling M is below the equilibrium price P. Producers will, therefore, reduce the quantity of goods supplied to the market place from Q to A. The

NOTES

quantity demanded will increase from Q to B, owing to the fall in price. The excess quantity demanded is therefore AB. To prevent an unfair allocation of the A units of the good that are available, the government might have to introduce *rationing*, eg petrol coupons, or a waiting list (as for council houses).

Rationing and *black marketeers* tend to go together. In Figure 2 consumers demand quantity B but can only get A. But for quantity A they are prepared to pay price Z, which is well above the official price M. The black marketeers step in to exploit the gap. The commodity may be sold at the official price M, but black marketeers may sell at price Z.

3.4 Minimum price regulations

Minimum price legislation or regulations aim to ensure that suppliers earn a minimum price for each unit of output they sell. Minimum prices are used in the European Union (EU). Farmers are guaranteed a minimum price for their output by the authorities if they cannot get a higher price on the free market.

If the minimum price is set below the market equilibrium there is no effect. But if it is set above the market price, it will cause an excess supply of AB (as in Figure 3). This was a recurring problem during the Seventies and Eighties for the EU, resulting in so-called 'butter mountains' and 'wine lakes'.

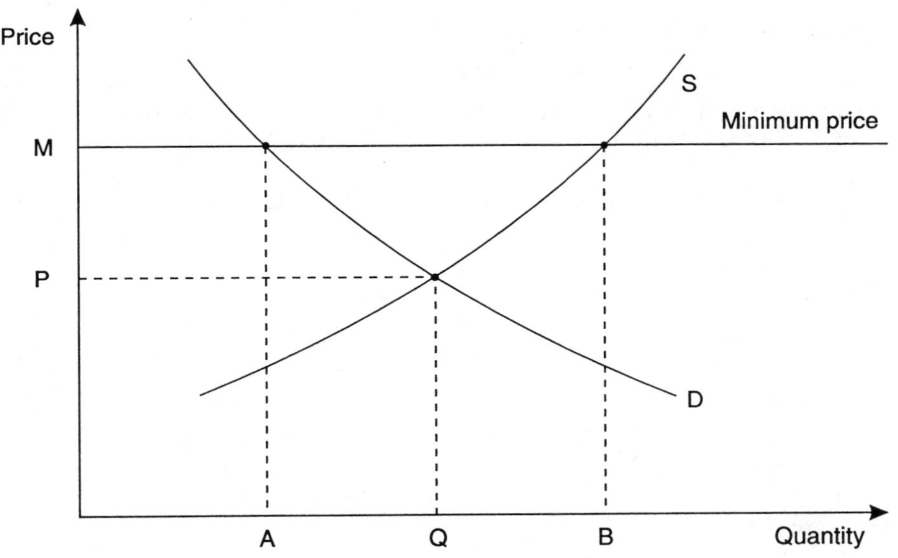

Figure 3

If the minimum price M is set above the equilibrium price P the quantity demanded falls from Q to A, but the quantity supplied increases to B. There is excess supply equal to the quantity AB.

When there is an excess of supply over demand, there is a danger that more of the good will be produced than can be sold at the minimum price. So surplus quantities will build up, which suppliers might sell off at low prices just to get rid of them. This has been a problem with oil production and OPEC's minimum price agreements in the past. To try to prevent over-supply and dumping of excess supply at low prices, a system of quotas might be introduced so that each supplier is allowed to produce up to a maximum quantity and no more. For some produce, the EU has tried to overcome the problem of excess supply by imposing quotas on farmers.

Now test yourself on the following activity.

NOTES

Activity 4

Many governments impose controls on the rents of private property with the object of assisting lower-paid workers. What are the likely consequences of such policies?

4 INDIRECT TAXES AND SUBSIDIES

Definition

Indirect taxation is an alternative form of price and output regulation: in other words taxation of expenditure on goods or services as opposed to direct taxation on incomes.

An indirect tax, which is imposed on some goods but not on others, is called a *selective* indirect tax.

If an indirect tax is imposed on one good, the tax will shift the supply curve to the left. This is because the price to consumers includes the tax, but the suppliers still only receive the net-of-tax price. For example, in Figure 4:

(a) the supply curve net of tax is S_0;

(b) the supply curve including the cost of the tax is S_1.

So if demand is for X_1 units, the price to suppliers will be P_2, but the price with tax to the consumer would be P_1 and the tax would be $(P_1 - P_2)$.

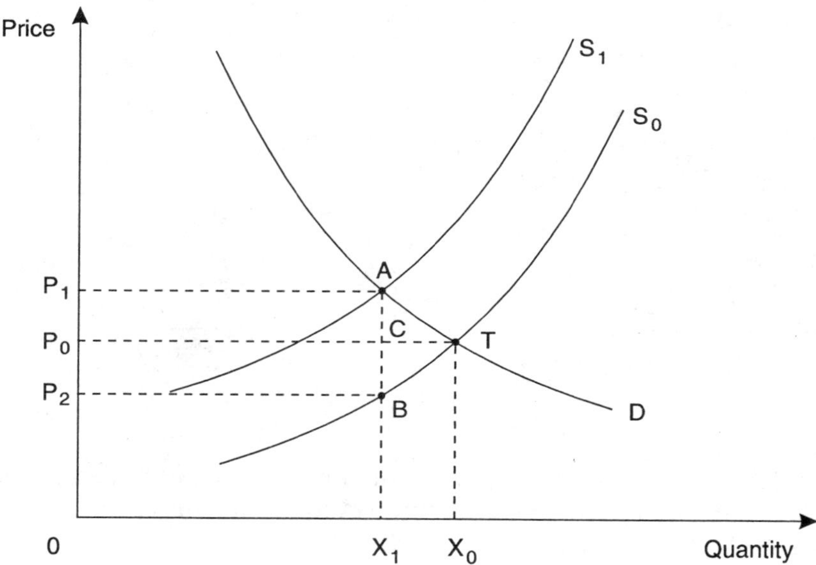

Figure 4

Without the tax, output would be X_0 and price P_0. Total expenditure is shown by the rectangle $0P_0TX_0$;

(c) After the tax has been imposed, output falls to X_1 and price with tax rises to P_1. Total expenditure is $0P_1AX_1$, of which P_2P_1AB is tax revenue and $0P_2BX_1$ is producers' total revenue;

(d) At the new equilibrium:

(i) price to the customer has risen from P_0 to P_1;

(ii) average revenue received by producers has fallen from P_0 to P_2;

(iii) the tax burden is therefore shared between the producers and consumers, with CB borne by the supplier and AC borne by consumers.

Consumers pay P_0P_1AC of total tax revenue and producers pay $P_2P_0CB_0$

The proportion of the tax passed on to the consumer rather than being borne by the supplier depends upon the elasticities of demand and supply in the market.

Figures 5(a) and 5(b) below illustrate the extreme cases of perfectly elastic demand and perfectly inelastic demand respectively.

Activity 5

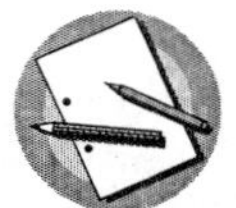

Try to work out yourself (from general principles, or from study of Figure 5) who bears the burden of taxation in each of these extreme cases.

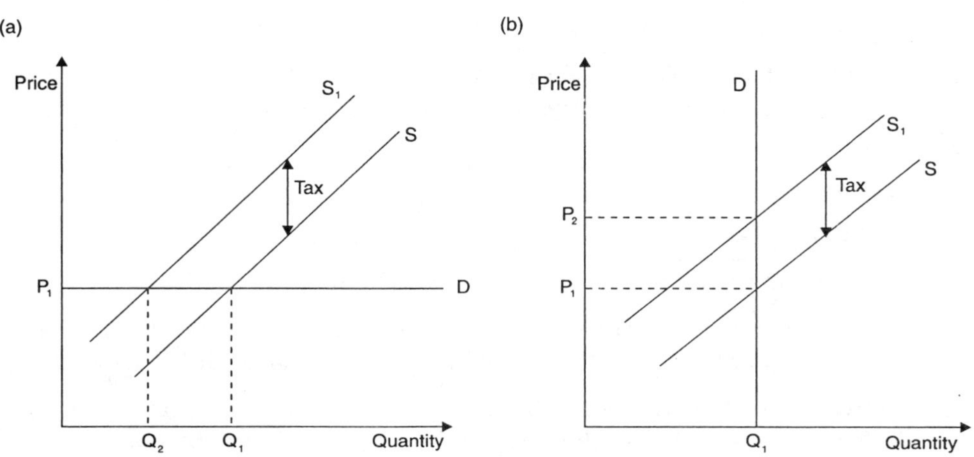

Figure 5

The elasticity of supply is also relevant. Figure 6 shows that for a given demand curve, the more inelastic is the supply curve, the greater the proportion of the tax that is borne by the supplier. Figure 6(a) shows a relatively inelastic supply curve S. The tax shifts the supply curve vertically upwards to S_1 and the equilibrium price rises from P_1 to P_2. The price to the consumer rises by AB per unit, while the supply price to the producer falls by BC per unit. Thus, the greater burden is borne by the supplier. Figure 6(b) in contrast shows a relatively elastic supply curve S_1, with a tax per unit as shown by the Tax line, the same amount of tax per unit as in Figure 6(a). The supply curve shifts to S_1 and the equilibrium price rises to P_2. The price to the consumer rises by AB per unit, and the supply price to the producer falls by BC per unit. It can be seen from Figure 6 that when the consumer bears a greater proportion of the tax burden, the more elastic is the supply curve. Figure 6 also shows that, for a given demand curve, the price rise and the fall in the equilibrium quantity will both be greater when the supply curve is more elastic.

NOTES

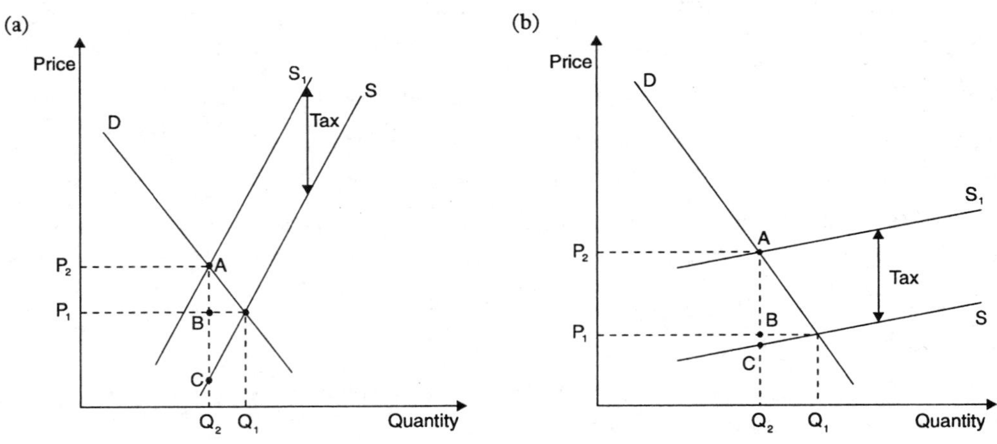

Figure 6

In general, the greater the elasticities of demand and supply, the greater will be the effect of a tax in reducing the quantity sold in, and therefore produced for, the market.

It can be shown that:

$$\frac{\text{consumers' share of tax}}{\text{producers' share of tax}} = \frac{\text{elasticity of supply}}{\text{elasticity of demand}}$$

(A proof of this is beyond the scope of this book, though not beyond the powers of a mathematically nimble student. You may like to try it as an additional exercise.)

So if a selective indirect tax of 10p is placed on a product where supply elasticity is 1.2 and demand elasticity is 0.8, the price of the good would rise by 6p, ie:

(a) the consumer would pay 6p of the 10p (ratio 1.2 : 0.8);

(b) the supplier would pay 4p because the price increase of 6p is not enough to pay the full tax of 10p per unit.

Further points to note are that:

(a) since such a tax reduces output, it may be harmful to an industry. For some companies, the reduction in quantities produced may lead to significant rises in the unit costs of production. This could have adverse consequences on the competitive position of the firm if it competes in domestic or overseas markets with foreign firms not subject to the same tax;

(b) indirect taxation may be used to create an improvement in the allocation of resources when there are damaging externalities.

4.1 Subsidies

Definition

A *subsidy* is a payment to the supplier of a good by the government.

The payment is made:

(a) to encourage more production of the good, by offering a further incentive to suppliers; or

(b) to keep prices on the market lower. Subsidised goods are cheaper to the consumer. Subsidised goods are therefore socially desirable goods whose production the government wishes to encourage; or

NOTES

(c) to protect a vital industry such as agriculture, when current demand in the short term is low and threatening to cause an excessive contraction of the industry.

A subsidy is rather like indirect taxation in reverse. In Figure 7:

(a) supply curve S_0 is what the supply curve would be if no subsidy existed;

(b) supply curve S_1, to the *right* of S_0, is the supply curve with the subsidy.

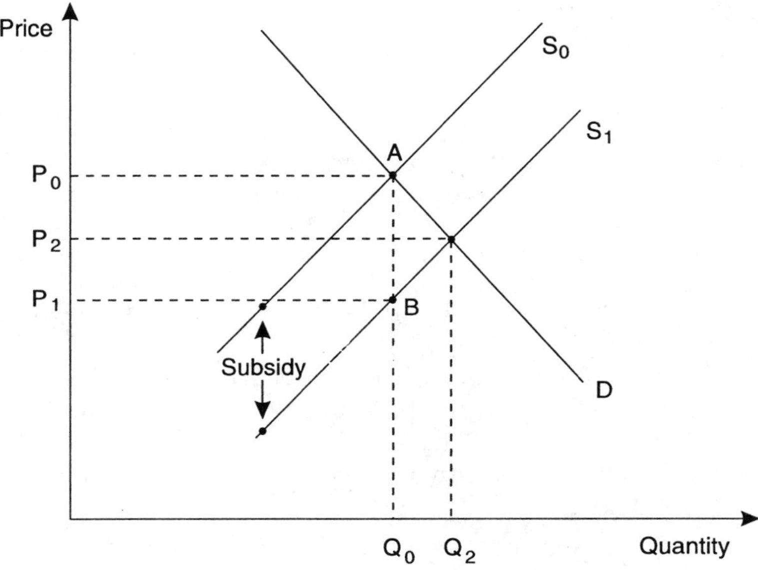

Figure 7

If there were no subsidy, the free market equilibrium price would be P_0, and output Q_0.

With a subsidy per unit equivalent to AB, suppliers would be willing to produce Q_0. If output were Q_0 then consumers need only be charged P_1, because the supplier will receive a subsidy of AB per unit produced. This reflects the fact that the supply curve shifts from S_0 to S_1. But, given the position of the demand curve, there will be a shift in the equilibrium quantity produced to Q_2, which can be sold on the market for P_2. So the effect of the subsidy will be:

(a) to increase the amount supplied in equilibrium; and

(b) to decrease the price, but the decrease in price will be less than the value of the subsidy itself.

Activity 6

By reference to Figure 7, analyse the extent to which the benefit of the subsidy falls to:

(a) the consumer;

(b) the supplier.

Who bears the cost of the subsidy?

Subsidies can be used to create an improvement in the allocation of resources when there are beneficial externalities.

When there is a beneficial externality, with the social benefits from supply of a good exceeding the private benefits, the ideal equilibrium price is at:

(a) a higher output; and

(b) a lower price;

than the free market equilibrium price and output.

The effect of a subsidy is to shift the market equilibrium to:

(a) a higher output; and

(b) a lower price.

If the amount of the subsidy were made equal to the size of the beneficial externality, the effect of the subsidy would be to regulate the market so that an ideal allocation of resources to the good is achieved. When the state does this, it might be said to be 'internalising the externality'.

Chapter roundup

- In this chapter, we have discussed why free markets may not lead to an ideal allocation of resources, and have discussed methods of regulating the market.
- Note in particular the following concepts.
  - *Market failure* – the failure of a market to produce a satisfactory allocation of resources.
  - *Public goods* – goods which by their nature need to be provided communally. Such goods cannot be provided privately because if they are provided at all, all will benefit from them: as a result, individuals would have no incentive to pay for them since they might as well be free riders.
  - *Social costs* – the costs to society of using economic resources.
  - *Social benefits* – the total gains to society as a whole flowing from an economic decision.
  - *Externalities* – the differences between private and social costs.
- Maximum or minimum prices may be set in attempts to regulate price and output, or policies of indirect taxation or subsidy may be employed. You should understand:
  - the effect of indirect taxation or a subsidy on the supply curve, and so on the equilibrium price and output for a good;
  - the incidence of the cost of an indirect tax, or the benefit of a subsidy, ie how the cost or benefit ends up divided between supplier and consumer;
  - the possibility of using a selective indirect tax to counter an adverse externality, or a subsidy when there is a beneficial externality, in order to re-allocate production resources in a better way.

Quick quiz

1 What is the general case in favour of allowing a free market to operate?

2 What is market failure, and what are its main causes?

3 What is an externality? What is the consequence of an externality?

4 Show, using a diagram, the difference between the free market price and output equilibrium, and the ideal equilibrium for a good, when there is an adverse externality with the good.

5 What is a public good? Give examples.

6 List various ways of regulating a market.

7 What determines the proportion of an indirect tax which is passed on to the consumer?

Answers to Activities

1 All of these are market imperfections. The point about (a) is that the consumer is behaving irrationally – paying more for a product without getting any greater total satisfaction from consuming it.

2 (a) Private costs of the company will presumably increase: the anti-pollution measures will have involved a financial outlay.

(b) External benefits will presumably increase: the public will benefit from a cleaner river.

(c) Social costs may stay the same: the increase in private costs may be balanced by the reduction in the external costs to society.

3 Item (b) is an external cost of the project, since increased volumes of traffic are harmful to the environment. Item (c) is a private benefit for the firm. Item (d) would only be an external benefit if a building is better for society than the use of open land, which is unlikely. Item (a) is correct because the benefits to local shops are additional to the private benefits of the sports firm and as such are external benefits.

4 You should see this question as a variation of maximum price legislation, which can be answered accordingly by supply and demand analysis. In addition, you could add points about:

(a) the deteriorating quality of rented accommodation if rents are held down, with landlords reluctant to pay for repairs and maintenance etc;

(b) the creation of a black market in rented property;

(c) discouraging new investment in building rented property.

5 In Figure 5(a), with perfectly elastic demand, demand falls to zero if the price is raised. Consequently, the supplier must bear the full burden of the tax with his supply price falling by the amount BC. In spite of the imposition of the tax, the market price remains the same but there is a fall in the quantity demanded from Q_1 to Q_2.

In the case of perfectly inelastic demand (Figure 5(b)), the supplier can pass on the full amount of the tax to the consumer by increasing the price from P_1 to P_2 by the full amount Q of the tax. The quantity supplied remains unchanged.

6 (a) Consumers benefit by the lowering of prices from P. to P_2.

(b) Suppliers benefit because they will receive a lower price, P_2 rather than P_0, but on top of this price they will receive the subsidy AB per unit.

(c) The cost of the subsidy is borne by the government (in effect, the taxpayer).

Case Study

'The price system cannot allocate resources efficiently when social costs such as pollution are becoming increasingly common.

Unless government intervenes in an attempt to correct the distortions in resource allocation that such social costs impose, society as a whole will be much worse off as a result of the actions of a few polluters upon the welfare of the majority of non-polluters.'

Explain what is meant by this statement.

Answer to Case Study

One important aspect of production and consumption in modern economics is that they frequently give rise to externalities. An externality may be defined as a difference between the private and social costs or benefits arising from a given activity, so it may be regarded as the spill-over effects of production and

NOTES

consumption which affect others, or society as a whole, rather than just the individual producers or consumers.

To get the full social costs of production we must, therefore, add the costs or benefits of these externalities to the private costs. A commonly quoted example of an externality imposing costs on society as a whole, which diverge from the private costs of production, is that of pollution. An industrial producer will take into account only its private costs of raw materials, labour and so on, whereas the total social cost of its activities will include the pollution arising from the dumping of waste materials.

The free operation of the price mechanism is claimed to lead to an optimum allocation of resources. This is because the price consumers are willing to pay for a given commodity represents the value they place on it. On the other hand, the cost of production is the amount that producers will pay to attract resources away from other uses (measuring the opportunity cost). An optimum allocation of resources exists when the value society places on another unit of the commodity, as measured by price, equals the cost of attracting resources away from alternative uses. This must be so because if alternatives were more highly valued, resources would move into their production as entrepreneurs would offer higher rewards.

The existence of externalities, however, has an important bearing on the allocation of resources to different uses in the economy. An efficient allocation can only exist when all prices in the economy reflect fully the social costs of production and consumption. Prices in a market economy, however, are based entirely on private costs. So, if a given activity imposes relatively large social costs on society, the free operation of the price mechanism will not lead to an optimum allocation of resources.

Where the social costs of production exceed the private costs, market price will be less than the real social opportunity cost of production, and the levels of consumption and production will be higher than if the full social costs of production were taken into account. In other words, society will tend to over-produce this commodity and under-produce others where the social costs of production are less than the private costs. The allocation of resources would be sub-optimal, as it would be possible to increase welfare by re-allocating resources from those goods which are over-produced in relation to the optimum level, to those which are under-produced.

A government might try to correct the distortions in resource allocation caused by social costs by bringing social costs and private costs into line.

Using pollution as an example, the output of polluting industries is generally greater than is optimal because the polluters often take little or no account of the costs imposed on others by their actions. If they were forced to pay for any externalities they impose, producers would be likely to change their techniques of production so as to minimise the pollution they generate. Also consumers would be likely to consume less of those goods which cause pollution. One approach for government is to levy a tax on polluters equal to the cost of removing the effects of the externality they generate. This will encourage firms to cut emissions and provide an incentive for them to research ways of permanently reducing pollution.

A second approach, which has tended to be more popular in the UK, is to impose regulations, under which waste emissions may be disposed of. Waste may only be disposed of with prior consent and if none is given, or if it is exceeded, the polluter is fined. Examples of legislation in this area include the Control of Pollution Act 1974 and the Environment Protection Act 1990. There may also be standards of, for example, air and water quality, with appropriate penalties for not conforming to the standards. Problems with this type of approach are the administrative burden it creates and the costs involved in monitoring and enforcement.

The government may also consider the use of subsidies to persuade polluters to cut back on their output and therefore pollution, or to assist with expenditure on new machinery, for example air filters, which reduce or eliminate pollution. The problem with subsidies is that they provide no incentive to reduce pollution any further. Indeed, profits are increased, which may have the opposite effect; encouraging more pollution to be generated in order to qualify for a subsidy. This is likely to be an expensive option for the government compared to using taxes, which provide additional revenue.

Further question practice

Now try the following practice questions at the end of this text.

Multiple choice questions	**37–48**
Exam style question	**4**

Chapter 5

THEORY OF THE FIRM: PRODUCTION AND COSTS

Introduction

In this chapter we shall look at the costs and output decisions of an *individual* firm. In other words, we shall look at what the costs of production are for a single firm, and how these are affected by both short-run and long-run factors.

We shall then go on to consider profit and how much output a firm will produce at a given market price. The aggregate amount of goods supplied by every individual firm adds up to the market supply; by studying an individual firm we are looking at the building blocks of market supply.

Your objectives

After completing this chapter you should:

(a) understand the concepts of total costs, average costs and marginal costs and be aware of their effects on short-run decision-making;

(b) understand the concept of economies of scale and how it affects decision-making in the long run.

NOTES

1 COSTS OF PRODUCTION AND THE FIRM

The firm is a wide term for any organisation which carries on business. In spite of their structural differences, firms will be treated as single, consistent decision-taking units, and we shall ignore any differences in decision-making procedures and economic structures between them. In particular, we will assume that the key objective of a firm is to maximise its profits.

Production is carried out using the factors of production, which must be paid for or rewarded for their use. The cost of production is the cost of the factors that are used.

Factor of production	*Its cost*
land	rent
labour	wages
capital	interest
entrepreneurship	normal or pure profit

It is very important to notice that normal profit is a cost. This may seem odd if you are used to thinking of profit as the *difference* between revenue and cost. We shall return to this point later.

Factors of production are discussed in greater detail in the next chapter.

1.1 Fixed and variable inputs and costs

Firms combine various input resources to produce a given level of output. By varying the amounts of inputs used, the level of output can be altered. However, not all inputs are equally flexible. Energy, raw materials, the number of labour hours and so on can be combined with each other with a great deal of flexibility, but the size of the factory or number of machines cannot be varied so quickly. For example, output can be increased in the short term by buying extra materials, hiring new labour or working overtime, but the extra work will still be done on the same machines and in the same factory.

Economists take the view that *in the short run* some factors of production (or production inputs) are variable in supply and so have variable costs. Typically, labour is regarded as a variable cost item. On the other hand, some factors of production (production inputs) are fixed in supply and so have fixed costs. Typically, capital is regarded as a fixed cost item.

More precisely, fixed costs are those costs which do not vary directly with output, but which remain constant whether anything is produced or not. Variable costs are those which *do* vary directly with the level of output.

In the long run, however, the supply of short-term fixed cost items can be made to vary and so all factors of production are variable. More land and buildings can be obtained, more capital obtained and more entrepreneurship stimulated.

In the short run, profit-maximising decisions must be taken within the limits of a fixed supply of resources. In the longer run, however, most costs are variable, because the supply of skilled labour, machinery, buildings and so on can be increased or decreased. Profit-maximising decisions in the long term are, therefore, subject to fewer restrictions about resource availability.

NOTES

1.2 Short-run costs: total costs, average costs and marginal costs

Let us now turn our attention to short-run costs – ie costs of output during a time period in which only some resources of production are variable in availability and some resources of production are fixed in quantity.

There are three aspects of cost to be considered.

(a) *Total cost* – TC.

(b) *Average cost* – AC. Average cost is simply the total cost divided by the total quantity produced.

   (i) Average cost is made up of an average fixed cost per unit plus an average variable cost per unit.

$$AC = \frac{TC}{n} = \frac{TFC}{n} + \frac{TVC}{n}$$

   (here n is the number of units produced)

   In other words, AC = AFC + AVC

   (ii) Average fixed cost per unit (AFC) will get smaller as more units are produced. This is because TFC is the same amount regardless of the volume of output, so as n gets bigger, AFC must get smaller.

   (iii) Average variable costs per unit (AVC) will change as output volume increases.

(c) *Marginal cost* – MC. For example, the marginal cost for a firm of producing the 50th unit of output is the extra cost of making the 50th unit, having already made the previous 49 units. In other words the MC of the 50th unit is the total cost of making the first 50 units minus the total cost of making the first 49 units.

Definition

Marginal cost is the extra cost of producing one more unit of output.

Activity 1

To test your understanding of these concepts, look at the three definitions given below. Which of them, if any, correctly describes the marginal cost of producing one extra unit of output?

(a) MC = increase in total cost of production

(b) MC = increase in variable cost of production

(c) MC = increase in average cost of production.

1.3 Numerical illustration of TC, AC and MC

Let us suppose that a firm employs a given amount of capital which is a fixed (invariable) input in the short run: in other words, it is not possible to obtain extra amounts of capital quickly. The firm may combine with this capital different amounts of labour, which we assume to be a variable input in the short term. So fixed capital and variable labour can be combined to produce different levels of output.

Here is an illustration of the relationship between the different definitions of the firm's costs: (the figures used are hypothetical).

NOTES

Table 1

Units of output n	Total cost TC £	Average cost AC £	Marginal cost MC £	
1	1.10	1.10	1.10	
2	1.60	0.80	0.50	(1.60 – 1.10)
3	1.75	0.58	0.15	(1.75 – 1.60)
4	2.00	0.50	0.25	(2.00 – 1.75)
5	2.50	0.50	0.50	(2.50 – 2.00)
6	3.12	0.52	0.62	(3.12 – 2.50)
7	3.99	0.57	0.87	(3.99 – 3.12)
8	5.12	0.64	1.13	(5.12 – 3.99)
9	6.30	0.70	1.18	(6.30 – 5.12)
10	8.00	0.80	1.70	(8.00 – 6.30)

(a) *Total cost* (TC) is the sum of labour costs plus capital costs, since these are assumed to be the only two inputs.

(b) *Average cost* (AC) is the cost per unit of output, ie AC = $\frac{TC}{output} = \frac{TC}{n}$

(c) *Marginal cost* (MC) is the total cost of producing n units minus the total cost of producing one less unit, ie (n–1) units.

Note the following points on this set of figures.

(a) *Total cost.* Total costs of production carry on rising as more and more units are produced.

(b) *Average cost.* AC changes as output increases. It starts by falling, reaches a lowest level, and then starts rising again.

(c) *Marginal cost.* The MC of each extra unit of output also changes with each unit produced. It too starts by falling, fairly quickly reaches a lowest level, and then starts rising.

(d) *AC and MC compared.* At lowest levels of output, MC is less than AC. At highest levels of output, though, MC is higher than AC. There is a cross-over point, where MC is exactly equal to AC. In this small example, it is at 5 units of output.

Activity 2

Complete the table below by calculating TC, MC, and AC at each level of output.

Output (units)	*Total FC*	*Total VC*	*TC*	*MC*	*AC*
0	15	0		–	–
1	15	30			
2	15	40			
3	15	60			
4	15	90			
5	15	130			
6	15	180			

1.4 Economists' and accountants' concepts of cost

To an economist, *cost* includes an amount for normal profit, which is the reward for entrepreneurship. To an accountant, there is no profit element within cost.

Definition

An *entrepreneur* is an economic agent who organises the exploitation of factors of production in a firm.

Another feature of *cost accounting* is that costs can be divided into fixed costs and variable or marginal costs. Total fixed costs per period are a given amount, regardless of the volume of production and sales. The variable cost per unit is a constant amount, so that the total variable cost of sales is directly proportional to the volume of sales.

Economists do not take this view. In the short run, there are fixed costs and variable or marginal costs, but the marginal cost of making each extra unit of output need not be the same for each extra unit that is made. In other words, the marginal cost per unit is not a standard value for every unit produced.

The following points are worth stressing.

(a) To the economist, cost includes an element for normal profit.

(b) To the economist, cost means opportunity cost. Normal profit, which is the cost of entrepreneurship, is an opportunity cost, because it is the amount of profit that an entrepreneur could earn elsewhere, and so it is the profit that he must earn to persuade him to keep on with his investment in his current enterprise.

(c) The short-run marginal cost per unit can change as more output is produced.

2 AVERAGE COSTS, MARGINAL COSTS AND DIMINISHING RETURNS

2.1 The relationship between AC and MC

The relationships between average and marginal costs are important.

(a) When the average cost schedule is rising, the marginal cost will always be higher than the average cost.

This makes sense. If the marginal cost of making one extra unit of output exceeds the average cost of making all the previous units, then making the extra unit will clearly cause an increase in the average unit cost.

(b) When the average cost curve is falling, the marginal cost lies below it.

(c) When the average cost curve is horizontal, marginal cost is equal to it.

Activity 3

(a) It is possible for the average total cost curve to be falling while the average variable cost curve is rising. True or false?

(b) Marginal fixed costs per unit will fall as output increases. True or false?

The marginal cost curve always cuts through the average cost curve at the lowest point of the average cost curve (Figure 1).

NOTES

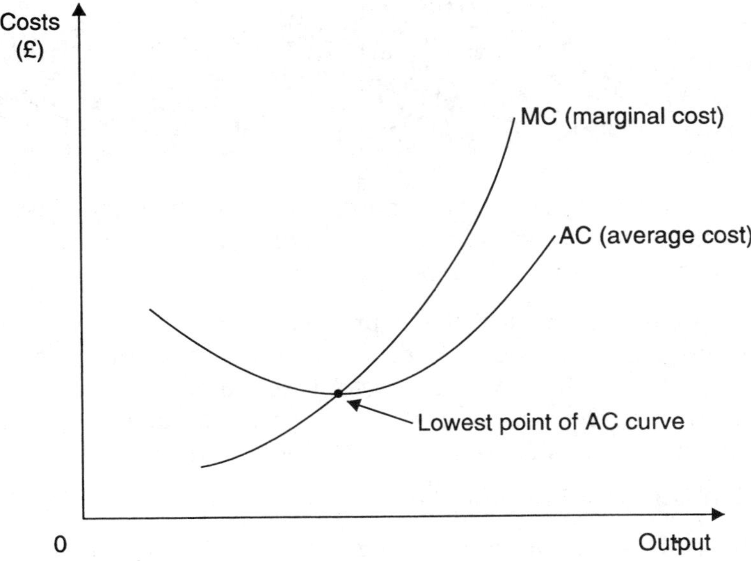

Figure 1

The short-run average cost (SAC) curve is always likely to be U-shaped. We now consider why.

Fixed costs per unit of output, ie average fixed costs, will fall as the level of output rises. Spreading fixed costs over a larger amount of output is a major reason why (short-run) average costs per unit fall as output increases.

Definition

Variable costs are made up from the cost of the factors of production whose use can be varied in the short run (for example wages, fuel bills and raw material purchases).

Total variable costs vary with output in the short run as well as in the long run.

(a) The standard belief about short-run variable costs is that *up to a certain level of output, the variable cost per unit is more or less constant* (eg wages costs and materials costs per unit of output are unchanged). If the average fixed cost per unit is falling as output rises and the average variable cost per unit is constant, it follows that the average total cost per unit will fall too as output increases.

(b) Even so, there is evidence that *average variable costs rise when output increases beyond a normal capacity level*. Beyond this level greater output can be attained only by using larger quantities of the variable factors of production, but this will lead to problems such as overcrowding, managerial problems and more frequent breakdowns of machinery from intensive use. Average variable costs will therefore begin to rise at some point, even assuming that there are no overtime payments or use of more skilled labour. With average variable costs per unit rising as output increases, the average total cost per unit will rise too.

Combining fixed and variable costs gives us the normal U-shaped short-run average cost curve.

2.2 The law of diminishing returns

Diminishing returns explain why a short-run average cost curve begins to rise at a certain level, and the average cost per unit of production gets higher as more output is produced.

NOTES

Definition

The *law of diminishing returns* states that, given the present state of technology, as more units of a variable input factor are added to input factors that are fixed in supply in the short run, the resulting additions to total production will eventually and progressively decline.

In other words, as more units of a variable factor are added to a quantity of fixed factors, there may be some *increasing returns or constant returns* as more units of the variable factor are added, but eventually, *diminishing returns* will set in.

The law of diminishing returns can also be expressed as the law of variable proportions. This states that as the proportions of a variable input factor to a fixed input factor are altered, and more of the variable factor is added to the fixed factor, the marginal product attributable to each extra unit of the variable factor will increase at first, but will later diminish and may eventually become negative.

Two important points to note about the law of diminishing returns are as follows.

(a) It relates to the short-run situation, when some inputs are in fixed supply. It does not relate to the long run.

(b) It is not a law that can be proved, but it has been found to apply frequently in practice.

Activity 4

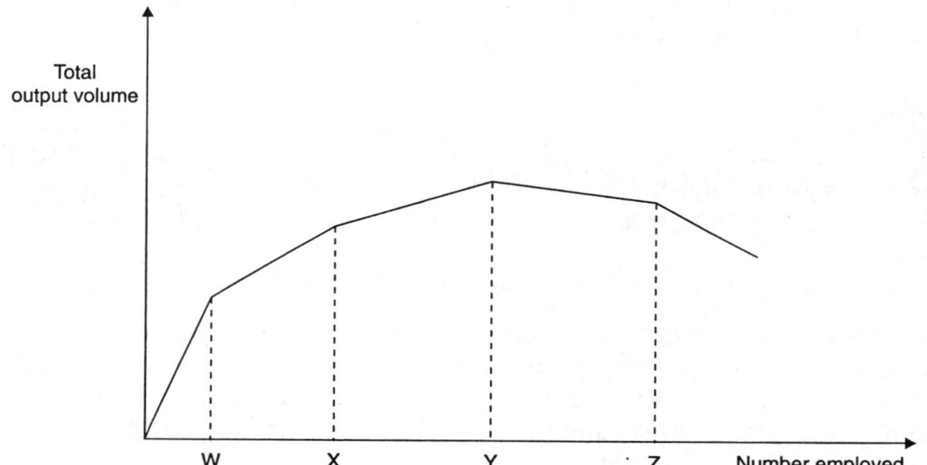

In the diagram above, from what level of employment do diminishing returns start to occur?

2.3 Marginal productivity

Diminishing returns can be explained by the marginal productivity of extra quantities of a variable factor of production.

Total physical product is the total output, measured by quantity rather than value, that is produced by a given quantity of (fixed plus variable) production factors.

If we combine a fixed factor of production (ie capital, or land) with increasing quantities of a variable factor (ie labour), the total volume of output should increase as more and more units of the variable factor are employed. In other words, total physical product will increase as extra units of the variable factor are employed.

The *average physical product* (APP) of the variable factor of production will be:

$$\frac{\text{Total physical product}}{\text{Quantity of variable factor units employed}}$$

In the short run, to produce more output, a firm must acquire extra quantities of variable factors of production, but fixed factors of production cannot be increased. Variable factors will be combined with fixed factors to produce the firm's output.

Definition

Marginal physical product is the addition to total output from employing an additional unit.

(a) The extra physical output produced by an extra unit of variable factor is called the *marginal physical product* (MPP). At low volumes of output, extra units of a variable factor might succeed in producing an increasing MPP.

(b) Eventually, extra units of variable factor will no longer be as productive, and MPP will start to get smaller. Returns from the extra quantities of variable factor will therefore get smaller or diminish – this gives us the name 'law of diminishing returns'.

(c) A declining MPP and a declining average physical product APP explain why *marginal* costs of extra units of production will eventually increase, and why *average costs* will start to increase beyond a certain level of output.

(d) This is why the law of diminishing returns explains the U shape of the short run AC curve.

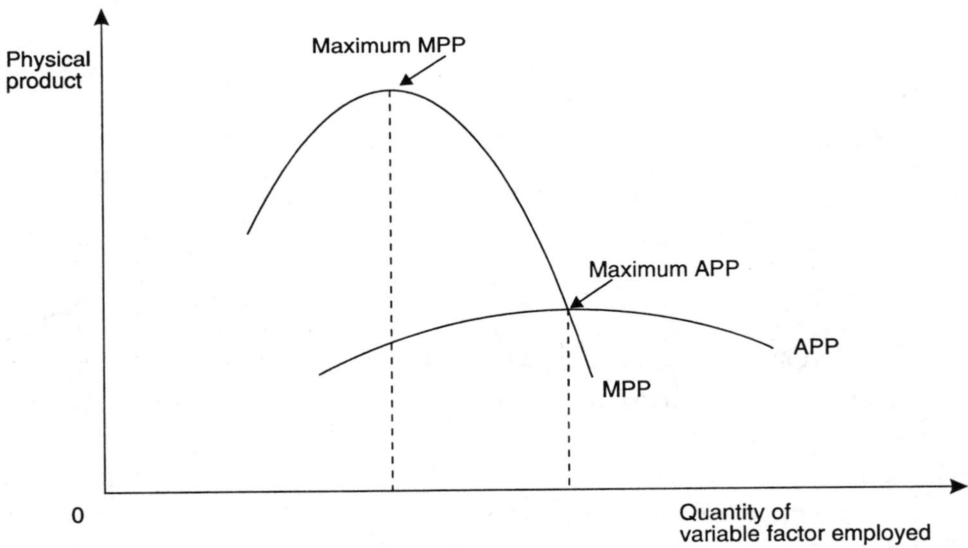

Figure 2 Average physical product and marginal physical product of a variable factor of production

3 PROFIT MAXIMISATION

3.1 Introduction

Before going on to consider long-run costs, let us think about the decision by an individual firm as to how much output it is going to produce in the short term.

NOTES

The common principle applying to competitive firms is the motive of *profit maximisation*: a firm is assumed to produce a volume of output that will enable it to maximise its profits.

Activity 5

Although this assumption (that firms always have the objective of maximising profits) provides a useful basis for discussing the output decisions of firms, it is not always the case in practice. Can you think of cases where firms are not necessarily aiming to maximise profits?

We can define profits as *total revenue minus total economic costs* at any level of output. Profits are at a maximum where the (vertical) distance between the total revenue (TR) and total cost (TC) curves in Figure 3 is greatest.

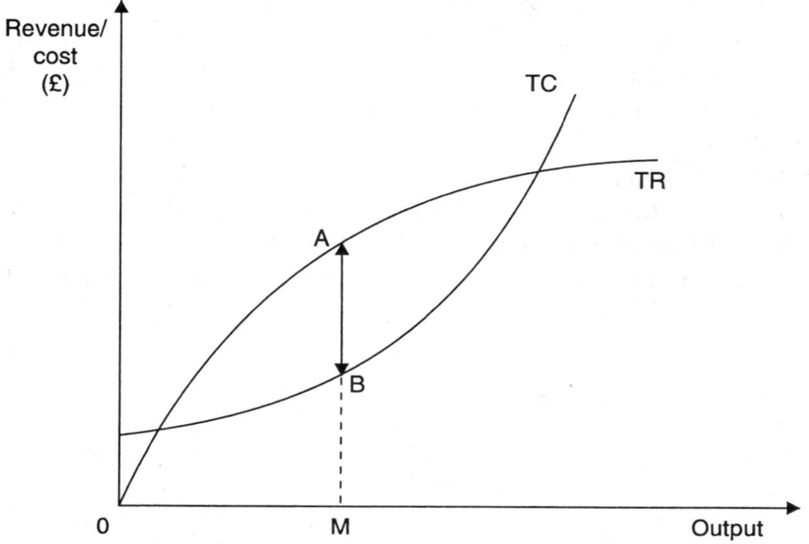

Figure 3

3.2 Total revenue, average revenue and marginal revenue

Before looking at how a firm decides its profit-maximising output, we must look at its revenues. There are three aspects of revenue to consider.

(a) *Total revenue* (TR), which is the total income obtained from selling a given quantity of output. We can think of this as quantity sold multiplied by the price per unit: $TR = P \times Q$.

(b) *Average revenue* (AR), which we can think of as the *price per unit* sold: $AR = \frac{TR}{n}$

(c) *Marginal revenue* (MR), which is the addition to total revenue earned from the sale of one extra unit of output: $MR = P = AR$.

When a firm can sell all its extra output at the same price, the AR curve will be a straight line on a graph, horizontal to the x axis. The marginal revenue per unit from selling extra units at a fixed price must be the same as the average price. (See Figure 4).

When the AR is falling as more units are sold, the MR must be less than the AR. In other words, if the price per unit must be lowered to sell more units, then the marginal revenue per unit obtained from selling the extra units will be less than the previous price per unit. (See Figure 5).

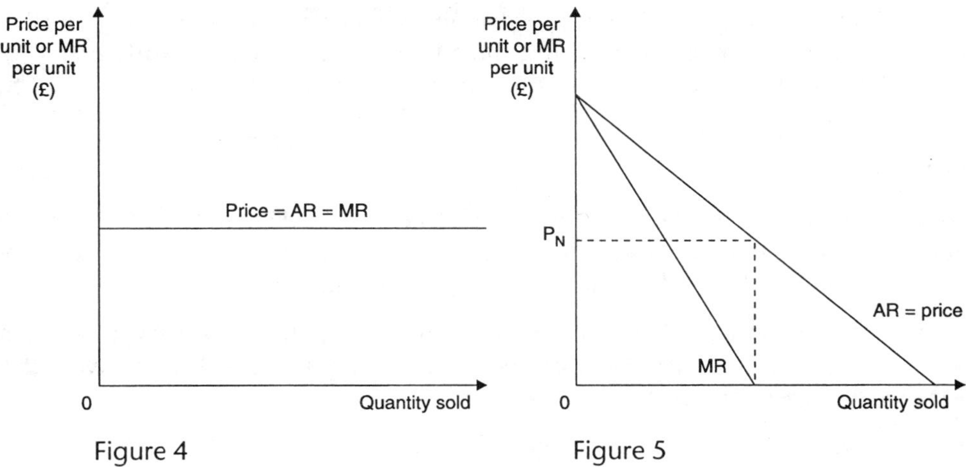

Figure 4

Figure 5

Note. In Figure 5, all units are sold at the same price. The firm has to reduce its price to sell more, but the price must be reduced for *all* units sold, not just for the extra units. This is because we are assuming that all output is produced for a single market, where a single price will prevail.

3.3 Illustration: AR and MR

This simple illustration shows how MR falls as AR falls, and MR is less than AR when this happens.

Units of sale Q	Price per unit AR	Total revenue (AR × Q)	Marginal revenue MR
	£	£	£
1	7.0	7	7
2	6.5	13	6
3	6.0	18	5
4	5.5	22	4
5	5.0	25	3

3.4 Profit maximisation: MC = MR

As a firm produces and sells more units, its total costs will increase and its total revenues will also increase (unless the price elasticity of demand is inelastic and the firm faces a downward sloping AR curve).

(a) Provided that the extra cost of making an extra unit is *less than* the extra revenue obtained from selling it, the firm will increase its profits by making and selling the extra unit.

(b) If the extra cost of making an extra unit of output *exceeds* the extra revenue obtainable from selling it, the firm's profits would be reduced by making and selling the extra unit.

(c) If the extra cost of making an extra unit of output is *exactly equal* to the extra revenue from selling it, bearing in mind that economic cost includes an amount for normal profit, it will be worth the firm's while to make and sell the extra unit. And since the extra cost of yet another unit would be higher (the law of diminishing returns applies) whereas extra revenue per unit from selling extra units is never higher, the profit-maximising output is reached at this point where MC = MR.

In other words, given the objective of profit maximisation:

(a) if MC is less than MR, profits will be increased by making and selling more;

(b) if MC is greater than MR, profits will fall if more units are made and sold, and a profit-maximising firm would not make the extra output;

(c) if MC = MR, the profit-maximising output has been reached, and this is the output quantity that a profit-maximising firm will decide to supply.

Activity 6

Working out a solution to the following numerical exercise will help to consolidate the points so far about short-run costs, the law of diminishing returns, marginal costs and marginal revenues and a firm's profit-maximising equilibrium.

A firm operates in a market where there is imperfect competition, so that to sell more units of output, it must reduce the sales price of all the units it sells. The following data are available for prices and costs.

Total output	*Sales price per unit (AR)*	*Average cost of output (AC)*
Units	£	£ per unit
0	–	–
1	504.00	720
2	471.00	402
3	439.00	288
4	407.25	231
5	377.40	201
6	346.00	189
7	317.07	182.5
8	288.375	180
9	259.00	186
10	232.20	198

The total cost of zero output is £600.

At what output level and price would the firm maximise its profits?

4 ECONOMIES OF SCALE AND LONG-RUN COSTS

4.1 Introduction

We have not yet considered a firm's *long-run costs* of output. In the long-run, all inputs are variable, so the problems associated with the diminishing returns to variable factors do not arise; in other words, the law of diminishing returns applies only to short-run costs and not to long-run costs. Whereas short-run output decisions are concerned with diminishing returns to scale given fixed factors of production, *long-run output decisions* are concerned with *economies of scale* when all factor inputs are variable.

Definition

Economies of scale are reductions in the average cost of producing a commodity in the long run as the output of the commodity increases.

NOTES

Output will vary with variations in inputs, such as labour and capital.

(a) If output increases in the same proportion as inputs (eg doubling all inputs doubles output), there are *constant returns to scale.*

(b) If output increases *more* in proportion to inputs (eg doubling all inputs trebles output), there are *economies of scale*. In the long run, average costs of production will continue to fall as output volume rises.

(c) If output increases less in proportion to inputs (eg trebling all inputs only doubles output), there are *diseconomies of scale*. In the long run, average costs of production will rise as output volume rises.

Returns to scale are, in effect, concerned with improvements or declines in productivity *by increasing the scale of production* (eg by mass-producing instead of producing in small batch quantities).

Figure 6 shows the shape of the long-run average cost curve (LAC) if there are increasing returns to scale up to a certain output volume and after that constant returns to scale It may be that the flat part of the LAC curve is never reached, or it may be that *diseconomies of scale* are encountered.

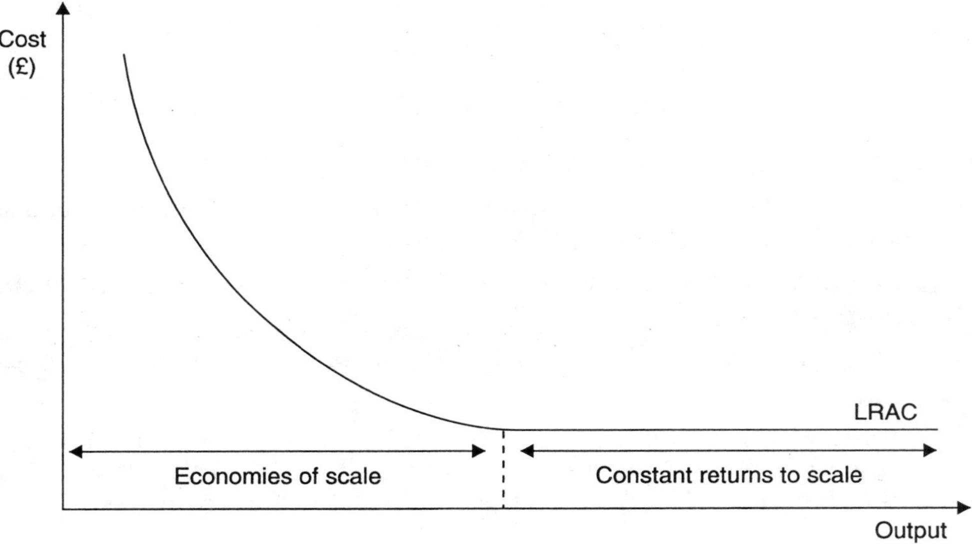

Figure 6

Definition

Diseconomies of scale arise when a firm gets so large that it cannot operate efficiently or it is too large to manage efficiently, so that average costs begin to rise.

NOTES

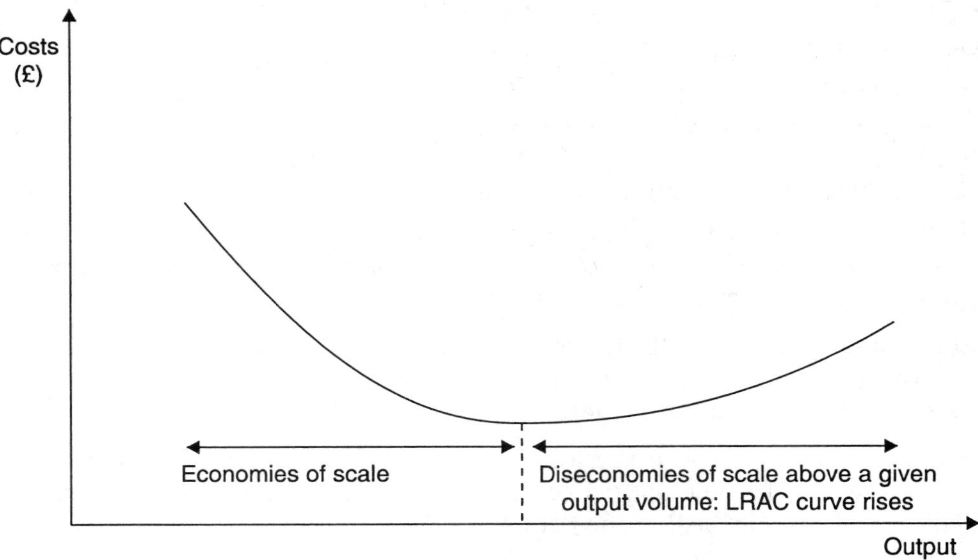

Figure 7

Activity 7

Which of the following items could be the cause of diseconomies of scale?

1. A firm has to lower its prices in order to sell a higher volume of output, and so producing more becomes unprofitable.
2. Expansion of the industry as a whole forces up the cost of production resources for firms in the industry.
3. Employees feel more and more left out and lose motivation as their firm gets bigger.

A profit-maximising firm will try to minimise its average costs in the long run. To do this it will try to produce output on a scale where the LAC curve is at its lowest point. While there are economies of scale, a firm will always be trying to grow.

The economies of scale attainable from large-scale production may be categorised as:

(a) *internal economies of scale:* economies arising within the firm from the organisation of production; and

(b) *external economies of scale:* economies attainable by the firm because of the growth of the industry as a whole.

Internal economies of scale arise from the more effective use of available resources, and from increased specialisation, when production capacity is enlarged.

(a) *Specialisation of labour:* in a large undertaking, a highly skilled worker can be employed in a job which makes full use of his skills. In a smaller undertaking, individuals must do a variety of tasks, none of which they may do very well ('Jack-of-all-trades – master of none').

(b) *Division of labour:* because there is specialisation of labour there is also division of labour, ie work is divided between several specialists, all of whom contribute their share to the final product. A building will be constructed, for example, by labourers, bricklayers, plumbers, electricians, plasterers, etc. Switching between tasks wastes time, and division of labour avoids this waste.

(c) Large undertakings can make use of *larger and more specialised machinery*. If smaller undertakings tried to use similar machinery, the costs would be excessive because the machines would become obsolete before their physical life

NOTES

ends (ie their economic life would be shorter than their physical life). Obsolescence is caused by falling demand for the product made on the machine, or by the development of newer and better machines.

(d) For a similar reason, large undertakings can use specialised tools, which small undertakings would find too costly.

Economists refer to large capital items that are only economically justifiable at high volumes of output as *indivisibles*.

(e) *Dimensional* economies of scale refer to the relationship between the volume of output and the size of equipment (eg storage tanks) needed to hold or process the output. The cost of a container for 10,000 gallons of product will be *much* less than ten times the cost of a container for just 1,000 gallons.

(f) *Buying economies* may be available, reducing the cost of material purchases through bulk purchase discounts.

(g) *Indivisibility of operations:* there are operations which:

   (i) must be carried out at the same cost, regardless of whether the business is small or large; these are fixed costs and *average* fixed costs always decline as production increases;

   (ii) vary a little, but not proportionately, with size (ie having semi-fixed costs);

   (iii) are not worth considering below a certain level of output (eg advertising campaigns, marketing structures).

Set-up costs for batch production are an example of fixed cost items for which average unit costs become lower as the size of the production run gets bigger.

(h) Specialisation of labour and machines result in simplification and standardisation of operations (ie *variety reduction*) which themselves result in lower costs.

(i) *Stock holding* becomes more efficient. The most economic quantities of inventory to hold increase with the scale of operations, but at a lower proportionate rate of increase.

Activity 8

The list above is by no means complete. Can you add to it?

External economies of scale occur as an *industry* grows in size. For example:

(a) a large skilled labour force is created and educational services can be geared towards training new entrants;

(b) specialised ancillary industries will develop to provide components, transport finished goods, trade in by-products, provide special services etc. For instance, law firms may be set up to specialise in the affairs of the industry.

The extent to which both internal and external economies of scale can be achieved will vary from industry to industry, depending on the conditions with respect to that industry. In other words, big firms are better suited to some industries than others.

4.2 Technological progress and shifts in the long-run cost curve

The U-shaped LRAC curve predicted by the economic theory of eventual diminishing returns to scale may not exist in fact because of technological progress. Technological progress would shift the LRAC curves over time, as shown in Figure 8, so the LRAC curve observed from observed data would be the L-shaped curve shown by the dashed line.

NOTES

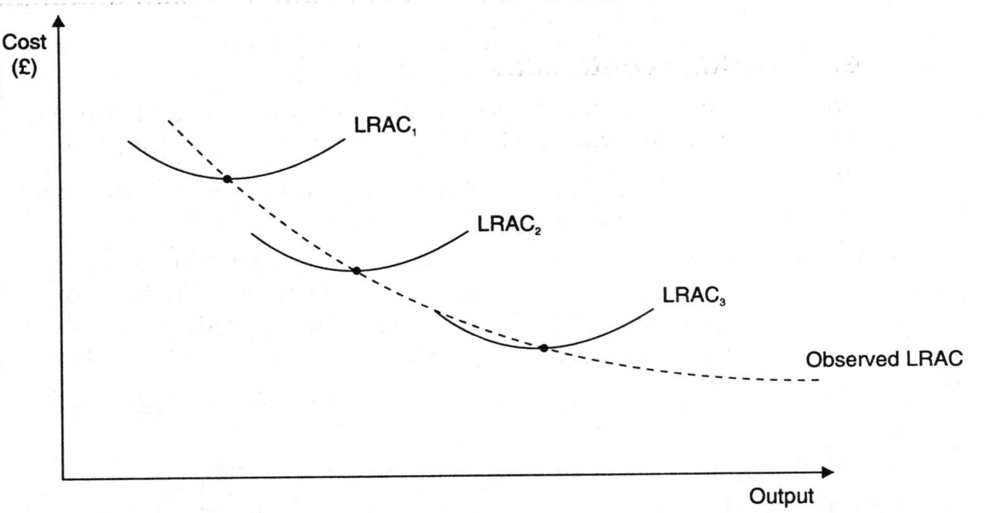

Figure 8

The reasons why technological progress reduces long-run costs are that new technology reduces short-run costs, and since the long-run average cost curve represents a series of short-run cost curves at different output volumes, there will be reductions in the LRAC too.

Short-run costs will fall because:

(a) the new technology might help in achieving greater economies of scale; it will improve labour productivity too, measured as output per employee over time;

(b) there might be a shift to using cheaper machines from relatively more expensive labour. In other words, new technology can result in lost jobs.

Chapter roundup

- Economic costs are different from accounting costs, and represent the opportunity costs of the factors of production that are used.
- A firm's output decisions should be seen in both (a) the short term, when some factors of production are fixed and (b) the long term, when all factors of production can be varied.
- In the short run, a firm's SAC curve is U shaped, owing to diminishing returns beyond a certain output level. In the short run, a firm will maximise its profits where (short run) MR = MC.
- In the long run, a firm's SAC curve can be shifted, and a firm's minimum achievable average costs at any level of output can be depicted by a long-run average cost curve (LRAC).
- The shape of an LRAC curve depends on whether there are increasing, constant, or decreasing returns to scale. There are some economies of scale, and even if increasing returns to scale are not achievable indefinitely as output rises, up to a certain minimum efficient scale of production (MES) there will be increasing returns to scale. Firms will reduce their average costs by producing on a larger scale up to the MES.
- Whether there are constant or decreasing returns to scale beyond the MES will vary between industries and firms. Similarly, whether economies of scale are significant will vary between industries.

NOTES

Chapter roundup (*continued*)

- Technological progress results in shifts in the LAC, and since technology changes are continual, a firm's LAC can probably never be stabilised and unchanging for long.
- Demand and supply have now been explained in the case of consumers by marginal utility theory, and in the case of producers by MC = MR. But consumption and output decisions (ie resource allocation decisions) are taken without regard to externalities, unless the government takes measures to allow for them.

Quick quiz

1 Explain the distinction between long-run and short-run costs.

2 Draw a graph showing the short-run average cost curve and the marginal cost curve of a good.

3 What is the law of diminishing returns?

4 What is the MPP of a variable factor of production?

5 Draw a graph showing the average revenue (price) and marginal revenue of a good.

6 Where is profit maximised?

7 Distinguish between constant returns, increasing returns and decreasing returns to scale.

8 Give examples of internal economies of scale.

9 Give examples of external economies of scale.

Answers to Activities

1 (a) and (b) are correct; (c) is incorrect. A numerical example might help. Suppose a firm has made 100 units of output, and now goes on to produce one more. The costs might be as follows.

	Cost of 100 units	*Cost of 101 units*
	£	£
Total variable cost	200	202
Total fixed cost	100	100
Total cost	300	302
Average cost	£3.00	£2.99

Marginal cost = 302p – 300p = 2p.

2

Output (units)	*Total FC*	*Total VC*	*TC (FC + VC)*	*MC*	*AC (TC/Output)*
0	15	0	15	–	–
1	15	30	45	30	45
2	15	40	55	10	27.5
3	15	60	75	20	25
4	15	90	105	30	26.25
5	15	130	145	40	29
6	15	180	195	50	32.5

NOTES

3 (a) True. Average total cost (ATC) comprises average fixed cost (AFC) and average variable cost (AVC). AFC falls as output rises, and the fall may be sufficient to outweigh a possible increase in AVC. In such a case, ATC will fall while AVC rises.

(b) False. It is *average* fixed costs per unit that fall as output increases. *Marginal* fixed costs = 0.

4 Diminishing returns occur when the marginal physical product of extra units of labour starts to decline. This begins to happen at output W, when the rate of increase in total output starts to decline as numbers employed continue to increase.

5 One possibility you may have thought of is nationalised industries, which are often forced to put considerations of public benefit before profit maximisation. Another possibility is the case of a firm which sets itself an objective of increasing market share, even if this leads to lower profits (or even losses) in the short term. And in a later chapter we look at monopoly and oligopoly firms, which likewise do not necessarily and always aim to maximise profits.

There are also wider considerations which are relevant here. We have talked about a firm as though it were a single rational individual. In practice, a firm is a totality of owners, managers and employees, all of them with their own individual objectives, which may or may not coincide with those of the firm as an entity. Decisions are frequently taken in business which indicate that profitability is not the sole aim of proprietors and managers – for example, a decision to site the business in an agreeable area, in spite of higher costs. Managers may take decisions which tend to increase their own salaries or profit shares, rather than increasing the profit earned by the firm. This behavioural conception of how a firm operates has given rise to the concept of *satisficing*: the idea that managers aim to make not the maximum profit, but a profit which is adequate, at the same time as permitting other aims to be fulfilled.

6

Units *Q*	*Price* *AR* £	*Total revenue* *= TR = AR × Q* £	*Marginal revenue* *MR* £	*Average cost* *AC* £	*Total cost* *TC* £	*Marginal cost* *MC* £
0	0	0	600			
1	504	504	504	720	720	120
2	471	942	438	402	804	84
3	439	1,317	375	288	864	60
4	407.25	1,629	312	231	924	60
5	377.4	1,887	258	201	1,005	81
6	346	2,076	189	189	1,134	129
7*	317.07	2,219.5	143.5	182.5	1,277.5	143.5
8	288.375	2,307	87.5	180	1,440	162.5
9	259	2,331	24	186	1,674	234
10	232.2	2,322	–9	198	1,980	306

* Profit is maximised at 7 units of output, since MR = MC = £143.5. The price would be £317.07 per unit and profit would be £(2,219.5 – 1,277.5) = £942.

7 Item 2 is an example of an external diseconomy of scale. If an industry grows in size, the competition for resources can push up their cost. For example, skilled labour shortages might occur and push up wage rates. Item 3 is an example of an internal diseconomy of scale. Employees who enjoy working for a smaller firm become demotivated and less productive as the firm grows into something more bureaucratic and less friendly. Item 1 is not a diseconomy of scale.

8 (a) Large firms attract better quality employees if the employees see better career prospects than in a small firm.

(b) Specialisation of labour applies to management, and therefore there are managerial economies; the cost per unit of management will fall as output rises.

(c) Marketing economies are available, because a firm can make more effective use of advertising, specialist salesmen and specialised channels of distribution.

(d) Large companies are able to devote more resources to research and development (R & D). In an industry where R & D is essential for survival, large companies are more likely to prosper.

(e) Large companies find it easier to raise finance and can often do so more cheaply. Quoted public limited companies have access to The Stock Exchange for new share issues. They are also able to borrow money more readily.

(f) A large firm can undertake more investments (in fixed assets and new operations) than a small firm; this allows the large firm to spread risks.

Case Study

'Economic analysis in terms of economies and diseconomies of scale can account entirely for variations in the number of firms in an industry and the degree of competition between them.'

Do you agree with the analysis in this extract?

Answer to Case Study

Economies of scale will cause average total costs of production, spread over the units produced, to fall as the size of the plant increases. Diseconomies of scale will tend to lead to average total costs being increased as plant size increases beyond a certain level. It is believed that economies of scale predominate as output rises from relatively low levels, leading to a downward-sloping curve of average total costs. As the plant size increases, certain diseconomies of scale begin to take effect, and this may lead the average total cost curve to rise at higher levels of output. An enterprise may grow through internal expansion, take-over, or mergers.

Economies of scale include those which result from the division of labour, from the ability to create specialisation in particular areas. There may be economies resulting from the technical advantages of larger scale production. A larger scale of production may enable economies to be gained in management costs, and there may also be financial economies: central services can be spread over a number of units without incurring additional costs in proportion to the number of units.

Economies can arise from external factors such as the growth of an industry overall. This may enable facilities to be established, of which the firms in the industry may take advantage.

It is believed that diseconomies of scale may result from too much bureaucracy and an increasing inability to co-ordinate activities effectively within the business. It is also thought that incentives may become eroded by the growth in size of organisations. Employees feel more remote from the organisation, and a diminishing of competition may inhibit management's willingness or ability to perform really effectively.

The minimum efficient scale in an industry is the lowest level of output at which long-run average costs are minimised. This is illustrated in Figure 9, in which it can be seen that long-run average total costs (LRAC) fall up to a particular level of output, Q_1.

NOTES

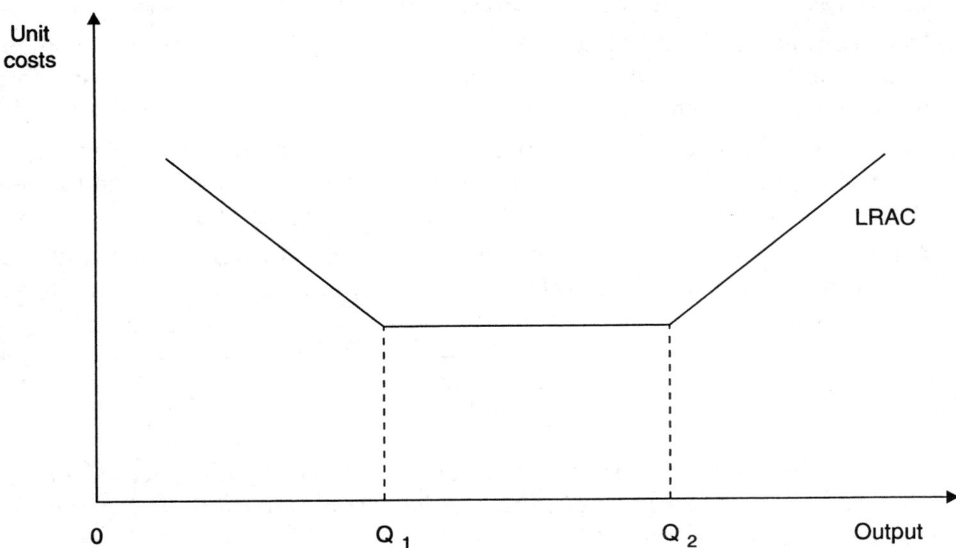

Figure 9

From this level up to Q_2, constant returns to scale are obtained and over that band of output, LRAC is flat. (In reality, it is to be expected that the curve will not completely flatten off at one particular point.) In the middle band of output, between Q_1 and Q_2, constant returns to scale are earned. In other words, efficiency cannot be improved by adjusting the scale of output within this range, and firms may coexist within the industry with plants of different sizes but similar unit costs.

If the band at which constant returns to scale are gained is relatively narrow, or if there is no flattening off to the curve at all, but a sharper minimum point as in Figure 10, there will be a single minimum efficient scale of operations at this minimum point. In an industry which has these conditions, producers are likely to operate with plants of similar sizes.

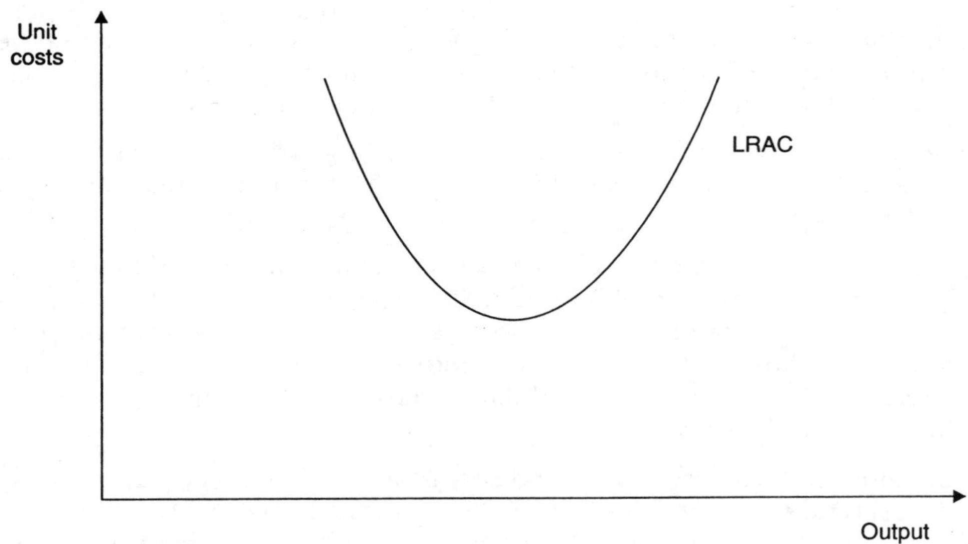

Figure 10

In many industries, it may be that there are few, if any, genuine diseconomies of scale. In such a case, the LRAC curve will flatten off, but will not rise significantly, as shown in Figure 11.

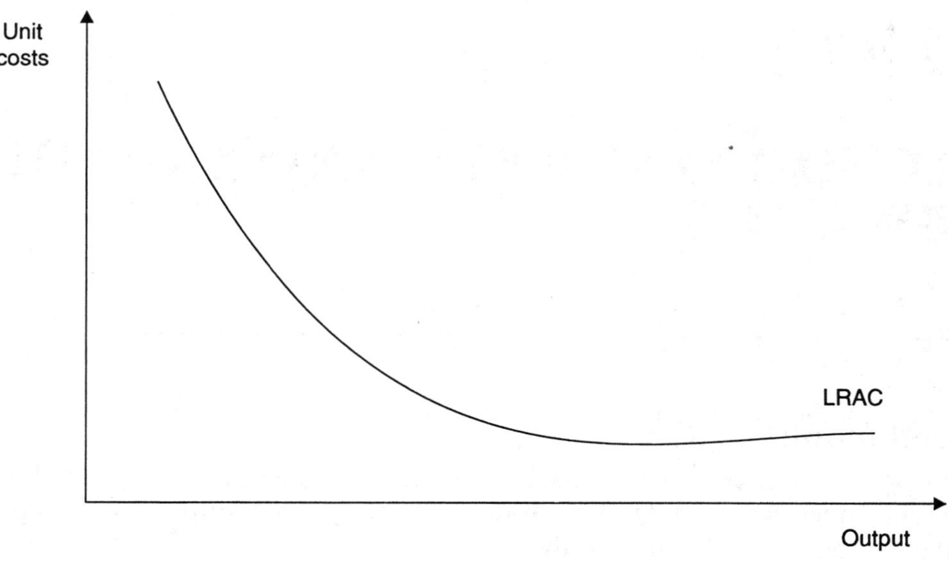

Figure 11

In such cases, the very large scale plants will be the most efficient. Competition may be reduced as production becomes concentrated among a few very large producers. Small firms will not be able to match the larger firms in efficiency and will not survive in the industry. A situation of natural monopoly may be enjoyed by a single producer if economies of scale can be gained indefinitely within the range of output in the whole industry. In this case, there will be no competition in the industry.

The structure of an industry is determined by various factors, including historical factors, regulatory and legislative restrictions, and the geographical spread of the business. As we have seen above, another significant factor in the structure of an industry, apart from competitiveness, is the extent of economies and diseconomies of scale in the industry.

Further question practice

Now try the following practice questions at the end of this text.

Multiple choice questions **49–60**

Exam style question **5**

Chapter 6

FACTOR MARKETS AND FACTOR REWARDS

Introduction

In the previous chapter we saw that the factors of production could be analysed into four categories: land, labour, capital and entrepreneurship. In this chapter we develop that analysis more fully.

Your objectives

After completing this chapter you should:

(a) be aware of the factors of production and the market of the rewards accruing to each of them;

(b) understand the application of supply and demand theory to factors of production.

1 FACTORS OF PRODUCTION AND THEIR REWARDS

Each scarce economic resource has a value, and the owner of the resource or factor of production is rewarded for giving it up to someone else. Firms are rewarded for the goods and services they produce by the price customers will pay for them. The resources used in production are also rewarded, by the price that firms pay for them.

Definition

Factors of production are the resources or inputs used in production

(a) *Land* is rewarded with *rent*. Although it is easy to think of land as property, the economic definition of land is not quite what you might suppose. Land consists not only of property (the land element only: buildings are capital) but also the *natural resources* that grow on the land or that are extracted from the land (ie the natural resources of the soil and woodlands and extracted minerals such as coal).

(b) *Labour* is rewarded with *wages*. Labour consists of both the mental and the physical resources of human beings. (Salaries as well as weekly-paid wages are defined collectively as 'wages' in economics.)

(c) *Capital* is rewarded with *interest*. It is easy to think of capital as financial resources, and the rate of interest as the price mechanism in balancing the supply and demand for money. However, capital in an economic sense is not money in the bank.

Capital refers to man-made items such as plant, machinery and tools which are made and used not for their own sake, but to aid the production of other goods and services. The cost of using machinery, plant and so on is interest.

(d) *Entrepreneurship*, or enterprise is the fourth factor of production. An entrepreneur is someone who undertakes the task of organising the other three factors of production in a business enterprise, and in doing so, bears the risk of the venture. Entrepreneurs create new business ventures and the reward for the risk taken is profit.

The cost of production (rent, wages, interest and profit) is the sum total of the rewards for all the factors of production that go into making a good.

Activity 1

Think carefully about what is, and what is not, a factor reward. Which of the following earnings are factor rewards?

(a) Commission charges earned by an insurance salesman.

(b) Dividends received on shares.

(c) Cash paid to a window cleaner.

(d) The pension earned by an ex-army officer now working for a security firm.

1.1 Distribution theory

Distribution theory is concerned with *how much* reward each factor of production gets. What determines the amount that is paid for land, labour, capital and entrepreneurship? How is the total income cake divided between them?

The total income earned by all factors of production within a national economy equals the *national income*. National income is the subject of a later chapter.

1.2 Factor prices

The prices paid for each factor of production are sometimes referred to as factor prices. The prices for land, labour and capital are determined by *supply and demand*. Entrepreneurship and profit are different, and these will be discussed later.

1.3 Factor demand as a derived demand

The demand for factors of production is a *derived demand*.

By this we mean that the factors of production are not demanded for their own sake. They are demanded because a firm needs them to make goods, which are then sold to households. It is the demand by households for goods from which the demand by firms for the factors of production is derived.

2 CAPITAL AND INTEREST

Interest is the reward for capital. Capital as a factor of production consists of:

(a) stocks of finished goods;

(b) producer goods (ie machines, tools, buildings, office equipment etc).

Definition

Interest rates are the percentage of a sum lent, which the borrower pays to the lender: in other words, the price of money.

The rate of interest, according to traditional economic theory, is determined by supply and demand.

(a) The demand for capital comes from firms, which expect to invest in stocks and equipment so as to create more output, make more sales and earn more profit.

(b) The supply of capital (ie finance to acquire stocks and equipment etc) comes from investors.

2.1 The marginal efficiency of capital

The *demand* by firms to borrow capital is explained in traditional economic theory by the marginal efficiency of capital. It is reasonable to assume that if firms borrow more and more capital to invest, the additional investments that they make will become less and less profitable.

Definition

Marginal efficiency of capital is the rate of discount that makes the present value of expected net returns from an investment equal to the capital sum invested.

Firms should always seek to invest in the opportunities that offer the biggest returns, and once these have been invested in, remaining opportunities will not offer returns quite as big. As more and more investments are made, the returns from additional capital investments will gradually decline. The marginal efficiency of capital refers to this declining size of return as the volume of investment increases.

NOTES

This can be illustrated by a marginal efficiency of capital curve (MEC curve) as shown in Figure 1.

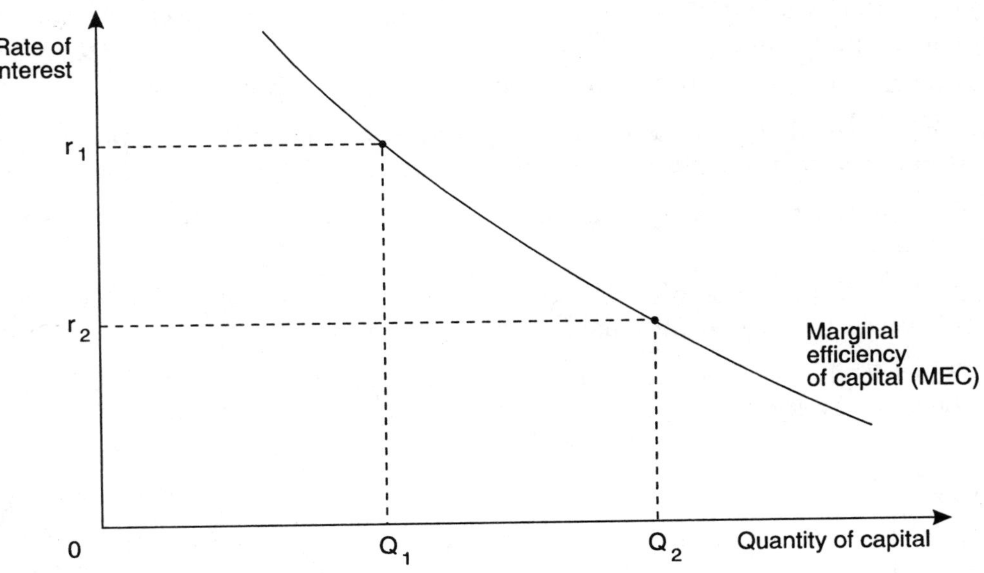

Figure 1 Marginal efficiency of capital curve

Firms should be willing to borrow capital up to the point where the MEC is equal to the interest rate because, on investments up to that amount, they would earn a return in excess of the rate of interest. In the diagram above, if the interest rate is r_1, firms should be willing to borrow up to £Q_1 of capital to invest.

The MEC curve is a demand curve for capital, with the demand being provided by firms.

Activity 2

Remembering the basic principles of supply and demand, how would an increased demand by firms (interest rates remaining unchanged) be represented on the above diagram?

The MEC curve for all the firms in an industry is the industry's demand curve for capital, and it is the sum of the demand curves (MEC curves) of all the individual firms in the industry. An industry's MEC curve and an individual firm's MEC curve have the same basic shape, as shown in Figure 1.

2.2 The supply of capital

The rate of interest also depends on the *supply* of capital from investors, and the interaction of supply and demand establishes interest rates.

The supply of capital comes from savers. Savings are the resources that are needed to produce capital (ie to pay for the materials and labour that produce the capital) and which could have been used for current consumption instead. Savings lead to investment and the creation of capital, but savings are only made by sacrificing some current consumption.

NOTES

Savers choose to save in order to make possible the production of even more outputs in the future, and so the amount of savings is determined by comparing:

(a) what the available wealth could be used to obtain now from the current consumption; and

(b) how much extra wealth will be obtained in the future from saving.

This extra wealth in the future, which makes savers prefer to save rather than consume their wealth now, is represented by interest.

Higher interest will make saving more attractive and the supply of savings will increase.

The price of capital (the interest rate) should be determined by the interaction of supply (savings) and demand (marginal efficiency of capital).

In Figure 2, the equilibrium interest rate would be r with quantity Q of capital supplied by savers and demanded by firms.

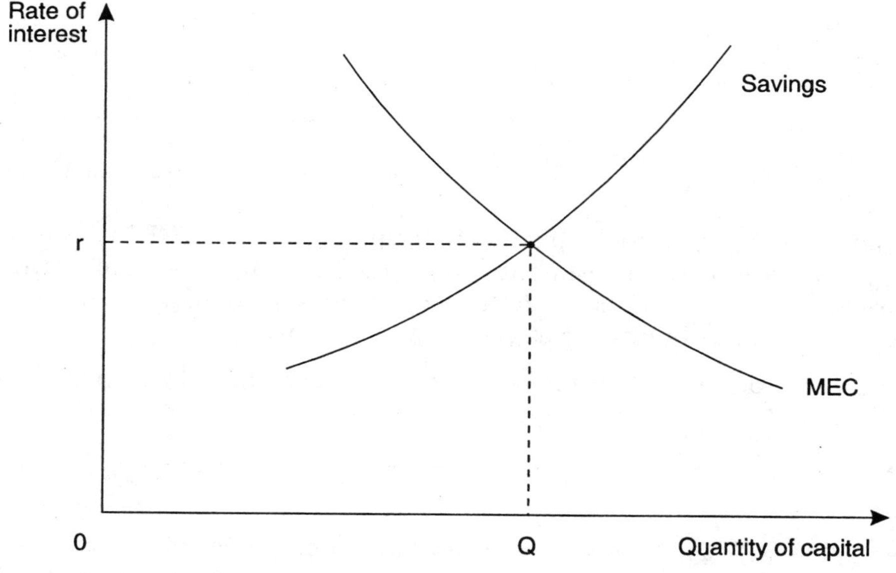

Figure 2

3 LABOUR AND WAGES

3.1 The demand for labour and marginal productivity theory

A similar demand and supply analysis can be made for labour and the price of labour (ie wages).

(a) Like the demand for capital, the demand for labour by firms is a derived demand, arising from consumer demand for the firms' output.

(b) Labour is employed to help to make the goods and services of the firm, and the more labour that is employed, the greater should be the total volume of goods or services produced.

(c) However, with labour the *law of diminishing returns* applies, because as more and more labour is hired, the productivity of the extra workforce will gradually decline. A firm cannot keep on hiring extra labour, in the short term at least,

NOTES

and expect every additional recruit to contribute the same extra output to the firm as others in the workforce.

In our basic analysis of marginal productivity theory, we shall assume that the amount of other factors of production is in fixed supply, so that any additions to a firm's output and revenue can only come from additions to the labour force. In other words, labour is a variable factor of production.

The *marginal physical product (MPP)* of labour is the additional units of output from one extra unit of labour. In accordance with the law of diminishing returns, the MPP of labour will decline as more and more output is produced.

The *marginal revenue product (MRP)* of labour is the marginal revenue value of the marginal physical product of labour. This is the extra revenue that firms in the industry would obtain from the extra output provided by each extra recruit to the workforce. Like the MPP, the MRP will be gradually declining. Table 1 below illustrates this relationship between MPP and MRP.

Table 1 MPP and MRP

Number of units of labour	Total output units	Revenue value of this output £	Marginal physical product units	Marginal revenue product £
1	60	700	–	
2	110	1,200	50	500
3	150	1,500	40	300
4	180	1,700	30	200

Activity 3

From the data below, calculate the MRP of the 12th employee.

Number of employees	*Total output (in units)*	*Unit price of output* £
10	300	10.00
11	400	9.50
12	450	9.00

The MRP of labour is similar in concept to the marginal efficiency curve of capital. It also represents the demand curve for labour by a firm (or by firms in the industry as a whole). Firms should be willing to pay for labour provided that the marginal revenue product of labour exceeds the cost of employing the labour. Quite simply, if a firm can make an extra £150 per week from hiring an extra employee, it should be willing to hire the employee, provided that the weekly wage does not exceed £150. In Figure 3, if the MRP of labour for a certain type of job, job type A, is as shown, and the wage level for job type A is W, then the industry would want to employ X employees in job type A, because the MRP of labour exceeds the wage rate up to X.

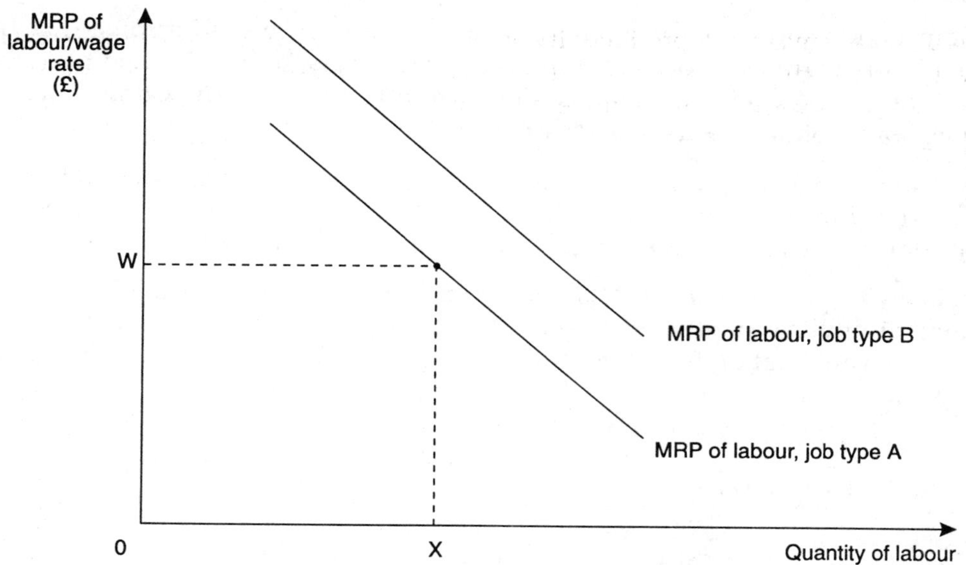

Figure 3

In contrast, job type B has a higher marginal productivity value than job type A, and so the industry would be willing either:

(a) to pay a higher wage for the same quantity of employees as job type A; or
(b) to employ more employees into job type B than job type A if the wage rate for both were W.

This analysis of the MRP of labour only considers the *demand* by firms for labour of different types and skills. It does not consider the *supply* of labour.

According to marginal productivity theory, wage levels are determined by the interaction of the demand for and the supply of labour. The supply of labour is influenced by wage rates. Higher wages will attract more people willing to do the work.

The supply curve for labour can therefore be shown as the marginal cost of the labour, ie the extra total wage payments needed to increase total labour supply by each marginal extra amount.

For example, suppose that at a wage level of £160 per week, the supply of labour into a job would be 8 men. At a wage level of £170 per week, the willing supply would be 9 men, and at £180 per week, 10 men would be willing to do the job. The marginal cost of the 9th and 10th men would be as in Table 2.

Table 2 Marginal cost

Wage = Average cost of labour (ACL) £	Supply (number of men)	Total wages £	Marginal cost of labour (MCL) £
160	8	1280	–
170	9	1530	250 (1530 – 1280)
180	10	1800	270 (1800 – 1530)

Although the example is small, the figures do show that when higher wages must be paid to attract more labour:

(a) the supply curve for labour, which is the marginal cost curve for labour (MC_L), will be positive and therefore rising; and

NOTES

(b) MC_L will be higher than the wage level (ie higher than the average cost of labour AC_L).

Returning to marginal productivity theory, we therefore have wage levels determined by the interaction of supply and demand, which is where the MCL curve intersects with the marginal revenue product curve for labour (MRP_L).

In a perfectly competitive industry, all extra quantities of labour can be obtained freely at a constant wage rate (for example, if a firm or an industry can hire limitless quantities of labour at a wage of £250 per week).

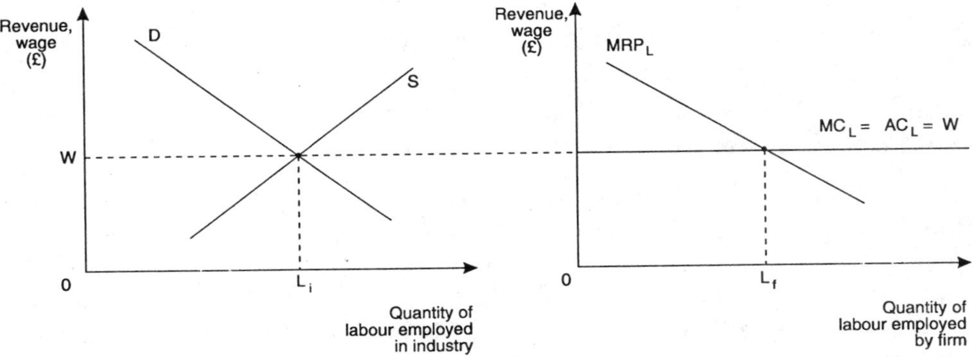

Figure 4 Competition among firms for labour

Figure 4 shows that an individual firm will continue to hire more labour at wage rate W until the MRP of labour falls to this level. The individual firm will therefore hire L_f units of labour. Total employment in the industry (L_i) is the sum of the employment of labour by the individual firms.

If the industry is dominated by a single firm, this firm is the only, or the main, buyer of labour in the industry. Such a firm is said to be a monopsonist buyer of labour.

In this situation, the firm will pay lower wages if it needs fewer employees and higher wages if it needs to attract more labour. The AC_L curve rises with output/numbers employed, and more significantly, the MC_L curve (the supply curve for labour) is also rising.

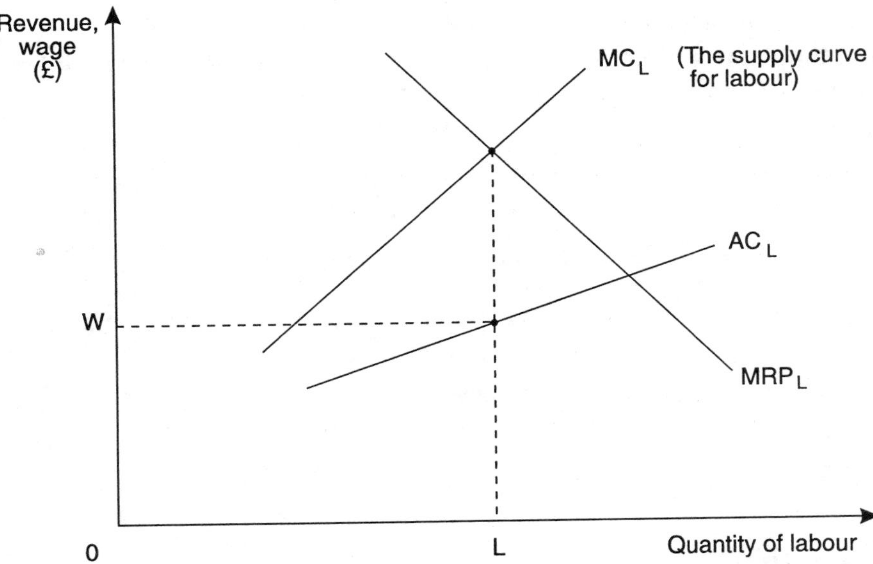

Figure 5 Wage levels and employment level where the firm is a monopsonist buyer of labour

Demand and supply analysis shows that the number employed will be L, which is the level where $MC_L = MRP_L$.

Activity 4

Study the above diagram carefully. For a monopsony buyer of labour, the marginal cost of labour is more than the wage rate. True or false?

3.2 Limitations of marginal productivity theory

The marginal productivity theory of wages cannot account wholly for the determination of wage rates and wage differentials because the assumptions on which it is based do not apply in reality.

(a) It is often impossible to calculate the marginal productivity of labour, especially in administrative work or service industries, eg bank clerks and shop assistants do not produce a measurable physical output.

(b) Marginal productivity theory for labour assumes that all other factors of production are held in constant supply. This is unlikely to be so, especially in the case of capital. As the amount of labour employed changes, so too would the amount of capital.

(c) A further assumption of the marginal productivity theory of wages is that labour is free to enter the market or leave it for alternative employment elsewhere. In practice, this might not be the case, and there might be imperfections in the labour market.

3.3 Imperfections in the labour market

Imperfections in the labour market prevent a free market in labour from operating, because of restrictions on the free *supply* of labour.

These labour supply restrictions include the following.

(a) Society, laws and customs. (For example, the social custom might be for women to work, or not to work; or for children to work from a certain age. Some jobs might be more socially acceptable than others.)

(b) Labour immobility. (This refers to the movement of labour from one industry to another and from one geographical region or country to another.)

(c) Barriers to entry into the trade or profession.

(d) Lack of freely available information about jobs and wages.

(e) Trade union influence on the supply of labour and wage rates.

We shall now consider some of these in more detail.

Activity 5

Try to think of some other social factors which might place restrictions on the supply of labour.

3.4 Wage differentials

Wage differentials are differences in the rate of pay between one type of job and another. Some jobs are more attractive than others. If wages were equal in all occupations the dirty and disagreeable jobs would attract few workers while most people would seek employment where conditions were pleasant. The tendency

NOTES

would therefore be for the wages in the disagreeable and dirty jobs to rise while wages in the more pleasant occupations would fall.

A theoretical explanation of wage differentials can be based on straightforward demand and supply analysis:

(a) the demand for a particular type of worker comes from employees (or customers)

(b) the supply of a particular type of worker comes from the individuals who are able and who choose to do that type of work.

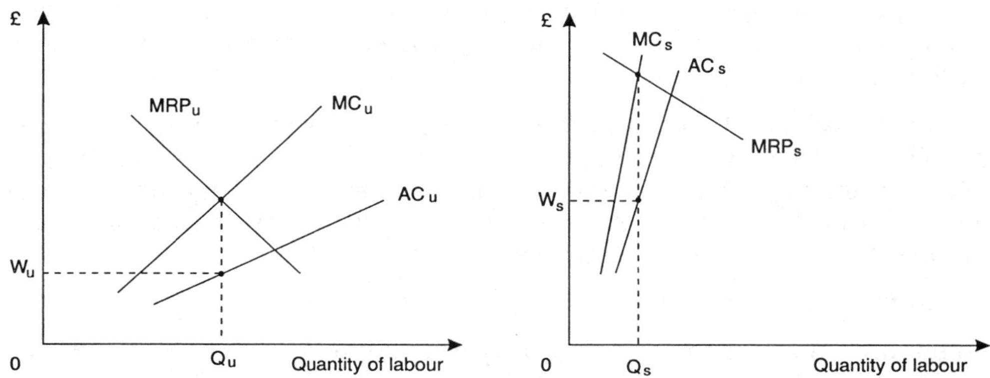

Figure 6

Skilled workers are more productive and add more value to a firm's marginal revenue product than unskilled workers. In Figure 6, we assume that employers effectively form a buyers' cartel or monopsony. The MRP of a skilled labour force is shown by MRP_s, and the MRP of an unskilled labour force is shown by MRP_u.

Skilled workers expect to be paid more for their skills. In order to attract a bigger supply of skilled workers, ie more people willing to acquire the necessary training, skills and qualifications, higher wages must be paid, and the supply curve of skilled labour (MC_s) will lie to the left of the supply curve of unskilled labour (MC_u). The supply of skilled workers will also be more inelastic, because the barriers to entry (eg the need to obtain suitable training and qualifications) are higher, or the availability of individuals with suitable talent will be restricted. As a consequence, there will be a wage differential between the skilled and the unskilled workers, with skilled workers earning W_s and unskilled workers earning W_u.

How might wage differentials be eliminated? If a group of low-paid workers wished to eliminate the wage differentials between themselves and more highly paid skilled workers, they might try strike action, or even ask for government support (minimum pay legislation, or income controls). However, according to marginal productivity theory, the solution would be to increase productivity.

If unskilled labour can become more productive, their MRP curve will shift to the right, and so they can justify higher wages. Wage differentials with other workers would be reduced and perhaps eliminated. This is why, in some highly profitable industries, unskilled workers might have such a high MRP that they earn higher wages than skilled workers in an unprofitable industry.

Marginal productivity theory is not the only way to explain wage differentials. Other factors affecting labour supply might help to influence wage levels for skilled workers; such as the willingness of some skilled labour to work for low wages, in spite of their skills and training (eg nurses and social workers).

NOTES

Activity 6

What factors determine the relative pay of a surgeon and a roadsweeper?

3.5 Trade unions and the bargaining theory of wages

Although we have looked at marginal productivity theory and the view that wage levels are set by demand and supply factors, it should also be recognised that trade unions try to negotiate higher wages for labour. There is a bargaining theory of wages, which states that wage levels are set by negotiation between unions and management.

Collective bargaining is a term which refers to the process by which unions negotiate and reach agreements with employers. It is common for collective bargaining to involve a single monopolist seller of labour (the trade union) and one buyer or monopsonist (a single firm or an employers' federation). As such, annual wage claims may be one of a trial of strength between two giants.

The role of trade unions, in economic terms, has two aspects:

(a) to put up and maintain barriers to entry into jobs in the industry, so ensuring high earnings for the existing members;

(b) to monopolise the supply of labour in the industry. If the demand for labour is in the hands of a single employer or employers' federation, this can influence the price at which labour is bought. If the supply of labour is in the hands of a collective body as opposed to individuals, this can influence the price at which it can be sold.

By restricting entry to the labour force, trade unions can force wages to move from W_0 to W_1 (see Figure 7) by effectively changing the supply curve from S_0 to S_1. This will however result in fewer jobs. The number employed will fall from L_0 to L_1.

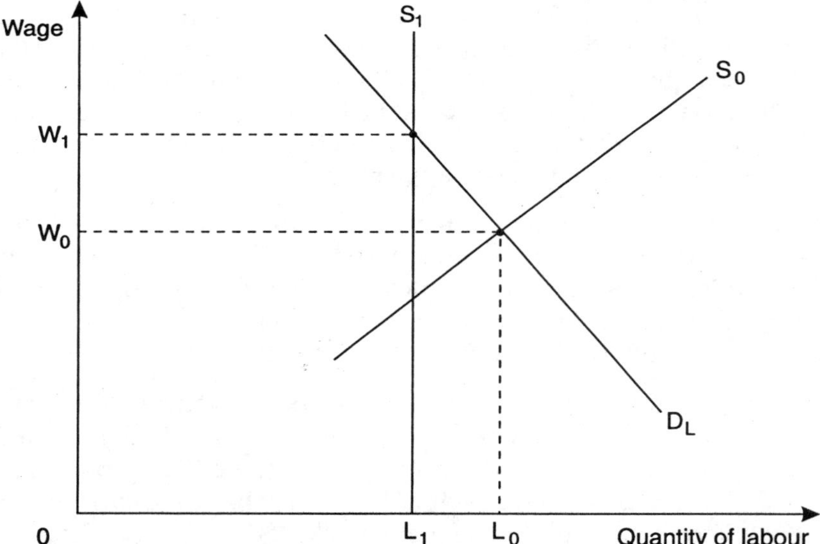

Figure 7

However, once wage rates have been given an *initial* increase by the unionisation of the work force, any *further* pay rises, given no change in the marginal revenue product (MRP) of labour, will probably reduce the total demand for labour by employers.

NOTES

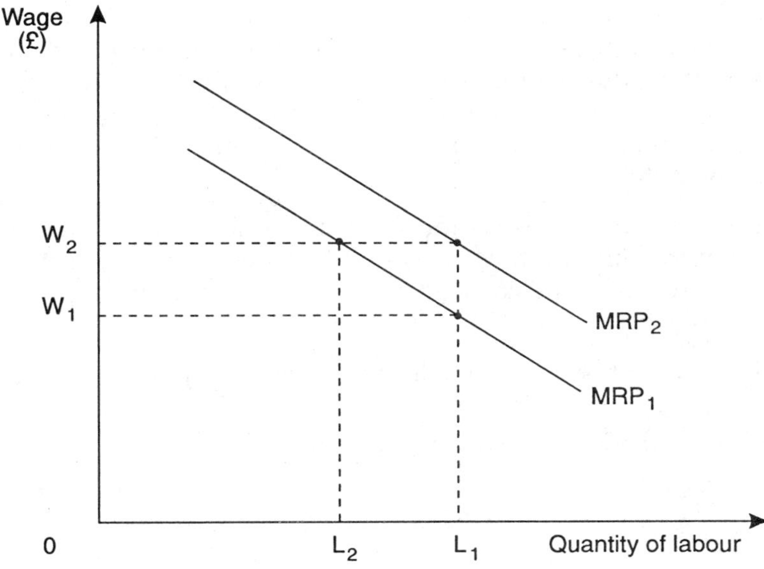

Figure 8

When wages rise from W_1 to W_2, the demand for labour will fall from L_1 to L_2 (Figure 8), given no change in the MRP of labour (initially MRP_1). However, if the labour force agrees to an *improvement in productivity* so that the marginal revenue product of labour shifts to MRP_2, an increase in wages from W_1 to W_2 could be achieved without changing the total workforce employed from L_1.

Activity 7

Trade unions are in a strong bargaining position with employees when:

(a) marginal revenue product is more than wages. True or false?

(b) there is elastic demand for the goods which the union members produce. True or false?

3.6 Wage rises and inflation

Consider again the wage rise from W_1 to W_2 in Figure 8. If the employer cannot raise the prices of his final product and the marginal revenue product of labour cannot be increased by improved productivity, the amount of labour demanded by the employer falls, from L_1 to L_2. However, if the employer can pass the extra labour cost on to the end customer by *raising the price of the end product*, the MRP of labour will be increased, and so the same quantity of labour, L_1, can be kept in employment at the new wage level.

Labour can often be substituted by capital. Higher wage costs in real terms make capital investment more attractive, as an alternative to labour. An example of this is the newspaper industry where high wages and inefficient work practices by printers eventually persuaded many employers to switch to new technology, and a smaller and newly-recruited work force.

On the other hand, in many industries, trade unions in the UK have responded in recent years to the problems of efficiency in production by discussing productivity improvements with management, in order to make firms more cost-efficient.

3.7 Minimum wages

In some industries of some countries, there is a minimum wage agreement, which means that all workers in the industry must earn at least the minimum wage. Some trade unionists have argued for a national minimum wage. The purpose of a minimum wage is to ensure that low-paid workers earn at least enough in wages to have a certain standard of living.

If a minimum wage is enforced by legislation or negotiated nationally for an industry by a trade union the minimum wage will probably be above the current wage level for the jobs concerned. The consequences of a minimum wage would then be:

(a) to raise wage levels for workers employed to a level above the equilibrium wage rate; but

(b) to reduce the demand for labour and so cause job losses.

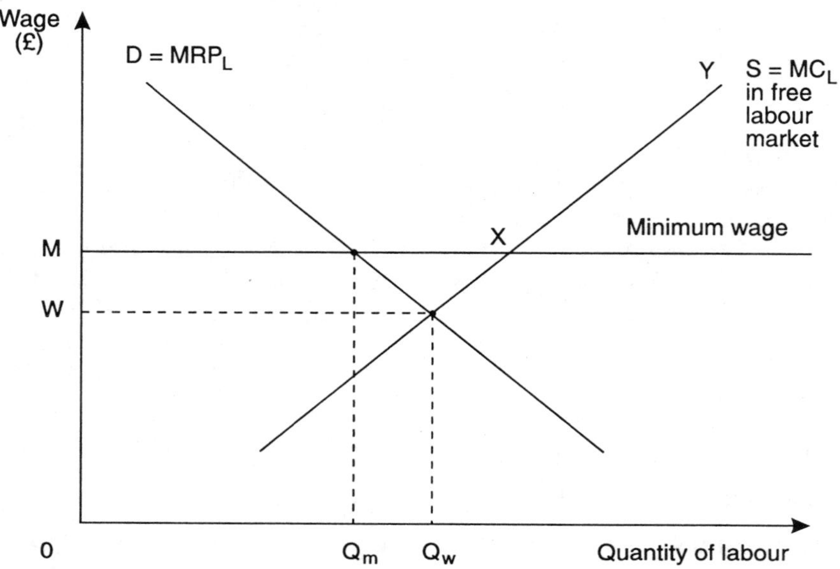

Figure 9

Without a minimum wage, $0Q_w$ workers would be employed at wage rate W (Figure 9).

Activity 8

By reference to Figure 9, work out what happens when a minimum wage M, higher than the existing rate W, is imposed.

3.8 Bargaining theory of wages: conclusion

It is probably fair to conclude that the bargaining theory of wages, that unions can fix a wage level by negotiating pay with employers, is not inconsistent with marginal productivity theory and the principles of demand and supply. The level of wages bargained by unions will help to determine employment levels (demand and supply). When conditions in the industry favour the employer with labour having low marginal revenue productivity, unions will find it difficult to bargain for higher wages or to preserve jobs in the industry.

3.9 Factors influencing demand for labour

As we have seen, demand for labour is influenced by the marginal productivity of labour. We now look at specific factors influencing demand and marginal productivity. These are:

(a) the efficiency or productivity of labour;

(b) the skills of labour;

(c) the substitutability of capital for labour.

The efficiency of labour

Improvements in productivity will increase the demand for labour, and productivity in turn depends on:

(a) the attitudes of the individual;

(b) the intelligence and skills of individuals;

(c) the attitudes of the work group to which the individual belongs;

(d) established work practices and trade union influence;

(e) the skill of management in getting the best out of a workforce;

(f) effective use of other factors of production;

(g) possibly, greater specialisation (ie an increasing division of labour).

Labour skills: specialisation of labour

Specialisation of labour helps to increase labour productivity. Work is divided up into small units and specialist labour concentrates on a particular unit of the overall work. Plant and equipment can be specialised too, and automation helps to increase labour productivity. Work can be organised effectively by assigning specialists to each aspect of what has to be done, and time is saved because workers do not have to keep switching from one job to another.

The substitutability of capital for labour

Substitution between factors of production (eg between labour and capital) will take place:

(a) provided that substitution is practical or technologically feasible (eg that machines can be made to do the work previously carried out by labour, or that labour can physically do the work of machines);

(b) when the price or productivity of one factor of production rises in relation to another. If wages go up, the marginal cost of labour will rise, and firms will want less labour at this higher cost. Labour will also become more expensive in relation to capital, and there will be some substitution of capital for labour. The net result of an increase in wages will be a reduction in the quantity of labour employed – unless the productivity of labour can be increased at the same time, to strengthen the demand for it.

3.10 The elasticity of demand for labour

The change in demand for labour in response to a change in wage rates can be measured by the elasticity of demand for labour. This is:

$$\frac{\text{\% change in numbers employed}}{\text{\% change in wages}}$$

The factors influencing the degree of elasticity of demand for labour are:

(a) *the technical ease with which employers could substitute other factors of production* (mainly *capital*) for labour;

(b) *the elasticity of demand for the final product.* If the product made by the work force has an inelastic demand, producers can pass on higher wage costs more easily to consumers by raising prices. However, if demand for the end-product has a high price elasticity, an increase in wages will result, through higher prices, in a sharp fall in demand for labour;

(c) *the elasticity of supply of alternative factors of production.* Even if it is technically possible to substitute labour with, say, capital, it might be too costly for producers to do so if the elasticity of supply of capital is low. An increase in supply would then only be achieved by paying significantly more for the substitute factor (capital), and so in spite of higher wages costs, it might still be less costly to use labour than to switch to capital as a substitute factor;

(d) *the proportion of labour costs to total costs.*

Activity 9

How does this last factor affect the elasticity of demand for labour?

4 LAND AND RENT

4.1 Rent

The price of land, which is rent, is also determined by supply and demand. In discussing land, it is important to get our basic definitions clear. In everyday language, if a person buys some land, we probably mean that the person buys some buildings with a supply of water, electricity and so on. To the economist, buildings and water supply are capital; land is the earth and its natural resources.

It is also usual to speak of renting a house, a car or a television. This is commercial rent paid to the landlord who is an owner of capital. Commercial rent is not the same as the more specific concept of economic rent, which refers to a payment made in excess of the payment needed to keep a factor of production, such as land, labour or capital, in current use. We shall return to this a little later.

4.2 The price of land

The special definitions of land and rent used by economists come from those first used by David Ricardo in the 19th century. Ricardo was concerned, not with how much rent is paid for land used for a particular purpose, but how much rent is paid for land as a whole. He argued that:

(a) the total amount of land available is fixed, therefore the supply of land is inelastic, regardless of how much rent is paid for it;

(b) since the supply of land is inelastic, the amount of rent will be determined by the price of the goods produced from the land for sale to markets.

NOTES

EXAMPLE: LAND AND RENT

As a simplified example, let us suppose that a piece of land (fixed in size) has only one use, which is to grow carrots. Suppose also that this fixed amount of land, which can only be used for growing carrots, has a perfectly elastic labour force to work on it and that no capital is employed.

Figure 10 shows:

(a) the wage rate of labour, W, which is constant regardless of the number of workers employed, because labour supply is perfectly elastic;

(b) the marginal revenue product of labour curves for two different price levels, P_0 and P_1 of a product, say carrots.

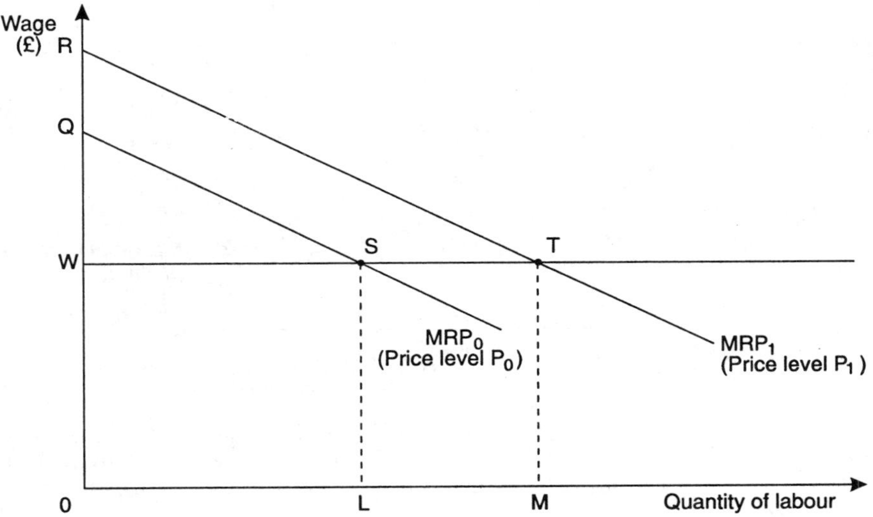

Figure 10

When the price of carrots is P_0 and 0L workers are employed at the given wage rate:

(i) the total cost of labour will be represented by the area 0WSL;

(ii) the total revenue from the sale of carrots will be 0QSL;

(iii) the difference, WQS, is rent;

(c) if the price of carrots rises to P_1, the MRP of labour will improve. 0M workers will be employed, and:

(i) the total cost of labour is now 0WTM;

(ii) the total revenue is 0RTM;

(iii) therefore rent has risen to WRT.

We conclude that when land is in fixed supply, the size of the rent depends on the price of the goods produced on the land.

4.3 The price of land for specific uses

We can extend this principle to cover the situation where the supply of land is *not* perfectly elastic. This situation arises where we are considering the supply of land for a particular purpose, for example, office development or agricultural use. Since it is usually possible to change the use of a piece of land, the supply of land for a particular purpose should not normally be considered fixed.

If the price of agricultural land in the UK went up we would expect a transfer of land from, for instance the domestic housing sector to the agricultural sector. In fact, the supply curve of agricultural land slopes upward from left to right. The equilibrium price and quantity of agricultural land are determined by the intersection of the demand curve (derived from the price of goods produced on the land) and the supply curve (derived from the price P which prevents a quantity of land Q being transferred to any other use).

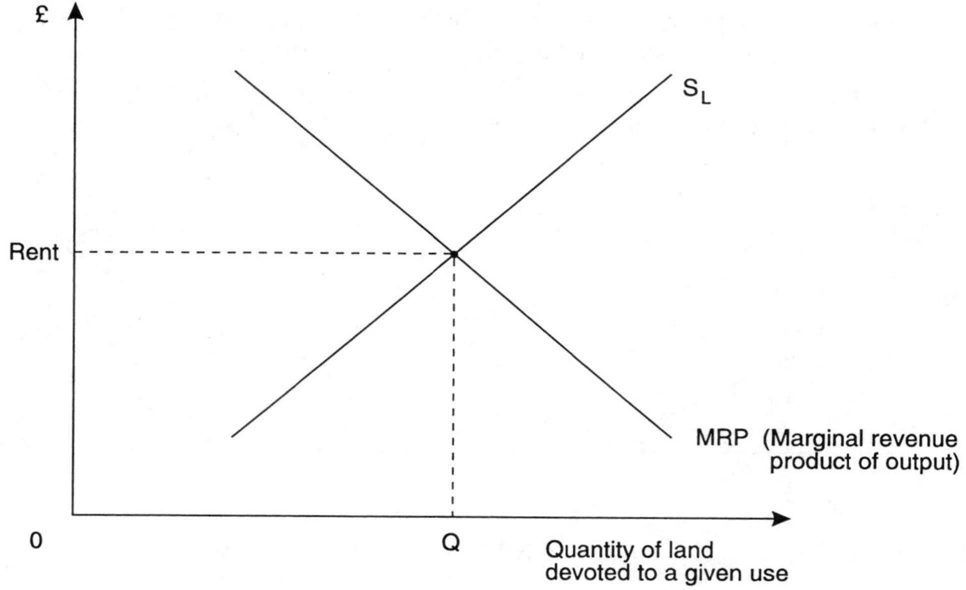

Figure 11 Price of land in a specific use

5 ENTREPRENEURSHIP AND PROFIT

5.1 The function of the entrepreneur

The function of entrepreneurs, as the fourth factor of production, is to combine the other three factors, land, labour and capital, so as to maximise the efficiency of resource utilisation and to maximise the firm's profits. Business enterprise involves risk and uncertainty and actual profits might be higher or lower than expected. It is the entrepreneur's role to bear the burden of this uncertainty. The reward, which is profit, is what is left over after the other three factors of production have been rewarded. If there is nothing left over the entrepreneur will make no profits, or even a loss.

We can identify two aspects of the role of entrepreneurs:

(a) they organise production and makes decisions about new business ventures;

(b) they earn the reward of profit.

These dual aspects of entrepreneurship are possibly most apparent in partnerships and small private limited companies, where the owners of the business (partners or shareholders) are often also the senior managers. They organise production, make the decisions and earn the profits for themselves.

5.2 The nature of profit

Unlike land, labour and capital, which are rewarded by rents, wages and interest respectively, entrepreneurs cannot be sure of gaining a reward (making a profit) because their business might make unexpected losses.

Profit is the reward of the entrepreneur for the risks taken. The entrepreneur bears the burden of business risk and uncertainty.

5.3 Normal profit

There ought to be an amount of pure profit which an entrepreneur should expect as a reward for the risks that he or she takes. This expected or appropriate profit is known as normal profit, and it is an economic cost of production.

Normal profit is earned when total revenues equal the total opportunity costs of *all* input resources.

If revenues are just enough to equal opportunity costs, this means that the input resources are being used as well as they could be used anywhere else.

If actual economic profit is below normal profit (ie a loss in economic terms), the firm would do better to leave the business it is in and put the resources at its disposal to better, more profitable use.

5.4 Supernormal profits

When total revenues exceed the total opportunity costs of input resources, the firm will be earning profit in excess of normal profits, and so resources are earning more than they could in an alternative occupation.

These excess profits are called supernormal profits, or monopoly profits (because monopoly firms are best able to exploit opportunities for earning supernormal profits). The supernormal profits of the monopolist are discussed in more detail in the next chapter.

Firms will obviously benefit from any supernormal profits that exist, and will wish to enjoy them if they are available. When a firm makes supernormal profits, however, other firms will want to enter the industry if they can, to grab a share of the high profits that are available. In competitive industries, supernormal profits therefore tend to be temporary, because they are eventually eroded by competition. Monopolies, however, might be able to earn supernormal profits indefinitely.

(a) Entrepreneurs of better ability should always be able to earn supernormal profits when others are making only normal profits.

(b) Monopolists can make supernormal profits by putting up entry barriers to prevent or deter rival firms from entering the market as competitors.

(c) Supernormal profits can indicate to entrepreneurs the best markets for new investments or for a switch of their existing investments.

5.6 Normal profit and risk and uncertainty

Firms in high-risk industries should expect to earn a higher return than firms in low-risk industries. The higher the risk, the higher the risk premium required. Risk premium can be defined as the additional return in excess of a risk-free return needed to compensate an investor for making the risky investment.

When the opportunity costs of a business are measured, the opportunity cost of capital tied up (ie the opportunity cost of alternative investments) will be higher for higher risk firms.

NOTES

Since normal profit means enough return to prevent the firm's owner from liquidating his or her investment and investing it elsewhere, normal profit must allow for the risk characteristics of the business and what could be earned from an alternative investment of comparable risk. So normal profit will be higher in a more risky market than in a less risky market.

Activity 10

Orson Cart is a business entrepreneur, operating a riding stables.

(a) He owns the land that the business uses. He does not charge the business any rent for using this land, which could have been put to another use to earn £30,000 per year.

(b) He owns the capital of the business, valued at £400,000, and a commercial rate of interest would be 10% per year.

(c) He pays himself a salary of £15,000 per year, but could earn £25,000 in alternative employment.

(d) The business earns revenue of £115,000 per year.

What are the annual economic profits of the business?

Chapter roundup

- The cost of capital is interest. The demand for capital is determined largely by the marginal efficiency of capital. It might be argued that supply and demand for capital interact (in a free market) to determine interest rates.
- The cost of labour is wages. The demand for labour is mainly determined by the marginal productivity of labour, which declines as more labour is employed, in accordance with the law of diminishing returns.
- In a market economy, wage levels are determined by the interaction of supply and demand. However, there are various imperfections in the labour market which influence the supply of labour and wage levels.
- The cost of land is rent. The level of rent is determined by the interaction of supply and demand.
- The reward of entrepreneurship is profit.

Quick quiz

1 What is derived demand?

2 What is the demand curve for capital?

3 List as many imperfections in the market for capital as you can.

4 What are the MPP and MRP of labour?

5 What are the problems in measuring the MRP of labour?

6 Show how wage and employment levels are determined, according to marginal productivity theory, in (a) a perfectly competitive market and (b) an imperfectly competitive market.

7 What factors restrict the free supply of labour (other than wage levels)?

8 What are the causes of labour immobility?

9 What is likely to be the consequence for employment of minimum wage levels in an industry?

10 What is normal profit?

Answers to Activities

1 All of these are factor rewards, with the exception of (d). The pension relates to a former employment.

2 The increase in demand would be represented by a rightwards shift in the MEC curve.

3

Employees	Output	Unit price	Total revenue
		£	£
11	400	9.50	3,800
12	450	9.00	4,050
MRP of 12th employee =			250

4 True. The wage rate is represented by the AC_L curve on the diagram, which is lower than the MC_L curve.

5 You might have thought of:

(a) the number of young people going into higher education, which affects the supply of 18–21 year old labour;

(b) general standards of education and training, which affect the supply of skilled labour;

(c) the tendency in many countries to pay women less than men for doing similar work.

6 A solution should be based on demand and supply analysis. Points to make could include:

(a) the restricted supply of surgeons' labour, due to the training and skills needed, and so the smaller number of people capable of doing this work, compared with road-sweeping;

(b) the restrictions on the opportunities to train as a surgeon;

(c) the higher MRP of surgeons;

(d) the greater demand for the services of surgeons, especially from private patients;

(e) greater union power. Control over entry to membership of the profession by the surgeons is more easily exercised than control over membership of the roadsweepers' trade union;

(f) the willingness of individuals to take the time, effort and cost to train as surgeons. Roadsweeping calls for little, if any, training and is an unskilled job.

7 (a) True. The employer has scope to raise wages while still making a profit.

(b) False. If demand is *inelastic* the firm can afford higher wages, because the cost can be passed on to consumers.

8 Demand for labour from employers will fall to $0Q_m$, but $0Q_m$ workers will at least earn a higher wage.

9 When labour costs are small in proportion to total costs, an increase in wages will be relatively insignificant and demand for labour will be only slightly affected. In this case, the demand for labour is inelastic. But if wage costs are a major part of total costs, demand for labour will be elastic.

10 The opportunity cost of the land is the revenue forgone from its next best use, that is £30,000.

Similarly, the capital he has invested could earn £40,000 elsewhere, and this is the appropriate opportunity cost.

Finally, the opportunity cost of his own services is £25,000 (and the fact that he only draws £15,000 in salary is irrelevant).

The economic profit of the business is therefore:

£115,000 – £30,000 – £40,000 – £25,000 = £20,000

NOTES

Case Study

'A major determinant of the pattern of wages in an economy is the existence and operation of minimum wage laws ... Three systems of minimum wages may be identified: statutory, collective agreements and selective. In France, Greece, the Netherlands, Portugal and Spain minimum wages are determined by statutory instruments, with higher minimum rates established in collective agreements extendible to non-signatories by government decision. In Belgium, Germany, Spain ... and for most workers in Ireland, minimum wages are set by collective agreements with extension again possible. In Denmark, collective agreements again set minimum wages but extension is not possible, whilst in the UK the previous selective minimum wage system of Wages Council, covering certain sectors including retailing, was abolished in 1993.

Comparisons between the US and continental Europe indicate that the crucial determinants of the impact of minimum wage laws on the structure of wages and employment are the level set relative to average wages, together with the frequency of adjustment and the coverage across the workforce'.

Adnett N: European Labour Markets: Analysis and Policy, 1996

Use this extract to consider the following.

- The problem of low pay and the concept of a statutory minimum wage.
- The use of supply and demand analysis to analyse the effects of a minimum wage, emphasising the factors affecting the elasticity of demand for labour.
- The effect of a statutory minimum wage on employment, costs and profitability.

Answer to Case Study

In a mixed economy such as the UK, it is well known that some groups of workers earn much less than the average wage. On the other hand some groups earn several times the average wage. It is not surprising that such wage differentials exist. Assuming that there is perfect mobility of labour and perfect knowledge, certain conditions would have to be fulfilled in order that wages in all jobs were equal. All workers, for instance, would have to be homogeneous, that is each worker would have the same level of skill in any occupation; and all jobs would have to provide identical non-monetary advantages and disadvantages.

Wages in all occupations would be equalised if this list of conditions were fulfilled. If the wage rate in one industry fell below the general level, there would be a transfer of workers into other industries, resulting in an excess demand for labour in this industry. This would force the industry wage rate up to the level in the economy as a whole. The opposite would apply if the wage rate in a single industry rose above the common wage rate. There would be a switch of workers to that industry and the excess supply of labour would drive down the industry wage to that in other industries.

Clearly, the conditions necessary for the equalisation of wage rates in a free market economy are not fulfilled in practice. In reality workers are not homogeneous, due to differences in natural ability, skills and training. A welder, for example, cannot switch to being a computer programmer overnight. Some people do not have the physical requirements or the natural ability required for particular jobs. An accountant, for example, needs to be good with figures while a driving instructor requires a lot of

NOTES

patience. Consequently, it can be argued that the labour market is separated into many distinct markets, so that different types of workers can be viewed as non-competing groups.

In addition, jobs do not offer identical non-monetary advantages and disadvantages. Some jobs mean working in pleasant conditions with convenient hours of work, while others require working in dirty and unpleasant conditions. Also, in practice neither employers nor employees are perfectly well-informed about conditions of service and pay in all occupations. Workers often do not know of all job opportunities that are available, particularly in other areas. Finally, there are several barriers to the mobility of labour, both geographical and occupational. These may take the form of workers not being willing to move to another part of the country; or barriers may exist because of the differing skill requirements of different jobs. Professional associations and trade unions sometimes put up entry barriers; perhaps the requirement of a long apprenticeship or period of training.

All these factors help to explain the differentials that exist between the wages earned in different occupations and why some individuals have high earnings while others are in low wage occupations. It is argued by its supporters that a statutory minimum wage is necessary to tackle the problem of low pay by ensuring that workers earn at least enough to attain a certain standard of living.

Assuming the UK government were to impose a minimum wage, the effect may be considered with reference to the diagram below. Curve DD_1 and SS_1 represent the free market demand and supply curves for a particular type of labour. The free market wage will be 0W and 0L people will be employed. If the minimum wage is set below 0W it will have no effect, as at a wage below 0W there will be excess labour demand. This would lift wages back to their equilibrium level of 0W. If, however, the government enforces a minimum wage of $0W_1$, it means that the part of the labour supply curve from S to X has no relevance. This is because although some workers will be willing to work for less than $0W_1$, they will not be allowed to do so. The supply of labour to the industry is now represented by the line W_1XS_1 and the equilibrium position is where the demand curve crosses this line. At this point $0L_1$ workers will be employed. The result of the introduction of the minimum wage is to reduce employment by LL_1 workers. The lucky workers who remain in employment will be better off than before as they now receive a higher wage rate. Those workers who lose their jobs will, however, be worse off.

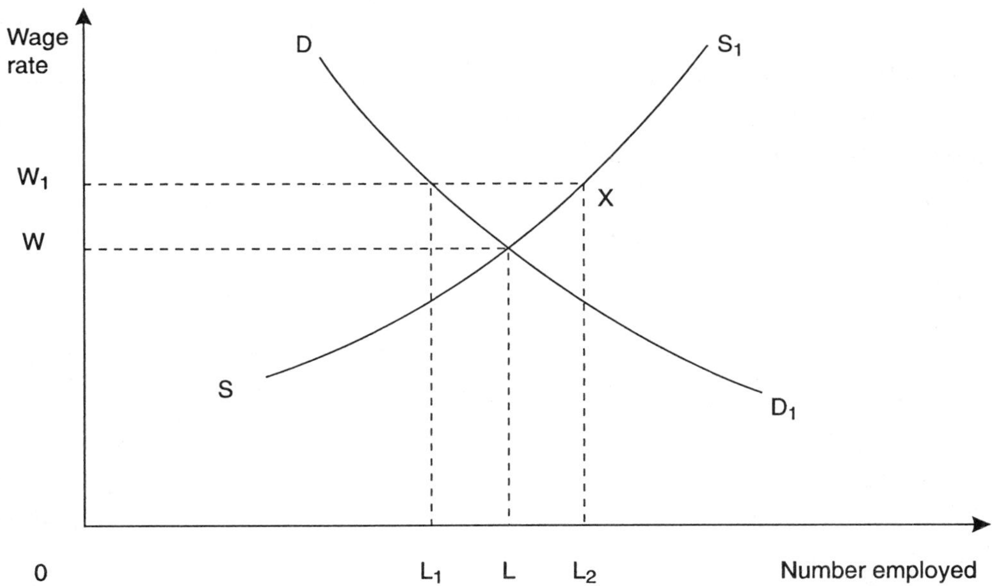

Figure 12

At the minimum wage of W_1 there is an excess labour supply of $(L_2 - L_1)$. Since firms cannot be forced to employ workers they do not want, employment will be at L_1 and the

NOTES

quantity of workers ($L_2 - L_1$) will be involuntarily unemployed. Workers are involuntarily unemployed if they are prepared to work at the going wage but cannot find jobs. So for low skill, low wage occupations a minimum wage in excess of the free market equilibrium wage will raise the wage for those lucky enough to find jobs, but will reduce the total amount of employment relative to the free market equilibrium level of employment. Minimum wage agreements may, in this way, explain involuntary unemployment among low-skilled workers.

Where the higher wage costs are passed on to consumers in the forms of higher prices, in an attempt by firms to maintain profit levels, the imposition of a statutory minimum wage may trigger an inflationary spiral. For this reason the opponents of minimum wage legislation argue against it because it tends to cause both inflation and unemployment.

The extent to which minimum wage legislation causes a fall in employment will to a large extent depend on the nature of the demand for labour in the industries where the minimum wage lies above the equilibrium wage rate. The elasticity of demand for labour depends on a number of features.

(a) The elasticity of demand for labour is directly related to the elasticity of demand for the product. If labour is producing a commodity which has a very inelastic demand, an increase in wages caused by the introduction of a minimum wage will have a relatively small effect on the demand for labour.

(b) The elasticity of demand for a given type of labour varies according to the proportion of total costs accounted for by labour costs. Where wages account for only a small proportion of total costs, the demand for labour will tend to be inelastic.

(c) The demand for labour will be more elastic the easier it is to substitute other factors for it. An increase in wage rates, all things being equal, will increase the cost of labour relative to the costs of the other factors. Where possible, therefore, firms will tend to substitute other factors for the now relatively dearer labour.

It should be noted that the supporters of minimum wage legislation argue that raising wage rates above the comparative equilibrium will lead in the end to an increase in the productivity of labour. Firms faced with higher wage rates might stimulate efforts to improve the productivity of labour. If this occurs the demand for labour will increase – which would be shown by a rightward shift of the demand curve in the diagram above. If this happens there might well be no net reduction in the numbers employed.

Further question practice

Now try the following practice questions at the end of this text.

Multiple choice questions **61–72**

Exam style question **6**

Chapter 7

MARKET STRUCTURES: FROM PERFECT COMPETITION TO MONOPOLY

Introduction

In Chapter 2 we set out the characteristics of a hypothetical perfect market. Consideration of such a market is useful although in fact it never exists in practice. The reason for this is that the underlying theory can be studied without the complicating factors that make real-life (imperfect) markets so complex. In this chapter we look at both perfect competition and its opposite, monopoly, and examine the effects of these market structures on the output decisions of firms. In the next chapter we look at two less extreme market structures: monopolistic competition and oligopoly.

Your objectives

After completing this chapter you should:

(a) understand the range of market structures that may exist;

(b) understand the main features of two extreme market structures: perfect competition and monopoly.

1 PERFECT AND IMPERFECT COMPETITION

Activity 1

Jot down the characteristics of perfect competition outlined in Chapter 2.

1.1 Characteristics of imperfect competition

One or more of a number of factors may make competition conditions imperfect.

(a) There may be one or just a few large firms dominating the market.

  (i) A single firm dominating the market is called a monopolist, or monopoly firm.

  (ii) When two or several firms dominate the market jointly, there is an *oligopoly* and firms are referred to as oligopolists. (A special case of oligopoly is *duopoly*: this is when precisely two firms dominate the market.)

  When only one or a few firms dominate the market, most of the market demand will be for their products and the firm can have a significant influence on the market price. The firm can make decisions on price as well as output and is a *price maker*.

(b) There may be shortages of information about prices and profit opportunities among some consumers or producers.

(c) In some markets, firms succeed in creating differences, real or imagined, between their own product and similar products of competitors. They seek to create customer demand for their own products in preference to competitors' products by emphasising these differences. Two ways of creating differences are *branding* and *advertising*. Another is small variations in product design. Creating such differences is called *product differentiation*, and it enables firms to become like monopolists or oligopolists in their own special corner of a large market. This type of competition is referred to as *monopolistic competition*.

(d) Free entry into the market might be prevented by existing firms in the market.

Definition

Oligopoly is a market dominated by a few suppliers.

2 EQUILIBRIUM UNDER PERFECT COMPETITION

2.1 Equilibrium in the short run

How are price, output and the maximisation of profit determined in the case of the firm operating under conditions of perfect competition in the short run?

Definition

Perfect market. A perfectly competitive market is one in which there is a large number of firms, each with a very small share of the market, producing a homogenous product, having perfect information and with free entry to and exit from the market.

The short run refers to a period in which the number of firms in the market is temporarily fixed. In these circumstances it is possible for firms to make supernormal profits or losses, as the following diagrams show.

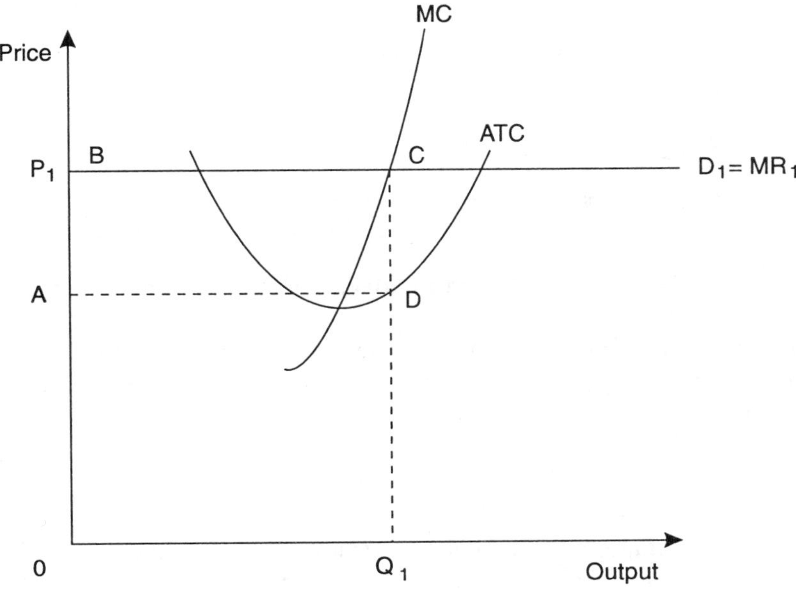

Figure 1 Perfect market in the short run: supernormal profits

Figure 1 shows the cost and demand curves of a firm in the short run making supernormal profits. The demand curve is the horizontal line D_1 at price P_1. The curve is a horizontal line indicating that the firm may not influence the price of the goods and has to accept the price that the market as a whole fixes for them. If the firm were to charge a higher price it would lose all its sales, and there is no point charging a lower price as it can sell all its output at the given price. The demand curve is also the marginal revenue curve; every new unit sold at price P_1 increases total revenue by an amount P_1.

Figure 1 also shows the average total cost curve (ATC) and the marginal cost curve (MC), with the MC cutting the ATC at the lowest point of the ATC. Given these cost curves and the demand curve D_1, the firm will produce the output Q_1, where the MC curves cuts the MR horizontal curve at the point C. This is the profit maximising point.

If the firm were to produce fewer units it would be producing at a point where MR was higher than MC and all additional units produced up to the point where MR = MC would similarly have MR greater than MC. The firm should produce these units because so long as MR is greater than MC, each unit shows a profit (additional revenue is greater than additional costs). Similarly it should not expand production past MR = MC because it will be producing where MC is greater than MR, in other words where the additional costs for each unit exceed the additional revenue earned.

At the output Q_1 the firm is making supernormal profits indicated by the rectangle ABCD. This will attract new firms into the industry and the price will be bid down, possibly to price P_2 as shown in Figure 2. Here the firm makes a loss shown by the rectangle WXYZ. Once again the firm produces where MC = MR giving an output of Q_2.

NOTES

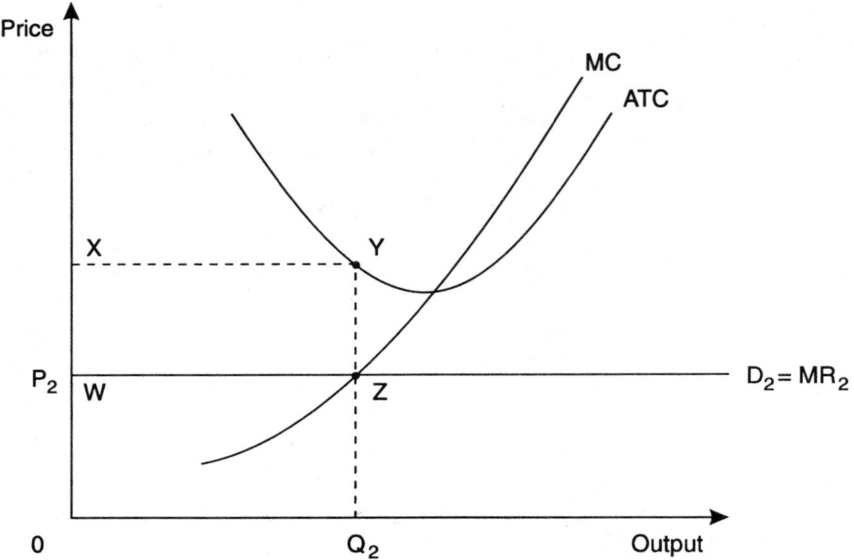

Figure 2 Perfect market in the short run: losses

In the long run, whenever profits are being made new firms will enter the industry and the price will fall. Similarly, when losses are made firms will leave the industry and the price will rise.

Activity 2

In conditions of perfect competition, the demand curve for a firm's product is:

(a) identical to the firm's marginal revenue curve. True or false?

(b) perfectly inelastic. True or false?

2.2 Equilibrium in the long run

In a perfectly competitive market in the long run, the firm cannot influence the market price and its average revenue curve is horizontal. The firm's average cost curve is U-shaped. The firm is in equilibrium and earns normal profits only (ie no supernormal profits) when the AC curve is at a tangent to the AR curve as shown in Figure 3(b). In other words, *long-term equilibrium* will exist when supernormal profits and losses are eliminated.

There is no incentive for firms to enter or leave the industry and the price will remain at P with the firm making normal profits only.

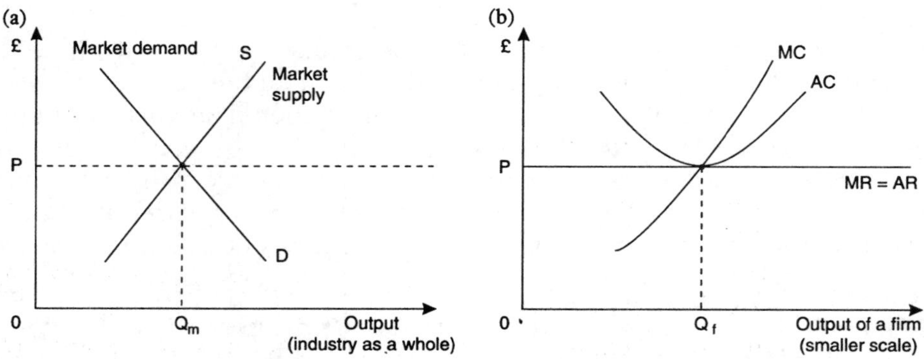

Figure 3

Note the following points about Figure 3.

(a) The market price P is the price which all individual firms in the market must take.

(b) If the firm must accept a given MR (as it must in conditions of perfect competition) and it sets MR = MC, then the MC curve is in effect the individual firm's supply curve (Figure 3(b)). The *market supply curve* in Figure 3(a) is derived by aggregating the individual supply curves of every firm in the industry.

Long-run equilibrium will, therefore, occur in the industry when there are no more firms entering or leaving the industry because no new firm thinks it could earn higher profits by entering and no existing firm thinks it could do better by leaving. So in the long run, all firms in the industry will have MR = MC = AC = AR as in Figure 3(b).

Activity 3

A perfectly competitive firm will be in equilibrium where price is equal to marginal cost. True or false?

3 EQUILIBRIUM FOR A MONOPOLY

3.1 The monopoly market

The long-run equilibrium of a firm in a perfectly competitive market is at a price and output level where only normal profits are earned. Price = MR = MC = AC, and the firm produces at the minimum average cost per unit.

Definition

Monopoly is a market with only one supplier of a product.

Monopoly is the opposite of perfect competition. In a monopoly, there is only one firm, the sole producer of a good which has no closely competing substitutes, so that the total market supply is identical to the single firm's supply.

In monopoly, the firm faces a downward-sloping average revenue curve because its average revenue curve is the same as the total market demand curve.

If average revenue is falling, marginal revenue will always be lower than average revenue; if the monopolist increases output by one unit the price per unit received will fall, so the extra revenue generated by the sale of the extra unit of the good is less than the price of that unit. So the monopolist faces a downward-sloping AR curve with an MR curve below the AR curve.

There is a useful technique for drawing the AR curve and the MR curve of a monopolist.

(a) For simplicity, assume that the monopolist's AR curve, which is the market demand curve too, is a straight line.

(b) Draw this AR curve from a point on the y axis (point A in Figure 4 below) to a point on the x axis (point B in Figure 4).

(c) You can now draw the MR curve from the same point on the y axis (point A) to a point on the x axis which is *half way* to point B. This is shown as point C in Figure 4, and 0C is one half the length of 0B (ie 0C = CB).

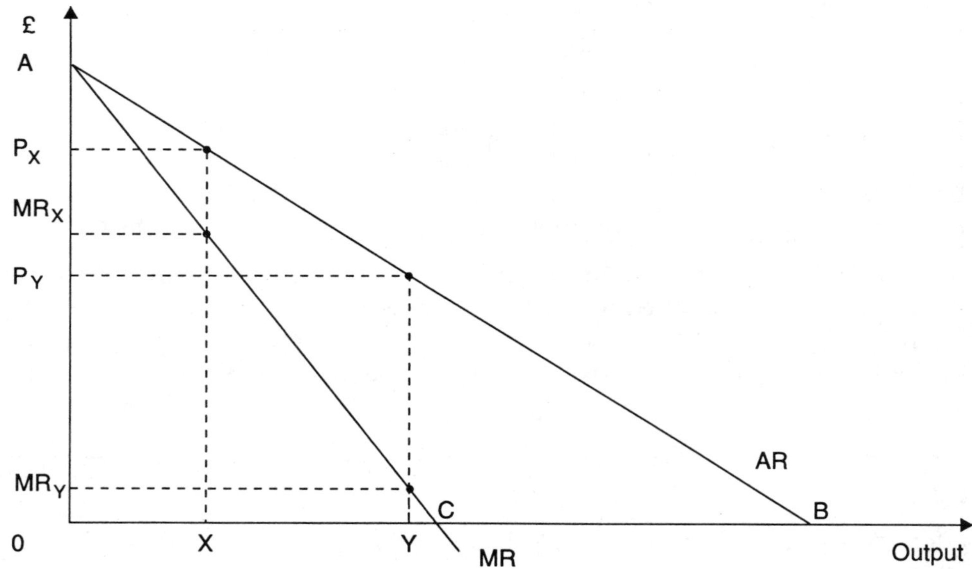

Figure 4 A monopolist's AR and MR curves

The marginal revenue can be negative. This is when the price elasticity of demand is inelastic; although lowering the price increases sales demand, the volume increase is small and so total revenue falls.

Activity 4

Study Figure 4 above. At what price and output level would the firm maximise its sales revenue?

It is important that you should understand what the MR and AR (demand) curves are showing us. In Figure 4:

(a) at output quantity X, the marginal revenue earned from the last unit produced and sold is MR_X, but the price at which all the X units would be sold is P_X. This is found by looking at the price level on the AR curve associated with output X;

(b) similarly, at output quantity Y, the marginal revenue from the last unit produced and sold is MR_Y, but the price at which all Y units would be sold on the market is, from the AR curve for Y output, P_Y.

3.2 Profit-maximising equilibrium of a monopoly

The condition for profit maximisation is, as we have seen, that marginal revenue should equal marginal cost. This is true for any firm. As long as marginal revenue exceeds marginal cost, an increase in output will add more to revenues than to costs, and therefore increase profits. A monopolist might maximise profits:

(a) but make no supernormal profits; or

(b) make supernormal profits.

Figure 5 shows a monopoly equilibrium where the monopolist is earning just *normal profits*, and so AC = AR. At this point (Q) the AC curve touches the AR curve at a tangent, at exactly the same output level where MC = MR. Since AC = AR and AC includes normal profits, the monopolist will be earning normal profits but no supernormal profits in this situation.

NOTES

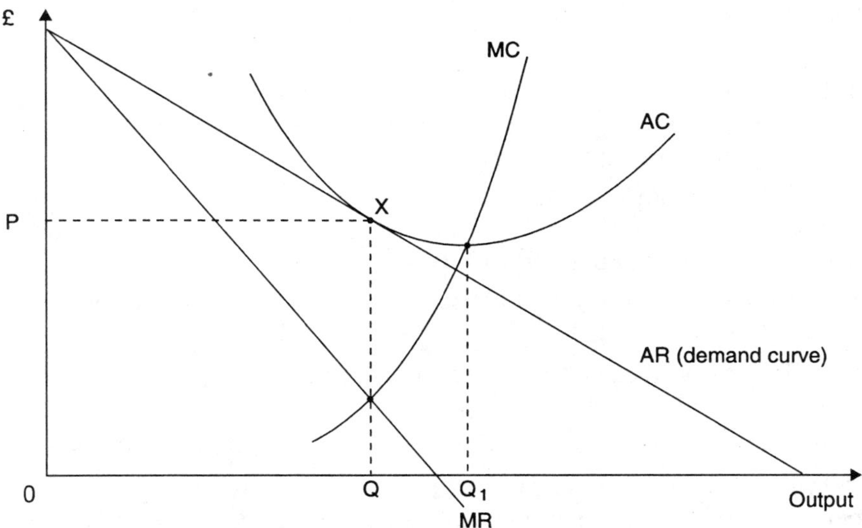

Figure 5 Equilibrium of a monopoly firm earning normal profits

In this situation, the monopoly will make a loss by producing at output higher than Q, and so it will have to produce at an output level which is below the capacity at which its average costs are minimised (output Q_1).

Monopolies are usually able to earn monopoly or supernormal profits in the long term as well as the short term, and the situation illustrated in Figure 5 will be rare for a monopoly. However, as we shall see later, it is a long-run equilibrium situation for firms in monopolistic competition. It *might*, however, represent the long-term equilibrium of some monopolies, where barriers to entry into the industry are low, and competition would be attracted into the market if supernormal profits were achievable. It might also be the case for a government-run monopoly which is required to cover costs rather than being required to make profits.

In perfect competition, a firm should not be able to earn supernormal profits in the long run because they would be competed away by new entrants to the industry. In monopoly, however, the firm can earn supernormal profits *in the long run* as well as in the short run, because there are *barriers to entry* which prevent rivals entering the market. Figure 6 shows a firm earning supernormal profits, equal to the area PCBA, which represents (P – A) × Q units produced and sold.

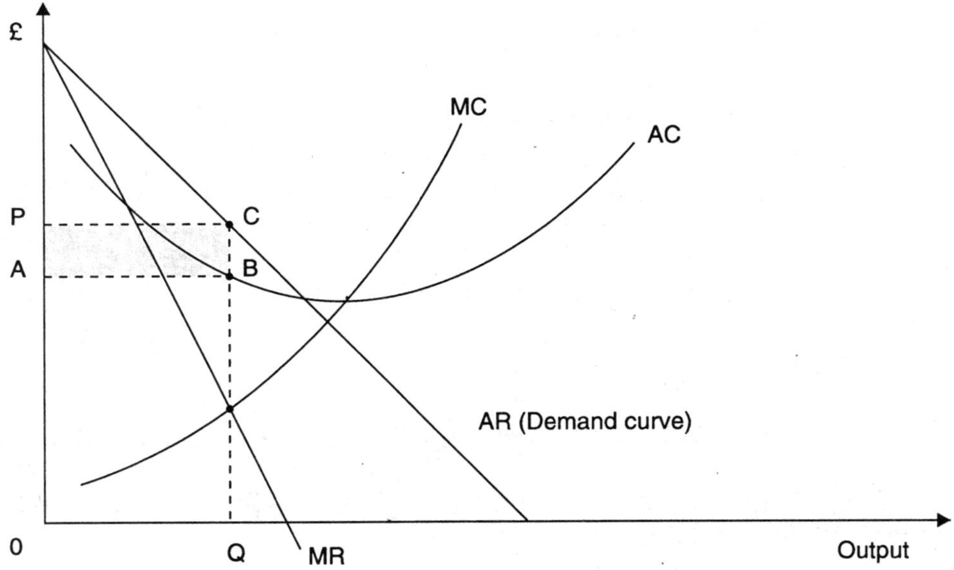

Figure 6 Equilibrium of a monopoly firm earning supernormal profits

NOTES

This is an important diagram that you should be able to reproduce yourself and explain clearly.

(a) First of all draw a U-shaped short-run average cost curve, AC, and a marginal cost curve MC, that is mainly upward-sloping and that cuts through the AC curve at the lowest point on the AC curve.

(b) Next, draw a downward-sloping demand curve (AR curve), as a straight line, that cuts through the AC curve. Draw a downward-sloping marginal revenue curve, MR – also a straight line, as explained in Figure 4.

(c) The profit-maximising output level Q is where MR = MC, ie where these two lines cross.

(d) The profit-maximising selling price P is found by reference to the demand curve (ie AR curve) at that output level.

(e) The average cost at this output level, A, is found by reference to the AC curve.

(f) You will find that at this level of output, the price, AR, exceeds average costs, AC, and so super-normal profits are earned (= unit price minus average cost (volume of output in units).

Activity 5

Now test your ability to reproduce the diagram. Without looking at the book, do a sketch and then refer back to the book to check your answer.

4 MONOPOLY AND PERFECT COMPETITION COMPARED

If there are no economies of scale for a large output-volume firm, output will be lower and costs and price higher under monopoly, compared with perfect competition.

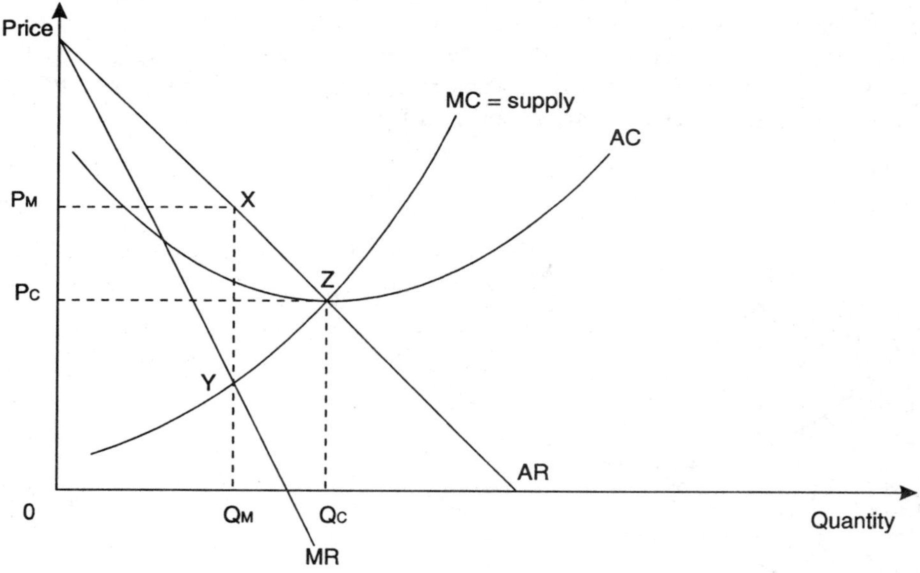

Figure 7 Monopoly industry and industry in perfect competition compared

Let us suppose that there are two industries identical in every respect, except that one has a monopoly supplier and the other has conditions of perfect competition. The demand curve of each industry is the same, and the marginal costs of production are the same, so that the MC curve of the monopolist and the supply curve of the perfectly competitive industry are the same.

(a) In the competitive industry, equilibrium is reached at a price level where the demand curve and supply curve intersect. All firms will sell their goods at price P_C, and total output for the industry will be Q_C. (Each firm individually, remember, faces a horizontal demand curve.)

(b) In the monopoly, the profit-maximising equilibrium is where MC = MR, so that price will be P_M and output Q_M.

In this way, a firm in a monopoly industry will produce less and sell at a higher price than firms in a perfectly competitive industry.

It is also significant that:

(a) in the perfectly competitive industry, equilibrium is reached when firms minimise their average costs (AC is at a minimum). Position Z is then the output/price level that gives an optimal allocation of resources;

(b) in the monopoly industry, profit-maximising equilibrium is *not* at the output level where AC is minimised, but at a lower output level with a higher AC.

At the monopolist's profit-maximising output, the difference between price and marginal cost is XY. It could be argued that if the firm were to produce more output, it would provide more marginal utility for consumers (as represented by the demand curve) than it would create marginal cost for the firm. There is a social cost that occurs because a monopoly produces only Q_M of output at price P_M, rather than Q_C of output at price P_C. The loss of social welfare, or social cost, is represented by the area XYZ in Figure 7, and is sometimes referred to as the *deadweight burden of monopoly*.

These conclusions *might* not be valid, however, if the monopolist is able to take advantage of its monopoly position to achieve economies of scale that perfectly competitive firms could not, owing to their relative smallness in terms of the total market output.

This is important, because it is a theoretical argument *in favour* of monopolies.

5 PRICE DISCRIMINATION

5.1 Price discrimination and market segmentation

Definition

The term *price discrimination* refers to a situation in which a firm sells the same product at different prices in different markets.

Market segmentation may involve elements of *product differentiation* (eg different brand names) in order to satisfy particular segments of the market.

Activity 6

You are likely to have encountered examples of price discrimination in practice. Can you remember any?

Three basic conditions are necessary for price discrimination to be effective and profitable.

(a) The seller must be able to control the supply of the product. Clearly, this will apply under monopoly conditions. The monopoly seller has control over the quantity of the product offered to a particular buyer.

(b) The seller must be able to prevent the resale of the good by one buyer to another. The markets must, therefore, be clearly separated so that those paying lower prices cannot resell to those paying higher prices. The ability to prevent resale tends to be associated with the character of the product, or the ability to classify buyers into readily identifiable groups. Services are less easily resold than goods, while transportation costs, tariff barriers, or import quotas may separate classes of buyers geographically, so making price discrimination possible.

(c) There must be significant differences in the willingness to pay among the different classes of buyers. This means that the elasticity of demand must be different in at least two of the separate markets, so that total profits may be increased by charging different prices.

We can see how the monopolist seller practising price discrimination can maximise revenue using a diagrammatic illustration (Figure 8).

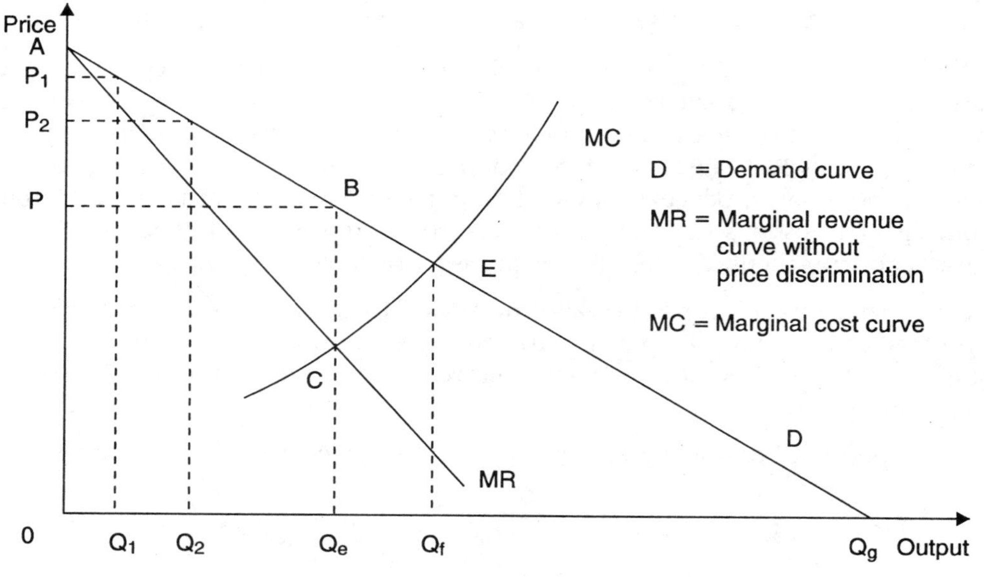

Figure 8

Figure 8 demonstrates firstly the equilibrium position of a monopolist that does not discriminate. He produces at the point C where marginal cost equals marginal revenue, producing output Q_e and selling at price P. His total revenue is given by the rectangle $0PBQ_e$.

Figure 8 also illustrates how the discriminating monopolist can improve on this position, both from the point of increased revenue and increased profits.

The discriminating monopolist does not charge the same price for all units sold. If we assume that monopolists can discriminate perfectly, then they can sell each unit for a different price, as indicated on the demand curve. So they can sell the first unit Q_1 at the price P_1, and the second unit Q_2 at the price P_2. This follows for all units sold so that the demand curve becomes the marginal revenue curve; each extra unit sold is sold for the price indicated on the demand curve, each previous unit being sold for the higher price relevant to that unit.

Perfectly discriminating monopolists will still maximise profits where MC = MR, but the marginal revenue curve is now the curve D, the demand curve. So they produce at the point E where marginal cost equals the new marginal revenue, producing Q_f units. The additional revenue of the discriminating monopolist is represented by the areas APB plus Q_eBEQ_f. Discriminating monopolists have therefore maximised their revenue (consistent of course with maximising profit). If monopolists did not wish to maximise profit, but simply to maximise revenue they would expand production to the point Q_g when total revenue would be the area $0AQ_g$.

Take care not to confuse maximising revenue with maximising profit. Increasing output beyond Q_f in the example will not increase profit, as marginal costs exceed marginal revenue for each additional unit sold.

Price discrimination often results where the market is separated by transport costs and tariffs; so firms may sell their products abroad cheaper than at home. An extreme example of this is known as dumping; this occurs when exports sell in foreign markets at prices below the cost of production. This pricing strategy is designed to drive domestic producers out of the industry so that the foreign producer may achieve monopoly power. The price differential cannot, of course, exceed the cost of transporting the good back to the home market, plus any tariff on imports.

Price discrimination also occurs where it is possible to separate buyers into clearly defined groups. Industrial users of gas and electricity are able to buy these fuels more cheaply from British Gas and electricity companies than are domestic users. Similarly, milk is sold more cheaply to industrial users, for example for making into cheese or ice cream, than to private households.

Activity 7

Explain why it is possible for a railway or airline to charge different fares for passengers using the same service.

6 PUBLIC POLICY TOWARDS MONOPOLIES

6.1 Public policy towards private enterprise monopolies

Monopolies might be harmful or beneficial to the public interest.

(a) A beneficial monopoly is one that succeeds in achieving economies of scale in an industry where the minimum efficiency scale is at a level of production that would mean having to get a large share of the total market supply.

(b) A monopoly against the public interest would be one in which cost efficiencies are not achieved, or are negligible. Oliver Williamson suggested that inefficiency in monopolies might occur if 'market power provides the firm with the opportunity to pursue a variety of other-than-profit objectives.'

There are other reasons for trying to control monopoly growth. A monopoly firm may be a multinational, with its head office in another country. Multinational firms are difficult to control within the context of a government's economic policy requirements; a government might prefer to see more national firms in a position of strength in the country's home markets.

Monopolies might also try to preserve their position by acting to prevent competition. They might create barriers to entry into the industry against other potential rivals (eg by taking over small new competitors or purchasing patents to secure a production monopoly). When competition between firms is killed off in this way, the public interest is harmed.

A monopoly may try to exploit its position by using price discrimination, to charge higher prices for the same good in a different segment of the market. Certain pharmaceuticals manufacturers, for example, have been accused of unfairly charging higher prices in one country than in another. This too can be against the public interest.

NOTES

6.2 Government control over monopolies, mergers and restrictive practices

There are several different ways in which a government can attempt to control monopolies.

(a) It can stop them from developing, or it can break them up once they have been created. In the past, there has been a history of trust-busting in the USA. Preventing monopolies from being created is the reason why a government might have a public policy on mergers.

(b) It can take them over. Nationalised industries are often government-run monopolies. Government-run monopolies are potentially advantageous because:

   (i) they need not have a profit-maximising objective so that the government can decide whether or not to supply a good or service to a household on grounds other than cost or profit;

   (ii) the government can regulate the quality of the good or service provided more easily than if the industry were operated by private firms;

   (iii) key industries can be protected (eg health, education).

(c) It can allow monopolies or oligopolies to operate, but try to control their activities in order to protect the consumer. For example, it can try to prohibit the worst forms of restrictive practice, such as price cartels. Or it may set up regulatory bodies to protect consumers' interests where conditions of natural monopoly apply, as in the recently privatised utility industries of the UK. The pricing of products in such industries may be controlled: in the UK, many of the large utilities have been required to limit price increases to a specified percentage *below* the Retail Prices Index over a number of years.

There are two basic principles in the thinking behind consumer protection policies.

(a) Control over markets can arise by firms eliminating the opposition, either by merging with or taking over rivals or stopping other firms from entering the market. The problem here is that when a single firm controls a big enough share of the market it can begin to behave as a monopolist even though its market share is below 100%.

(b) Several firms could behave as monopolists by agreeing with each other not to compete. This could be done in a variety of ways (for example by exchanging information, by setting common prices or by splitting up the market into geographical areas and operating only within allocated boundaries).

In a perfect monopoly, there is only one firm that is the sole producer of a good that has no closely competing substitutes, so that the firm controls the supply of the good to the market. The definition of a monopoly *in practice* is rather more extensive than this, because governments seeking to control the growth of monopoly firms will probably choose to regard any firm that acquires a certain share of the market as a potential monopolist.

Activity 8

In recent years, the government has tried to increase competition by removing monopoly status in a number of industries. Can you think of any?

6.3 The Monopolies and Mergers Commission in the UK

In the UK, the Monopolies and Restrictive Practices Act 1948 provided that any firm controlling more than one third of the market for its goods should be investigated as a potential monopoly, which was against the public interest. Under the Fair

Trading Act 1973, the Director General of Fair Trading is allowed to refer cases to the Monopolies and Mergers Commission if any firm controls one quarter of the market, or if any proposed takeover or merger would create a firm that controlled more than one quarter of the market. The Commission will then investigate the proposed merger or takeover and recommend whether or not it should be allowed to proceed.

Another aspect of the work of the Monopolies and Mergers Commission (MMC) is to investigate cases where a monopoly is suspected of operating against the public interest and to recommend to the government the steps that should be taken to make the monopoly alter its practices.

6.4 UK government policy on monopolies and mergers

It is significant, however, that a government department, the Office of the Director General of Fair Trading, has the power to refer cases to the Commission, which can then prevent a merger or takeover from taking place if it is considered to be against the public interest. The strength of anti-monopoly and anti-takeover activity, therefore, depends on the attitude of the government of the day.

The office of the Director General has the help of the Consumer Protection Advisory Committee which advises the Director General and the Minister whether trading and commercial practices referred to it are harmful to the interests of the consumers. (The activities of this committee are not directed against monopolies as such, but it is a focus of consumer protection activity, which is one of the reasons why anti-monopoly controls might be required.)

6.5 Mergers

Mergers, or prospective mergers, can also be referred to the MMC if they are thought likely to create or strengthen a monopoly. Companies do not have to seek permission before merging, nor can permission be given in advance of the full details being known. But it is common practice these days for mergers to be proposed subject to MMC approval.

6.6 Public policy in favour of monopolies and mergers

One aspect of the UK government's policy has been an attempt to control the development of monopolies that are against the public interest. But opinions differ about which monopolies would be good for the country and which would be harmful. Another aspect in recent years has been the establishment of consumer watchdog bodies to regulate the recently privatised utility industries. These usually operate under conditions of natural monopoly.

In the modern world of multinational companies, companies need to be big to survive and prosper. Arguably, the UK's industrial strength has declined over the years because the country has failed to nurture enough multinational companies (strengthened by virtual monopolies in their own country) to compete successfully in world markets.

There have been signs in recent years that the UK government has wanted to encourage the growth of companies in the UK, and many of the proposed mega-mergers (ie mergers between big companies) have not been referred to the Monopolies and Mergers Commission. Government anti-monopoly policy in the UK has accordingly been relatively mild in recent years.

6.7 European Union regulations on mergers

The European Commission has the power to intervene and either to block or to authorise larger mergers.

The regulation provides that mergers with a world wide aggregate turnover of over 5 billion ecu (approximately £3.5 billion) between undertakings with EU-wide turnover of over 250 million ecu (approximately £175 million) require prior clearance from the European Commission.

If the Commission finds that the merger might not be compatible with the European common market, it will start proceedings to block it.

7 PRIVATISATION OF NATIONALISED INDUSTRIES

Definition

Privatisation is the policy of transferring economic activities to private ownership

Privatisation takes three broad forms.

(a) The deregulation of industries, to allow private firms to compete against state-owned businesses where they were not allowed to compete before (eg deregulation of bus and coach services, possible deregulation of postal services).

(b) Contracting out work to private firms, where the work was previously done by government employees (eg refuse collection, hospital laundry work).

(c) Transferring the ownership of assets from the state to private shareholders (eg the denationalisation of British Telecom and British Gas).

The UK government has carried out a policy of denationalisation in recent years. British Gas, British Telecom and the regional water companies have been among the enterprises which have been privatised.

Activity 9

Possible disadvantages for consumers have been at least partially guarded against by the creation of regulatory bodies for the above industries (and for others). Do you know what they are called?

Privatisation may improve efficiency, but there are other possible advantages of privatisation.

(a) Denationalisation provides an immediate source of money for the government.

(b) Privatisation reduces bureaucratic and political meddling in the industries concerned.

(c) There is a view that wider share ownership should be encouraged. Denationalisation is one way of creating wider share ownership, as the sale of shares in British Telecom, British Gas and some other nationalised industries proved in the UK.

There are arguments against privatisation too.

(a) State-owned industries are more likely to respond to the public interest, ahead of the profit motive. For example, state-owned industries are more likely to cross-subsidise unprofitable operations from profitable ones; for example, the Post Office will continue to deliver letters to the isles of Scotland even though the service might be very unprofitable.

(b) Encouraging private competition to state-run industries might be inadvisable where significant economies of scale can be achieved by monopoly operations.

The advantages of having a controlled or centrally planned economy, rather than a free enterprise economy, can also be advanced as reasons in favour of having nationalised industries.

Chapter roundup

- Market structures range from perfect competition at one extreme to pure monopoly at the other. Monopolistic competition and oligopoly are examples of market structures falling between these extremes.
- In perfect competition, the long-run outcome is that firms will have:

  $$MR = MC = AC = AR = \text{price}$$

- In a monopoly, the monopolist's average revenue curve (the market demand curve) is downward-sloping. At the profit-maximising equilibrium, MC = MR, and at this level of output the monopolist is likely to earn supernormal profits.
- In the absence of economies of scale, a monopolist's output will be lower, and costs and price higher, than in conditions of perfect competition.

Quick quiz

1 What are the characteristics of perfect competition?

2 How can a firm in perfect competition make supernormal profits?

3 Draw an AR curve and an MR curve for a monopolist.

4 Draw a graph which shows the profit-maximising equilibrium of a monopolist.

5 Draw a graph which compares the profit maximising equilibrium of an industry with a monopoly firm as an identical industry which has perfect competition. What is the deadweight burden of monopoly?

6 What is price discrimination?

7 Why might a government wish to control monopolies?

8 How might a government control monopolies?

9 What forms can privatisation take? What are the economic arguments for and against privatisation?

Answers to Activities

1 The characteristics of perfect competition are as follows.

(a) A large number of buyers and sellers: individual firms are price takers, unable to influence market prices.

(b) There is perfect communication. All buyers and sellers have the same information and it costs them nothing to acquire it.

(c) Producers and consumers act rationally.

(d) The product is homogeneous.

(e) There is free entry to and exit from the market.

(f) There are no transport costs.

2 (a) True. The firm can sell whatever output it produces at the market price.

(b) False. (a) above implies that the demand curve is perfectly elastic.

3 True. Price is average revenue (AR) which will be equal to MC at equilibrium.

4 At the point where MR = 0. Further sales will lead to negative MR, and so a reduction in total revenue.

NOTES

5 Refer to Figure 6 to check your answer.

6 You might have thought of:

   (a) telephone calls (different prices for peak and off-peak calls);

   (b) rail travel (there are often many different tickets you can buy for a particular journey);

   (c) package holidays (more expensive during school holidays).

7 (a) *Consumers' ignorance.* Not all consumers may be aware of the availability of low-rate tickets such as lower prices for booking in advance, special offers and so on. This means that two customers on the same journey and in similar seats might pay different prices because one of the customers is unaware that a cheaper price could have been obtained.

   (b) *The nature of the good.* Prices can be varied according to the time of day or day of the week. Many customers will be forced to travel at peak times and pay top prices and some will switch to travelling at a cheaper time when the railway or airline has spare capacity to be filled. Demand for journeys at peak times will be relatively inelastic, since demand will be from commuters who must travel in these periods in order to reach their workplace on time. A cheaper rate might be offered to children. Since a child cannot transfer his ticket to an adult there is no danger that adults can buy cheaper tickets by using children to obtain tickets on their behalf.

   (c) *Distance.* A railway can sell cheap travel to customers travelling from say, Manchester to London, but still charge full rates to customers travelling from London to Manchester.

8 You might have mentioned telecommunications, television franchises, electricity supply and others.

9 Inevitably, OFGAS, OFTEL and OFWAT.

Case Study

'British and European buyers of compact discs (CDs) get a raw deal by comparison with music lovers on the other side of the Atlantic. Prices in Europe are about 40% higher than in North America. The Director General of Fair Trading is considering referring the matter to the Monopolies and Mergers Commission. So far the industry has failed to give a convincing explanation of why CD prices are so high. The industry's argument that the costs of supplying CDs in the UK are higher than in the US does not ring true. On the other hand, no evidence has emerged of a cartel among either record companies or retailers.

A price-fixing cartel is not necessary to achieve this because one company's music cannot normally be substituted for another's. Each title is effectively a mini-monopoly, at least where protected by copyright. Copyright law also supports market segmentation by allowing record companies to ban retailers from buying CDs at cheaper wholesale prices in other countries. This enables the industry to maintain wide differentials in wholesale prices between the US and the UK, which are then reflected in retail prices.

Market segmentation and price discrimination are not in themselves always against the public interest. Record companies have a high proportion of fixed costs. To recoup these fixed costs the industry has to charge a mark-up on top of marginal costs. Rather than charging the same mark-up for each customer, it may be more efficient to charge a higher mark-up for those who receive more value from the product, hence the higher price of the better quality CDs compared to tape cassettes.

Case Study (continued)

But a similar argument cannot justify price discrimination between Europe and America. Market segmentation in this case works against consumer interests and the competition authorities should act to remove it.'

Financial Times, 4 May 1992

Use this extract to answer the following questions.

(a) What are the conditions necessary for firms to be able to operate a policy of price discrimination?

(b) What is the extent of price discrimination in the market for CDs? Identify the factors that enable record companies to practise this discrimination.

(c) Assess whether or not the Monopolies and Mergers Commission should intervene to prevent price discrimination in the CD market. Suggest the best form such intervention could take.

Answer to Case Study

(a) The term *price discrimination* refers to a situation in which a firm sells the same product at different prices in different markets.

Three conditions are necessary for price discrimination to be effective.

(i) First, the seller must be able to control the supply of the product, a condition which will apply under monopoly conditions. The monopoly seller has control over the quantity of the product offered to a particular buyer.

(ii) The seller must be able to prevent the resale of the good by one buyer to another. This means that the markets must be clearly separated so that those paying lower prices cannot resell to those paying higher prices. The ability to prevent resale tends to be associated with the character of the product, or the ability to classify buyers into readily identifiable groups. Services are less easily resold than goods while transportation costs, tariff barriers or import quotas may separate classes of buyers geographically and so make price discrimination possible.

(iii) There must be significant differences in the willingness to pay among the different classes of buyers. In effect, this means that the elasticity of demand must be different in at least two of the separate markets so that total profits may be increased by charging different prices.

(b) The average prices of CDs in Europe is around 40% higher than CD prices in North America, which appears to indicate significant price discrimination. The prices of different CD titles also vary widely in each of these markets. However, there is only limited substitution between different titles and therefore these price differences do not represent price discrimination.

It will be found that there are significant differences in price for the same CD titles in Europe compared with North America, and there are two reasons why record companies are able to practise this price discrimination.

(i) Copyright law makes it easier for record companies to segment the market by prohibiting retailers from buying CDs at lower wholesale prices in other countries for re-sale at home.

(ii) Physical separation between the European and North American markets reduces the extent to which European consumers can easily buy CDs in the lower-priced North American market.

(c) The Monopolies and Mergers Commission (MMC) can carry out an investigation into an industry if the case is referred to it by the Director General of Fair Trading or by the President of the Board of Trade, a government minister.

NOTES

An MMC investigation can be called for to see whether a monopoly situation exists in an industry, or if the industry is following practices which are against the public interest. The UK CD industry cannot be said to be a monopoly, although by the nature of the product a mini-monopoly can be said to exist for each title, reinforced by copyright law. There is also lack of evidence of a price-fixing cartel. Reference to the MMC would need to be on the grounds that the large price difference between European and North American CD prices is against the public interest.

Some would argue that the price discrimination which exists is in the best interests of consumers, since it allows a wider range of music to be marketed than would otherwise be the case. However, this argument will only be borne out if it can be shown that the price differential allows a wider range of music to be available in Europe than in North America.

To reduce or eliminate price discrimination, the MMC would need to address the issue of why the price discrimination is taking place.

Obviously, it is not possible to reduce the physical distance between the European and North American markets. However, it might be possible for the MMC to press for changes in copyright law so that it is possible for retailers to source CDs from wholesalers in either market. This might intensify price competition in European markets and lead to a lower price differential between Europe and North America.

Further question practice

Now try the following practice questions at the end of this text.

Multiple choice questions **73–84**

Exam style question **7**

Chapter 8

MONOPOLISTIC COMPETITION AND OLIGOPOLY

Introduction

Actual market structures usually do not correspond with either of the extreme cases of perfect competition and monopoly. This leads to a discussion of forms of imperfect market structure, including a form known as 'monopolistic competition'.

Your objectives

After completing this chapter you should:

(a) understand the main features of monopolistic competition and their implications for firms' marketing and output decisions;

(b) understand the main features of oligopoly and their implications for firms' marketing and output decisions.

1 MONOPOLISTIC COMPETITION AND NON-PRICE COMPETITION

1.1 Monopolistic competition

Firms in monopolistic competition (as well as oligopoly, discussed later in this chapter) will try to avoid competition on price in order to preserve their position as a price maker. They will often resort to non-price competition instead. This can take several forms, including:

(a) product differentiation;

(b) branding;

(c) advertising and sales promotion;

(d) creating add-on services.

1.2 Product differentiation

Product differentiation describes a situation in which there is a single product being manufactured by several suppliers, and the product of each supplier is basically the same. However, the suppliers try to create differences between their own product and the products of their rivals or between different brands of the product they sell. These differences might be real (eg small or large design differences) or imaginary, created largely by advertising and brand image.

Differentiation may take a number of forms, including:

(a) different physical or technical characteristics, satisfying different buyer needs, or the same needs in different ways;

(b) different packaging;

(c) different conditions of sale with respect to guarantees, after-sales services, and so on;

(d) different geographical location;

(e) different perceptions of the product created through advertising and promotion. This includes *branding of goods*.

Activity 1

You will certainly have come across many examples of product differentiation yourself. Jot down a few.

1.3 Other forms of non-price competition

There are other ways in which non-price competition can be developed.

Definition

Non-price competition involves competition between firms for customers in the same market, but not on the basis of lowest price (or, at least, not on the basis of lowest price only).

(a) *Advertising and sales promotion, or brand imagery*

   (i) The aim of advertising, sales promotions or brand image is to increase demand for the good, often at the expense of demand for the goods of other firms in the market.

NOTES

(ii) When one firm advertises, others will retaliate. As a result, an advertising or sales promotion campaign might have little or no effect on demand, and so incur cost for little or no benefit.

(b) *Incidental services*. Incidental services are extra services that come as an add-on to the basic good. A firm might make its product more attractive than its rivals' product by, for example, superior sales services or personal attention. Rival firms can retaliate by also offering incidental services.

(c) *Innovation and technical differences*. A firm may improve its market share by creating genuine differences through innovation: Brand X is made to have more features than Brand Y, so that customers for Brand Y are encouraged to switch. Here, the opportunity for retaliation by other firms must be limited because innovation is easily the most effective form of non-price competition. However, this is not easily available to firms which produce basic commodities like petrol or farm produce (eg milk or wheat).

Activity 2

Consider the example of a motorist wishing to buy petrol.

(a) What factors affect the motorist's choice of petrol stations?

(b) How do petrol stations compete for business?

1.4 Profit-maximising equilibrium of a firm in monopolistic competition

A firm which operates in conditions of monopolistic competition:

(a) has a downward-sloping demand curve. The quantity demanded responds to the price at which the firm is prepared to sell. The downward-sloping curve is possible because of product differentiation;

(b) unlike a monopoly firm, is often *unable* to create barriers to entry to other firms. (Indeed, the firm already competes with rivals, who can take retaliatory competitive action if the firm makes big profits).

A firm will therefore have:

(a) a short-run equilibrium, in which it can make supernormal profits; and

(b) a long-run equilibrium.

In the *long run*, the monopolistic competitor cannot earn supernormal profits because there are no entry barriers. Its short-run supernormal profits will be eroded by new entrants. So the firm eventually will only be able to achieve normal profits.

The short-run equilibrium for a firm in monopolistic competition is illustrated in Figure 1 below. This diagram is the same as a diagram which shows the equilibrium of a monopoly firm earning supernormal profits. The firm makes supernormal profits of (P–A) × Q units, shown by the area PCBA.

NOTES

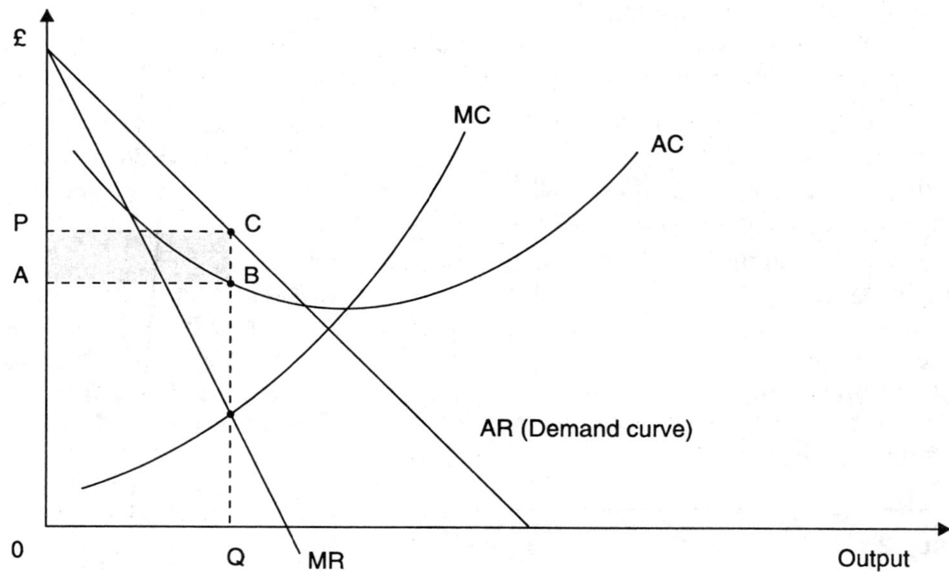

Figure 1 A firm's short-run equilibrium in monopolistic competition

The long-run equilibrium for a firm in monopolistic competition is illustrated in Figure 2. This diagram is the same as a diagram that shows the equilibrium of a monopoly firm which earns no supernormal profits, only normal profits (Figure 5 of the previous chapter).

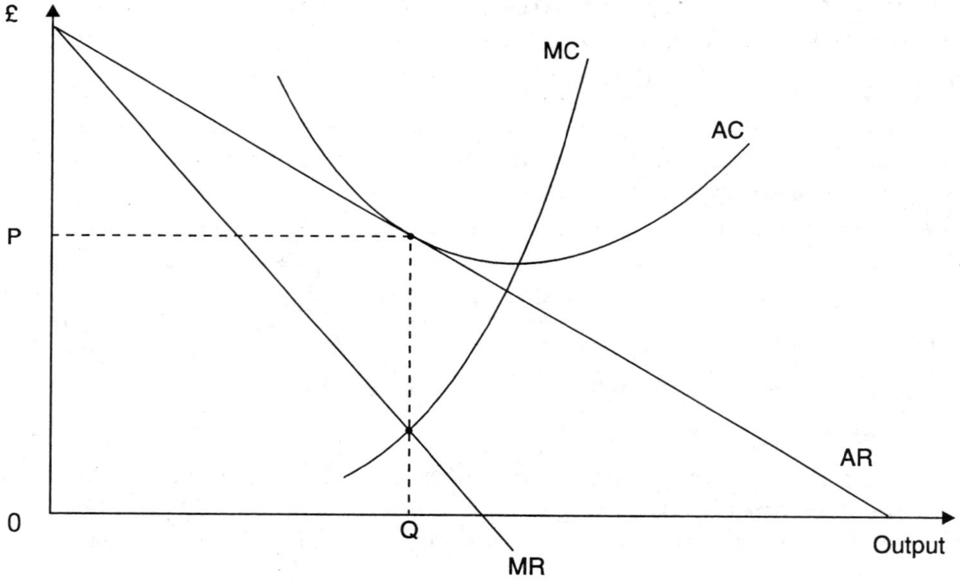

Figure 2 The long-run equilibrium of a firm in monopolistic competition

Price is higher and output lower than in perfect competition for the same reasons described earlier when comparing monopoly with perfect competition.

Because profit-maximising output is lower in a market with monopolistic competition, and at a point where average costs are not minimised, monopolistic competition, like monopoly, is arguably more wasteful of resources than perfect competition.

1.5 Characteristics of monopolistic competition: a summary

Monopolistic competition is characterised by the following.

(a) Equilibrium output below the level at which average costs are a minimum, in the long run. Monopolistic competitors are said to have *excess* or *unused* capacity.

(b) Since firms in monopolistic competition cannot expand their output to the level of minimum average cost output without making a loss, the *excess capacity* theorem predicts that industries marked by monopolistic competition will always tend to have excess capacity. Check this in Figure 2, where profit is maximised at output Q, and output Q is lower than the output level where AC would be minimised.

(c) A higher price and lower output than in perfect competition.

(d) An equilibrium price above marginal cost.

(e) Product differentiation.

(f) Other forms of non-price competition such as advertising and sales promotion.

1.6 Is monopolistic competition wasteful of economic resources?

There are several reasons for suggesting that monopolistic competition is wasteful of economic resources.

(a) It can be argued that it is wasteful to produce a wide variety of differentiated versions of the same product. If a single version of the same product were made, firms might be able to achieve economies of scale with large-volume production (and so shift their cost curves to the right).

(b) Some methods that are used to create product differentiation are a waste of resources. Advertising costs can be said to be an example of this, although some would argue that promotional activity informs potential customers and actually adds utility to a product.

(c) Firms in monopolistic competition, like monopolists, produce at an output level below that at which AC is minimised.

Activity 3

These arguments against monopolistic competition are not universally accepted. Can you put forward objections to them?

---

2 OLIGOPOLY

2.1 The nature of oligopoly

Oligopoly differs from monopoly in that there is more than one firm in a market, although the number of firms is small. Oligopoly differs from monopolistic competition because in oligopoly the number of rival firms is small. An oligopoly consisting of only two firms is sometimes referred to as a *duopoly*.

Oligopolists may produce a homogeneous product (eg oil), or there may be product differentiation (eg cigarettes, cars).

NOTES

The essence of oligopoly is that *firms' production decisions are inter-dependent.* One firm cannot set price and output without considering how its rivals' response will affect its own profits. How oligopolists will actually set their output and price depends on what assumption firms make about their competitors' behaviour.

2.2 Price cartels by oligopolist producers

Definition

A *price cartel* or price ring is created when a group of oligopoly firms get together to agree on a price at which they will sell their product to the market.

The market might be willing to demand more of the product at a lower price, while the cartel agreement tries to impose a higher price (for higher unit profits). It does this by restricting supply to the market to a level consistent with the volume of demand at the price it wishes to charge.

Each oligopoly firm could increase its profits if all the big firms in the market charge the same price as a monopolist would, and split the output between them. This is known as *collusion*, which can be unspoken or openly admitted.

Cartels are difficult to outlaw. There might still be collusive price leadership. This occurs when all firms realise that one of them is setting up a price change that will be of benefit to them all, and so they follow the leader and change their own price in the same way.

2.3 Cartels: output as well as price collusion

Figure 3 shows that:

(a) in a competitive market, with a market supply curve S_1 and demand curve D, the price would be P_1 and output Q_1;

(b) a cartel of producers might agree to fix the market price at P_2, higher than P_1. But to do so, the cartel must also agree to cut market supply from Q_1 to Q_2, and so fix the market supply curve at S_2.

Establishing a cartel depends on:

(a) the firms in the cartel being able to control supply to the market;

(b) agreeing on a price (P_2);

(c) agreeing on how much of the output each firm should produce. In Figure 3, if the market price is fixed at P_2, firms would want to supply output Z in a free market. This cannot be allowed to happen; otherwise market price P_2 could not be sustained.

NOTES

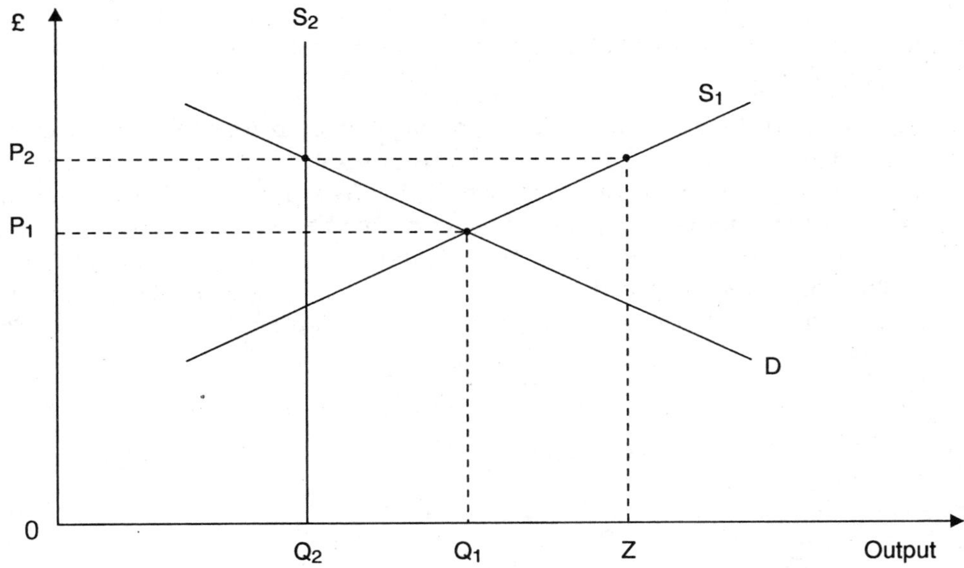

Figure 3 Price cartel

Activity 4

At least one cartel is regularly in the business news. Can you name it?

The main weakness of cartels is that each firm is still seeking the best results for itself, and so there is an incentive for an individual firm to break the cartel agreement by secretly increasing its output and selling it at the fixed cartel price.

However, if all firms increased their output in this way the cartel would collapse, because the high price could not be kept up without a restricted output, and excess supply on the market would force down the price.

This has been the experience in recent years among the oil-producing countries of the Organisation of Petroleum Exporting Countries (OPEC). Attempts to agree on a restricted output quota for each country in order to push up oil prices have often broken down, because some member countries exceeded their quota, or sold below the cartel's agreed price.

The success of a price cartel will depend on:

(a) whether it consists of most or all of the producers of the product;

(b) whether or not there are close substitutes for the product. For example, a price cartel by taxi drivers might lead to a shift in demand for transport services to buses, private cars and trains;

(c) the ease with which supply can be regulated. (In the case of primary commodities, such as wheat, rice, tea and coffee, total supply is dependent on weather conditions and even political events in the producing country);

(d) the price elasticity of demand for the product. An attempt to raise prices might result in such a large a fall in demand that the total income of producers also falls (ie price elasticity is greater than 1);

(e) whether producers can agree on their individual shares of the total restricted supply to the market. This is often the greatest difficulty of all.

2.4 The kinked oligopoly demand curve

Price cartels, whether official or unspoken and collusive, do not always exist in an oligopoly market. So how does an oligopoly firm which is competing with a rival oligopoly firm decide on its price and output level? A feature of oligopoly markets, remember, is that each firm's pricing and output decisions are influenced by what the firm's rivals might do.

When demand conditions are stable, the major problem confronting oligopolists in fixing their price and output is judging the response of their competitors to the prices they have set. Oligopolists are faced with a downward sloping demand curve, but the nature of the demand curve is dependent on the reactions of their rivals. Any change in price will invite a competitive response. This situation is described by the kinked oligopoly demand curve in Figure 4, in which the oligopolist is currently charging price P, for output 0Q, which is at the kink on the demand curve DD.

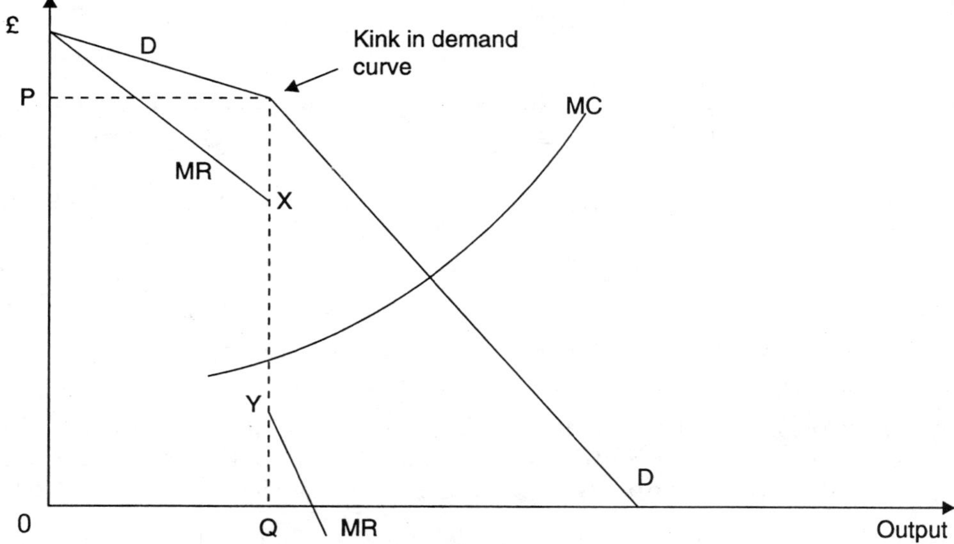

Figure 4 Kinked oligopoly demand curve

The kinked demand curve is used to explain how an oligopolist might have to accept price *stability* in the market.

If the oligopolist were to raise his prices above P, his competitors would keep their price lower and so many consumers would buy from them instead. An example is the difficulty which individual petrol companies have in raising the price of petrol at garages. If competitors do not raise their prices too, usually the firm has to restore its prices to their previous level. The demand curve would therefore be quite elastic at these higher prices.

If, on the other hand, the oligopolist were to reduce his prices below P, competitors would probably do the same. Total market demand might rise, but the increase in demand for the oligopolist's products would probably be quite low, unless demand in the market as a whole were elastic. The elasticity of demand at prices below P will be less than the elasticity at prices above P (shown by the kink in the demand curve).

The MR curve breaks off at the output level where there is the kink in the demand curve. The kink in the demand curve explains the nature of the marginal revenue curve MR. At price P, output 0Q, the MR curve falls vertically. This is because at higher prices the MR curve corresponds to the more elastic demand curve, and at prices below P the MR curve corresponds to the less elastic demand.

A firm maximises its profit at the point where MR = MC. There is a strong probability that the MC curve will cut the MR curve somewhere between points X and Y (the broken off part of the MR curve). The more inelastic the demand curve is below price P, the longer the broken off portion (XY) of the MR curve will be.

The oligopolist's cost structure can change, with worsening or improved efficiencies, but as long as the MC curve cuts the MR curve through its vertical portion XY, the oligopolist's price and output decision should not alter. So there will be price and output stability, with cost changes for the oligopoly firm, which change its MC curve and do not affect output and price.

Only if marginal costs rise far enough for the MC curve to pass through the MR curve above point X in Figure 4 is there a case for raising price. Only if MC falls far enough to pass through the MR curve below point Y is there a case for lowering price.

In general, oligopoly prices will rise only if all the firms follow the lead of a rival in raising its price, so that the AR curve shifts outwards. The kink rises to the new common price level, which is again stable. The opposite holds for price falls, perhaps occurring because of technological advance.

2.5 Price leadership and price wars in oligopoly markets

In oligopoly markets there is a tendency for one firm to set the general industry price, with the other firms following suit. This is called *price leadership*. It is one source of stability in a market where there may be cartels which tend to be undercut, and price wars.

When demand conditions change, the situation becomes somewhat different and price stability might no longer exist.

(a) If total market demand falls, oligopolists might try to increase their share of the market by cutting prices.

(b) Similarly, if oligopolists begin to lose their *share* of the market, they might try to restore it by cutting prices. The consequence would be a price war. In the UK in recent years there have been price wars by supermarkets and oil companies, for example. The effect of price wars is usually good for consumers, but they do not last long. This is because it is not in the interests of oligopolists to keep them up for long.

2.6 Oligopoly: conclusion

We can conclude that oligopoly will lead to equilibrium prices and output between the levels that would arise from monopoly and perfect competition. However, if there is collusion there will be the same results as in monopoly.

Activity 5

A group of firms in oligopoly decide to agree a price. Would they need to have an agreement about total output of the industry? Would it be easy to keep to such an agreement? What pressures might there be to break it up?

Definition

Contestable markets are markets with freedom of entry for firms and no exit costs.

The theory of contestable markets is that although there might be just a *few firms* in the market, the market might operate more efficiently than an oligopoly (or monopolistic competition). In equilibrium, a firm in a contestable market will:

(a) earn normal profits only, and no supernormal profits;

(b) produce at an output level where AC is minimised.

Thus at equilibrium MR = MC = AC = AR, just as in perfect competition.

Firms in contestable markets are forced into this situation because there are:

(a) no entry barriers into the market; and

(b) no exit barriers from the market.

If they were to be inefficient and produce at a level where AC is not minimised, or if they were to raise prices to earn supernormal profits, other firms would quickly enter the market knowing they could just as easily leave if supernormal profits were to be eroded by the extra competition.

Chapter roundup

- When price competition is restricted, firms usually go in for other forms of competition, eg advertising, product differentiation and market segmentation/price discrimination.
- In some industries, there are many firms, but competition is reduced because each firm tries to achieve some product differentiation. As a result:
  - it is more difficult for new competitor firms to break into the market;
  - each firm can build up a customer loyalty or market niche and act in many ways like a monopolist (ie making prices and facing a downward-sloping demand curve).
- In advanced economies, many industries and markets display characteristics of monopolistic competition and/or oligopoly. When industries consist of a small number of firms, the one thing that managers will have to consider is the reaction of rivals to their own pricing and output decisions and to the non-price competitive activities they pursue. (This is referred to as *competitor analysis*).
- The kinked oligopoly demand curve may explain why there is price stability (and non-price competition) in many oligopoly markets.
- Oligopolies might collude and make a formal or informal cartel agreement on the price for the industry and output levels for each firm.

Quick quiz

1 What forms can non-price competition take?

2 What is product differentiation? What forms might it take?

3 Draw a graph to show the long-run profit-maximising equilibrium of a firm in monopolistic competition.

4 What is a price cartel? Draw a diagram to show the effect of a cartel on price and output to the market.

5 Draw a graph to show a kinked oligopoly demand curve. Why is there a kink in the demand curve? What is the implication of such a curve for price and output by an oligopoly firm?

Answers to Activities

1 Food manufacturers (eg of baked beans or frozen peas) rely heavily on brand image and advertising to create product differentiation. Soft drinks can be sold in cartons, bottles and ring-pull cans, and the price differences do not just reflect the cost of each type of packaging. The major manufacturers of soap powder each ensure that they maintain a substantial share of the market by each selling a number of different brands of a broadly similar product.

2 (a) Locations, convenience, brand loyalty, free gifts – and price.

(b) Petrol stations in the same area tend to compete on non-price factors: opening hours, number of pumps, shopping facilities, giveaways etc.

3 (a) Some product differentiation is 'real' (ie there are technical differences between similar goods from rival firms). Buyers/consumers therefore have more to choose from. Their requirements are likely to be satisfied better than if there were just a single, basic, low-price good, without any choice.

(b) If product differentiation is entirely 'imaginary', created by brand image and advertising when the goods of rival firms are exactly the same, rational buyers should opt for the least-cost good anyway.

4 The Organisation of Petroleum Exporting Countries (OPEC).

5 The previous discussion illustrates that an agreement on output *would* be necessary, and that the cartel would be difficult to sustain. Among the pressures to break up you might have cited the activities of rogue members, breaching the agreement.

Further question practice

Now try the following practice questions at the end of this text.

Multiple choice questions	**85–96**
Exam style question	**8**

Chapter 9

MONEY AND BANKING

Introduction

We have been considering in earlier chapters the prices of goods (which, for these purposes, covers services also), the incomes of customers and the costs and revenues of firms. All of these are important elements in economic exchange. In carrying out economic exchange in a modern economy, money is obviously important, and in this chapter we turn to consider its functions and those of the banking system.

Your objectives

After completing this chapter you should:

(a) understand the nature and functions of money;

(b) be aware of the main monetary aggregates and how they are made up;

(c) understand the role of banks in creating credit.

NOTES

1 MONEY AND ITS FUNCTIONS

Activity 1

Surely 'money' is a concept very easily understood? Yet we will see in this chapter that it is not necessarily as simple as you might think. Before beginning on the chapter, try to analyse what constitutes money (for example, is a bank deposit account money?) and what are the functions of money. Revise your answers in the light of what you learn while reading this chapter.

Definition

Money is used as a means of paying for goods and services, and paying for labour, capital and other resources.

Money is important in an economy because:

(a) it oils the wheels of economic activity, by providing an easy method for exchanging goods and services (ie buying and selling);

(b) the total amount of money in a national economy may have a significant influence on economic activity and inflation.

In this chapter, we shall consider:

(a) the functions of money;

(b) different means of quantifying the amount of money in an economy; and

(c) how money is lent and borrowed, to move it from people who have more money than they can use to people who want to use it.

1.1 The functions of money

Attempts to define money have traditionally started with identifying what money does, ie what are the *functions* of money? We can identify four different functions of money.

Money acts as:

(a) a means of exchange;

(b) a unit of account;

(c) a standard of deferred payment;

(d) a store of value.

Money as a means of exchange

Without money, the only way of exchanging goods and services would be by means of *barter*, ie by a *direct exchange* of goods or services. If a shoemaker wanted to buy a horse, he would have to either:

(a) find a horse-owner prepared to exchange a horse for a sufficient quantity of shoes of equal value to the horse; or else

(b) find other people willing to exchange different goods (eg food, clothes etc) for shoes, and then trade these goods in exchange for a horse from the horse-owner.

A monetary economy is the alternative to a barter economy, and it provides a means of encouraging economic development and growth.

(a) People are prepared to organise and work for an employer, and in return receive money wages.

(b) A business will exchange its goods or services for money.

(c) People will pay out money to obtain goods or services.

Money as a unit of account

This function of money is associated with the use of money as a means of exchange. Money should be able to measure exactly what something is worth. It should provide an agreed standard measure by which the *value* of different goods and services can be compared.

For example, suppose that only four products are traded in a market: pigs, sheep, hens and corn. The relative value of these products must be agreed before exchange can take place in the market. It might be decided that:

(a) 1 pig has the same value as 0.75 sheep, 3 hens or 1.5 bags of corn;

(b) 1 sheep has the same value as 1.33 pigs, 4 hens or 2 bags of corn;

(c) 1 hen is worth 0.33 pigs, 0.25 sheep or 0.5 bags of corn;

(d) 1 bag of corn has the same value as 0.67 pigs, 0.5 sheep or 2 hens.

The function of money in the economy would be to establish a common unit of value measurement, or account, by which the relative exchange values or prices of goods can be established.

Activity 2

In the above example of a four-product market, simplify the value relationships by expressing the worth of a pig, a sheep, a hen and a bag of corn in terms of a common unit of money.

Money as a standard of deferred payment

When people buy a good or service, they might not want to pay for it straightaway, perhaps because they have not yet got the money. Instead, they might ask for credit. Selling goods on credit is not an essential feature of an economy, but it certainly helps to stimulate trade.

Definition

Credit establishes, by agreement between buyer and seller, how much value will be given in return at some future date for goods provided/received now.

Similarly, when a buyer and seller agree now to make a contract for the supply of certain goods in the future, the function of money is to establish the value of the contract, ie how much the buyer will eventually pay the seller for the goods.

In order to provide an acceptable standard for deferred payments, it is important that money should maintain its value over a period of time.

Suppose, for example, that a customer buys goods for an agreed sum of money, but on three months' credit.If the value of money falls in the three-month credit period, the sum of money which the seller eventually receives will be worth less than it was at the time of sale. The seller will have lost value by allowing the credit.

When the value of money falls (or rises) over time, sellers (or buyers) will be reluctant to arrange credit, or to agree the price for future contracts. Money would then be failing to fulfil its function as a standard for deferred payments.

Money can lose value as the result of price inflation.

Definition

Inflation is a sustained rise in the general level of prices.

When inflation is high:

(a) sellers will be reluctant to allow credit to buyers. For example, if a buyer asks for three months' credit, and inflation is running at 20% per annum, the real value of the debt that the buyer owes will fall by about 5% over the three month credit period;

(b) sellers will be reluctant to agree to a fixed price for long-term contracts. For example, a house-builder might refuse to quote a price for building a house over a 12-month period, and instead insist on asking a price, which is index-linked and rises in step with the general rate of inflation.

Money as a store of value

Money acts as a store of value, or wealth. So too do many other assets (eg land, buildings, art treasures, motorcars, machinery) some of which maintain or increase their money value over time, and some of which depreciate in value.

This means of course that money is not the only asset which acts as a store of wealth, and we need to extend our definition of this function of money.

Money is more properly described as acting as a *liquid* store of value. This definition has two parts to it.

(a) Money is a store of value or wealth. A person can hold money in the *certainty* that its value does not fall and that it will have the same exchange value in the future that it does now, in normal terms at least (ie ignoring inflation).

(b) Money is a liquid asset.

The erosion of the value of money due to inflation is one good reason why someone with wealth to store should hold assets which are *not* money.

1.2 Liquidity

A liquid store of value means that the wealth can be converted immediately (or at least very quickly) into a means of exchange for obtaining goods or services. Liquidity is therefore 'the ability to transform wealth holding into any form without loss of face value or delay'.

Definition

Liquidity is sometimes defined as 'readily convertible into cash', and the most liquid asset of all is cash itself.

There are two parts to this definition of liquidity. A liquid asset is one which can be converted into cash (or into a means of exchange for goods or services):

(a) without significant delay; and

(b) without significant penalty or loss of face value.

Let us look at each part of the definition in turn.

Delay

Liquidity is the ability to transform an asset into a means of exchange with minimum delay.

A liquid store of wealth can therefore be drawn on by its owners to obtain goods and services whenever they want, and without having to wait to convert the store of wealth into a means of exchange. A painting is a store of wealth, but if its owner wishes to use this wealth to buy something else, he or she must first sell the painting and then use the proceeds from the sale to make the purchase. Since selling a painting takes time, it is not a liquid asset (and nor is a house).

Loss of face value, or significant penalty

A non-cash asset is liquid if it can be converted into cash within a short period of time without significant penalty. Significant penalty means:

(a) loss of capital value, or face value; or

(b) loss or forfeit of a substantial amount of interest, (for instance, loss of 14 days' interest or more).

Activity 3

Shares in a quoted company can be bought and sold very rapidly. Could they therefore serve as a form of money?

1.3 Liquidity and interest

An alternative to holding money as banknotes, or money in a non-interest-bearing current bank account, is to hold on to an *interest-bearing financial asset.* Examples of such assets are:

(a) a time deposit with a bank, or an interest-bearing current account;

(b) a bond or debenture.

These provide the holder with:

(a) an interest yield on the value of the asset;

(b) the certainty of a money repayment to the holder of the asset at the end of a certain period of time or after a certain period of notice has been given by the asset holder.

Holders of a financial asset sacrifices some liquidity in exchange for an interest yield on their store of wealth.

1.4 Narrow money and broad money

It is not always easy to decide whether a particular financial asset (eg a bank deposit) is money or not. In defining money, we can distinguish between narrow money and broad money.

Narrow money. Narrow money refers to financial assets (including cash) which perform the functions of money when a fairly narrow definition of liquidity is applied. Financial assets must have a high degree of liquidity to be regarded as narrow money.

A definition of narrow money is 'money balances which are readily available to finance current spending, that is to say for "transactions purposes"'.

Broad money. In contrast, broad money includes financial assets which are relatively liquid, but not as liquid as narrow money items. A financial asset which would be regarded as narrow money would also fall within the definition of broad money; but broad money, as its name implies, extends the range of assets which are regarded as money.

Broad money refers generally to 'money held for transactions purposes and money held as a form of saving. It provides an indicator of the private sector's holdings of relatively liquid assets – assets which could be converted with relative ease and without capital loss into spending on goods and services'.

2 MONETARY AGGREGATES

2.1 Introduction

Definition

The *money supply* is the total amount of money in the economy. It is also referred to as the money stock.

A monetary aggregate is a total of the money stock or money supply. In the UK, there are four different monetary aggregates which are published by the Bank of England. These are:

M0, M2, M4 and M3H.

Various other aggregates, including M1, M3 and M5 have been published at various times in the past.

The main purpose of measuring a monetary aggregate is to discover by how much (and how rapidly) the money supply is rising in the economy, and

(a) to predict from this rise what future changes in economic activity might be;

(b) also to discover whether past changes in the money supply help to explain changes in economic activity which have already occurred.

There is also the view that by controlling the rate of increase in the money supply, inflation can be brought under control and economic conditions made more suitable for achieving economic growth and fuller employment.

Activity 4

This view has been hotly debated over the last decade or so in the UK. You should be able to attach a name to it, and also to identify which political party has adopted it.

2.2 A comparison of the different aggregates

The definitions of the different monetary aggregates currently in use in the UK are shown in the diagram below.

NOTES

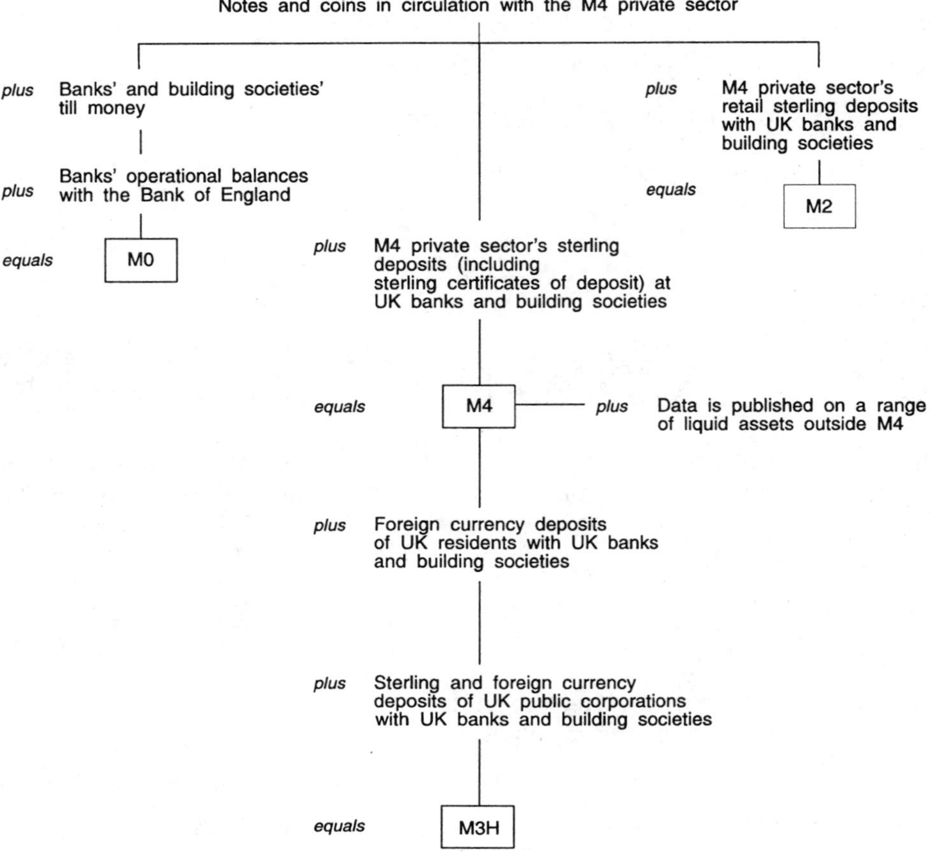

Figure 1 Current UK monetary aggregates

Note the following points about the monetary aggregates in current use.

(a) M0 is the narrowest definition of money, the great majority of which is made up of notes and coin in circulation outside the Bank of England. M0 is now the only monetary aggregate for which a growth target range is set by the government.

(b) M2 is effectively a measure of all sterling deposits used for *transaction* purposes (as distinct from investment purposes).

(c) M4 is a broad definition of money, including deposits held for savings as well as spending purposes. The Bank of England also now publishes statistics for various 'liquid assets outside M4' (discussed below), for the benefit of those who are interested in a still broader definition of the money stock. The government does not set a target for growth in M4, although it does monitor its growth.

(d) M3H is a monetary aggregate created for the UK in 1992, although figures going back to 1985 are available. It results from work by officials of European central banks to produce a harmonised broad monetary aggregate, which could be used for making comparisons among EU member states. M3H grows broadly in line with M4.

2.3 Liquid assets outside M4

With the ending of the publication of the broad monetary aggregates M4C and M5 during 1991, the Bank of England adopted a new approach to broad money statistics of providing information about the various 'liquid assets outside M4'.

These series of data are expected to be used as building blocks from which users of monetary statistics can create their own aggregates if they wish.

Note, however, that M4 itself contains some comparatively illiquid elements. For example, M4 contains deposits of any maturity with banks and building societies and certain paper and other capital market instruments of not more than five years' original maturity. In practice the bulk of M4 is of under three months' residual maturity.

Activity 5

Which of the following, if any, would tend to result in a reduction in the rate of growth of M4?

(a) An increase in the rate of interest offered on National Savings.

(b) A reduction in the public sector borrowing requirement.

(c) The sale of long-term government bonds by the government to the banking sector.

3 FLOWS OF FUNDS WITHIN AN ECONOMY

3.1 Introduction

The flow of funds describes the movement of funds or money between one group of people or institutions in the economic system and other groups.

If we begin by ignoring imports and exports and foreign investments, we can start to build up a picture of the flow of funds by identifying three sectors of the economy:

(a) the personal sector (ie individuals);

(b) the business or industrial and commercial sector (ie companies and other businesses);

(c) the government sector (ie central government, local government and public corporations).

Within each of these three sectors, there is a continual movement of funds. For example:

(a) individuals will give or lend money to other individuals;

(b) companies will buy goods and services from other companies, and may occasionally lend money direct to other companies;

(c) central government will provide funds for local government authorities and loss-making nationalised industries.

As well as movements of funds within each sector, there is also a flow of funds between different sectors of the economy.

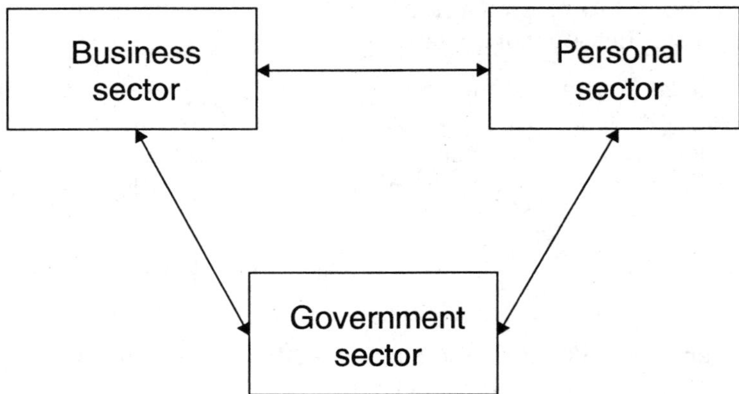

Figure 2 Flow of funds in a closed economy, ignoring financial intermediation

But reality is not quite so simple, and our analysis of the flow of funds in the UK has to take account of:

(a) the *overseas sector*, ie businesses, individuals and governments in other countries who:
   (i) sell goods or services to the UK;
   (ii) buy goods or services from the UK;
   (iii) invest capital in the UK; or
   (iv) obtain investment capital from individuals or businesses in the UK;

(b) *financial intermediaries*.

3.2 Financial intermediaries

An intermediary is a go-between, and a financial intermediary is an institution which links lenders with borrowers, either (as principal) by obtaining deposits from lenders and then re-lending them to borrowers or (as broker) arranging a transaction. Here, we are concerned with the former type of intermediary.

The basic process of financial intermediation can be shown by simple diagrams.

(a) If no financial intermediation takes place, lending and borrowing will be direct.

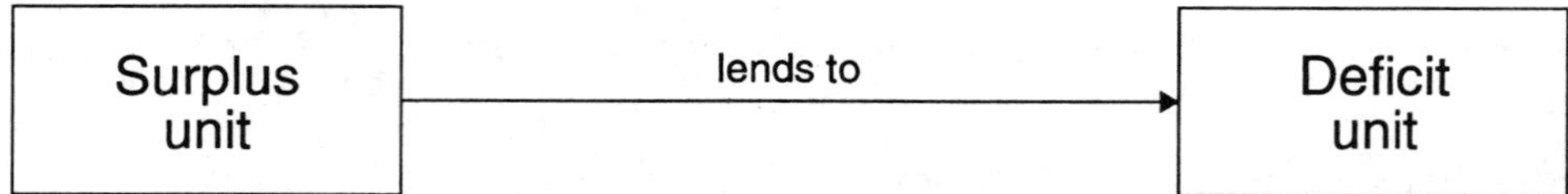

(b) If financial intermediation does take place, the situation will be:

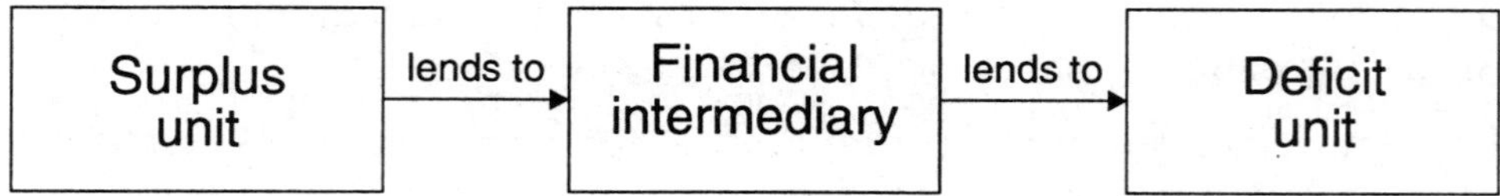

For example, a person might deposit savings with a bank, and the bank might use its collective deposits of savings to provide a loan to a company.

Financial intermediaries might also lend abroad or borrow from abroad, and a final version of the diagram of the flow of funds is now as follows:

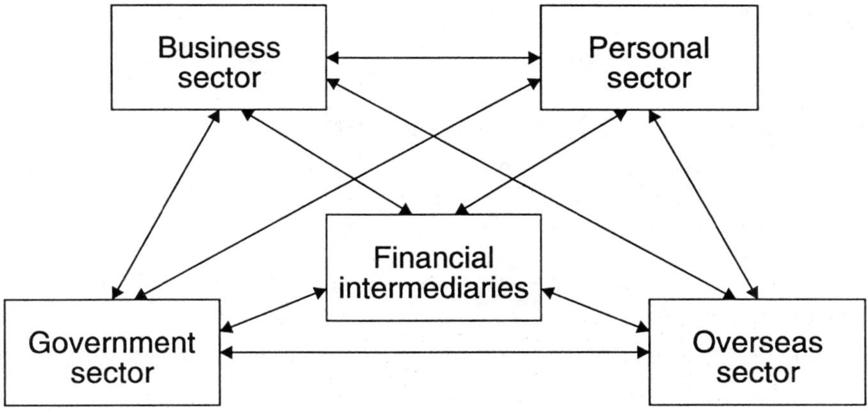

Figure 3 Flow of funds in an open economy, showing the role of financial intermediation

In the UK financial intermediaries include:

(a) banks;

(b) building societies;

(c) insurance companies, pension funds, unit trust companies and investment trust companies.

3.3 The importance of banks as financial intermediaries

In spite of competition from building societies, insurance companies and other financial institutions, banks are still the major financial intermediaries in the UK.

(a) The clearing banks dominate the retail banking market, although competition from the building societies has been growing in the UK.

(b) There is greater competition between different banks (overseas banks and the clearing banks especially) for business in the wholesale lending market.

3.4 Risk reduction and maturity transformation

It is useful to understand what the benefits of financial intermediation are.

(a) Financial intermediaries provide obvious and convenient ways in which a lender can save money. Instead of having to find suitable borrowers for their money, lenders can deposit money with a bank, building society, pension fund, investment trust company, National Savings scheme etc. All lenders have to do is decide for how long they might want to lend the money and what sort of return is required, and they can then choose a financial intermediary that offers a financial instrument to suit their requirements.

(b) Financial intermediaries aggregate (ie package up) the amounts lent by savers and lend on to borrowers in bigger amounts.

(c) Provided that the financial intermediaries are themselves financially sound, lenders would not run any risk of losing their investment. Bad debts would be borne by the financial intermediary in its re-lending operations.

(d) They provide a ready source of funds for borrowers. Even when money is in short supply, a borrower will usually find a financial intermediary prepared to lend some.

(e) Financial intermediaries, most importantly, provide *maturity transformation*; in other words they bridge the gap between the wish of most lenders for liquidity and the desire of most borrowers for loans over longer periods. They do this by providing investors with financial instruments which are liquid enough for the investors' needs, and by providing funds to borrowers in a different longer-term form.

4 BANKING

4.1 The banks and the banking system

Bank deposits are an important feature within most definitions of the money supply. There are different types of bank, and you will probably have come across a number of terms which describe them.

(a) *Clearing banks* are the banks which operate the so-called clearing system for settling payments (eg payments by cheque by bank customers).

(b) The term *retail banks* is used to describe the traditional High Street banks. The term wholesale banks refers to banks which specialise in lending in large quantities to major customers. The clearing banks are involved in both retail and wholesale banking, but are commonly regarded as the main retail banks.

(c) *Merchant banks* are banks which offer services, often of a specialised nature, to corporate customers.

(d) *Commercial banks* are any banks which make commercial banking transactions with customers. They are distinct from the country's central bank.

Activity 6

In the balance sheet of a retail bank, which one of the following items do you think would constitute the largest asset?

(a) Customers' overdrafts and bank loans.

(b) Customers' deposits.

(c) Land and buildings.

4.2 Credit and banking

Before we go on to consider the role of banks in creating credit, it is worth giving some attention to the importance of credit in the economy.

Credit means owing money or being owed money.

(a) Taking or obtaining credit involves an arrangement whereby someone either:

   (i) borrows money, with an undertaking to pay it back in time with interest;

   (ii) buys goods or services without paying for them immediately, but with an undertaking to pay for them in the future. Firms often buy goods from each other under this sort of credit arrangement, which is then referred to as trade credit.

(b) Lending or giving credit is the other side of the transaction. The person or organisation giving credit is the creditor and the borrower is the debtor.

Our main interest in credit for the purpose of this chapter concerns lending and borrowing money, rather than buying goods on trade credit.

4.3 The functions of credit

The functions of credit can be seen from the point of view either of the borrower or the lender.

(a) For borrowers, the reason for borrowing money is to be able to purchase goods or services now that they would not otherwise be able to afford. The borrower wants to buy now and pay later.

NOTES

(b) For lenders, the reason for lending money is that there is nothing that they particularly wants to spend their money on, and by lending it, they can earn some interest.

The borrower can be described as a 'deficit unit' with not enough money to buy all the goods and services he or she wants. The lender can be described as a 'surplus unit' with more money at the moment than he or she needs to spend.

Credit involves the transfer of money from a surplus unit to a deficit unit, in return for a promise to pay interest.

4.4 Bank deposits and the creation of money

Banks are major providers of credit. Banks create money when they give credit, and so bank lending has two aspects which are important for the economy:

(a) credit and therefore expenditure in the economy;

(b) increases in the money supply.

When a bank lends money, most of the money will find its way back into the banking system as new customer deposits. This adds to the money supply if we include bank deposits within our definition of the money stock.

Suppose, for example, that in a country with a single bank, customer deposits total £100,000. The bank, we will assume, re-lends all these deposits to other customers. The customers will use the money they have borrowed to buy goods and services and they will pay various firms and individuals for these purchases. If the firms and individuals receiving payment then put the money into their own accounts with the bank, the bank's deposits will have doubled.

The fact that most additions to bank lending end up as money in someone's bank account, adding to total customer deposits with the banks, gives banks the special ability to create money. It is an ability that is also shared in the UK by building societies, since building society deposits are included in definitions of the money supply (eg M2 and M4).

4.5 Fractional reserve systems

A bank could, in theory, go on re-lending all the deposits it receives, and if all the money re-lent then finds its way back into bank accounts, there is theoretically no limit to the amount of extra money that banks can create.

'This seeming power of the banking system to create apparently unlimited quantities of money has troubled economists and banking practitioners for many years. They have held up the spectre of an uncontrolled banking system creating money in such quantities that inflation would run riot and the value of money become debased.'

Crockett: *Money, theory, policy and institutions*

This theoretical situation does not exist in practice, and there are two major reasons why this is so.

(a) Banks do not re-lend all the extra deposits they receive. One obvious reason for this is that they need some liquidity to meet demands for withdrawals by customers. One way of ensuring adequate liquidity is to maintain a safe proportion of the bank's assets in the form of cash or liquid assets. If a bank does try to maintain a minimum ratio (fraction) of cash or liquid assets to total assets, it is said to be operating a fractional reserve system, or is said to be using a cash ratio or reserve asset ratio. A reserve asset ratio is the ratio of a bank's reserve assets to its total assets. Reserve assets can be thought of as liquid assets or near-liquid assets, and so a reserve asset ratio is similar to a cash ratio.

(b) Not all the money lent as bank loans to customers finds its way back into the banking system: there are leakages (discussed later in this chapter).

Activity 7

Try to think of ways that money can leak from the banking system. You will come across some suggestions later in the chapter.

A simplified illustration of a fractional reserve system cannot show the complexity of the financial system and the wide range of liquid and near-liquid assets in which a bank can invest. In the illustration which follows, simplifying assumptions have had to be made for the sake of clarity.

4.6 Minimum cash ratio system illustrated: credit creation

We shall assume for simplicity that there is only one bank in the banking system, and that all money lent by the bank is re-deposited by various customers.

A customer depositing £1,000 in cash with the bank creates a personal asset, in the sense that the bank, in return for the deposit, gives the customer an IOU (a promise to pay on demand), or subject to notice, the £1,000 deposited. The IOU is reflected in the account opened under the name of the client. To the bank, the deposit is a liability. However, the deposit provides funds for the bank to acquire assets. We shall begin by assuming that the bank holds these assets entirely in the form of cash.

If the bank keeps the full £1,000 and does nothing with it, then it would simply operate as a cloakroom for the client and the money so deposited. However, if the bank believes that the client is unlikely to claim the full £1,000 for some time, there will be an incentive to use the money rather than to keep it idle. One possibility would be to lend it; the bank would be taking a risk that it will not have the cash when its customer wants to have it back, but at the same time it would expect to make a profit, by charging interest on the sum of money so lent.

So there is the liquidity/security/profitability conflict in the motives of the bank. On the one hand the deposit of the £1,000 creates the opportunity for the bank to make a profit in the form of the interest that it can charge on the money it lends (the incentive being all the stronger if the bank is paying interest on the deposits it accepts), but on the other hand there is a risk that when the money is out on loan the client may claim it back. The bank will then be unable to meet its obligation to repay the cash to the client unless it can recall the loan instantly, which is unlikely.

As long as the bank feels that it is unlikely that its depositors will demand a substantial proportion of their deposits in cash, it faces an acceptable risk in lending some of the money. In other words, there is a balancing act between the desire to play it safe and keep the cash and the desire to make profits by lending. In practice, banks can be confident that in normal times, provided that there is not a serious loss of confidence in the banking system, most depositors will not demand substantial proportions of their deposits as cash.

In the example in the table below, it is assumed that the bank has decided on the basis of past experience and observation to keep 50 pence in cash for every £1 deposited, and then lend out the other 50 pence. In other words, the bank in this example is operating a 50% cash ratio.

	Bank's liabilities (= customer deposits)	*Bank's assets (= cash or loans to customers)*
(1)	£1,000 deposits	£1,000 cash

The bank has £1,000 in cash. This is enough to support total assets of £2,000 and maintain a 50% cash ratio. If the bank now lends £1,000, and if all of that £1,000 is then spent by the borrowers but ends up back with the bank as deposits of other customers, the new situation for the bank will be as in (2) below.

(2)	£2,000 deposits	£1,000 cash £1,000 loans

4.7 Money creation and the cash ratio: credit multiplier

If the bank decided that the 50% cash ratio was too conservative and reduced it to 25%, then for £1,000 cash deposited with the bank deposits could be expanded fourfold. It is important to understand that banks in the process of lending are also potentially creating money, because clients either borrowing or receiving the proceeds of borrowers' expenditure can use their deposits to make money transactions. In a modern economy a large proportion of money transactions are by cheque, or other bank transfer such as direct debits or standing order. Bank deposits are transferred from person to person or from firm to firm in this way and consumers and producers use the liabilities of a private institution (which is what bank deposits are) as money.

The fact that banks do not need to keep a 100% cash ratio, automatically implies that they have the capacity to create money out of nothing. The size of this credit expansion depends on the size of their cash ratio.

We can summarise the quantitative side of credit creation in banks by writing the credit multiplier as:

$$\text{Deposits} = \frac{\text{cash}}{\text{cash ratio}} \quad \text{or } D = \frac{c}{r}$$

The smaller the cash ratio the bigger the size of the deposits that a given amount of cash will be able to support.

This theoretical description of the *credit multiplier* applies to some extent in practice, but there are other factors which operate to restrict the volume of expansion in bank deposits. In other words, if a bank decides to keep a cash reserve ratio of 10%, and it receives additional deposits of £1,000, the total increase in bank deposits will not be £1,000 ÷ 10% = £10,000, but considerably less than this.

Activity 8

Suppose all the commercial banks in an economy operated on a cash reserve ratio of 20%. How much would have to be deposited with banks for the money supply to increase by £80 million?

The constraints on the growth of a bank's deposits are:

(a) leakages of cash out of the banking system;

(b) the nature of customer demand for loans. Customers might not want to borrow at the interest rates the bank would charge;

(c) prudent management of lending operations by the banks themselves. Banks should not lend to high-risk customers without good security.

NOTES

4.8 Leakages, reducing the size of the credit multiplier

Leakages are caused by a few factors, including the decision by the public (firms and individuals) to hold some of their extra money in cash (ie notes and coin in their hands). For example, if a bank lends £10,000 to a customer, who then uses the money to buy a car, the car dealer who is then paid the £10,000 might decide to hold some of this extra money in cash instead of putting it all into the bank.

If we assume that the total amount of cash held by the public increases or decreases as the total volume of bank deposits rises or falls, it can be shown mathematically that the effect of the credit multiplier on total bank deposits is

$$D = \frac{C}{c + r}$$

where D is the eventual total increase in bank deposits

C is the initial increase in bank deposits

r is the banks' cash reserve ratio

c is the ratio of cash held by the public to the volume of bank deposits.

For example, if the banks aim to have a cash reserve ratio of 10% and the public chooses to have a cash to bank deposits ratio of one-sixteenth (6.67%), then the total increase in bank deposits arising from an initial increase of £1,000 would be:

$$\frac{£1,000}{0.0667 + 0.10} = £6,000$$

The credit multiplier is now only times 6, not times 10.

4.9 Credit control and government policy

If the government is worried about growth in the money supply, or inflation in the economy, it might consider the growth in credit to be a major cause of the problem.

This might suggest that all a government has to do to control inflation and growth in credit spending is to stop banks from lending too much, ie to place controls over bank lending.

Credit control policies have been attempted in the past in the UK, without any long-term success. The main problems in applying direct controls over bank lending are as follows.

(a) Enforcing the controls could be difficult. Financial institutions might try to bend or avoid the rules, in order to continue lending. There might also be more direct lending between investor and borrower.

(b) The development of a strong capital market in the UK will be damaged by government restrictions on lending, given the liberalisation of capital markets around the world in recent years.

(c) Restrictions on certain forms of lending (eg investment loans to small companies, or mortgage lending to house buyers) could have harmful economic or social consequences.

5 THE BUILDING SOCIETIES

The building societies developed in the UK as mutual organisations to enable members to save or to borrow money to finance house purchase. Building societies are now allowed by the Building Societies Act 1986 to provide certain banking services as well, such as personal lending to customers for purposes other than house buying. Building societies now offer cheque book accounts, cash cards and many other facilities that compete directly with the retail banks.

The growing similarity between banks and building societies is further evident in:

(a) the inclusion of building society deposits in the broad monetary aggregates M4 (as well as M2);

(b) the ability of building societies to become public limited companies and, in effect, banks. The Abbey National was the first UK building society to do this in 1989. The Halifax Building Society followed the same course in 1997 after its merger with the Leeds in 1995.

The previous description of banks, and the ability of banks to create money by giving credit, also applies to a large extent to building societies. However, building societies are still mainly engaged in mortgage lending for house purchase, and are not yet fully comparable with banks.

Chapter roundup

The key points in this chapter are as follows.

- Money has four functions: as a means of exchange, a unit of account, a standard of deferred payments and a liquid store of value.
- There are many different types of financial instrument. Some fit into a definition of money better than others. This is why there are several different definitions of the money stock. In the UK there are M0, M2 and M4.
- Banks and building societies create money when they lend or grant overdrafts, and contribute significantly to the increase in the money supply.
- Credit lending is done mainly through financial intermediaries, such as banks.
- Banks provide financial intermediation, but they also provide a payments mechanism (ie a means for payments to be made from one person or firm to another) and a place for households or firms to store their wealth.
- The aim of banks, in performing these functions, is to balance the conflicting aims of profitability, liquidity and security.
- Lending is profitable, but restricted by the need for liquidity and security. Banks are therefore likely to try to maintain a minimum cash ratio or reserve assets ratio.
- The total increase in the broad money supply that will occur through credit lending by banks depends, among other things, on the size of this cash ratio. A credit multiplier operates.

Quick quiz

1 What are the functions of money?
2 What is narrow money? What is broad money?
3 How does inflation affect the functions of money?
4 Compare the different monetary aggregates published by the Bank of England.
5 What are the benefits of financial intermediation?
6 What are the functions of commercial banks?

NOTES

7 What are the three conflicting aims of banks? Why do these aims conflict?

8 Why does bank lending add to the broad money supply?

9 What is a fractional reserve system?

10 What is the credit multiplier?

Answers to Activities

2 You might have calculated as follows.

A pig	=	3 units
A sheep	=	4 units
A hen	=	1 unit
A bag of corn	=	2 units

Other results (such as 6, 8, 2 and 4 respectively) would work just as well.

3 No. Although shares can indeed be sold rapidly, the cost of doing so may be a loss on sale.

4 The view is, of course, an important tenet in the monetarist school of thought adopted by the Conservative Party (at least under the leadership of Margaret Thatcher – more recently there has been far less emphasis on control of the money supply).

5 (a) and (b). National Savings are, in effect, lending by individuals to the government. As more people are attracted to do this, the amount of money in circulation will decrease. Reductions in the PSBR will also reduce the money supply. Borrowing from banks by the government (item (c)) has a neutral effect on the money supply.

6 The answer is (a). Item (b) is not an asset of a bank – it is a liability (a sum of money owed by the bank to its customers). It might be tempting to choose item (c), if you think about the large number of High Street sites owned by the retail banks, but in fact the value of this asset is dwarfed by the financial assets of the banks.

8 Call the extra cash £C. Then:

$$\frac{C}{20\%} = 80 + C$$

$$C = 20\%\,(80 + C)$$

$$0.8C = 16$$

$$C = £20 \text{ million}$$

If an extra £20 million is deposited, the total volume of cash will rise to £20 million ÷ 20% = £100 million. This includes the initial £20 million, so the increase is £80 million.

Case Study

The following data and extract refer to the structure of assets of United Kingdom commercial banks.

Distribution of commercial banks' main assets (May 1993)

Cash	0.5%
Balances with Bank of England	0.2%
Market loans	24.0%
Bills of exchange	1.8%
Investments	6.7%
Advances	62.0%
Miscellaneous	4.8%

Creating deposits enables a bank to lend money and make profits. However, this involves risks. The obvious risk is non-payment by the borrower – the risk of bad debts. In addition, there is the risk that depositors may withdraw their funds in cash; if the bank could not meet all these cash demands, customer confidence would collapse and there might be a run on the bank. So the bank must keep some liquid assets – a reserve of cash, plus other assets which can be converted into cash quickly and easily. A bank which kept all of its assets in long-term loans and advances would be acting most unwisely.

However, highly liquid assets earn relatively low rates of interest: cash held by banks earns no interest at all. As these assets are relatively unprofitable for the bank. They will aim to maintain the minimum level of liquid assets in order to remain in liquidity.

Banks will also try to ensure that the risks involved in lending are minimised. They will avoid lending if there is a possibility of non-repayment; they often require collateral in order to ensure repayment of loans. This may take the form of physical assets (eg houses), but is more likely to be other financial assets, since these are more liquid.

Liquidity and profitability operate against each other: short-term loans are more liquid than long-term loans, but the rate of interest charged is lower. So banks must compromise and maintain a portfolio of different assets.

Using the material above do the following.

(a) Explain the importance of security, liquidity and profitability for the structure of bank assets.

(b) Identify the principal sources of risk for commercial banks and how these may be minimised.

(c) Explain the relationship between the liquidity of an asset and its profitability.

Answer to Case Study

(a) *Security* involves maintaining the bank's financial stability and confidence in the bank's ability to meet valid claims upon it by depositors and others, as they arise. Banks help to make themselves secure by ensuring formal security, ie collateral, in respect of most loans advanced by them. The security of banks also requires the maintenance of a sizeable base of capital reserves as protection against bad debts and operating losses (capital adequacy).

Liquidity is the ability of a bank to meet due claims upon it as they arise. The bank must be able to convert enough of its assets speedily into cash without sustaining a capital loss. Under normal banking conditions, funds will be needed to provide cash for withdrawal by depositors as well as to provide for the settlement of amounts owing to other banks. Supplementary liquidity will be required to deal with exceptional demands upon the bank. This may be provided by borrowing in the inter-bank market or by the issuing of certificates of deposit. In practice, banks keep a significant part of their assets in near-liquid form, which can be converted into cash as necessary.

Profitability. As commercial institutions owned by shareholders, the banks also have a need to be profitable. A sufficient return on capital needs to be earned to allow for an acceptable dividend to be paid to shareholders and to minimise the threat of takeover. Banks also need to increase their capital reserves in order to allow for inflation and to improve their security. Funds may also be needed to finance strategic development in a competitive global economy.

The assets of a bank range from already liquid cash to longer-term, somewhat illiquid loans. Generally, the more liquid the asset, the lower the return which will be earned by the bank. To help profitability, banks try to keep as high a proportion of assets as is prudent in non-liquid form, such as advances to customers. These advances generally earn the highest rates of return for the bank.

(b) Banks face the following risks of losses.

(i) *Credit risk:* the possibility that debts owed to the bank will not be repaid on the due date at their full value (eg individuals being unable to repay loans made to them) or that a firm which has obtained an advance from the bank might go into liquidation and be unable to clear the loan.

(ii) *Investment risk:* that investments held as assets by a bank will fall in realisable value below their purchase price or book value.

(iii) *Forced sale risk:* the risk that the market may be so unfavourable as to make it necessary to sell the asset below book value.

To meet or minimise such risks, the banks keep an array of assets, including cash and highly liquid assets. The banks also phase their loans and advances, so that loan repayments are spread and are not unduly concentrated on certain points in time. Care should be taken in relation to individual risks and commitments. In addition, the Bank of England capital adequacy requirements stipulate against over-exposure to any one form of debt.

(c) The biggest profits of a bank come from lending at higher interest rates. Usually longer-term lending will earn higher rates of interest than short-term lending. Lending to higher-risk customers will be at higher interest rates than lending to low-risk customers. Cash, as the most liquid of assets, earns zero return. Market loans, eg to discount houses, are short-term (sometimes as short as overnight) and also very secure; therefore they tend to earn lower rates of interest. Investment in gilts provides a higher rate of return, but there may be delay in turning them into cash. Loans to individuals and businesses generally will earn the highest rates of return, but such loans may be for several years and borrowers may default on repayment.

Although collateral may have been obtained, its effectiveness may be subject to sharply falling asset values (eg real property, plant and machinery), as in an economic recession. So the more profitable an asset, the less liquid or secure it is likely to be.

In reality, the banks try to maintain a balanced portfolio of assets reflecting the mix of liquidity, security and profitability considerations.

Further question practice

Now try the following practice questions at the end of this text.

Multiple choice questions	**97–108**
Exam style questions	**9** and **10**

Chapter 10

THE CENTRAL BANK AND THE FINANCIAL MARKETS

Introduction

From looking at the functions of money and the banking system in the previous chapter, we move on in this chapter to look at the main financial markets in the modern economy. We also describe the role of the central bank which acts on behalf of the government.

Your objectives

After completing this chapter you should:

(a) understand the functions of the Bank of England and the methods it uses to fulfil them;

(b) understand the role of the capital markets and the money markets.

NOTES

1 THE FUNCTIONS OF THE BANK OF ENGLAND

1.1 Introduction

A central bank is a bank which acts on behalf of the government. In the UK, the central bank is the Bank of England. The Bank of England is a nationalised corporation and is the central bank of the UK. It is run by a Court of Directors, consisting of the Governor, Deputy Governor, and some Executive Directors and part-time Directors.

The Bank of England, as the UK's central bank, has a variety of functions.

(a) It acts as banker to central government and holds the public deposits. Public deposits include the National Loans Fund, the Consolidated Fund and the account of the Paymaster General, which in turn includes the Exchange Equalisation Account.

(b) It is the central note-issuing authority in the UK; it is responsible for issuing bank notes.

(c) It is the manager of the National Debt (ie it deals with long-term and short-term borrowing by central government and the repayment of central government debt).

(d) It is the manager of the Exchange Equalisation Account (ie the UK's foreign currency reserves).

(e) It acts as the administrator of any exchange control regulations that might be in force.

(f) It acts as advisor to the government on monetary economic policy.

(g) It acts as agent for the government in carrying out its monetary policies and, from May 1997, has operational responsibility for setting interest rates.

Up to 1997, the Bank of England has also acted as supervisor of the banks. However, under reforms announced in May 1997, the Bank will hand over this role to a separate regulatory body, the Securities and Investments Board. This change will take the UK closer to meeting the European Union criterion of having an independent central bank without supervisory powers in preparation for European economic and monetary union ('EMU').

In the UK, the Bank of England is also:

(a) a banker to the commercial banks. Each of the commercial banks keeps accounts with the Bank of England;

(b) a lender to the banking system. When the banking system is short of money, the Bank of England will provide the money the banks need at an appropriate rate of interest. As we shall see, it does this mainly by purchasing eligible bills and other short-term money-market instruments from financial institutions, and it might very occasionally lend direct to institutions as a *lender of last resort*. This aspect of the Bank's activities is very important, because it provides the means by which it can influence or control the level of interest rates.

1.2 The Bank of England as a banker

The Bank's customers are:

(a) the government;

(b) other banks in the financial system, in particular the clearing banks.

Each clearing bank has a bank account with the Bank of England. Banks use these deposits to settle debts between each other. They also use these deposits to pay amounts due to the government, and when the government makes payments to the banks, there will be a transfer of funds from the government's account with the Bank to the banks' accounts with the Bank.

A feature of the Bank's role as a banker is therefore:

(a) daily transfers of funds between the deposits of the banks as inter-bank debts are settled;

(b) daily transfers of funds between the government's public deposits and the bankers' deposits.

1.3 The Bank of England as the central note-issuing authority in the UK

The Bank of England is the central authority in the UK for the issue of banknotes. The profits from note issues are paid to the Exchequer. These profits arise from the fact that notes are interest-free, but the funds obtained by the Bank from the commercial banks as payment for the issue of notes are used to acquire interest-bearing securities.

1.4 The Bank of England as manager of the National Debt

The Bank of England issues government securities to raise funds on behalf of the government, and is active in the gilt-edged market and money markets, buying and selling government (and other) securities. The Bank also administers the repayment of government debt when these debts reach their maturity (redemption date).

Long-term government debt instruments are referred to collectively as gilt-edged securities or gilts. Gilts are interest-bearing securities which are issued by the government and bought by investors. Short-term government debt takes the form of Treasury bills, which are issued by the government and bought largely by the banks and securities firms.

1.5 The Bank of England as manager of the Exchange Equalisation Account

This account represents the deposits of the nation's gold and foreign currency reserves. The Exchange Equalisation Account can be used to influence the exchange rate of sterling against other foreign currencies. The exchange value of sterling is allowed to float (ie rise or fall in value) against other currencies in response to market supply and demand, but when the government considers that sterling's value is too high or too low, the Bank will intervene.

Activity 1

Such intervention by the Bank is frequently reported in the press. The Bank will buy or sell sterling in exchange for foreign currencies. Think back to the basic principles of supply and demand to analyse which way round the process works: if sterling's exchange rate is too low, will the Bank buy sterling or sell it?

The Bank of England is a major active participator in three markets:

(a) the gilt-edged market;

(b) the money market (more specifically, the short-term money market); and

(c) the foreign exchange market.

NOTES

1.6 The Bank of England's role as administrator of exchange controls and other duties

Exchange controls are restrictions on the flow of money into or out of a country. At the moment, there are no such controls at all in force in the UK because they were removed by the government in 1979. However, should they ever be re-introduced, the Bank would have the responsibility for administering them. Similarly, the central bank of any country where exchange control regulations *are* in force would have the responsibility of enforcing them.

The important function of the Bank as administrator or agent for the government's monetary policy will be described later.

1.7 The Bank of England as lender of last resort to the commercial banking system

In the UK, the short-term money market provides a link between the banking system and the government (Bank of England): the Bank of England lends money to the banking system when banks which need cash cannot get it from anywhere else (eg from other banks).

(a) The Bank will supply cash to the banking system on days when the banks have a cash shortage. It does this by buying eligible bills from the institutions in exchange for cash. Eligible bills are bills (ie debt instruments) which the Bank will be prepared to buy. Most of these are bills that have been issued by banks which are on the Bank's list of eligible banks.

(b) The Bank will remove excess cash from the banking system on days when the banks have a cash surplus. It does this by selling bills to the institutions, so that the institutions obtain interest-bearing bills in place of the cash that they do not want.

The process whereby this is done currently is known as *open market operations*. This simply describes the buying and selling of eligible bills between the Bank and the short-term money market.

1.8 Open market operations and short-term interest rates

One aspect of open market operations is that they enable the Bank of England to influence short-term interest rates.

When bills are bought and sold, they are traded at a discount to their face value, and there is an implied interest rate in the rate of discount obtained. Interest rates on bills traded in open market operations have an immediate influence on other money market interest rates, such as the London Inter-Bank Offered Rate (LIBOR), and these in turn influence the banks' base rates.

This means that if interest rates in the discount market's open market operations went up, there would very soon be an increase in other money market rates. Then the banks' base rates would increase and so would lending rates on bank loans and overdrafts.

You might sometimes hear on the television or radio news that banks have lowered or increased their base rates in response to a signal from the Bank of England. Such a signal comes from a change of interest rate at which the Bank of England will deal that day in its open market operations.

The Bank's aim is two-fold:

(a) to provide a mechanism whereby the Bank can regulate the cash position of the banking system; and in doing so

(b) to control or influence the level of short-term interest rates.

NOTES

1.9 How does the Bank influence short-term interest rates?

By operating as a lender of cash in the short-term money market, the Bank's stated aim is to influence very short-term interest rates, and so indirectly influence the general level of interest rates.

Because the assets that the Bank of England acquires in its money market operations are short-term assets, a proportion matures each day. The market is then obliged to redeem these claims and must seek further refinancing from the Bank. This continued turnover of assets gives the Bank the opportunity to determine the level of interest rates day by day.

Institutions must compete with each other to sell bills to the Bank when they are short of money, or buy bills from the Bank when they have a cash surplus. The institutions must, therefore, select the interest rates at which they wish to buy or sell, and offer this rate to the Bank. The Bank will say yes or no, ie it will agree to buy or sell, or it will refuse. (If it refuses, the institutions can offer a new price.)

By rejecting offers, the Bank will influence money market interest rates. If the Bank is satisfied with the pattern of rates implied by the offers, it is generally prepared to accept enough to balance the market. But if the rates which are offered conflict with the Bank's interest rate objective, all or part of the offers may be rejected.

Open market operations occur daily, although general large interest rate changes only occur occasionally.

Activity 2

The following events occur in open market operations by the Bank of England in the money markets. Try to put them into their correct sequence.

Event

1. Bank of England buys eligible bills for cash. Interest rate implied in the purchase price.
2. Institutions become short of cash.
3. Cash enters the banking system from the Bank of England.
4. Institutions compete with bids to sell eligible bills to the Bank of England.

---

2 THE CAPITAL MARKETS AND THE MONEY MARKETS

2.1 Introduction

A distinction is usually made between:

(a) capital markets, which are financial markets for raising and investing long-term capital; and

(b) money markets, which are financial markets for lending and borrowing short-term capital.

Long term and short term are rather arbitrary distinctions. What do we mean by long-term and short-term capital?

(a) By short-term capital, we mean capital that is lent or borrowed for a period which might range from as short as overnight up to about one year, and sometimes longer.

(b) By long-term capital, we mean capital invested or lent and borrowed for a period of about five years or more, but sometimes shorter.

There is a grey area between long-term and short-term capital, which is lending and borrowing for a period from about one to two years up to about five years. This is not surprisingly sometimes referred to as medium-term capital.

It is not just the term of the lending and borrowing that distinguishes the capital markets from the money markets. Another important difference is the financial instruments that are dealt in by each market.

Definitions

Capital market is a market, or group of interrelated markets, for investing and raising capital in financial form, largely on a long-term basis. *Money market* is a market for lending and borrowing, mainly short-term capital, but where the amount lent and borrowed in one transaction will be large.

Activity 3

Try to think of some of the markets that firms can use to obtain finance. A number of them will be listed in the next few paragraphs.

Firms obtain long-term or medium-term capital in one of the following ways:

(a) as share capital;

(b) as loan capital.

The *government* borrows from a variety of sources, but the major method of capital borrowing by central government is the issue of gilt-edged securities or gilts. These are government loan stock, on which interest is paid until maturity of the loan, when the capital is then repaid in full. Another method is through National Savings. National Savings, which operates through Post Offices, is a government institution set up to borrow from individuals on behalf of the government.

2.2 Capital markets in the UK

There are several market places for raising capital. In the UK there are:

(a) *the Stock Exchange.* The Stock Exchange provides the main market where:

  (i) quoted companies (ie public limited companies whose shares are quoted on the Stock Exchange) can raise new funds by issuing new shares or loan stock;

  (ii) investors can buy and sell second-hand stocks and shares – ie stocks and shares that are already in issue;

(b) *the Alternative Investment Market.* This is a 'second tier' market where smaller companies that do not meet the stringent requirements needed to obtain a full listing on the Stock Exchange can raise new capital by issuing shares. Like the main market, the AIM is also a market for second-hand shares, regulated by the Stock Exchange;

(c) *the gilts or gilt-edged market.* This is the market for the government's long-term debt securities;

(d) *banks.* Banks can be approached directly by firms and individuals for medium-term and long-term loans as well as short-term loans or overdrafts;

(e) *building societies*. This is a capital market where individuals can obtain capital to buy a home with a mortgage, as well as personal loans;

(f) *National Savings*. This is a capital market where the government obtains capital by borrowing from private investors.

2.3 The contribution of the Stock Exchange to the economy

The Stock Exchange is an organised capital market which plays an important role in the functioning of the UK economy. It is the main capital market in the UK.

(a) It makes it easier for large firms and the government to raise long-term capital, by providing a market place for borrowers and investors to come together.

(b) The Stock Exchange publicises the prices of quoted (or listed) securities, which are then reported in daily national newspapers such as the *Financial Times*. Investors can therefore keep an eye on the value of their stocks and shares, and make buying and selling decisions accordingly.

(c) The Stock Exchange tries to enforce certain rules of conduct for its listed firms and for operators in the market, so that investors have the assurance that companies whose shares are traded on the Exchange and traders who operate there are reputable. Confidence in the Stock Exchange will make investors more willing to put their money into stocks and shares.

(d) The general level of share prices on the Stock Exchange acts as an indicator of the state of the country's economy.

2.4 Share prices on the stock market

The price of shares on a stock market goes up and down.

(a) The price of shares in a particular company which are not traded much might remain unchanged for quite a long time; alternatively, a company's share price might vary continually throughout each day.

(b) The general level of share prices, as measured by some form of index (eg in the UK, by the All-Share Index and the FT-SE 100 Index or 'Footsie' Index, which includes 100 leading shares), will go up or down each day.

Activity 4

From your reading of business pages (which should be a central feature in anyone's study of economics) what factors have you noticed as having an influence on share prices?

Stock markets are nowadays international in character, with major investors buying and selling shares on stock markets in different parts of the world (eg New York, Tokyo, Hong Kong, London). So share price movements reflect international views on the performance of a particular country's economy and industries.

2.5 Lenders of capital: institutional investors as financial intermediaries

The *lenders* of capital include private individuals, who buy stocks and shares on the Stock Exchange, or who invest in National Savings or building societies. However, there are some important *institutional investors*, ie institutions which specialise in lending capital in order to make a return. These institutions, which are financial intermediaries themselves, include the following:

(a) *pension funds*. Pension funds invest the pension contributions of individuals who subscribe to a pension fund, and of organisations with a company pension fund;

(b) *insurance companies*. These invest insurance premiums paid on insurance policies by policy holders. If you think about it, insurance companies, like pension funds, must do something with the premiums they receive, and in practice, they invest the money to earn a return;

(c) *investment trust companies*. These are companies whose business is investing in the stocks and shares of other companies and the government. In other words, they trade in investments;

(d) *unit trust companies*. These are similar to investment trust companies, in the sense that they invest in stocks and shares of other companies. They then sell portions or units of these investments to individual investors;

(e) *venture capital organisations*. These are organisations that specialise in raising funds for new business ventures, such as management buy-outs (ie. purchases of firms by their management staff). These organisations are therefore providing capital for fairly risky ventures. A venture capital organisation that has operated for many years in the UK is Investors in Industry or the 3i group. In recent years, many more venture capital organisations have been set up, and there is an active British Venture Capital Association.

2.6 The effectiveness of the capital markets as providers of capital to businesses

The functions of the capital market are to enable investors to lend money and borrowers to raise money, in such a way that new investments can take place. These help to stimulate or add growth to the economy. Although the market exists and is active, it is perhaps doubtful whether it is as effective as it should be in providing a means of raising money for new investments.

(a) In recent years, high rates of interest have made it difficult for companies to issue new loan stock. This will change with lower interest rates when this kind of capital becomes cheaper.

(b) Public limited companies have been able to raise new funds from share issues on the stock market, but the stock market remains mainly a market for second-hand shares rather than new issues. Only public limited companies are permitted to issue shares in this way, and in spite of the AIM, smaller firms have much more difficulty in finding investors who will subscribe for new shares. Venture capital organisations are not large enough to supply the volume of equity finance to small firms that would probably be needed for an effective capital market.

(c) Several large firms experienced difficulties during the economic recession of the early 1980s and were taken into intensive care by their bank. To this extent, the capital market functioned effectively to prevent an even deeper recession.

(d) Bank lending and lending by other financial institutions are often accused of being excessively conservative, avoiding risky investments. Since economic growth will probably depend on the success of risky ventures, a conservative approach is likely to reduce the prospects of successful ventures in large numbers. However, the large number of receiverships in the early 1980s recession suggest that this reputation of the banks for conservatism may not be entirely deserved. During the economic boom period of 1986 to 1988, the banks lent to numerous businesses which faced serious financial difficulties in the years that followed.

2.7 The money markets

The money markets in the UK are operated by the banks and other financial institutions. Although the money markets largely involve wholesale borrowing and lending by banks, some large companies and the government are also involved in these operations. The money markets consist of:

(a) the *discount market*. This is a market where some specialist money market banks, called the discount houses, buy and sell bills of exchange. An important aspect of trading in bills is the daily trading in certain eligible bills for cash between financial institutions and the Bank of England. As we saw earlier, the Bank uses this trading, known as open market operations, both to control or influence the level of short-term interest rates and to ensure that the banking system as a whole has an adequate daily supply of cash with which to operate. However, from 1997, the Bank of England has extended the counterparties with which it will deal in these open market operations to include various banks, building societies and securities firms, and so the discount houses have lost their privileged position.

(b) the *interbank market*. This is the market in which banks lend short-term funds to one another, and is a very important money market.

    A key interest rate in the UK money market is the London Inter-Bank Offered Rate (LIBOR), the rate of interest at which the largest London banks will lend to each other short term. The level of the 3-month LIBOR influences clearing banks' base rates, and much big money (or wholesale) lending of short-term funds to banks' customers is fixed at a certain margin above LIBOR (eg 1% above the 3 month LIBOR);

(c) the *eurocurrency market*. This is the market operated by banks for lending and borrowing in foreign currencies. Most of the trading is done by banks. Firms wishing to borrow in a foreign currency will usually do so from a bank;

(d) the *Certificate of Deposit market*. This is a market for trading in Certificates of Deposit;

(e) the *local authority market*. This is a market in which local authorities borrow short-term funds from banks and other investors, by issuing and selling short-term 'debt instruments';

(f) the *finance house market*. This refers to the short-term loans raised from the money markets by finance houses (eg hire purchase finance companies);

(g) the *inter-company market*. This refers to direct short-term lending between companies, without any financial intermediary. This market is very small, and restricted to the treasury departments of large companies. It has largely been overtaken by the sterling commercial paper (CP) markets;

(h) the *commercial paper/MTN market*. This is a market in which companies issue debt securities, known as commercial paper (CP) and medium-term notes (MTNs). The paper carries a rate of interest, and is purchased by investors.

A distinction is sometimes made between the discount market and all the other money markets, (b) to (h), which are referred to collectively as the *parallel markets* or wholesale markets.

Chapter roundup

- The Bank of England has various roles:
  - as a banker;
  - as the central banknote issuing authority;
  - as manager of the National Debt;
  - as manager of the Exchange Equalisation Account;
  - as administrator of exchange controls;
  - as advisor and agent to the government regarding monetary policy;
  - as the supervisor of the banking system;
  - as informal supervisor of other institutions;
  - as lender of last resort.
- The money markets comprise:
  - the discount market; and
  - the parallel or wholesale money markets.

Quick quiz

1 What are the functions of the Bank of England?

2 What are open market operations?

3 What is the difference between capital markets and money markets?

4 What are the capital markets in the UK?

5 What are the money markets in the UK?

Answers to Activities

1 The exchange rate is the price paid for sterling. If this price is too low, it can be forced up by restricting the supply of sterling. In other words, the Bank will *buy* sterling to prop up the exchange rate. On the other hand, if the exchange rate is too high, the Bank will *sell* sterling.

2 The order is 2, 4, 1, 3.

On days when the banking system as a whole is short of cash, so that cash needs can not be met by inter-bank lending, the banks must get cash from the Bank of England (Event 2). The institutions, to obtain the cash, sell eligible bills to the Bank of England (Event 4).

If the Bank accepts the prices offered, it will buy the bills in exchange for cash (Event 1) and cash will then flow into the banking system (Event 3). If the Bank rejects the tendered prices, it could be giving a signal to the market that it wants interest rates to change, and the institutions would be invited to put in fresh bids.

4 Share prices respond to:

(a) factors related to the circumstances of individual companies, eg news of a company's annual profits, or a proposed takeover bid;

(b) factors related to the circumstances of a particular industry, eg new government legislation or regulations for an industry, such as new laws on pollution controls or customer protection measures;

(c) factors related to the circumstances of the national economy, eg changes in interest rates, the latest official figures for the balance of trade, or price inflation.

NOTES

Further question practice

Now try the following practice questions at the end of this text.

Multiple choice questions	**109–119**
Exam style question	**11**

Chapter 11

NATIONAL INCOME ANALYSIS

Introduction

We start our analysis of issues in macroeconomics by looking at how to measure the total level of economic activity in a country. We also look at how income and expenditure flows around the economic system.

Your objectives

After completing this chapter you should:

(a) be aware of the different ways of measuring a nation's economic wealth;

(b) understand the way in which income flows between households and firms;

(c) understand how national income is measured.

1 MEASURING THE CREATION OF ECONOMIC WEALTH

1.1 Introduction

Three key measures of the total amount of economic activity in a country are:

(a) national income;

(b) gross national product (GNP);

(c) gross domestic product (GDP).

Activity 1

These are terms which are often encountered in news reports, and yet are often only vaguely understood. Jot down what you think is the meaning of each, and review what you have written once you come to the end of the chapter.

These are related but different measures of the economic wealth that a country creates or earns over a period of time, usually one year.

1.2 Why is national income so important?

Definition

National income is a measure of the value of goods and services available to the people in an economy at a given period.

National income is an important measure because it is an aggregate of personal incomes. The bigger the national income in a country, the more income its individual inhabitants will be earning on average. More income means more spending on the output of firms, and more spending (ignoring inflation) means more output of goods and services.

National income provides information of great importance to governments in setting their macroeconomic objectives. Such objectives typically include:

(a) *full employment*. In the UK in recent years employment has been at levels way above the 3% which is sometimes argued to be the absolute minimum for this country. Some commentators believe the reason for this to be the low priority given by the Conservative government to full employment as a macroeconomic objective;

(b) *economic growth*. This is an upward trend in the total output of a nation. Most governments will try to achieve a satisfactory rate of growth by adopting policies to encourage investment, research and development and so on;

(c) *stable prices*. Rapid rates of price increases are thought to be undesirable for reasons discussed in a later chapter. Governments aim to maintain prices at a stable level or, if that is not possible (and it rarely is), at least to keep increases to a minimum;

(d) a *satisfactory balance of payments*. This is discussed in detail in a later chapter.

1.3 Who creates economic wealth?

Economic wealth is created by:

(a) the people or organisations that *spend* money to buy the goods and services:

(i) consumers (or households);

(ii) the government; and

(iii) foreign buyers (the overseas sector); or

(b) the people who *earn* the wealth:

(i) labour, who earn wages for the work they do;

(ii) providers of capital, who earn interest on the capital they invest;

(iii) owners of land, who earn rent on the land they provide for economic use;

(iv) entrepreneurs, who earn profits for the business risks that they take.

As has often been stressed earlier in this book, the scarcity of these factors of production, and the need for decisions on their allocation, is the fundamental problem of economics;

(c) the creators of wealth can also be identified as the firms (or government departments and corporations) which *produce* the goods or services in the national economy.

The three approaches (a), (b) and (c) give rise to three ways of defining economic wealth:

(a) the expenditure approach;

(b) the income approach; and

(c) the value added approach.

These are defined and discussed later in this chapter.

2 THE CIRCULAR FLOW OF INCOME

2.1 Introduction

Income in a country's economy flows between households and firms.

(a) The income of firms is the *sales revenue from the sales of goods and services.*

(b) The income of households is the *income arising from the ownership of the factors of production.*

Activity 2

Before going on, try to remember from an earlier chapter what the factors of production are, and what reward is earned by each.

Firms must pay households for the factors of production, and households must pay firms for goods. This creates a circular flow of income and expenditure, as illustrated in Figure 1.

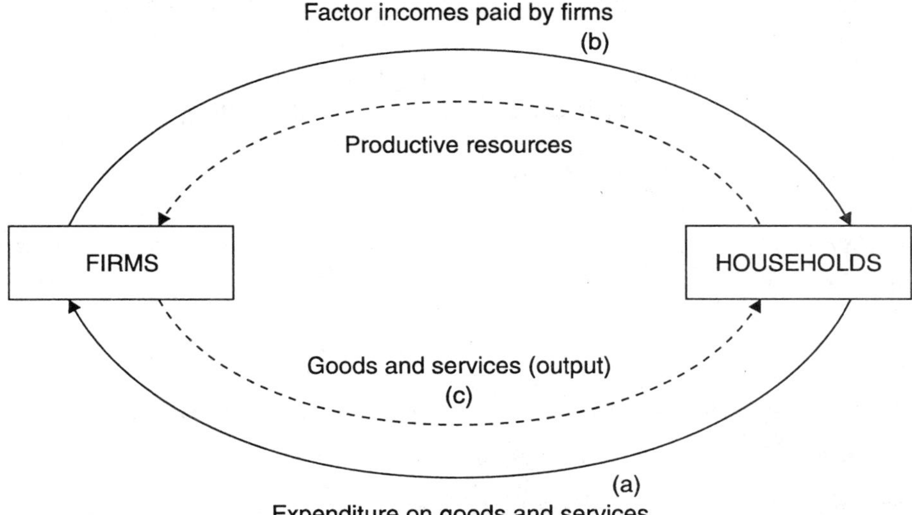

Figure 1 Circular flow of income

The total sales value of goods produced should equal the total expenditure on goods (a), assuming that all goods that are produced are also sold. The amount of expenditure should also equal the total income of households (b), because it is households that consume the goods and they must have income to afford to pay for them.

Households earn *income*. They earn income because they have provided the factors of production which enable firms to *output* goods and services (c). The income earned is used as *expenditure* on these goods and services that are made.

2.2 Withdrawals and injections into the circular flow of income

Our simplified diagram of the circular flow of income needs to be amended to allow for:

(a) *withdrawals* from the circular flow of income. These are movements of funds out of the cycle of income and expenditure between firms and households;

(b) *injections* into the circular flow of income. These are movements of funds in the other direction.

There are three types of *withdrawal* from the circular flow.

(a) *Savings (S)*. Households do not spend all their income. They save some, and these savings out of income are withdrawals from the circular flow of income, simply because savings are not spent.

(b) *Taxation (T)*. Households must pay some of their income to the government, as taxation. Taxes cannot be spent by households, because the funds go to the government.

(c) *Imports (M)*. When we consider national income, we are interested in the economic wealth that a particular country is earning. Spending on imports is expenditure, but on goods made by firms in other countries. The payments for imports go to firms in other countries, for output created in other countries. Spending on imports therefore withdraws funds out of a country's circular flow of income.

There are also three types of *injection* into the circular flow of income.

(a) *Investment (I)*. Investment in capital goods is a form of spending on output, which is additional to expenditure by households. Just as savings are a withdrawal of funds, investment is an injection of funds into the circular flow of income, adding to the total economic wealth that is being created by the country.

(b) *Government spending (G)*. Government spending is also an injection into the circular flow of income. In most mixed economies, total spending by the government on goods and services represents a large proportion of total national expenditure. The funds to spend come from either taxation income or government borrowing.

(c) *Exports (X)*. Firms produce goods and services for export. Exports earn income from abroad, and therefore provide an injection into a country's circular flow of income.

2.3 Three approaches to measuring national income

As already mentioned, these are as follows.

(a) *The expenditure approach*. The economic wealth created in a period can be measured by the amount of expenditure on the goods and services that are produced by the nation's economy.

   (i) The expenditures will be incurred by consumers, the government and foreign buyers (ie exports). Expenditures on imports represent wealth created by other countries, and so the value of expenditure on imports must be deducted from the total expenditure figure.

   (ii) Expenditures by firms (eg companies) are *excluded*, to avoid double-counting.

(b) *The income approach*. This approach measures the income of individuals from employment and from self-employment, the profits of firms and public corporations and rent on property. (Interest earnings will be included within the profits of companies or the income of individuals.)

(c) *The value added approach*. This approach is to measure the (sales) value of output produced by firms and other organisations in the period.

All three approaches will, in theory, result in the same total amount for economic wealth created in the period, which we call Gross Domestic Product or GDP. In practice, statistical discrepancies arise, which cause differences between the alternative figures.

Activity 3

We stated above that, in the expenditure approach to measuring national income, expenditures by firms are excluded to avoid double counting. Think carefully about this and make sure that you understand exactly what is meant. Jot down an explanation.

2.4 The government and national income

The government has several functions within the national economy, and so plays several different roles in the circular flow of income.

(a) It acts as the *producer* of certain goods and services instead of privately-owned firms. The production of public administration services, education and health services, the police force, armed forces, fire brigade services and public transport are all aspects of output. The government in this respect acts as a producer, in the same way as firms, and must, like them, pay wages to its employees.

(b) It acts as the *purchaser* of final goods and services and adds to total consumption expenditure. National and local government obtain funds from the firms or households of the economy (eg in the form of taxation) and then use these funds to buy goods and services from other firms.

NOTES

(c) It *invests* by purchasing capital goods (eg building roads, schools and hospitals).

(d) It acts as a means of transferring wealth or income from one section of the economy to another, eg by taxing workers and paying pensions, unemployment benefits and social security benefits ('transfer payments') to other members of society.

Items (a), (b) and (c), but not (d), contribute to the creation of national income.

3 NATIONAL INCOME STATISTICS

3.1 What is national income?

The UK national income can be defined as:

> ***the sum of all incomes of residents in the UK which arise*** **as a result of economic activity,** ***that is from the production of goods and services. Such incomes, which include rent, employment income and profit, are known as*** **factor incomes** ***because they are earned by the so-called factors of production: land, labour and capital.***
>
> *CSO*

National income is also called *net national product.*

(a) The terms 'income' and 'product' are just two different aspects of the same circular flow of income.

(b) The term 'net' means 'after deducting an amount for capital consumption or depreciation of fixed assets'. We shall return to this point later.

3.2 Gross domestic product (GDP)

Most UK national income is comes from economic activity within the UK. Economic activity within the UK is referred to as total *domestic income* or *domestic product.* It is measured gross (ie before deducting an amount for capital consumption or depreciation of fixed assets) and the term *gross domestic product* therefore refers in the UK to the total value of income/production from economic activity within the UK.

3.3 Gross national product (GNP)

> ***Some national income arises from overseas investments while some of the income generated within the UK is earned by non-residents. The difference between these items is*** **net property income from abroad.**
>
> *CSO*

Gross national income or gross national product (GNP) is therefore the gross domestic product (GDP) plus the net property income from abroad, or minus the net property income from abroad, if it is a negative value.

3.4 The relationship between GDP, GNP and national income

The relationship between GDP, GNP and national income is as follows.

NOTES

	GDP
plus	Net property income from abroad
equals	GNP
minus	Capital consumption
equals	National income (net)

Activity 4

Which of the following may cause an increase in national income?

(a) A rise in exports.

(b) An increase in saving.

(c) A fall in consumer spending.

3.5 The expenditure approach to measuring national income

Probably the most widely used measure of national income is the measurement of total spending or expenditure and it is worth looking at this in some detail.

UK NATIONAL INCOME 1992: EXPENDITURE APPROACH	£bn
At current market prices	
Consumers' expenditure	382.7
General government consumption	132.4
Gross domestic fixed capital formation	92.9
Value of increase/(decrease) in stocks and work in progress	(2.0)
Total domestic expenditure	606.0
Exports of goods and services	139.8
Imports of goods and services	(149.2)
Statistical discrepancy	(0.4)
Gross domestic product at market prices	596.2
Taxes on expenditure (indirect taxes)	(87.7)
Subsidies	6.1
GDP – gross domestic product at factor cost	514.6
Net property income from abroad	5.8
GNP – gross national product at factor cost	520.4
Capital consumption (depreciation)	(64.0)
National income at factor cost	456.4

(Source: CSO Blue Book)

Note the following points.

(a) National income is calculated by subtracting a fairly arbitrary amount for depreciation from a total value known as Gross National Product, or GNP.

(b) GNP itself is calculated by measuring total expenditure within the national economy (which we call Gross Domestic Product or GDP) and then adding an amount for income from property (assets) abroad.

(c) The three measures, national income, GNP and GDP are therefore closely related. When we distinguish between the expenditure approach, the income approach and the value added approach, we are really talking about three approaches to calculating GDP.

(d) We might refer to any of the three measures, national income, GNP or GDP. Where a government seeks to increase national income, it is also seeking increases in GDP and GNP.

Notes on the expenditure approach

Total spending consists of consumption spending, government spending, investment spending, spending by foreigners on our goods and services minus spending by us on foreign goods and services. This is often symbolised as C + I + G + (X – M) where:

C = consumption expenditure
I = investment expenditure
G = government expenditure
X = expenditure on our exports by foreigners
M = expenditure by us on imports

From the table it can be seen that when we calculate C + I + G + (X – M), the total we arrive at is called the gross domestic product at market prices. This measure (GDP at market prices) is one way of expressing the level of economic activity in the UK.

If a government is planning its economic policy, and wishes to increase the country's GDP and GNP, it might wish to turn its attention to any of these items:

(a) trying to increase consumer spending, C;

(b) trying to increase private investment, I;

(c) deciding to increase government spending, G and/or I;

(d) trying to improve the balance of payments on overseas trade, (X – M).

Since the prices of many goods and services are distorted by sales taxes (eg alcohol and cigarettes) and some are distorted by subsidies (eg many agricultural products) we often wish to view the situation without these distortions and convert GDP at market prices to GDP at factor cost:

(a) expenditure at *market prices*, ie the actual amounts paid for the goods by their buyers; and

(b) expenditure at *factor cost*, ie expenditure at market prices minus indirect taxes plus any government subsidies.

As you can see from the table this is still not the end of the story. Many statisticians, economists, governments and international agencies like to include property income from abroad to give a fuller picture of what is happening in the domestic economy. When this extra item is included we now have a measure called gross national product or GNP.

Although technically national income has a particular definition, generally you will find both measures (GDP and GNP) loosely referred to as national income.

Activity 5

Gross national product at factor cost, plus indirect taxes on expenditure, minus subsidies equals what?

3.6 The income approach to measuring national income

The second method of calculating national income is the income method. Since money spent by an individual or firm must become income to another we should not be surprised to find that, except for a residual error, the results of the two methods are the same.

UK NATIONAL INCOME 1992: INCOME APPROACH	£bn
At current factor cost	
Income from employment (wages and salaries, plus employers' national insurance contributions)	341.0
Income from self-employment	58.1
Gross trading profits of companies	64.6
Gross trading surplus of public corporations	1.8
Gross trading surplus of government enterprises	0.1
Rent	51.0
Total domestic income	516.6
Less stock appreciation	(2.2)
GDP – income based	514.4
Statistical discrepancy	0.2
GDP – expenditure based (see earlier table)	514.6

(Source: CSO Blue Book)

More about the income based approach

When we refer to national income, it might seem more obvious to consider the *income*-based approach rather than an expenditure-based approach to measuring the statistics.

The table showing the income-based approach displays as separate items:

(a) income from employment (ie wages and salaries before deducting tax and including employers' National Insurance contributions);

(b) income from self-employment;

(c) pre-tax profits of companies;

(d) pre-tax profits of public corporations (including state-owned industries);

(e) the pre-tax surplus of other government enterprises.

You might notice that these income figures do not include:

(a) income from government pensions or social security payments;

(b) any value for work done by individuals for no monetary reward, such as housework done by housewives or do-it-yourself home improvements. These are activities for which no money value can be given, and so are not economic activities.

3.7 Transfer payments (transfer incomes)

Definition

Transfer payments are payments that are not made in return for goods or services: student grants and social security payments are examples. They are payments which involve the transfer of wealth, rather than a reward for creating new economic wealth.

Transfer payments do not lead directly to any increase in marketable output of goods.

NOTES

Most transfer payments are made by the government, which collects taxes and uses some of its tax income to make payments for:

(a) old age pensions, and

(b) social security payments.

Transfer payments are not included in GNP because they do not add to marketable output of goods.

Government expenditure figures within GNP are *net* of transfer payments.

Activity 6

Which of the following is or are transfer payments?

(a) Salaries paid to members of parliament.

(b) Invalidity benefit.

3.8 Rent

Rent is the profits (or operating surplus) from the ownership of land and buildings.

3.9 Imputed income and expenditure

Although the income figures exclude most work that is done for no monetary reward (eg housework and do-it-yourself activities) the definition of production/economic activity in the UK does include some activities which are not carried out for a money reward.

The main one of these activities is the provision of owner-occupied houses. When a person buys his own home and lives in it, no money will be exchanged between the owner and the occupier because they are one and the same person. However,

> ***the services of the house do nevertheless have a value equivalent to the net income which could have been obtained by letting it commercially. A figure based on this approach is included in the national income. In effect, the owner-occupier is divided into two separate transactors. It is supposed that as owner, he lets the house to himself as occupier for a certain rent.***
>
> ***CSO***

This process of inventing a transaction is known as *imputation*. In the case of owner-occupied dwellings an imputed amount of rent is included in the income statistics as rent (income-based approach) or consumers' expenditure (expenditure-based approach).

3.10 The value added method of measuring national income

The third method of calculating national income is the value added method. Since the goods and services we spend our money on must have been produced by some industry or another it is not surprising to find the amount we have all spent is the same as the value of the goods and services produced (except for a residual statistical discrepancy).

NOTES

UK NATIONAL INCOME 1992: VALUE ADDED APPROACH	£bn
At current prices	
Agriculture, forestry and fishing	9.3
Mining and quarrying, oil and gas exploration	9.8
Manufacturing	114.7
Electricity, gas and water supply	13.7
Construction	32.0
Transport, storage and communication	41.6
Wholesale and retail trade, hotels, catering, repairs	72.5
Financial intermediation, real estate, renting and business activities	121.7
Public administration, national defence, compulsory social security	36.6
Education, health and social work	52.5
Other services	32.9
Gross domestic product (GDP) value added based	537.3
Adjustment for financial services	(22.9)
GDP income based	514.4
Residual error (as with income approach)	0.2
GDP expenditure based – as shown above	514.6

(Source: CSO Blue Book)

As we have seen, there are three ways of measuring GDP and national income – the expenditure, income and value added methods. Since expenditure, income and value added are three ways of looking at the same events, they ought to produce the same total value for GDP and national income. In practice, they do not. This is because collecting statistics is liable to error.

Estimates have to be made when accurate figures are unobtainable. There are omissions in obtaining some figures and deliberate errors in others – for example, fiddling tax returns might occur on a large scale. Because of errors, the three approaches will produce slightly different figures, and one of them must be taken as correct. In practice, the expenditure-based figures are considered most reliable. The income based and value added based GDP figures are adjusted to the expenditure based GDP figure, by inserting a balancing item known as a residual error.

Activity 7

Which of the following items is or are included in the calculation of GNP at factor cost?

(a) The cost of building new government offices.

(b) Valued added tax on business services.

3.11 National income and inflation

Inflation is a particular problem in using national income as a measure of national wealth. Price inflation increases the *money* value of national income.

We should be careful not to interpret this as meaning that there is more economic activity in our economy. All that has happened is that the prices of the things we are measuring have gone up. To see if there has been any *real* change in the level of activity we must deduct any influence due to inflation. Although this is not a simple operation, the standard method for turning money GDP or GNP into real measures, is to use what is called the 'GDP deflator' to take inflation out of the figures.

When comparing one year's national income with another's it is very important that we use real figures if we are to reach any worthwhile conclusions. This is because with real comparisons of national income from one year to the next, we compare like with like.

Chapter roundup

- There is a circular flow of income in an economy, which means that expenditure, output and income will all have the same total value.
- There are withdrawals from the circular flow of income (savings, taxation, import expenditure) and injections into the circular flow (investment, government spending, export income). In formula terms:

$$W = S + T + M$$

$$J = I + G + X$$

- National income can be measured by an expenditure method, income method or value added method. Allowing for statistical errors in collecting the data, all three methods should give the same total for GDP, GNP and national income.
- A useful formula to learn is the expenditure method:

$$Y = C + I + G + (X - M).$$

- National income figures can be used to measure growth in the economy, although real growth can only be measured by taking out inflation and using figures on a common price basis.
- Economic wealth is perhaps best measured by GDP, GNP or national income per head of the population. However, national income is a measure of *annual* income, not the nation's total stock of wealth.

Quick quiz

1 What are the withdrawals from and injections into the circular flow of income?
2 What are the three approaches to calculating national income?
3 Define:
 (a) national income;
 (b) Gross Domestic Product;
 (c) Gross National Product.
4 Explain the relationship between national income, GDP and GNP.
5 What is the meaning of GDP = C + I + G + (X – M)?
6 What is capital consumption?
7 What are transfer payments (or transfer incomes)? Are they included in national income statistics?
8 What is imputed income? Give an example.
9 What are the difficulties in calculating national income?

Answers to Activities

3 Firms buy goods and services which become costs of the goods or services that they produce and sell themselves. If we included expenditure by firms, we would be double-counting the value of the wealth created by the suppliers of raw materials and components and the providers of services to other firms.
4 Only (a). Both (b) and (c) are reductions in national income.
5 Gross national product at market prices.

NOTES

6 (a) is *not* a transfer payment. MPs are like any other employees – they just happen to be employed by the government.

(b) *is* a transfer payment. It falls within the category of social security payments.

7 (a) of course, *is* included.

(b) is *not* included: GNP at factor cost is calculated by removing taxes on expenditure, such as VAT.

Case Study 1

In this case we will look a little more closely at the single largest component of GDP, consumption.

Consider the following data and try to answer the following questions.

(a) What have been the main trends in consumer expenditure in the UK since 1970?

(b) Give possible explanations for these trends in consumption.

(c) Why would you expect the demand for consumer durable goods to fluctuate more than the demand for food?

Consumer expenditure in the United Kingdom (£ billion in 1985 prices)

	1970	**1980**	**1990**
Consumer durable goods	9.4	15.5	27.8
Food	29.1	30.5	33.2
Drink and tobacco	19.7	24.2	23.2
Clothing and footwear	8.9	11.9	17.5
Energy products	14.4	17.3	20.5
Other goods	15.2	20.0	30.6
Rent, water and rates	20.7	25.4	29.3
Other services	40.6	52.4	90.9
Total expenditure	158.0	197.2	273.0

(Source: Economic Trends, HMSO)

Answer to Case Study 1

(a) The table shows the component parts of consumer expenditure in the UK between 1970 and 1990 expressed at 1985 prices. This means that the increases shown are real increases in consumer expenditure. Expressing the figures using a common base year removes the effect of inflationary price rises on consumer expenditure in money terms.

Total consumer expenditure rose by 73% over the twenty years to 1990. The largest rises were recorded for consumer durables (196%), other services (124%), other goods (101%) and clothing and footwear (97%). Rises below the average were recorded for energy products (42%), and rent, water and rates (42%). The slowest growing categories were drink and tobacco (18%) and food (14%). For inferior goods, consumption falls as incomes rise. The fact that all sectors showed positive growth indicates that no sector was inferior overall, in this technical sense.

As a result of these changes, by 1990 the other services sector had grown to 33.3% of total expenditure compared with 25.7% in 1970, and consumer durable goods made up 10.2% of the total compared with 5.9% in 1970. The share of total expenditure represented by food, drink and tobacco declined from 30.9% in 1970 to 20.7% in 1990.

Working

	Increase on 1970		*Percentage of total*		
	1980	**1990**	**1970**	**1980**	**1990**
	%	%	%	%	%
Consumer durable goods	65	196	5.9	7.9	10.2
Food	5	14	18.4	15.4	12.2
Drink and tobacco	23	18	12.5	12.3	8.5
Clothing and footwear	34	97	5.7	6.0	6.4
Energy products	20	42	9.1	8.8	7.5
Other goods	32	101	9.6	10.1	11.2
Rent, water and rates	23	42	13.1	12.9	10.7
Other services	29	124	25.7	26.6	33.3
Total expenditure	25	73	100.0	100.0	100.0

(b) The period from 1970 to 1990 was a period of rising real incomes, along with some reduction in levels of direct personal taxation. So there was a rise in real disposable incomes after tax over the period. As well as having more to spend from income, people had increasing confidence to borrow more; there was an expansion of consumer credit and a decline in the personal savings ratio over the period. Individuals' confidence was encouraged by rising levels of employment and rises in asset values, particularly in the case of owner-occupied housing.

The pattern of expenditure is influenced by the income elasticities of demand for different types of product. Income elasticity of demand is a measure of the responsiveness of demand to changes in income. Food, drink and tobacco have relatively low income elasticities of demand. There is a limit to the amount of these products which individuals can consume. So in a country where almost everyone has enough to eat, it is only by substitution of cheaper foods with more expensive goods that expenditure on food will increase significantly. The rising share of consumer durables and other services reflects the fact that households consume more of these as income rises, and therefore income elasticity of demand is high. As incomes rise, households are able to acquire more durable goods and to buy more services to deal with tasks they might previously have carried out themselves.

Consumer durables also have a high price elasticity of demand, and so falls in real prices of these goods resulting from cheaper production methods would be expected to have led to an overall increase in expenditure on them. Additionally, the process of technological advance has expanded the market for consumer durable products over the period.

Expenditure on energy products has risen over the 20 years to 1990, although their share of total expenditure has fallen. This reflects the development of more energy-efficient products, such as in domestic heating, over a period when the real price of oil and other fuels has risen.

(c) Food represents a relatively stable part of household expenditure, and this is reflected in its relatively low income and price elasticities of demand. This is because food is regarded as an essential and, in a relatively affluent country, there is no need for people to go without enough food. As incomes or prices rise or fall, households will not change their expenditure on food by very much, and so there will be relatively stable demand.

Consumer durables are different in that their income and price elasticities of demand are higher. They often represent major items of expenditure, such as a television set or a dishwasher, and many are considered to be luxury items. If real incomes fall in a recession, households will readily postpone expenditure on consumer durables until they feel that they can afford them. As the trade cycle moves on to the recovery phase, people will feel more confident and will make purchases which were previously postponed. They may also have increased confidence to make new major purchases out of borrowings. The trade cycle can thus lead to relatively large fluctuations in the demand for consumer durables.

NOTES

Case Study 2

This case looks a little more closely at the structure of output in the UK.

Consider the data and try to answer the following questions.

(a) Describe the main changes in the structure of output in the UK economy, both within and between sectors.

(b) Explain the shifts in the structure of output that you have identified in the first part.

(c) Describe the economic problems that might arise as a result of large changes in the economic structure of an economy.

Distribution of UK national output

	% share of GDP in each sector		
	1969	**1979**	**1989**
Primary sector	4.3	6.7	3.8
of which:			
Agriculture, forestry, fishing	1.8	2.2	1.3
Mining	2.5	1.3	0.7
Oil and gas	–	3.2	1.8
Secondary sector	42.0	36.7	31.3
of which:			
Manufacturing	30.7	27.3	22.4
Construction	8.4	6.2	6.2
Energy and water	2.9	3.2	2.7
Tertiary sector	53.0	56.5	64.8
of which:			
Distribution, hotels, catering	13.3	12.7	13.2
Transport and communications	6.3	7.3	6.9
Banking, finance, insurance	8.6	11.0	18.4
Public services	14.1	14.2	15.0
Others	10.7	11.3	11.3

(Source: Economic Trends)

Answer to Case Study 2

(a) The *primary sector* of the economy consists of industries which produce raw materials such as crops and minerals. Over the long term, the trend is one of decline in this sector when measured in terms of its share of gross domestic product (GDP). Viewed against the process of economic growth, this declining share reflects the rising absolute level of output of other industries.

The data show how, within the primary sector, the beginning of North Sea oil and gas production in the 1970s increased the overall importance of the sector within the UK economy. By 1989, however, the share of oil and gas within GDP had fallen to 56% of its 1979 share. Agriculture, forestry and fishing increased its share of GDP slightly from 1969 to 1979, but the fall in share from 2.2% in 1979 and to 1.3% in 1989 is more consistent with the long-term trend of declining importance for these industries. Mining shows a progressive decline over the period from 1969 (2.5%) to 1989 (0.7%), reflecting the progressive rundown of the coal industry in favour of other fuels. The relatively high share of 6.7% for the primary sector as a whole in 1979 mainly reflects the advent of North Sea oil.

The *secondary sector* consists of industries which process raw materials, and is sometimes referred to as 'industry'. This sector normally grows rapidly during the early stages of economic development; the data show how the UK has reached a later stage of decline in this sector. The major part of the decline in GDP share for the sector from 42.0% in 1969 to 31.3% in 1989 is attributable to a decline in manufacturing, which is the part of the sector most heavily involved in international trade, as opposed to construction and energy and water.

The *tertiary sector* is made up of goods distribution and service industries. This sector has become the predominant provider of employment and output in the UK economy in recent decades, growing from a 53% share in 1969 to a 64.8% share in 1989.

The data show that the main reason for the continuing growth in this sector during the 1970s and 1980s has been the rapid expansion in the banking, finance and insurance sectors, which expanded their GDP share by approximately 110% (from 8.6% to 18.4%) between 1969 and 1989.

(b) Within the primary sector, the most significant factor affecting the change in GDP shares over the period from 1969 has been the discovery and exploitation of North Sea oil and, later, gas. In the earlier years, as well as benefiting from the peak in absolute output from the North Sea, this sector benefited from relatively high energy prices compared with more recent years.

The term *de-industrialisation* is often used to describe the long-term decline in the importance of the manufacturing industry and the secondary sector in general. Although we have so far considered GDP shares of the different sectors of the economy, as remarkable as the decline in the share of manufacturing is the fact that the level of manufacturing output has shown no upward trend in the UK since the early 1970s.

Some argue that the decline of the secondary sector and the rise of the tertiary sector is an inevitable consequence of economic development. As in earlier stages of economic development, the agricultural sector declines with the growth of the secondary sector, and so the latter sector declines as demand shifts, relatively, from goods to services. International comparisons offer some support for this explanation, since recent years have seen a decline in the share of employment accounted for by manufacturing in almost all advanced capitalist economies. However, a special feature to note regarding the UK is that manufacturing employment reached its peak rather earlier (1955) than in many other countries, including West Germany (1970). Some point out that Britain was the first country to industrialise and, during much of this century, relative economic decline has been apparent in the UK, with many other industrialised countries overtaking the UK in GDP per head.

It is important to note that domestic output supplies both domestic demand and exports. A relative decline in manufacturing output may be the result of a shift of demand away from UK-manufactured goods towards foreign-manufactured goods, coupled with a failure of UK manufacturing industries to meet demand. This explanation is borne out by the shift from a UK trade surplus in manufactured goods during the 1970s to significant deficits in manufactured goods during the 1980s.

Within the tertiary sector, the rising share of banking, finance and insurance reflects a number of factors. First, London has built on its reputation as one of the leading financial centres of the world, and in some areas (eg the foreign exchange markets) it is pre-eminent. The strong position of the City makes it a large exporter of financial services. Secondly, increasing affluence and changing social factors (eg increasing levels of owner-occupation of housing during the 1970s and 1980s) have increased domestic demand for financial products of various kinds (eg current accounts, mortgages and insurance products). Thirdly, the abolition of exchange controls in 1979 and the deregulation of financial markets during the 1980s (eg the Stock Exchange 'Big Bang' and the Building Societies Act of 1986) served to free up supply as well as intensify competition in this subsector.

(c) Major changes in the economic structure of an economy may make the economy ill-equipped to respond to future economic changes. For example, a country might take the opportunity to exploit substantial oil and gas resources. The effects of increasing employment in this industry and a buoyant exchange rate fuelled by the oil and gas exports might lead to decline in other sectors, such as manufacturing. When the oil and gas resources run down, the diminished manufacturing industry may be poorly placed to take advantage of the new situation; it may be unable to make up for the lost oil and gas output rapidly enough. To the extent that domestic manufactured goods are replaced by imports, the balance of payments will suffer.

Another change which may adversely affect an economy in which economic activity has become concentrated in particular sectors, is a change in world market conditions, for example a change in commodity prices. Just as a firm can reduce overall risk by diversification, so an economy may gain in the long run from having a widely-based economic structure, rather than one which relies heavily on particular sectors.

However, it needs to be recognised that some changes in economic structure reflect the process of dynamic change which economic and technological progress brings about. There are so-called sunrise industries, such as information technology and genetics, whose importance is increasing worldwide. Sunset industries in the western economies include heavy industries such as steel and shipbuilding, whose prices have been undercut for many years by more efficient producers in the Pacific Basin.

The decline of industries can bring the problem of unemployment in the regions affected, particularly where there is heavy geographical concentration, as in the case of shipbuilding and coal mining. If industries on which a region is economically reliant are closed down rapidly, the effects can be severe. As well as the immediate problem of unemployment, there may be knock-on effects for the rest of the region's businesses as consumers' spending power is reduced and people begin to leave the area. Such problems may be eased by government policies on training, support for new employment opportunities in the affected areas and the encouragement of geographical and occupational mobility of labour.

Just as the rundown of certain industries brings problems for the regions in which they are concentrated, so the rapid expansion of certain sectors may present problems. During the 1980s, the rapid expansion of the banking, finance and insurance industries put strains on the economic infrastructure and brought high house price inflation in the South East region where those industries are concentrated.

Further question practice

Now try the following practice questions at the end of this text.

Multiple choice questions	**120–131**
Exam style question	**12**

Chapter 12

NATIONAL INCOME AND UNEMPLOYMENT

Introduction

You may well be aware that there has been some difference of opinion between economists as to how real economic growth can be achieved. Broadly speaking, economists can be divided into two camps, the Keynesians and the monetarists. These two camps have had differing ideas about how national income can be made to grow, how full employment can be achieved and how booms and slumps of trade cycles can be smoothed out. They differ in their views about the causes of inflation, the extent to which inflation creates unemployment and prevents economic growth, and the effectiveness of government measures to stimulate the economy, for example by borrowing and spending heavily to create new investment and jobs. In this chapter we look at the basic elements of the Keynesian model for national income determination and equilibrium.

Your objectives

After completing this chapter you should:

(a) understand the relationship between aggregate demand, aggregate supply and equilibrium national income;

(b) understand the impact of consumption, savings and investment on national income;

(c) understand the link between the level of national income and the level of employment.

1 AGGREGATE DEMAND AND SUPPLY AND EQUILIBRIUM NATIONAL INCOME

1.1 Introduction

Keynesian economics originated with John Maynard Keynes, an English economist whose book *The General Theory of Employment, Interest and Money* (1936), revolutionised economic analysis. Keynes put forward his ideas following a period in which there was an economic boom (after the First World War), followed by the Wall Street Crash in 1929, and the Great Depression in the 1930s when unemployment levels soared.

1.2 Aggregate demand and aggregate supply

Keynes argued that the level of overall output and employment depends on the level of *aggregate demand* in the economy. His basic idea was that demand and supply analysis could be applied to macroeconomic activity as well as microeconomic activity.

Definition

Aggregate demand means the total demand in the economy for goods and services.

Definition

Aggregate supply means the total supply of goods and services in the economy.

Aggregate supply depends on physical production conditions – the availability and cost of factors of production and technical know-how. Keynes was concerned with short-run measures to affect the economy, and he also wrote in a period of high unemployment when there was obviously no limit on the availability of factors of production. His analysis therefore concentrated on the *demand side*. Supply side economics (discussed later) describe the views of economists who do not agree with the Keynesian approach to the problems of national income and employment. They prefer to concentrate on supply side (ie production) factors.

The *aggregate supply curve* will be upward sloping, for the reasons applying to the microeconomic supply curves mentioned in earlier chapters. A higher price means that it is worthwhile for firms to hire more labour and produce more because of the higher revenue-earning capability. So at the macroeconomic level, an increasing price level implies that many firms will be receiving higher prices for their products and will increase their output.

In the economy as a whole, supply will at some point reach a labour limit, when the entire labour force is employed. When there is full employment, and firms cannot find extra labour to hire, they cannot produce more even when prices rise, unless there is some technical progress in production methods. The aggregate supply curve will therefore rise vertically when the full employment level of output is reached (AS in Figure 1).

Aggregate demand (AD) is total desired demand in the economy, for consumer goods and services and also for capital goods. It makes no difference whether the buyers are households, firms or government. Aggregate demand is a concept of fundamental importance in Keynesian economic analysis. Keynes believed that national economy could be managed by taking measures to influence aggregate demand up or down.

NOTES

Aggregate demand is the total desired demand, just as a 'microeconomic' demand curve represents the desired demand for a particular good at any price level. The AD curve will be downward-sloping because at higher prices total quantities demanded will be less.

Keynes argued that a national economy will reach equilibrium where the aggregate demand curve and aggregate supply curve intersect.

The actual level of national income will be at the intersection of the AD curve and AS curves, ie at Y in Figure 1. The difference between the equilibrium national income Y and the full employment national income Y_F shows how much national income could be increased with the resources at the economy's disposal. This gap between actual equilibrium national income and full employment national income (the level of national income at which the entire labour force would be employed) is called a deflationary gap. Price levels will be P. So Y represents the level of satisfied demand in the economy.

You should note that the aggregate demand function assumes constant prices.

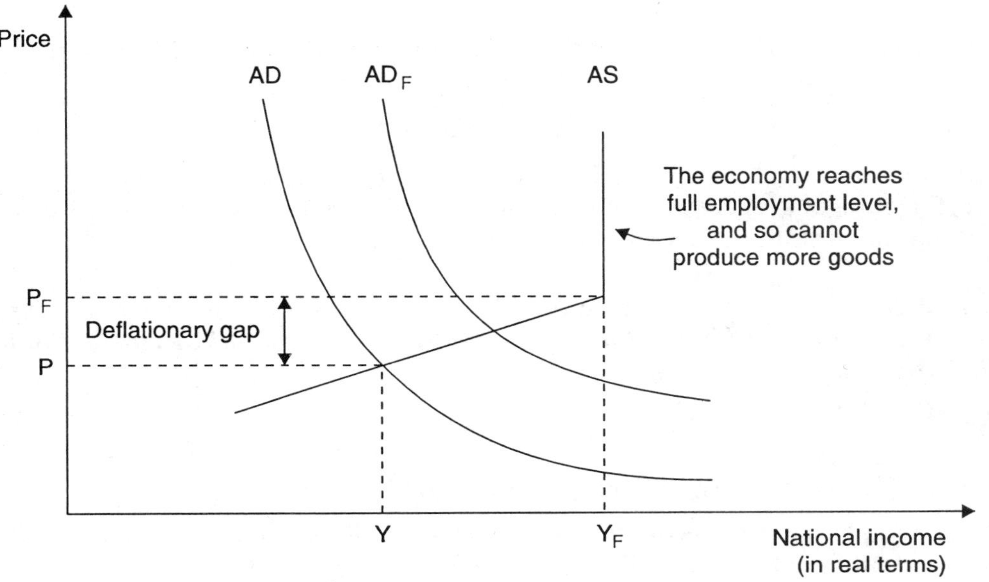

Figure 1 Equilibrium national income, using aggregate supply and aggregate demand analysis

Activity 1

What happens if equilibrium national income is *above* full employment national income? Sketch the outcome, basing your diagram on Figure 1 above. What can you deduce about price levels in this scenario?

1.3 Shifts in the AD curve

As with demand and supply analysis in microeconomics, we can predict in macroeconomics that equilibrium national income can be increased by:

(a) shifting the AD curve to the right; or

(b) shifting the AS curve to the right;

ie, expanding either AD or AS in the economy. As suggested already, Keynesian economists concentrate on shifts in AD.

The Keynesian economic argument is that if a country's economy is going to move from one equilibrium to a different equilibrium, there needs to be a shift in the aggregate demand curve. To achieve equilibrium at the full employment level of national income, it may therefore be necessary to shift the AD curve to the right (upward) or the left (downwards).

Activity 2

Go back to the sketch you prepared in Activity 1. Show the effect of moving the demand curve so that it intersects the supply curve at the point where the latter becomes vertical.

1.4 Deflationary and inflationary gaps

In a situation *where there is unemployment of resources* there is said to be a *deflationary gap* (Figure 1). Prices are fairly constant and real output changes as aggregate demand varies. A deflationary gap can be described as:

the extent to which the aggregate demand function will have to shift upward to produce the full-employment level of national income.

***Lipsey:* An Introduction to Positive Economics**

In a situation where resources are fully employed, there is said to be an inflationary gap, for changes in aggregate demand will cause price changes and not variations in real output. An inflationary gap can be described as:

the extent to which the aggregate demand function would have to shift downward to produce the full employment level of national income without inflation ....

Lipsey

1.5 The ideal equilibrium national income

If one aim of a country's economic policy is full employment, the ideal equilibrium level of national income will be where AD and AS are in balance at the full employment level of national income, without any inflationary gap. This is where aggregate demand at current price levels is exactly enough to encourage firms to produce at an output capacity at which the country's resources are fully employed. This is shown in Figure 2, where equilibrium output will be Y (full employment level) and price levels P.

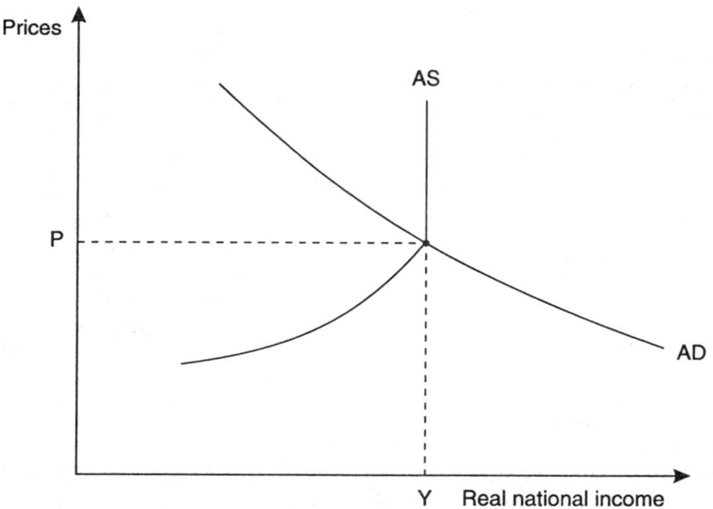

Figure 2

1.6 Demand management

For Keynesian analysis to have practical value for the management of a national economy, it is necessary to establish how aggregate demand can be shifted.

To understand shifts in AD, we need to turn our attention to expenditure in the economy. *Satisfied* aggregate demand is the actual level of national income, and one way of expressing national income is as the total expenditure in the economy.

A formula for the GNP (= total national expenditure) which was described in the previous chapter is:

$$E = C + I + G + (X - M)$$

Definition

Demand management is an approach to economic policy making, which tries to control the level of aggregate demand through fiscal and/or monetary policy.

Demand management involves the manipulation of E (eg achieving economic growth) by influencing C, I, G or net exports.

If we ignore capital consumption, we can equate E (GNP) with national income. This is what we shall do in our analysis of the Keynesian model.

1.7 Withdrawals and injections into the circular flow of income

For a national economy, there are certain withdrawals from and injections into this circular flow of income. Withdrawals divert funds out of the circular flow and injections add funds into it.

Activity 3

Think back to the previous chapter. What were the three categories of withdrawals and injections identified there?

Keynes argued that for an equilibrium to be reached in the national income, not only must AD = AS, but also total *planned* withdrawals from the circular flow of funds must be equal to total *planned* injections. In other words, for equilibrium:

W = J and so M + T + S = X + G + I.

In the long term, W will always equal J.

(a) The difference between the value of imports M and the value of exports X is the *balance of payments deficit*. Even in the short term, this difference must be balanced by borrowing or lending abroad, as we shall see in a later chapter.

(b) The difference between government spending and taxation can only be made up by government borrowing. Loans are eventually repaid.

(c) In the long run, savings will also equal investments, even though the people who save and the firms who invest are not the same. We shall look more closely at savings and investment later.

However, although W and J will be equal retrospectively and in the long run, it does not follow that *planned* J and *planned* W will equal each other *in the short run*, since injections and withdrawals are made by different people.

It is precisely this frustration of plans in the short run that causes national income to change with time. The imbalance between J and W creates factors which can make the level of national income change. Keynes argued that the imbalance between planned withdrawals and planned injections explained *trade cycles*, ie booms and slumps in the economy which prevent it from settling down at an equilibrium level.

2 CONSUMPTION, SAVINGS AND INVESTMENT

2.1 Consumption and savings (C and S)

Let us now go into a bit more detail of Keynesian analysis, and concentrate particularly on consumption, savings and investment. To simplify our analysis, we shall ignore government spending, taxation, imports and exports for the time being. By ignoring imports and exports, we are concentrating on a *closed economy*, ie a national economy which is not in any way dependent on foreign trade.

If we ignore G, T, X, and M, we can look at a circular flow of income in which households divide all their income between two uses:

(a) consumption on goods and service; or

(b) saving.

Provided that national income is in equilibrium, we will have:

Y = C + S (ie Y is the same as C + S)

where Y = national income, C = consumption and S = saving

This should seem logical to you. Income can only be spent or saved. Since we have a closed economy, consumption must be of goods produced by the economy itself.

2.2 Savings

What people do not spend out of their income, they will save.

Definition

Savings are the part of income that is not spent on current consumption

There are two ways of saving. One is to hold the income as money (banknotes and coin, or in a current bank account). The other way is to put money into some form of interest-bearing investment.

In the long run, there is no reason for people to hold banknotes or keep money in a current bank account, unless they intend to spend it fairly soon. If this is so, income that is not spent will be saved and income that is saved will, eventually, be invested.

We can therefore conclude that in *conditions of equilibrium* for national income:

$$
\begin{aligned}
Y &\equiv C + S \text{ and} \\
Y &\equiv C + I \text{ and so} \\
I &\equiv S
\end{aligned}
$$

In the short run, however, savings and investment might not be equal and so there might not be equilibrium.

NOTES

Activity 4

What do you think are the main factors which influence the amount that people will save?

2.3 The propensities to consume and save

In aggregate, the population will spend a certain proportion of total income on consumption. This proportion is known as the *average propensity to consume* (APC).

If there is an increase in total income, some of this extra income will be spent and the rest saved. The proportion of the additional total income spent is called the *marginal propensity to consume* (MPC). The proportion of the increase in income that is saved is the *marginal propensity to save* (MPS).

Since in our analysis (ignoring G, T, X and M) saving and consumption are the only two uses for income, MPC + MPS = 1.

It is often assumed that the marginal propensity to consume and the marginal propensity to save are constant proportions, and that a household will spend (consume):

(a) a fixed amount of money every period (£a);

(b) plus a constant percentage of its income (b% of Y);

Similarly, a *national economy as a whole* will spend a fixed amount (a), plus a constant percentage (b%) of national income Y.

We can then state a *consumption function* as C = a + bY. This can be illustrated diagrammatically (Figure 3 below, in which ΔC represents the increase in consumption arising from an increase of ΔY in the national income).

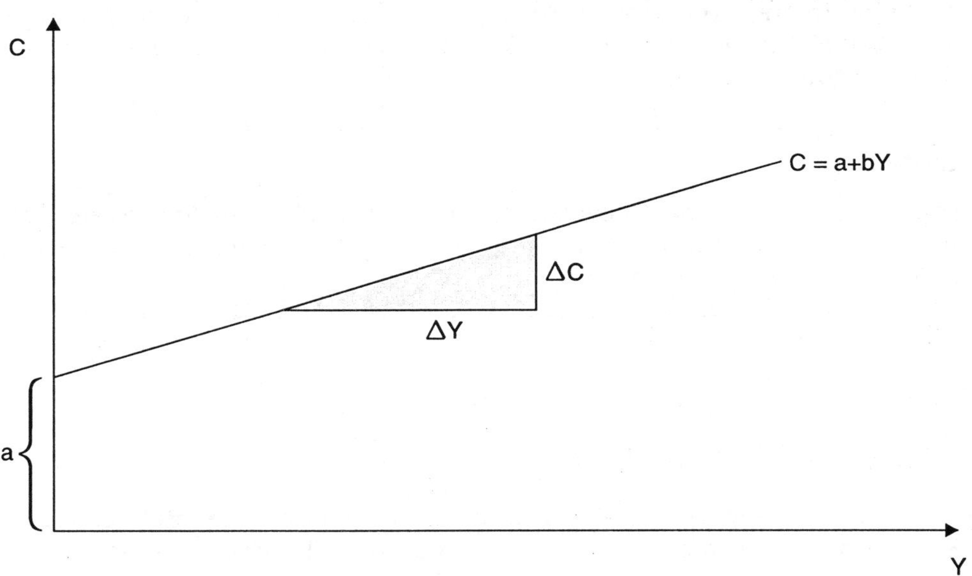

Figure 3 Consumption function and the marginal propensity to consume

Given a consumption function C = a + bY:

(a) the marginal propensity to consume is b, where b is the proportion spent on consumption of each extra £1 earned.

(b) the average propensity to consume will be the ratio of consumption to income, ie:

$$\frac{C}{Y} = \frac{a + bY}{Y}$$

For example, if an individual household has fixed spending of £100 per month, plus extra spending equal to 80% of its monthly income:

(a) when its monthly income is £800, its consumption will be:

£100 + 80% of £800 = £740

(b) when its monthly income is £1,000 its consumption will be:

£100 + 80% of £1,000 = £900.

Activity 5

Calculate this household's average propensity to consume:

(a) when its income is £800; and

(b) when its income is £1,000.

Changes in the marginal propensity to consume and the marginal propensity to save will involve a change of preference by households between current consumption and saving for future benefits. A cause of such a change might be an alteration in interest rates, which makes the investment of savings more, or less, attractive than before.

2.4 Investment (I)

The total volume of desired investment in the economy depends on such factors as the rate of interest on capital, the marginal efficiency of capital invested, expectations about the future, business confidence and the strength of consumer demand for goods.

Activity 6

An open economy, which has a government sector, is in equilibrium. Imports are greater than exports. We can conclude that investment plus government spending is less than savings plus taxation. True or false?

3 THE MULTIPLIER

Keynes wanted to suggest why the volume of national income might change, by how much, and what would be the consequences of such a change. When national income grows, we have economic growth. Since economic growth might be an economic objective of government, the reasons for economic growth will obviously be of crucial importance for the government's economic planners.

The level of national income might increase or decrease for a number of reasons; for example, there might be a pay rise for workers or an increase in the country's exports. Keynes showed that if there is an initial change in expenditure, say an initial increase in exports, or government spending or investment or consumer spending, a new equilibrium national income level will be reached.

The eventual total increase in national income will be greater in size than the initial increase in expenditure.

This is an important point. A small initial increase in expenditure will result in a bigger total increase in national income before equilibrium is re-established.

Definition

The ratio of the total increase in national income to the initial increase in national income is called the *multiplier.*

$$\text{Multiplier} = \frac{\text{Total increase in national income}}{\text{Initial increase in national income}}$$

The multiplier can be defined as a measure of the effect on total national income of a unit change in some component of aggregate demand. In particular, I, G or X, ie investment spending, government spending or exports.

3.1 Numerical illustration of the multiplier

A numerical illustration of the multiplier might help to explain it more clearly. In this example, we shall again ignore taxes, government spending, exports and imports, and assume a simple closed economy in which all income is either spent on consumption (C) or saved (S). Let us suppose that in this closed economy, marginal propensity to consume (MPC) is 90% or 0.9, ie out of any addition to household income 90% is consumed and 10% saved.

(a) If income goes up by £200, £180 would be spent on consumption, and £20 saved.

(b) The £180 spent on consumption increases the income of other people, who spend 90% (£162) and save £18.

(c) The £162 spent on consumption in turn becomes additional income to others, so that a snowball effect on consumption (and income and output) occurs, as follows:

		Increase in expenditure	*Increase in savings (withdrawals)*
		£	£
Stage 1	Income rises	200.00	–
2	90% is consumed	180.00	20.00
3	A further 90% is consumed	162.00	18.00
4	"	145.80	16.20
5	"	131.22	14.58
	etc...		
Total increase in income		2,000.00	200.00

In this example, an initial increase in income of £200 results in a final increase in national income of £2,000. The multiplier is 10.

This multiplier is the reciprocal of the marginal propensity to save. Since MPC = 0.9, MPS = 0.1.

$$\text{Multiplier} = \frac{1}{\text{MPS}}$$

$$\text{Increase in national income} = \frac{\text{Initial increase in expenditure}}{\text{MPS}} = \frac{£200}{0.1} = £2{,}000$$

NOTES

Notice that at the new equilibrium, savings of £200 equal the initial increase in expenditure of £200 but national income has risen £2,000.

If the marginal propensity to consume were 80%, the marginal propensity to save would be 20% and the multiplier would only be 5. Because people save more of their extra income, the total increase in national income through extra consumption will be less.

The multiplier in a national economy works in the same way. An *initial* increase in expenditure will have a snowball effect, leading to further and further expenditures in the economy.

A downward multiplier, or de-multiplier effect also exists. A reduction in investment will have repercussions throughout the economy, so that a small disinvestment (reduction in expenditure/output) will result in a multiplied reduction in national income.

Activity 7

Up to now we have simplified our analysis of the multiplier by, among other things, ignoring leakages from the circular flow (eg taxes, spending on imports). If we take such leakages into account, would you expect the effect of the multiplier to increase or decrease?

3.2 The importance of the multiplier

The importance of the multiplier is that an increase in one of the components of aggregate demand will increase national income by more than the initial increase itself. So if the government takes any action to increase expenditure (eg by raising government current expenditure, or lowering interest rates to raise investment) it will set off a general expansionary process, and the eventual rise in national income will exceed the initial increase in aggregate demand.

This can have important implications for a government when it is planning for growth in national income. By an initial increase in expenditure, a government can engineer an even greater increase in national income (provided that the country's industries can increase their output capacity), depending on the size of the multiplier.

The size of the multiplier depends on:

(a) the marginal propensity to save (MPS);

(b) the marginal propensity to import. Imports reduce national income and if households spend much of their extra income on imports, the snowball increase in total national income will be restricted. This is because imports are a withdrawal out of the circular flow of income. One of the reasons for a low multiplier in the UK is the high marginal propensity to import that exists in the UK; and

(c) tax rates – because taxes reduce the ability of people to consume and so are likely to affect the marginal propensity to consume and the marginal propensity to save.

Chapter roundup

- To achieve full employment national income, it might be possible for a government to take measures to boost aggregate demand in the economy, although some price inflation will probably result.
- When there is inflation in the economy, measures should be taken to suppress aggregate demand.
- A consumption function can be expressed as a + bY, where a is a fixed minimum amount of consumption spending and b is the marginal propensity to consume, so that total consumption varies with national income (Y).
- Changes in national income begin with a small change in expenditure, leading to an even larger eventual change in national income, due to the multiplier effect.

Quick quiz

1 Draw a diagram to show aggregate demand and aggregate supply in a national economy, and the equilibrium national income and general price level:
   (a) when equilibrium national income is below the full employment national income level;
   (b) when equilibrium national income is at the full employment national income level, but there is an inflationary gap.

2 What is a deflationary gap?

3 What is an inflationary gap?

4 For an equilibrium national income level to be reached, withdrawals from and injections into the circular flow of income must be equal. Why are they not always in balance?

5 What are the marginal propensity to consume and the marginal propensity to save?

6 What factors influence the amount of consumption?

Answers to Activities

1

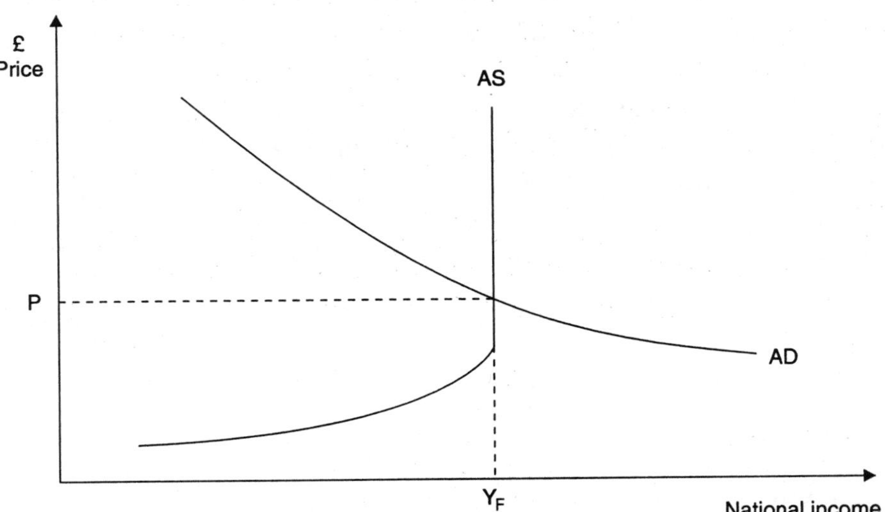

To begin with, the economy will be fully employed, but prices will be higher than they need be (P). There will be inflationary pressures in the economy.

NOTES

2

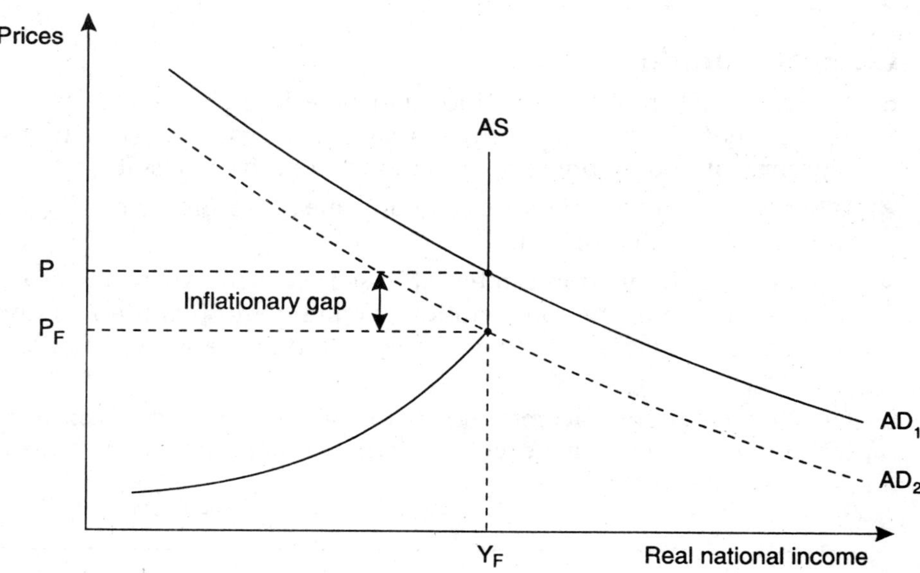

3 (a) *Withdrawals* (W) from the circular flow of income consist of imports (M), taxation (T) and savings (S).

(b) *Injections* (J) into the circular flow of income consist of exports (X), government spending (G), and investment spending by firms (I).

4 The amount that people save will depend on:

(a) how much income they are getting, and how much of this they want to spend on consumption;

(b) how much income they want to save in case they need it in the future;

(c) interest rates. If the interest rate goes up we would expect people to consume less of their income, and to be willing to save and invest more.

5 (a) $\text{APC} = \dfrac{740}{800} = 92.5\%$

(b) $\text{APC} = \dfrac{900}{1{,}000} = 90\%$

6 False. In equilibrium, withdrawals equal injections, ie I + G + X = S + T + M. Since imports M exceed exports X, it follows that I + G must be *greater* than S + T.

7 The effect of the multiplier would decrease. The reasons for this are described in the next few paragraphs of the text on page 198.

Further question practice

Now try the following practice questions at the end of this text.

Multiple choice questions **132–143**

Exam style question **13**

Chapter 13

UNEMPLOYMENT AND INFLATION

Introduction

One of the problems that a national economy might face is a high level of unemployment. High unemployment means that there is a large amount of wasted labour resource, and governments will often try to reduce unemployment to an 'acceptable' level. Another macroeconomic problem is inflation. We discuss these two topics, and the possibility of a 'trade-off' between unemployment and inflation, in this chapter.

Your objectives

After completing this chapter you should:

(a) be aware of some of the main categories of unemployment and their causes;

(b) understand the relationship between unemployment and inflation;

(c) be aware of the main explanations of why inflation occurs;

(d) be aware of the arguments for and against prices and incomes policies.

1 UNEMPLOYMENT

To understand why unemployment arises, and in order to suggest remedies, it is important to distinguish between a number of different categories of unemployment.

(a) *Frictional unemployment.* It is inevitable that some unemployment is caused not so much because there are not enough jobs to go round, but because of the *friction* in the labour market, ie the difficulty in quickly matching workers with jobs, caused perhaps by a lack of knowledge about job opportunities. Frictional unemployment occurs where there is a shortage of a given type of worker in one region, but a surplus of the same type in another (eg clerical staff may be plentiful in Wales but in short supply in London). In general, it takes time to match prospective employees with employers, and individuals will be unemployed during the search period for a new job. Frictional unemployment is temporary, lasting for the period of transition from one job to the next.

(b) *Seasonal unemployment.* This occurs in certain industries, eg building, tourism and farming, where the demand for labour varies in seasonal patterns throughout the year.

(c) *Structural unemployment* occurs where long-term changes in the conditions of an industry occur, eg an industry may decline, leaving many workers redundant and reluctant to move to a new industry (labour immobility). The feature of structural unemployment is high regional unemployment in the location of the industry affected.

(d) *Technological unemployment.* This is a form of structural unemployment, which occurs when new technologies are introduced.

With automation, employment levels in an industry can fall sharply, even when the industry's total output is increasing.

(e) *Cyclical unemployment.* It has been the experience of the past that domestic and foreign trade go through cycles of boom, decline, recession, recovery, then boom again, and so on.

Cyclical unemployment can be long term, and a government might try to reduce it by doing what it can to minimise a recession or to encourage faster economic growth.

Seasonal employment and frictional unemployment will be short term. Structural unemployment, technological unemployment, and cyclical unemployment are all longer term, and more serious.

1.1 Government policies to influence employment

Governments are anxious to influence unemployment levels for a number of reasons. Unemployment is a waste of economic resources, and it leads to individual hardship. Politically, the level of unemployment is seen as a key indicator of a government's success or failure.

A government's policies to influence employment will probably be aimed either at reducing the total number of unemployed people to an acceptable level, or at creating more jobs. Job creation and reducing unemployment should often mean the same thing.

(a) It is possible to create more jobs without reducing unemployment. This can happen when there is a greater number of people entering the jobs market (school leavers etc) than there are new jobs being created. For example, if 500,000 new jobs are created during the course of one year, but 750,000 extra school leavers are looking for jobs, there will be an increase in unemployment of 250,000, even though 500,000 new jobs have been created.

(b) It is also possible to reduce the official unemployment figures without creating jobs. For example, in the UK, individuals who enrol for one of the government-financed job training schemes is taken off the unemployment register, even though he or she does not have a full-time job.

A government can try to create jobs or reduce unemployment by:

(a) spending more money directly on jobs, ie hiring more civil servants;

(b) encouraging growth in the private sector of the economy. When aggregate demand is growing, firms will probably want to increase output to meet demand, and so will hire more labour;

(c) encouraging training on job skills. There might be a high level of unemployment among unskilled workers, and at the same time a shortage of skilled workers. A government can help to finance training schemes, in order to provide a pool of workers who have the skills that firms need and will pay for.

Activity 1

Match the terms (a), (b) and (c) below with the definitions A, B and C.

(a) Structural unemployment.

(b) Cyclical unemployment.

(c) Frictional unemployment.

A Unemployment arising from a difficulty in matching unemployed workers with available jobs.

B Unemployment occurring in the downswing of an economy in between two booms.

C Unemployment arising from a long-term decline in a particular industry.

2 THE PHILLIPS CURVE

2.1 Unemployment and inflation

The problems of unemployment and inflation have been very severe for many countries over recent years.

It has been found from experience that:

(a) full employment cannot be achieved without some price inflation, and to increase the level of employment might cause a higher rate of inflation;

(b) growth in unemployment might sometimes be associated with a rising rate of inflation.

2.2 Inflationary gaps and deflationary gaps

As we saw in Chapter 12 on the Keynesian model, one method of showing equilibrium national income was by means of:

(a) an aggregate demand curve (AD), where AD is the total demand for all goods in the economy, at different price levels; and

(b) an aggregate supply curve (AS) where AS is the total supply of all goods in the economy, at different price levels.

The ideas of a deflationary gap and an inflationary gap were also described in Chapter 12. According to Keynes, demand management by the government could be based on government spending:

(a) to eliminate a deflationary gap and create full employment;

(b) to eliminate an inflationary gap, to take inflation out of the economy.

Activity 2

According to the Keynesian analysis, how could each of these aims be achieved?

A significant point to note from the Keynesian analysis is that when there is unemployment (a deflationary gap), Keynesians accept that reductions in unemployment can only be achieved if prices are allowed to rise. That is to say, reducing unemployment goes hand in hand with allowing some inflation.

2.3 Relationship between unemployment and inflation: the Phillips curve

A W Phillips discovered (1958) a statistical relationship between unemployment and the rate of money wage inflation which implied that, in general, the rate of inflation fell as unemployment rose and vice versa.

Definition

A *Phillips curve* shows a relationship between the level of unemployment and inflation in prices or wages.

A Phillips curve can be drawn linking inflation and unemployment (Figure 1).

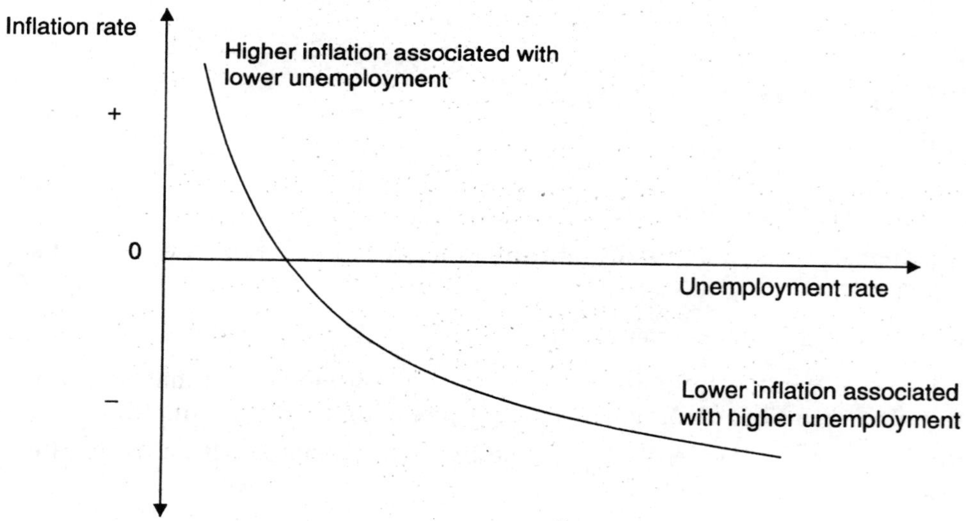

Figure 1 Phillips curve

Two points should be noticed about the Phillips curve.

(a) The curve crosses the horizontal axis at a positive value for the unemployment rate. This means that zero inflation will be associated with some unemployment; it is not possible to achieve zero inflation and zero unemployment at the same time.

(b) The shape of the curve means that the lower the level of unemployment, the higher the rate of increase in inflation.

However, the Phillips curve relationship between inflation and unemployment broke down at the end of the 1960s when Britain began to experience rising inflation at the same time as rising unemployment. In other words, the new curve seemed to be upward sloping.

2.4 Inflationary expectations: refinements to the Phillips curve

An explanation of rising inflation rates combined with rising unemployment was put forward, based on inflationary expectations. This natural rate hypothesis is supported by monetarist economists.

Inflationary expectations are the rates of inflation that are expected in the future. The inflationary expectations of the workforce will be reflected in the level of wage rises that is demanded in the annual round of pay negotiations between employers and workers.

(a) If the workforce expects inflation next year to be 3%, they will demand a 3% wage increase in order to maintain the real value of their wages.

(b) If we now accept that any increase in wages will result in price inflation (which is the monetarist argument), then a 3% pay rise to cover expected inflation will result in an actual rate of inflation of 3%.

(c) The workforce might also try to achieve some increase in the real value of wages. If inflation next year is expected to be 3%, the workforce might demand a pay rise of, say, 4%. According to monetarist economists, a pay rise of 4% would simply mean inflation of 4%. If workers wish to achieve a 1% increase in real wages each year, then during each successive period the rate of inflation will begin to accelerate from 5% to 6% to 7% and so on, and the real increases in wages will not happen.

(d) To compound the problem of inflation still further, it is argued that if mistakes are made over expectations, then money wages will be adjusted upwards next period in order to rectify the mistake made in the last period.

The example used here is simplified because expectations change and adapt and there are both economic and statutory limits to changes in prices and wages. However, many economists believe that events in the UK from about 1967 well into the 1970s followed a sequence of events not unlike that described above.

Activity 3

Which of the following conclusions is supported by the Phillips curve?

(a) Higher inflation causes unemployment.

(b) Higher unemployment causes inflation.

(c) Full employment and low inflation cannot be achieved together.

2.5 The natural rate hypothesis

The natural rate hypothesis incorporates these views on inflationary expectations, to produce a refinement of the Phillips curve.

Suppose that the economy is represented by the Phillips curve PC_1 in Figure 2. Initially, say, that is at an unemployment rate of 5%, with zero price and wage inflation.

NOTES

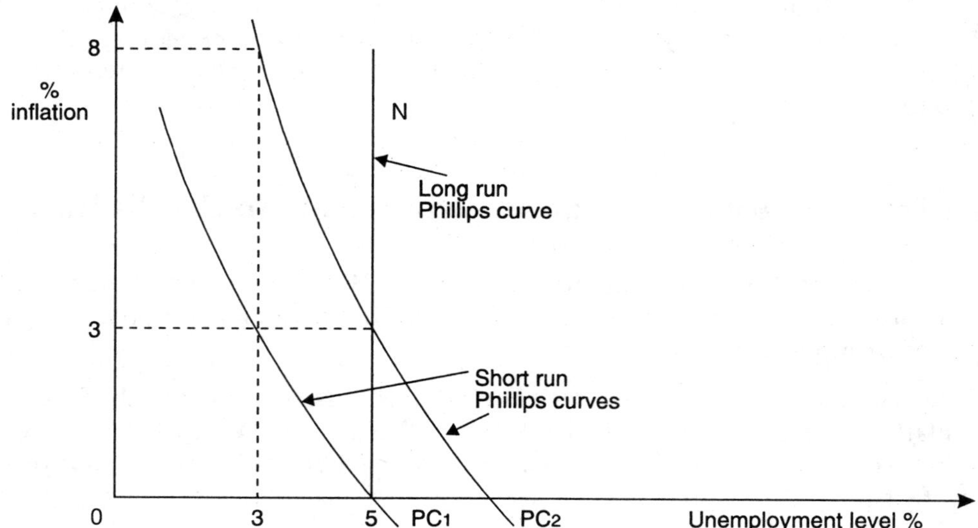

Figure 2 Natural rate hypothesis

(a) Suppose now that the government expands aggregate demand so as to reduce unemployment to 3% of the labour force. There is a movement along the Phillips curve, and the new unemployment level turns out to be associated with 3% inflation.

(b) As employers realise that they are paying higher wages as well as receiving higher prices, and as workers realise that the real value of their wages has not risen, the unemployment rate rises to 5% again.

(c) But in the meantime, the period of positive inflation has generated inflationary expectations and 5% unemployment is now associated with 3% inflation, because the Phillips curve has shifted from PC_1 to PC_2.

In effect, the *short-run* Phillips curve has shifted outwards from PC_1 to PC_2 in Figure 2.

Monetarist economists state that the *long-run* Phillips curve is vertical at the *natural rate of unemployment*. In our example, monetarists would claim that the long-run Phillips curve is N in Figure 2, so that there is a natural unemployment rate of 5% (but note that this figure of 5% is simply being used as an example here).

In the long run, unemployment will revert towards its natural level. The rate of inflation, however, will be determined by the short-run Phillips curve, which will shift upwards as inflationary expectations increase. The distinction between short- and long-run Phillips curves can help explain why in Britain unemployment and inflation have often both risen at the same time.

Monetarist economists argue that:

(a) the only way to reduce the rate of inflation is to get inflationary expectations out of the system. In doing so, excessive demands for wage rises should be resisted by employers;

(b) a firm approach to reducing the rate of inflation could mean having to accept high levels of unemployment for a while;

(c) attempts to get the unemployment level below its natural rate (whatever this is) will only result in higher inflation in the long run.

Activity 4

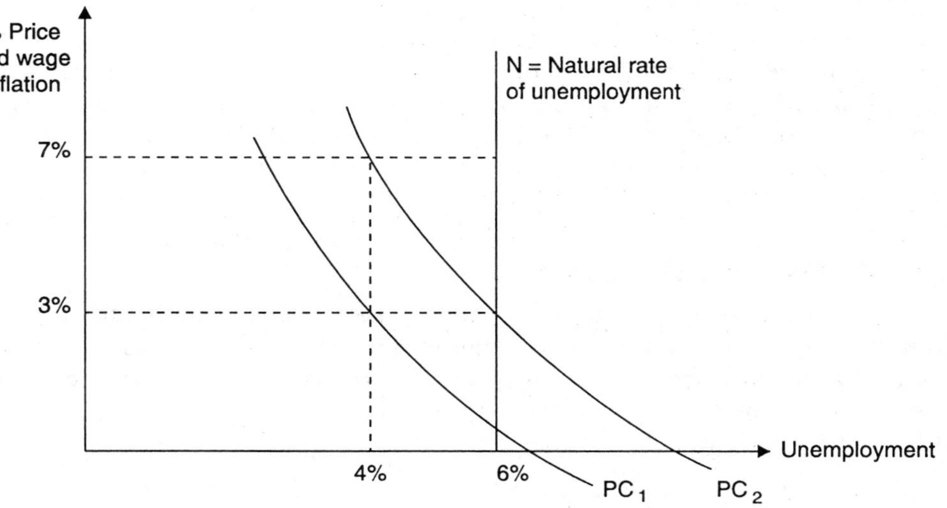

In the diagram above, the vertical line N represents the long-run Phillips curve for an economy. The short-run Phillips curve is initially PC_1, the rate of inflation is 0% p.a. and unemployment is a little over 6% of the working population.

The government takes measures to reduce the rate of unemployment to 4%. According to monetarist economists, what will the rate of inflation and unemployment become?

3 INFLATION AND ITS CONSEQUENCES

Definition

Inflation is a sustained rise in the general level of prices.

Inflation has a number of undesirable consequences.

(a) *Redistribution of income and wealth.* Inflation leads to a redistribution of income and wealth in ways which may be undesirable. Redistribution of wealth might take place from creditors to debtors. This is because debts lose real value with inflation. For example, if you owed £1,000, and prices then doubled, you would still owe £1,000, but the real value of your debt would have been halved.

    In general, in times of inflation those with economic power tend to gain at the expense of the weak, particularly those on fixed incomes.

(b) *Balance of payments effects.* If a country has a higher rate of inflation than its major trading partners, its exports will become relatively expensive and imports relatively cheap. As a result, the balance of trade will suffer, affecting employment in exporting industries and in industries producing import-substitutes.

(c) *Uncertainty of the value of money and prices.* If the rate of inflation is forecast inaccurately, no one really knows the true rate of inflation. As a result, no one has certain knowledge of the value of money or of the real meaning of prices.

(d) *Resource costs of changing prices.* A fourth reason to aim for stable prices is the resource cost of frequently changing prices. In times of high inflation substantial labour time is spent on planning and implementing price changes. Customers may also have to spend more time making price comparisons if they want to buy from the lowest cost source. The term 'menu costs' is sometimes applied to the costs of revising prices; the term refers to the costs of changing prices on restaurant menus.

(e) If price rises include rises in the rate of interest, people will hold less of their wealth in the form of cash, and more in the form of interest-bearing assets. Cash holdings will need to be topped up more regularly, and this too causes a financial cost (sometimes referred to as a 'shoe-leather cost', the image being that of people wearing out their shoes with frequent trips to the bank).

3.1 Measuring inflation

In order to measure changes in the real value of money as a single figure, we need to group all goods and services into a single price index. This process is subject to statistical error and misrepresentation. However, the government measures changes in the prices of a number of groups of goods and services and publishes a number of different price indices.

3.2 The retail prices index (RPI)

The most important measure of the general rate of inflation in the UK is the retail prices index (RPI).

There are also other government-produced price indices for the prices of more specific items and commodities, such as wholesale prices indices and capital goods prices indices, which we shall not consider in detail here.

The RPI measures the percentage changes month by month in the average level of prices of the commodities and services, including housing costs, purchased by the great majority of households in the UK. These include practically all wage earners and most small and medium salary earners. The weights used for combining the indices for the various groups (of commodities) are revised annually on the basis of information from the Family Expenditure Survey for the year ended in the previous June.

The items of expenditure within the RPI are intended to be a representative list of items, current prices for which are collected at regular intervals.

3.3 Underlying inflation

There are drawbacks in using the RPI as an indicator of inflationary pressures in the economy. The RPI includes households' mortgage costs and the local authority tax known as the Council Tax (previously the community charge or poll tax). This makes it difficult to make comparisons with inflation statistics of other countries which exclude these elements.

A further problem is that mortgage costs depend on interest rates. In the UK in recent years, the government has adopted a policy of raising market rates of interest in order to reduce consumer demand and damp down inflation. Yet such a policy has an effect on mortgage costs which moves the RPI in the opposite direction from the one intended. When interest rates are then brought down again, any fall in RPI is more rapid than it would be if mortgage costs were excluded from the inflation measure. It is also worth noting that the UK has a higher level of home ownership than many other countries, making the effect of mortgage rate movements on price indices much greater than in those countries.

High interest rates, therefore, work rather like a medicine whose use, in the short term at least, makes worse the symptoms of the disease which it is supposed to cure.

In the longer term, the disease may be made better, but stopping the medicine (lowering the interest rates) will make the recovery from the disease (the lowering of inflation) appear to happen more quickly than it really is.

The term 'underlying rate of inflation' is usually used to refer to the RPI adjusted to exclude mortgage costs, and sometimes other elements as well (such as the Council Tax). The effects of the interest rate changes noted above help to make the RPI fluctuate more widely than the underlying rate of inflation. Because of the distorting effects of mortgage interest rates on the RPI, the underlying rate of inflation could be called a better barometer of the inflationary pressures present in the economy.

EXAMPLE: RPI AS A MEASURE OF INFLATION

Quoted rates of inflation are usually annual rates, calculated as the percentage change in the index concerned during the twelve months up to the date quoted. Suppose that the RPI on 1 January was 330 and on 31 December was 348.

(a) The decline in real terms of £100 in banknotes during the year would be:

$$\left(\frac{348-330}{330}\right) \times 100\% = 5.45\%$$

In other words, the decline in the buying power or 'purchasing power' of money would be 5.45% over the course of the year.

(b) The amount of money needed on 31 December to maintain spending power as at 1 January would be:

$$\frac{348}{330} \times £100 = £105.45$$

The general rate of inflation during the year was about 5½% (precisely, 5.45%).

3.4 The causes of inflation

The causes of inflation are complex, because there will be several factors operating simultaneously, each having some effect on price levels.

The causes of inflation might be:

(a) demand pull factors;

(b) cost push factors;

(c) expectations;

(d) growth in the money supply.

Definition

Demand pull inflation occurs when the economy is buoyant and there is a high aggregate demand, which is in excess of the economy's ability to supply.

(a) Because aggregate demand exceeds supply, prices rise.

(b) Since supply needs to be raised to meet the higher demand, there will be an increase in demand for factors of production, and so factor rewards (wages, interest rates, and so on) will also rise.

(c) Since aggregate demand exceeds the output capability of the economy, it should follow that demand-pull inflation can only exist when unemployment is low. A feature of inflation in the UK in the 1970s and early 1980s, however, was high inflation coupled with high unemployment.

Traditionally, Keynesian economists saw inflation as being caused by demand-pull factors. However, they now accept that cost-push factors are involved as well.

Definition

Cost-push inflation occurs where the costs of factors of production rise regardless of whether or not they are in short supply. This appears to be particularly the case with wages: workers anticipate inflation rates and demand wage increases to compensate, so starting a wage-price spiral. Interest rate rises can also add to the rate of inflation, because mortgage costs will rise.

A further problem is that once the rate of inflation has begun to increase, a serious danger of expectational inflation will occur.

The monetarists argue that inflation is caused by *increases in the supply of money*. There is a considerable debate as to whether increases in the money supply are a *cause* of inflation or a *symptom* of inflation. The monetarists argue that since inflation is caused by an increase in the money supply, it can be brought under control by reducing the rate of growth of the money supply.

Activity 5

(a) A government can help to counter demand-pull inflation by reducing interest rates. True or false?

(b) A government can help to counter demand-pull inflation by increasing value added tax. True or false?

(c) A government can help to counter cost-push inflation by increasing income tax rates. True or false?

(d) A government can help to counter cost-push inflation by linking wage increases to productivity improvements. True or false?

3.5 High interest rates and inflation

A government may adopt a policy of high interest rates as a means of trying to reduce the rate of inflation, when inflation is being caused by a boom in consumer demand. This means when demand rises faster than the ability of industry to increase its output to meet the demand.

If interest rates are high enough, there should eventually be a reduction in the rate of growth in consumer spending. This reduction should occur because:

(a) people who borrow must pay more in interest out of their income. This will leave them less income, after paying the interest, to spend on other things;

(b) high interest rates might put people off borrowing, and so there would be less spending with borrowed funds;

(c) high interest rates should encourage more saving, so that people spend less of their income on consumption;

(d) high interest rates will tend to depress the values of non-monetary assets, such as houses. The reduction in people's perceived wealth may make them feel poorer and consequently reduce the amounts they spend on consumer goods.

NOTES

4 PRICES AND INCOMES POLICY

The first prices and incomes policy was introduced in Britain in 1962, by the then Prime Minister, Harold Macmillan. There were several attempts to find a successful policy after then, the last being the 'social contract' under the Labour government of James Callaghan.

Definition

Prices and incomes policy means a policy which aims to restrain both prices and incomes.

4.1 The need for co-ordinated prices and incomes controls

If prices but not wages are controlled the results would be a profit squeeze and/or a rise in unemployment, with firms shedding labour in order to remain profitable.

This suggests that wages ought be kept under control as well as prices. This would be particularly important if wage rises are a major cause of cost-push inflation.

The structure of a prices and incomes policy can take various forms, but it is usually possible to make a clear distinction between types of incomes control and types of price control.

4.2 Incomes/wages controls

The broad types of wage controls which could be attempted by a government are:

(a) *statutory restrictions* on the amount of wage increases allowed;

(b) government *wage policy guidelines*, which it is hoped that wage negotiators will stick to voluntarily;

(c) a *social contract* between the government and trade unions in which the unions accept a voluntary restraint on wage increases in return for other favours from the government.

Statutory controls are more direct and, if enforceable, more likely to work effectively. *Voluntary* controls depend on the willingness of trade unions and individual workers to accept the controls. A social contract, if agreed, is likely to be more morally binding on them than wage policy guidelines.

4.3 Problems with wage controls

Problems with wage controls include:

(a) non-comparable wages between work groups. Some groups are likely to feel cheated;

(b) reduction of pay differentials;

(c) rewarding productivity improvements. Improved productivity should be encouraged, but wage controls might prevent this;

(d) evading the controls;

(e) trade union resistance.

4.4 Price controls

A policy of controlling wages cannot work unless prices are controlled as well, because workers will not readily accept enforced controls on their earnings when prices are rising more rapidly. In Britain it has always proved to be much easier to control prices than wages. For example, the Price Commission in Britain, until it was disbanded by the Thatcher government in 1980, had some success in reducing and/or delaying price rises.

A policy for controlling prices also has particular problems to overcome.

(a) The government must decide what prices should be controlled. It is administratively impossible to control all prices charged by all firms, especially small firms. Controls must therefore be applied to selected products, companies or markets, in the hope that if these prices are controlled, other prices will also remain in check.

(b) It might be necessary to allow exceptions to the rule, so that certain prices can rise in excess of the government's norms or limits.

(c) Many raw materials, products and services are imported. If the prices of these imported goods go up (eg because of a fall in the value of the domestic currency) firms must be allowed to pass on the increased costs into their prices. Rules for permissible price increases must, therefore, be established.

(d) If price controls are too rigid, the government might face the problem that a black market economy might develop in certain goods, with its prices rising to levels that are far above the government's limits.

(e) There is the enormous practical problem of establishing a policing agency or agencies to monitor, control and approve increases in prices (and this applies equally to controls on incomes).

Chapter roundup

- Demand management is defined as a fiscal policy of the government to influence the economy by altering aggregate demand and so raising or lowering the equilibrium national income level, in order to close an inflationary or deflationary gap. However, there appears to be a connection between the rate of inflation and unemployment. The Phillips curve has been used to show that when there is zero inflation, there will be some unemployment.
- Monetarist economists would argue that a Keynesian government policy to boost demand in the economy is likely to be inflationary and inflation will create more unemployment. They prefer to concentrate on the supply side of the economy – ie pursue policies which will affect supply and the costs of production, rather than policies for influencing demand.
- A conclusion from the link between unemployment and inflation is that if the government wants to reduce unemployment, it must accept a faster rate of inflation in the economy, which will damage prospects of economic growth. On the other hand, by trying to reduce inflation in order to stimulate economic growth and more employment in the longer term, there will have to be some unemployment in the short term.
- Efforts to control inflation might be directed at high taxes or high interest rates to reduce consumer demand, exchange rates to control the cost of imported goods, control of the money supply, or direct controls over price and wage increases.

Quick quiz

1 How may unemployment be categorised?

2 What does a Phillips curve show?

3 What are inflationary expectations?

4 Draw a graph to illustrate the natural rate hypothesis of unemployment and inflation. What are the main conclusions of this hypothesis?

5 What are the undesirable consequences of inflation?

6 What are the possible causes of inflation?

Answers to Activities

1 The pairings are (a) C, (b) B and (c) A.

2 To eliminate a deflationary gap, Keynesians would recommend an increase in government spending which, aided by a multiplier effect, would boost aggregate demand.

To eliminate an inflationary gap, government spending could be reduced.

3 The answer is (c). The Phillips curve expresses an assumed relationship between unemployment and inflation. It is not intended to offer a causal explanation of the link.

4 Initially, unemployment at 4% will mean inflation at 3%. Over time, unemployment will revert to its long-term natural rate of 6%, but now be associated with 3% inflation. In effect, the short-run Phillips curve will shift from PC_1 to PC_2.

5 (a) False. On the contrary, this would increase consumer borrowing and so stimulate demand-pull inflation.

(b) True. This might increase total spending on goods and services inclusive of the tax, but spending *net* of tax will probably fall.

(c) False. Increasing direct taxation will reduce consumers' disposable income, and is therefore a measure aimed at countering demand-pull inflation, not cost-push inflation.

(d) True. This will reduce the unit costs of production.

Case Study 1

The following data refer to the UK economy and are drawn from HMSO Economic Trends. Consider the data and answer the following questions.

Year	*Inflation* (1)	*Unemployment* (2)	*Growth of money supply* (3)
1980	21.0	4.4	9.1
1981	11.3	7.7	5.6
1982	9.2	9.3	–0.6
1983	3.7	10.4	5.9
1984	5.1	10.6	5.5
1985	7.0	10.9	5.2
1986	2.5	11.1	3.4
1987	4.2	10.5	4.3
1988	4.6	8.4	7.1
1989	8.3	6.5	5.4
1990	9.8	5.6	6.3
1991	5.8	7.7	1.9
1992	3.9	9.6	1.3

(1) = % rise in retail price index over previous year.
(2) = Unemployment as % of total labour force.
(3) = % increase in money supply M0 over previous year.

NOTES

Case Study 1 (continued)

(a) What are the main trends in the rate of inflation and the level of unemployment since 1980?

(b) What is the relationship between changes in the rate of inflation and changes in the money supply?

(c) What is the relationship between changes in the rate of inflation and changes in the level of unemployment.

Answer to Case Study 1

(a) At the beginning of the 1980s, RPI inflation was at very high levels before falling rapidly, during the early 1980s, reducing from 21% per annum in 1980 to 3.7% in 1983. After a rise to 7.0% in 1985, annual inflation fell to a low point of 2.5% in 1986. The inflation rate rose again in the years which followed, with a particularly marked rise between 1988 and 1989, before peaking at 9.8% in 1990 and then falling back to 3.9% by 1992.

The level of unemployment as a percentage of the total labour force rose annually throughout the period from 1980 (4.4%) to 1986 (11.1%). The steepest rise was between 1980 and 1982, when the percentage of the labour force without employment more than doubled from 4.4% to 9.3%. In the years following 1986, unemployment fell to half of its 1986 peak level by 1990 (5.6%). A fairly rapid rise in unemployment followed that, with the level reaching 9.6% by 1992.

The figures show that the inflation rate and the level of unemployment were moving in opposite directions over the period from 1980 to 1992.

(b) The data for growth in the money supply show only the percentage increase in M0, which is a measure of narrow money, consisting mainly of notes and coin in circulation.

It can be seen from the data that the year with the highest inflation – 1980 – was also the year in which monetary growth was greatest, at 9.1%. The two-year period with lowest monetary growth – 1991 to 1992 – was a period in which the inflation rate was falling. However, periods of high monetary growth are not consistently those with rising inflation and low monetary growth is not always matched by falling inflation. For example, in spite of a fall in inflation from 9.2% to 3.7% between 1982 and 1983, the same period showed a rise in M0 growth from –0.6% to 5.9%. To take a second example, the rise in inflation from 4.6% to 8.3% between 1988 and 1989 occurred when money supply growth fell from 7.1% to 5.4%.

The monetarist viewpoint would suggest that changes in the money supply will affect the inflation rate, perhaps with a lag of one or two years. If monetary growth is high, there will be too much money chasing too few goods and prices will rise as a result.

Steep falls in the rate of growth of M0 compared with the previous year occurred in 1982 and in 1991. In each of these cases, there was a fall in the inflation rate in the following years. However, no consistent lagged relationship between M0 growth and inflation can be discerned. In some years, there is a contrary relationship between the two variables: in 1984 and 1989, M0 fell while the rate of inflation rose in the following years in these two cases.

The lack of a consistent relationship between M0 growth and the inflation rate may indicate that M0, as a narrow money measure, is an unsatisfactory measure of monetary growth. It may be that growth of some other measure, such as the broad money aggregate M4, which includes private sector bank balances, produces a closer relationship with the rate of RPI inflation. It should also be remembered that the RPI is not a perfect indicator of inflationary conditions in the whole economy.

This is because it is influenced heavily by changes in mortgage rates, which follow interest rate changes brought about by government policy actions.

(c) As described in part (a) above, the data suggests that there is an inverse relationship between the rate of inflation and the rate of unemployment. Rises in the level of unemployment occurred while the inflation rate was falling, from 1980 to 1983 and from 1990 to 1992. Unemployment fell when the rate of inflation was rising, in the period 1986 to 1990.

This relationship is consistent with the Phillips curve, which is depicted below, supporting a Keynesian demand-side interpretation of the data rather than a monetarist one.

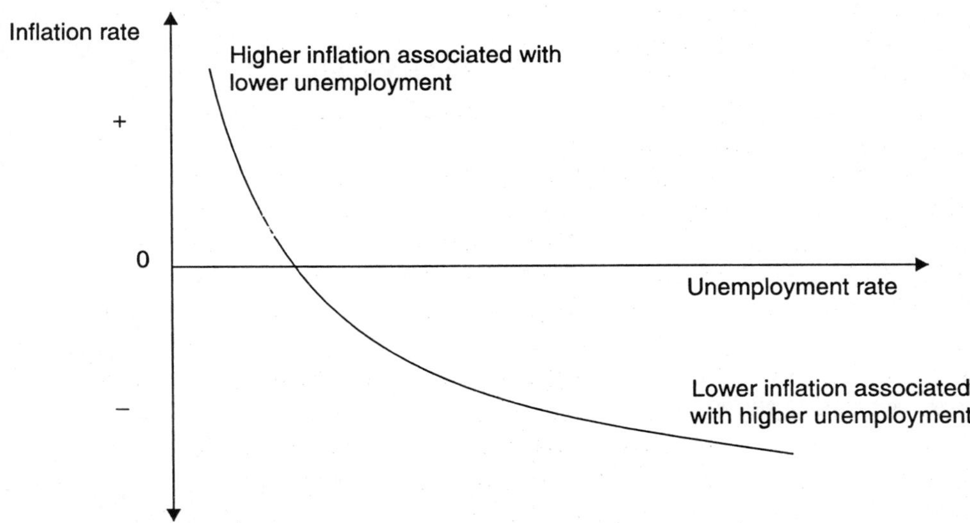

Figure 3

When aggregate monetary demand is rising, there will be an increased demand for labour. Real wages will start to rise, which will tend to increase unit costs and the level of prices. This effect on costs and prices will become particularly significant as the economy reaches its full employment level and unemployment is low.

In conditions where unemployment rises, demand will be falling in factor (labour) markets as well as product markets. Workers will be less able to negotiate increases in real wages, and consequently the rate of increase in unit costs and prices will fall.

Case Study 2

The Bank of England produces a quarterly report which includes a forecast for inflation. The October 1994 report indicated that the prospects for lower inflation in the UK economy had improved in the previous six months.

The report identified three main reasons for expecting that inflation would remain relatively low.

(1) Recent rises in UK interest rates had slowed the growth of consumer spending to a more manageable rate.

(2) Recent inflation figures were less than had been expected by the Bank and it had responded by adopting a lower starting point for its forecasts.

(3) The growth of average earnings was below that expected and therefore the upward pressure on companies' labour costs had been lessened.

Case Study 2 (continued)

The report also noted that, partly due to competitive pressures, companies were not yet passing cost increases on to the consumer in the form of higher prices. Therefore, the current low rate of inflation should continue. However, the report also pointed out that if production costs rose significantly, companies might raise prices and this might produce a rise in the rate of inflation.

A further source of inflation was identified in the report: overseas demand for UK exports was rising strongly. This was the result partly of economic recovery in Europe and the USA, and partly of the fall in the sterling exchange rate over the previous year.

Use the extract to answer the following questions.

(a) What is meant by the term *inflation*; show how it can be measured.

(b) What is meant by *demand pull inflation*?

(c) What is meant by *cost push inflation*?

Answer to Case Study 2

(a) Inflation is defined as a continuing or persistent tendency for the general price level to rise. It is measured through the use of price indices constructed to be representative of the mix of goods/services bought or consumed over the period in question.

The price index used for adjusting national income for the effects of inflation – the GDP deflator – is calculated by weighting the rise in the prices of goods and services according to their relative importance in the economy at the base date. The indices are periodically updated to take account of changes in the structure of the economy.

The retail prices index (RPI), published monthly, is the main official measure of how the average household in the UK has been affected by changes in the prices of goods and services. It includes 600 items and involves 130,000 prices quotations each month. The weights in the RPI are calculated from the spending patterns of 7,000 households representing different income groups (although pensioners and households in the top 4% of incomes are excluded). The main limitation of the RPI is that it takes no account of the effect upon disposable income of direct tax, eg income tax.

The tax and price index (TPI) shows how the purchasing power of income is affected by changes in direct taxes, including national insurance contributions, as well as by changes in retail prices. It covers a range of households in different tax positions and is intended to express what is happening to households in general.

Other price indices include official indices of changes in wholesale prices and of changes in basic commodity prices. At times there may be significant differences in price changes between these different sectors. In 1994, commodity prices were rising and to some extent this was reflected in a rise in the index of wholesale prices. However, as the result of restrained consumer demand, the RPI was rising markedly less. The point was made in the extract that 'partly due to competitive pressures, companies were not yet passing cost increases on to the consumer in the form of higher prices'.

(b) Demand-pull inflation occurs when aggregate demand is persistently rising above aggregate supply at the existing price level. In consequence, the price level will be bid upwards. In Keynesian terms, as the economy approaches full employment further increases in aggregate monetary demand will exert an upward pressure on prices. For a time, supply can continue to increase, although possibly only by the use of more marginal, less efficient resources. At full employment there is no more scope for increasing output, so that any further increase in aggregate demand merely leads to higher prices.

Expectations will be important in fuelling demand-led inflation: if prices are expected to rise noticeably, potential buyers will be keen to anticipate the price and buy now. At times, if necessary, buyers will draw upon their savings to add to their effective purchasing power and this will increase the demand-led inflationary pressure.

Point (1) in the extract states that the (recent) rises in interest rates had slowed the growth of consumer spending. The rises in interest rates had raised the cost of borrowing and, in particular, mortgages.

Point (3), 'the growth of average earnings was below that expected', shows that the rise in mortgage and other borrowing costs was not being offset by increased take-home pay.

In addition, the rise in interest rates further undermined consumer confidence, while tax increases also came into effect. The overall effect was disinflationary: demand-led inflation was virtually non-existent. Against this, 'overseas demand for UK exports was rising strongly'. This served to offset partly the low home demand. For the most part, the effect of rising export demand was not inflationary, thanks to the spare capacity then existing within many UK firms. (Since that time there has been some falling off in the level of UK exports.)

(c) Cost-push inflation comes about when the source of upward pressure on price is rising costs. With labour costs accounting for approximately 70 per cent of total costs in the UK, it is not surprising that wage increases in excess of productivity increases are commonly blamed for being the source of inflation. The widespread practice in the UK of centralised wage bargaining has undoubtedly reinforced the power of labour groups to obtain relatively high wage increases. Yet the effective power of labour groups is constrained by economic conditions: the nearer the economy is to full employment, or the greater the scarcity value of particular categories of workers, the greater the bargaining power of such labour groups.

Other factors may bring about cost pressures. A rise in the price of commodities imported into the UK, resulting from rising world demand, may force up selling prices of manufactured goods within the UK. The increases in world oil prices experienced in the 1970s is a glaring example of the effects of imported inflation. Inflationary cost pressures could also result from rises in the cost of imported capital equipment. Any fall in the value of sterling will raise the price of imports. This will lead to input costs of British manufacturers rising and also to the upward adjustment of selling prices of British-made goods, workers will seek higher wages to offset the increased cost of imported foods, and so on.

The extract relates to cost-push inflation by stating in point (3) that 'the upward pressure on companies' labour costs had been lessened', and that 'partly due to competitive pressures, companies were not yet passing cost increases on to the consumer in the form of higher prices' (implying that with a change to more favourable selling market conditions, those price increase could be expected to take place). 'If production costs rose significantly, companies might raise prices ... .' The fall in the sterling rate over the previous year is also mentioned as a source of inflation. Overall, the prospects for UK inflation are considered to be quite favourable.

Further question practice

Now try the following practice questions at the end of this text.

Multiple choice questions	**144–155**
Exam style question	**14** and **15**

Chapter 14

THE DEMAND FOR AND SUPPLY OF MONEY

Introduction

This chapter deals with some of the main views of monetarism, which we have so far only touched on, as well as discussing Keynesian ideas on the demand for and supply of money.

Your objectives

After completing this chapter you should:

(a) understand the main features of the monetarist view of money supply and demand;

(b) understand the main features of the Keynesian view of money supply and demand;

(c) understand the implications of these views for interest rates and inflation.

NOTES

1 THE QUANTITY THEORY OF MONEY

There are two broad schools of thought about monetary theory which you need to know about, and economists are not in unanimous agreement. The two broadly differing views are:

(a) the *monetarist view*. The monetarist view of money supply and demand, and of the influence of money on interest rates and inflation, comes from the so-called quantity theory of money;

(b) the *Keynesian view*. Keynes developed a theory of the demand for money in the 1920s, known as liquidity preference theory, which challenged the quantity theory of money.

1.1 The quantity theory of money

Monetarist economists stress the significance of the role of money in the workings of the economy, and base their arguments on the old quantity theory of money.

The classical *quantity theory of money* was developed by Irving Fisher in 1911 at a time when Britain was on the gold standard, and the quantity of money therefore changed little. It was the generally accepted view, until the 1930s, about the relationship between the amount of money in the economy and the level of prices. It is a theory about how much money supply is needed to enable the economy to function.

Definition

The *quantity theory* is that money is used only as a medium of exchange, to settle transactions involving the demand and supply for goods and services.

This is quite important to remember. Whereas the quantity theory states that the demand for money is simply for spending on foreseeable transactions (and monetarist economists agree with this view), Keynesian economists argue that there are other reasons for wanting to hold money, as we shall see later.

If the number of transactions in the economy is fixed, and independent of the amount of the money supply, then:

The total money value of transactions will be PT

where P is the price level of goods and services bought and sold; and
T is the number or quantity of transactions.

The amount of money needed to pay for these transactions will depend on the *velocity of circulation*.

Definition

Velocity of circulation is the average frequency with which money is passed between one economic agent and another.

Money changes hands. People receiving money can use it to make their own purchases. For example, if A pays B £2 for transaction X, B can use the £2 to pay C for transaction Y and C can use the same £2 to pay D for transaction Z. If the three transactions X, Y, and Z all occur within a given period of time then the money value of the transactions is:

PT = £2, × 3 transactions = £6.

The total amount of money is the same £2 in circulation for all three transactions but this money has exchanged hands three times. The velocity of circulation is 3 and MV = 6

where M is the money supply; and
V is the velocity of circulation.

This brings us to the identity of the quantity theory of money: $MV \equiv PT$.

MV *must* equal PT because they are two different ways of measuring the same transactions. In practice, the velocity of circulation V is calculated as the balancing figure where:

$$V = \frac{PT}{M}$$

Activity 1

Which of the following definitions correctly describes the velocity of circulation?

(a) The money stock in a given time period divided by the level of prices.

(b) The number of times in a given period that a unit of money is used to purchase final output.

(c) The total value of transactions in a given time period divided by the average price level.

1.2 Conclusion from the quantity theory of money

The identity (or equation) of the quantity theory of money does not really say very much. It is assumed that M is both the quantity of *demand* for money and also the money *supply*.

Definition

Money supply is the amount or stock of money in an economy.

(a) An increase in M would reduce V or increase either P or T.

(b) An increase in V would reduce M or increase either P or T.

(c) An increase in P would reduce T or increase either M or V.

(d) An increase in T would reduce P or increase either M or V.

However, three further assumptions can be made.

(a) V has a roughly constant value. The velocity of circulation of money remains the same at all times, or at least only changes very slowly. There were reasons for making this assumption which we need not go into here. Whether V is constant or not is discussed later.

(b) T is either given or it is independent of the amount of money, M. The reason why T should be a given total was that the supporters of the quantity theory argued that in the economy, full employment of resources is the norm and if all resources are fully utilised the volume of transactions T, must be a constant value.

(c) The amount of M is determined by other factors and is independent of V, T, or (most significantly) P. The money supply could be controlled by government authorities (eg the central bank).

Given these assumptions, the quantity theory of money becomes a theory of price levels because, since MV = PT

$$\text{then } P = \frac{MV}{T}$$

If V and T are roughly constant values, P will vary directly with increases or decreases in the amount of M. It is changes in the money supply M that cause prices P to change, not changes in price that cause changes in the money supply. In other words, inflation would be directly related to the money supply, and a 10% increase in the money supply would result in 10% inflation.

1.3 The money supply and inflation

There is an argument that the link between the money supply and inflation is a misleading one. But before we look at this counter-argument, let us summarise the points made so far.

Important conclusions from the quantity theory of money equation are that:

(a) if the velocity of circulation of money, V, is more or less constant, any growth in the money supply, M, over and above the potential in the economy to increase T, will cause inflation;

(b) if output in the economy, T, is growing and if the velocity of circulation, V, is constant, then a matching growth in the money supply, M, would be needed to avoid deflation (ie falling prices).

A further conclusion from the quantity theory is that government's monetary policy should be to allow some growth in the money supply if the economy is growing, but not to let the growth in the money supply get out of hand.

The extent to which these conclusions are valid depends largely on whether the velocity of circulation of money is roughly constant. For example, if the money supply increases by 10%, and the real growth in the economy – ie the increase in the volume of transactions – is 3%, we could predict that inflation will be about 7% but only if the velocity of circulation is constant.

Activity 2

In one year, the broad money supply in a certain country was $6,500 million. During the course of the year, the money supply increased to $7,000 million. The country's economy did not grow or decline in real terms, so that the volume of transactions was the same as the year before. The velocity of circulation of broad money had fallen from 5.2 in the first year to 4.9 in the second.

What would the rate of price inflation be for the year?

1.4 Is the velocity of circulation constant?

The velocity of circulation can be measured. It is measured in the UK as the ratio of gross national product at current market prices (this is PT) to the average money stock for the quarter (this is M).

The money stock is measured by the various monetary aggregates, eg in the UK, as M0, M2 and M4. There is a different measure of the velocity of circulation for each definition of the money stock.

Measurements of the velocity of the circulation of money in the UK show that V is subject to continual variations up and down. The following table gives some indication of these variations over a six year period.

NOTES

Table 1 Velocity of circulation ratios

Fourth quarter of year	*Money stock*	
	M0	M4
1983	24.2	1.82
1985	25.8	1.64
1987	28.1	1.47
1989	29.7	1.27

(*Source:* Financial Statistics)

Monetarist economists have argued that in spite of short-term fluctuations, the velocity of circulation V is constant in the long term. Keynesian economists disagree, and argue that V is variable so there is no direct connection between the money supply and inflation. In the UK, statistics show that the velocity of circulation for M4 increased during the 1970s, but slowed down during the 1980s and early 1990s.

Even so, it is probably reasonable to suppose that *over a longer period*, V should remain fairly stable.

1.5 Another view of the money supply and inflation

It was mentioned earlier that there is a counter-argument to the view that growth in the money supply causes inflation.

The equation, or identity $MV \equiv PT$ must be correct, but instead of increases in M causing inflation, some economists would argue that it is inflation which happens first, causing the money supply to rise in step. And if the money supply does not increase at once, V will increase instead. The economists who believe in this argument conclude that the authorities should not put so much effort into controlling the money supply, because they will be tackling a symptom of inflation rather than its cause.

In the same way, if the money supply M is increasing, there might be no change in PT, and indeed, it could be V that is decreasing.

1.6 What makes the money supply grow?

We have looked at the demand for, and supply of, money without yet asking what it is that makes the money supply grow in the first place.

If we define money broadly, to include bank deposits, the main factors that contribute to money supply growth are:

(a) government borrowing (the public sector borrowing requirement (PSBR));

(b) who the government borrows from, banks or non-banks;

(c) bank lending; and

(d) flows of money between the country and foreign traders/investors.

The PSBR is usually a positive amount, adding to the growth in the money supply, because in most years, the government has been a net borrower of money. In some periods in the late 1980s, however, the UK government borrowed less than the amount of debt it repaid, so there was a negative PSBR. A negative PSBR has a contractionary effect on the money supply.

NOTES

1.7 Approaches to controlling the growth of the broad money supply

The broad approaches that a government might take to control the growth of the money supply, if this were to be part of its monetary policy, are:

(a) to reduce or control the size of the PSBR;

(b) to finance as much government borrowing as possible by borrowing from the UK non-bank private sector (eg by encouraging National Savings in preference to issuing gilts);

(c) to control the increase in bank lending. There are various ways in which the government can try to do this, some of which were mentioned in Chapter 9;

(d) to control external and foreign currency items – eg by keeping the balance of payments under control.

Activity 3

Jot down what you can remember about controls on bank lending, particularly the use of a fractional reserve system. Refer to Chapter 9 if you cannot remember.

The government can follow a policy of trying to limit the PSBR, perhaps by cutting government expenditures, but possibly also by increasing tax revenues. To the extent that the government must borrow, it can try to sell as much debt as possible to the non-bank private sector and achieve overfunding. Both of these policies have been followed by the UK government in fairly recent times.

1.8 The demand for money: what do we mean by 'money'?

We shall now look more closely at the *demand* for money, which will take us further into the conflicting theories of Keynesian and monetarist economists.

It helps to start by getting a clear idea of what we mean by money. When we consider the theories of demand for money, we take money to mean a *non-interest bearing store of wealth*.

(a) Bank notes and current (bank) accounts (sight deposits) are money.

(b) Funds in a bank time deposit account are not money. Nor are building society deposits.

Our definition of money has now therefore switched from a broad money definition (M4) to a *narrow money* definition.

2 KEYNESIAN VIEWS ON THE DEMAND FOR MONEY

2.1 Liquidity preference

Liquidity means assets in the form of cash or near-cash, in particular notes, coin and money in a current bank account. Liquidity preference refers to the preference of people to hold on to their savings as money (ie in liquid form) rather than investing it.

Keynes used the concept of liquidity preference, which refers to the demand for money, to explain:

(a) how savings and investment might be temporarily different and;

(b) how interest rate levels in the economy are arrived at.

In addition, Keynes argued that if households did not hold their savings in the form of money, they would invest it to earn interest. The choice was between money and bonds. (This is a view since disputed by monetarist economists.)

Keynes identified three reasons, or motives why people hold wealth as money rather than as interest-bearing securities. These were:

(a) *the transactions motive*: households need money to pay for their day-to-day purchases. The level of transactions demand for money depends on household incomes;

(b) *the precautionary motive*: people choose to keep money on hand or in the bank as a precaution for a 'rainy day' when it might suddenly be needed;

(c) *the speculative motive*: some people choose to keep ready money to take advantage of a profitable opportunity to invest in bonds which may arise (or they may sell bonds for money when they fear a fall in bonds' market prices).

The speculative motive for holding money needs explaining a bit further.

(a) The reason for holding money instead of investing in bonds is that interest rates are expected to go up. If interest rates go up, bond prices will fall.

   For example, if the current market price of bonds which pay 5% interest is £100, and interest rates doubled to 10%, the market value of the bonds would fall, perhaps to £50. So if interest rates are expected to go up, any bonds held now will be expected to lose value, and bond holders would make a capital loss. So it makes sense to hold on to money, for investing in bonds later, *after* interest rates have gone up.

(b) What causes individuals to expect interest rate changes in the future?

Keynes argued that each individual has some expectation of a *normal* rate of interest. This perception of a normal interest rate reflects past levels and movements in the interest rate, and expectations of the future rate level, obtained from available market information.

Activity 4

Following this Keynesian analysis, how would you expect individuals to act if:

(a) they think that the current level of interest is below the normal rate?

(b) they think that the current level of interest is above the normal rate?

Keynes argued further that people will need money to satisfy the transactions motive and precautionary motive regardless of the level of interest. It is only the speculative motive which alters the demand for money as a result of interest rates.

(a) If interest rates are high, people will lend more money (eg by buying government stocks) hold little cash, and will have *low liquidity preference*.

(b) If interest rates are low and people expect them to rise, there is a danger that current bond prices will fall when interest rates go up. People will therefore hold money to satisfy the speculative motive. They will want to invest in bonds later and their *liquidity preference will be high*.

The conclusion is that the demand for money will be high (ie liquidity preference will be high) when interest rates are low. This is because the speculative demand for money will be high when interest rates are low. Similarly, the demand for money will be low when interest rates are high, because the speculative demand for money will be low.

There is a minimum fixed demand for money (transactions and precautionary motives) and some demand for money that varies with interest rates (speculative motive).

2.2 Keynesian view on interest rates and money demand and supply

If the money supply is assumed to be fixed by government decision, the size of the money supply is perfectly inelastic with respect to changes in the rate of interest. Keynes argued that the level of interest rates in the economy would then be reached by the interaction of money supply (fixed) and money demand (liquidity preference), as follows (Figure 1).

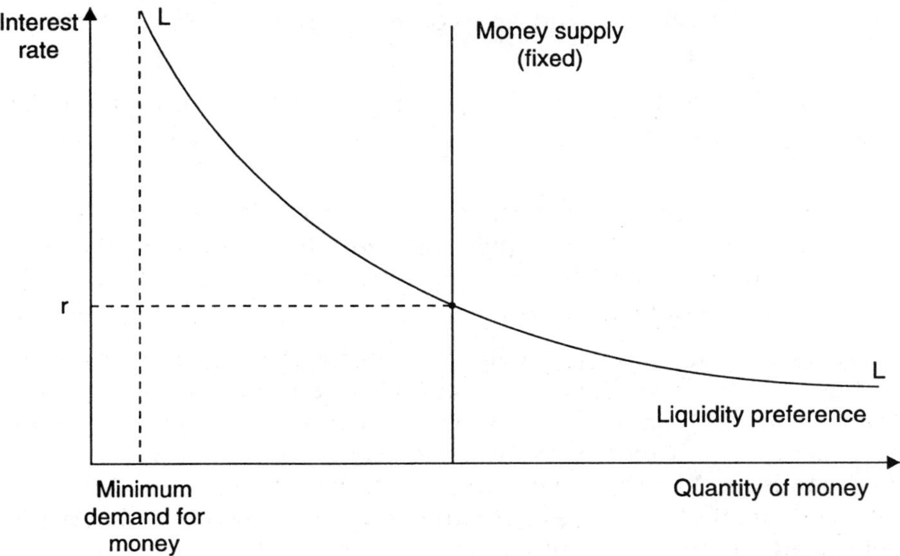

Figure 1 Interest rates, money demand and the money supply

If the money supply is fixed, it follows that interest rates in the economy would be determined by the demand for money.

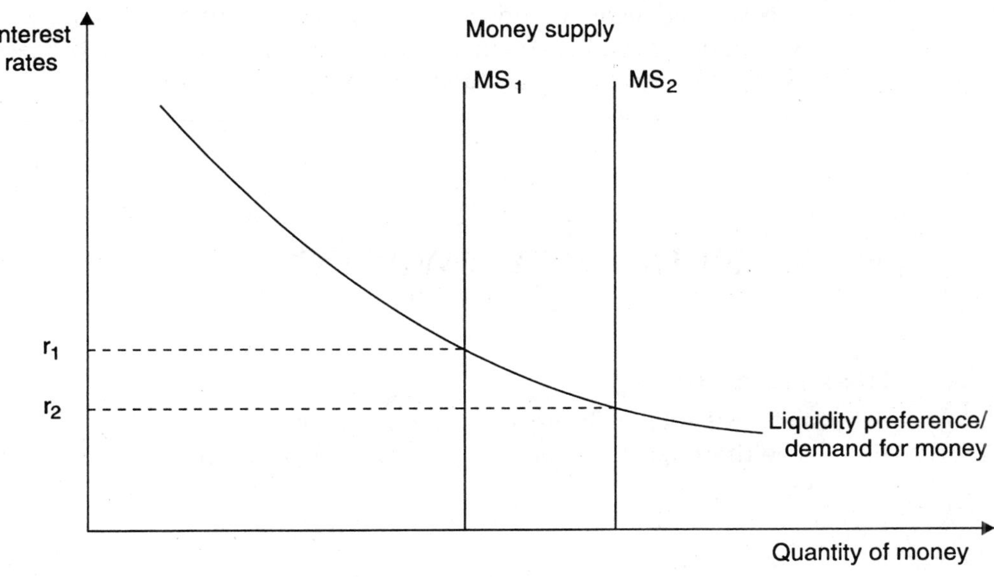

Figure 2 Consequence of an increase in the money supply: Keynesian views

If there is an increase in the money supply, from MS_1 to MS_2 in Figure 2, interest rates will fall from r_1 to r_2. There will be some increase in the level of investment spending, since it now becomes more profitable for firms to invest in new capital. The increase in investment, being an injection into the circular flow of income, causes some increase in the level of national income through the multiplier process.

According to the Keynesians, therefore, an increase (or decrease) in the money supply only affects the demand for goods and services (and therefore the level of income) indirectly, via a change in the rate of interest.

So the impact on the economy of the increase in the money supply depends on the effect that the fall in interest rates produces. According to the Keynesian view, both investment demand and consumer spending are relatively insensitive to interest rate changes, that is, they are relatively interest inelastic. The volume of investment depends heavily, Keynes argued, on *technological changes* and also *business confidence and expectations*. It follows that the increase in the money supply will have only a limited effect on aggregate demand and consequently relatively little effect on output and employment.

If the rate of interest is at a point where the demand for money is in the so-called liquidity trap, an increase in the money supply would have a very small effect on interest rates.

Investment would then be hardly affected at all. Keynes explained this by saying that the increases in the money supply would be offset by a reduction in the velocity of circulation, so that the increase in the money supply would have a neutral effect on the economy.

Keynesians argued that monetary policy to control the money supply would possibly, though not always, have an effect on interest rates. An increase in the money supply without an increase in the demand for money would make individuals use the extra money available to buy more bonds, and the higher demand for bonds would push down interest rates. In the longer term, changes in interest rates might affect investment. In other respects, however, monetary policy would not really affect the economy and national income. This is because increases in the money supply would be neutralised by reductions in the velocity of circulation, leaving PT unaffected.

Activity 5

In an earlier chapter we identified four functions of money: a means of exchange, a unit of account, a standard of deferred payment and a store of value. Which one of these is central to the Keynesian analysis of the demand for money?

3 THE MONETARIST VIEWPOINT

3.1 Introduction

Monetarist economists such as Professor Friedman revived the quantity theory of money and argued that there is a much more direct link between the money supply and national income.

NOTES

Definition

Monetarism is a school of thought in economics which takes the view that instability in the economy is mainly caused by factors within the monetary sector.

Whereas Keynes argued that an increase in the money supply would merely result in lower interest rates, with no immediate effect on national income, monetarists argue that an increase in the money supply will lead directly and quickly to changes in national income and PT, with the velocity of circulation V remaining fairly constant.

Friedman's first major work, entitled *The quantity theory of money: a re-statement* was published in 1956.

Friedman argued that money is just one of five broad ways of holding wealth. The five ways are:

(a) money;

(b) bonds;

(c) equities;

(d) physical goods;

(e) human wealth.

(Human wealth here is a special concept of wealth and may be ignored for the purpose of our analysis.)

Each method of holding wealth brings some form of return or yield to the holder.

(a) The yield from money might include some interest, such as on bank deposit accounts, but the main yield from money is a *convenience* yield. This is the convenience of having ready money when it is needed instead of having to go to the bother of converting other assets into cash. The convenience yield cannot be measured in money terms.

(b) Bonds stand for fixed-interest investments. The return on bonds is not just the interest yield, but also the capital gain or loss as a consequence of a change in market interest rates.

(c) Equities are financial assets, which should provide a yield (dividends and capital growth) that keeps ahead of the rate of inflation, ie a real return to investors.

(d) Physical goods are houses and consumer durables such as furniture, paintings etc. These are all physical assets which do not waste away through use (because assets which are consumed cannot be a store of wealth).

Friedman argued that the demand for money is related to the demand for holding wealth in its other forms. Money is a direct substitute for wealth in the form of bonds, equities or physical goods. In this respect, he argued against the Keynesian view that holding money is only a substitute for holding financial assets (bonds).

Whereas Keynes believed that if people did not want to hold money, they would invest it to earn interest, monetarists believe that people would possibly invest it to earn interest, but they might also use it instead to buy equities or physical assets.

Friedman argued that money gives a convenience yield, but it is not an asset which is held for its own sake. It is a temporary abode of purchasing power waiting to be spent on other types of financial or physical asset. The portfolio of assets held by any person should be a balance between money, bonds, equities and physical assets, ie the full range of financial assets and physical assets, so that the marginal interest or yield from the last £1 invested in every type of asset is the same.

The *demand for money* is therefore a function of the yield on money and the yield on other forms of holding wealth. Remember, however, that the yield as defined here includes non-monetary yield such as convenience and enjoyment.

Monetarists would argue, further, that the demand for money is fairly interest-elastic. The demand for money is related to a transactions motive, but not to any speculative motive. An expected rise in interest rates might persuade individuals to sell bonds and buy other assets, but not to hold speculative money!

3.2 Monetarists and the loanable funds theory of interest rates

According to Keynesians, the level of interest rates is determined by the interaction of the demand for money and the money supply.

Monetarists disagree: after all, they hold the view that the reasons for demanding money are for transactions only, not speculation about future investment. Monetarists argue instead that interest rates are determined by the demand and supply of *loanable funds*.

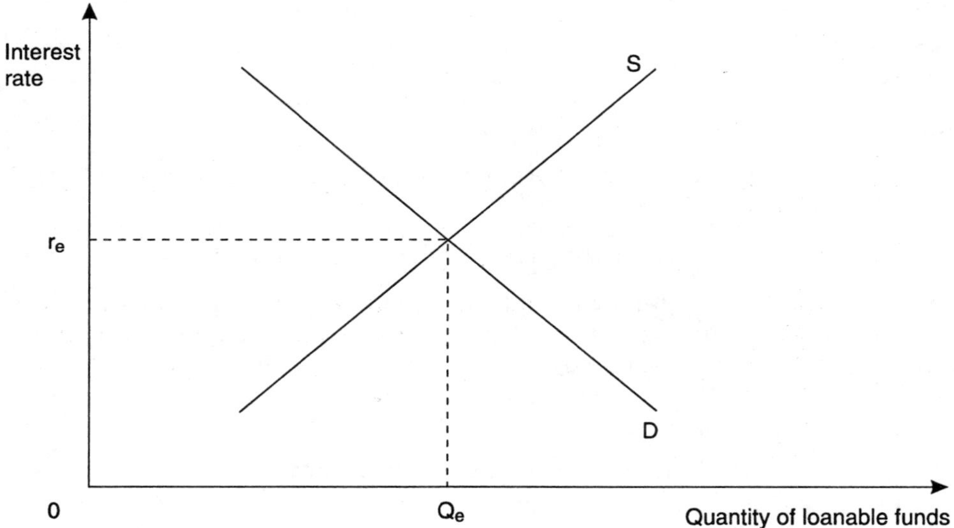

Figure 3 Loanable funds theory of interest rates

An increase in the money supply, without any increase in demand for money, will increase the amount of loanable funds available. Interest rates will fall, and investment will rise.

3.3 Monetarists, the transmission mechanism and imbalances between money supply and demand

So what is the connection between the demand for money, the money supply and national income, according to monetarists?

This can be explained by the *transmission mechanism*. The transmission mechanism describes the process where any excess of money demand over money supply, or any excess of money supply over money demand, cause a change in the aggregate expenditure in the economy (ie a change in national income).

Starting from a position of equilibrium holding of assets of all kinds, *an increase in the money supply* would leave individuals holding an excess of money balances. In order to restore the level of money holdings to its desired level, individuals will substitute assets of all kinds for money. This means the demand for all commodities will increase, not just demand for financial assets.

(a) The increase in the price of financial assets means a fall in the rate of interest. This will not lead to an increase in the demand for money, according to the monetarists, because they believe that the demand for money is interest-inelastic.

(b) The increase in direct spending on goods and services will, however, lead to a rise in the level of money national income.

By assuming that money is a substitute for all assets, the monetarists conclude that variations in the money supply have a great influence on the level of national income.

In terms of the quantity theory of money, if M goes up, and MV = PT, there will be an increase in PT, but this could mean an increase in either real output (T) or in prices and inflation (P).

Suppose that the demand for money goes up, but the authorities stop the money supply from increasing, so that there is an excess demand for money.

The transmission mechanism will work the other way. Households will sell bonds, equities and reduce consumption on other goods in order to acquire more money. Interest rates will go up. There will be a decline in total spending in the economy until money supply and demand are again in equilibrium. Since MV = PT, a decline in PT will have one of two effects:

(a) if the economy is operating below its full employment national income level, a decline in T (ie even less output and so more unemployment);

(b) if the economy has an inflationary gap, a decline in P (ie inflation will be brought under control).

Conclusion: for monetarists, changes in the money supply cause changes in national income. This contrasts with the Keynesian view that changes in the money supply are caused by changes in national income, not vice versa.

Activity 6

According to monetarist economists, which of the following consequences will result from an increase in the money supply?

1. Households will have excess money.
2. Households will use this money to buy more bonds, equities and physical goods.
3. Interest rates will rise.
4. The demand for money will respond to the change in interest rates.
5. Expenditure in the economy will increase.

3.4 The monetarist view of money supply and inflation in the economy

Monetarists argue that since money is a direct substitute for all other assets, an increase in the money supply, given a fairly stable velocity of circulation, will have a direct effect on demand for other assets. This is because there will be more money to spend on those assets. If the total output of the economy is fixed, an increase in the money supply will lead directly to higher prices.

Monetarists, therefore, reach the same basic conclusion as the old quantity theory of money. A rise in the money supply will lead to a rise in prices and probably also to a rise in money incomes. (It is also assumed by monetarists that the velocity of circulation remains fairly constant, again taking a view similar to the old quantity theory.)

NOTES

In the short run, monetarists argue that an increase in the money supply might cause some increase in real output and so an increase in employment. In the long run, however, all increases in the money supply will be reflected in higher prices, *unless* there is longer-term growth in the economy.

3.5 Weaknesses in monetarist theory

There are certain complications with the monetarist views. For example:

(a) the velocity of circulation is known to go up and down by small amounts;

(b) increases in prices will not affect all goods equally. Some goods will rise in price more than others,so the relative price of goods will change. For example, the price of houses might exceed the average rate of inflation, but the price of electronic goods might rise more slowly;

(c) a higher rate of inflation in one country than another might affect the country's balance of payments and currency value. This introduces complications for the economy from international trade movements;

(d) prices in the economy might take some time to adjust to an increase in the money supply.

Nevertheless, monetarists would still argue that inflation has been a major problem for many national economies, including that of the UK. High rates of inflation are impossible without a comparable increase in the money supply. V and T cannot adjust quickly enough, given the identity $MV \equiv PT$. Inflation cannot be brought under control unless the money supply is also controlled.

4 A COMPARISON OF THE TWO VIEWS

4.1 Which view of money is correct?

Keynesians and monetarists disagree and one key point of difference is the substitutability of money for bonds, with liquidity preference influenced by the rate of interest on bonds. Surely, therefore, it is a simple matter of testing to see whether this is the case? In other words, all we need to do is to find out whether there is a significant statistical relationship between the quantity of money and the rate of interest. There might be some practical difficulties in setting up the test in the first place, for example defining money and defining bonds, but this should not be impossible.

As you might imagine, tests have been carried out to find out whether the direct relationship between money supply and interest rates exists (in which case Keynesians are correct) or does not (in which case monetarists are correct). Unfortunately, these tests have not been conclusive. A relationship does exist, but it is not certain whether it is statistically significant or not. Given the view of the monetarists that in the short run interest rates might fall when the money supply is increased, some fall in interest rates after an increase in the money supply would still be consistent with monetarist theory! The Keynesian versus monetarist argument has not been resolved.

Both approaches agree that:

(a) great economic uncertainty explains the high cost of capital in recent years;

(b) high rates of inflation are largely responsible for high nominal interest rates;

(c) government monetary policy has some effect on the rate of inflation and so on the cost of capital;

NOTES

(d) although they have different views about:

'the speed and the mechanism by which interest rate adjustments occur, there is general agreement that interest rates are sometimes rather sticky. Smooth adjustment of interest rates to changing economic conditions depends on the participants in capital markets recognising the changes that are required'.

Wilson Committee

It is probably also generally agreed that the interest rate which produces an equilibrium balance between the supply and demand for investment (flow of funds approach) and the interest rate which brings into balance the supply and demand for money (liquidity preference approach) will tend to move towards each other and in the longer term become the same interest rate. The liquidity preference approach, however, is perhaps more concerned with *short-term* movements in interest rates.

Chapter roundup

- The Quantity Theory of Money is based on the identity $MV \equiv PT$. On the assumption that V is constant and T can only increase slowly, large increases in the money supply M will be inflationary.
- According to monetarists, if there is an increase in the money supply:
  - individuals will have more money than they want;
  - they will spend this excess money, buying not just 'bonds' (as Keynes believed) but also equities and physical goods;
  - the greater demand for physical goods will boost expenditure in the economy (and so the money value of national income);
  - however, a rapid increase in the money supply will increase spending at a faster rate than the economy will be able to produce more physical output;
  - a rapid increase in the money supply will therefore inevitably be inflationary.
- Keynes argued that money is held for transactions and precautionary motives (ie for spending) and for speculative reasons. Transaction spending is independent of the money supply. Changes in the money supply will have implications for speculative holdings of money, and interest rates, but will have little or no consequence for spending on goods and services.
- Keynesians argue that interest rates are determined by the interaction of the supply of money and the demand for money (rather than bonds), ie liquidity preference. Monetarists argue that interest rates are determined by the supply and demand for loanable funds.
- Keynes argued that increases in the money supply will affect interest rates and the demand for money, but changes in interest rates only have a limited and relatively insignificant effect on consumer spending and investment spending. This is a view which is now *not* generally favoured – you might be aware, for example, how the UK government used a policy of high interest rates during the late 1980s to help reduce consumer spending.

NOTES

Quick quiz

1 Write the equation for the quantity theory of money.

2 What assumptions must be made if the quantity theory of money is to become an explanation of price inflation?

3 According to Keynes, what are the three motives for wanting to hold money?

4 What will be the consequence for bond prices of an increase in interest rates?

5 Draw a liquidity preference schedule.

6 Use a liquidity preference schedule to show Keynes's explanation of the effect of an increase in the money supply on interest rates.

7 According to monetarists, what affects the demand for money?

8 What is the loanable funds theory of interest rates?

9 What is the transmission mechanism? Explain the consequences of an increase in the money supply on national income, according to monetarist views of the transmission mechanism.

10 What will be the effect of an increase in the money supply on inflation, according to monetarists?

Answers to Activities

1 According to the quantity theory, $V = \frac{PT}{M}$. This is described by (b), which is therefore the correct answer.

Answer (a) implies that $V = \frac{M}{P}$, and answer (c) implies that $V = \frac{PT}{P}$ PT, both of which are incorrect.

2 MV in Year 1 = $6{,}500 \times 5.2 = 33{,}800$

MV in Year 2 = $7{,}000 \times 4.9 = 34{,}300$

But MV = PT

Given no change in T, the increase in price levels (P) between Year 1 and Year 2 is:

$$\frac{34{,}300 - 33{,}800}{33{,}800} = 1.48\%$$

4 (a) If someone believes that the normal rate of interest is above the current level, he will expect the interest rate to rise and will therefore expect bond prices to fall. To avoid a capital loss the individual will sell bonds and hold money.

(b) Conversely, if an individual believes that the normal rate of interest is below the current market interest rate, he will expect the market interest rate to fall and bond prices to rise. Hence he will buy bonds, and run down speculative money holdings, in order to make a capital gain.

5 It is the function of money as a liquid store of value or wealth which is central to the concept of liquidity preference.

6 Consequences 1, 2 and 5 (but not 3 and 4) will result. According to monetarists, an increase in the money supply creates excess supply over demand. Households use the excess money to buy bonds (and so interest rates *fall*), equities and physical goods (and so expenditure in the economy rises). The demand for money is interest-rate inelastic, according to monetarists (but not according to Keynesians) and so this does not increase in response to any interest rate fall.

Case Study

'The purpose of monetary policy is to influence monetary variables in the economy such as the rate of interest and the supply of money. The intention is to achieve the targets set for the government's main policy objectives.

Economic theory suggests that *the rate of interest* is important because for firms it is the cost of both their short-term borrowing for cash flow purposes and of long-term borrowing to finance investment. Also, consumer spending on durable goods may be influenced by the rate of interest since it affects the cost of hire-purchase finance. Household decisions on the portfolio of assets that they hold may be affected by the rate of interest; low interest rates may discourage savings and encourage consumption. Changes in interest rates may also have implications for the balance of payments since international movements of capital reflect differences in interest rates between countries.

Both monetarist and Keynesian economists recognise the importance of *the money supply*. In the Keynesian approach, changes in the money supply affect output and unemployment. However, for monetarists, the main impact, especially in the long run, is on the level of prices. Thus, for governments, measuring and controlling the money supply has been an important policy instrument.'

Use this summary of the role of monetary policy to:

(a) explain the mechanisms by which changes in interest rates can influence:

(i) expenditure by firms,
(ii) expenditure by consumers;

(b) explain the monetarist theory that changes in the money supply affect mainly prices;

(c) show how a change in interest rates might affect the exchange rate for a country's currency.

Answer to Case Study

(a) (i) Interest rates represent the cost of borrowing funds. According to the loanable funds theory, the demand for funds is inversely related to movements in interest rates.

At interest rate r_1 in the diagram below, the demand for funds is Q_1. At the lower rate of r_2, the demand for funds is Q_2.

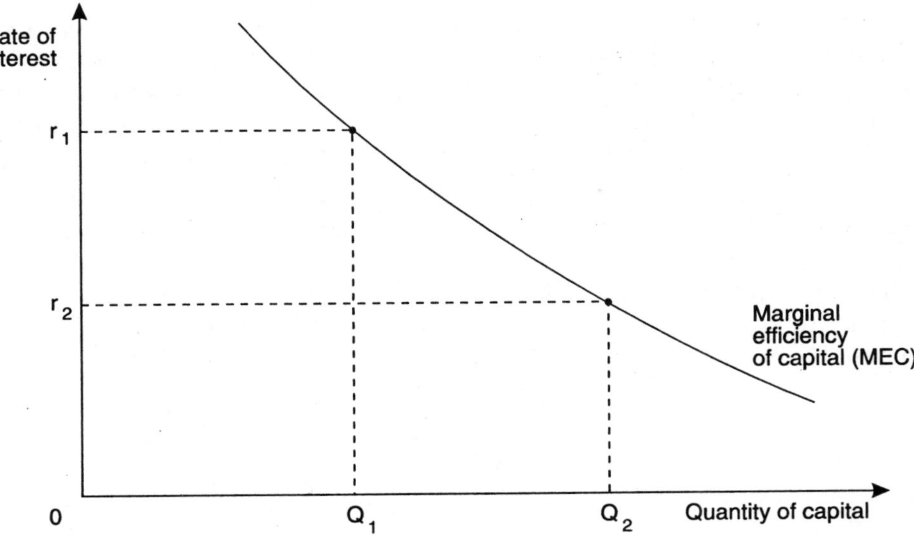

Figure 4

The curve shown represents the marginal efficiency of capital (MEC) – the return on funds available to the borrower of funds. At a lower borrowing cost, the productivity of capital rises, as a higher return overall is obtainable. The demand for funds in the private sector comes from firms as well as from consumers.

The impact of changes in interest rates on the expenditure of firms will be various. Capital expenditure decisions are more likely to be affected by movements in longer-term interest rates, especially long-term projects. However, in times of financial stringency, changes in the cost of shorter-term funds will be of importance in some investment decisions.

Decisions on stock levels may also be affected by movements in short- to medium-term interest rates. If interest rates were to rise substantially, the additional borrowing costs and the wider effects on the demand for sales could lead to fewer concessions on wage demands.

Interest rates are one of several factors which need to be considered in investment decisions. Forecast consumer demand, selling price levels, inflationary effects and general business confidence will also be taken into account.

(ii) Interest rates changes will also influence consumer expenditure. This may be through the effect on mortgage interest rates, affecting the demand for housing as well as for all the wide range of products and services associated with residential property. For those on existing mortgages, a rise in monthly interest rates will mean less income available to spend in other sectors.

Generally, higher interest rates will tend to encourage saving and discourage borrowing or entering into hire purchase contracts in order to buy consumer durables. Again, the relationship or response is unlikely to be direct or automatic. In a period of rising incomes, and general business confidence, a substantial rise in interest rates may be necessary to reduce consumer demand. Conversely, if consumers are wary from the bitter experience of a recession, a fall in interest rates may, in itself, do little to stimulate consumer demand.

(b) The monetarist theory that changes in the money supply affect mainly prices was stated by Irving Fisher in the *quantity theory of money*. The nucleus of the relationship is expressed in his equation of exchange:

$$MV = PT$$

where M = the quantity of money in the economy

V = the velocity of circulation of money, ie the speed at which money moves through the economy over a given period

P = the general price level

T = the total number of transactions over a given period

Since M is the quantity of money and V is the number of times that each unit of money is used on average over a given time period, it is clear that MV equals the total value of expenditure during that time period. Since P is the average value of each transaction and T is the volume of transactions during a given time period, it is evident that PT equals the total value of expenditure during the time period. MV must equal PT.

The Fisher equation is definitionally true; it shows two different ways of measuring the same group of transactions. It begins to have practical value when valid assumptions are made regarding the variables. If it is assumed that the velocity of circulation is constant and the volume of transactions is fixed, it follows that any change in the quantity of money will be matched by a change in the price level. Changes in M bring about changes in P, with V and T unchanged.

$$M\bar{V} = P\bar{T}$$

The argument is that, at least in the short run, V is constant or at any rate predictable: it is determined by institutional factors such as the payment intervals for wages or business accounts. T, the volume of transactions, is determined by the productive capacity of the economy, and a further assumption of monetarist theory is that an economy tends naturally towards full employment.

Given that V is a constant and that T is fixed, at least in the short term, the consequence of a change in M must be a change in P. Therefore, an increase in the money supply under conditions of full employment will have an impact on prices rather than on output, provided that the velocity of circulation is unchanged.

(c) A given exchange rate is determined by the demand for and, supply of that country's currency on the foreign exchanges.

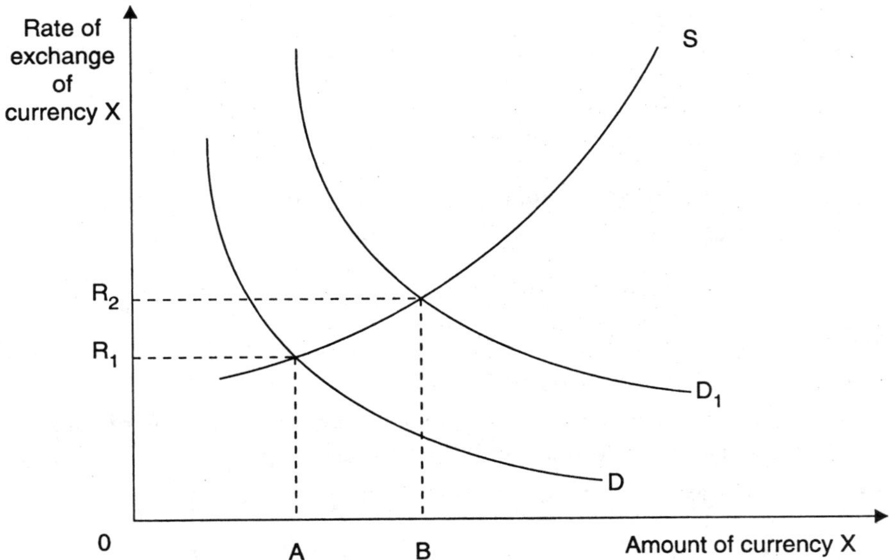

Figure 5

A rise in the demand for currency X, from OA to OB in Figure 5, pushes up the rate of exchange from R_1 to R_2.

In practice, there is a world-wide complex structure of interest rates. Any change in interest rates in the UK, unless matched by similar changes in interest rates in the other main trading and financing nations, will affect the relative position of the UK economy. So a rise in the UK interest rates, unmatched abroad, would encourage portfolio-type investment into the UK as well as money looking for marginally high or short-term returns (hot money). This would lead to a rise in the value of sterling, as the demand for sterling to place within the UK increases. In point of fact, much of this rise in sterling might already have taken place through speculation in sterling on the foreign exchange markets, the markets having anticipated the rise in the UK interest rates. Any fall in the value of sterling would have the reverse effects.

The effect upon longer term-investment into the UK could be quite different. Such investment is looking for a return by way of profits rather than the reward of interest. It may not be deterred by shorter-term movements in interest rates. On the other hand, it may be discouraged if, for instance, the rise in interest rates is part of a package of deflationary measures: setting up or operating costs within the UK might rise and selling markets there might be depressed.

There could be less direct effect upon the value of sterling from, for instance, an initial rise in UK interest rates. The initial rise in the value of sterling would raise the effective price of British exports. This would make exporting more difficult. Any consequential fall in the demand for UK goods/services would, in turn, have some downward effect on the value of sterling. Any major effect upon the UK economy resulting from the initial rise in interest rates could, in turn, lessen UK demand for imported goods. This would tend to result in an upward movement of the value of sterling, as the balance of payments deficit is lessened.

Further question practice

Now try the following practice questions at the end of this text.

Multiple choice questions **156–167**

Exam style question **16**

Chapter 15

FISCAL POLICY

Introduction

In this chapter, we look at how government spending and taxation policies can be used to influence the economy, and at the forms and characteristics of taxation.

Your objectives

After completing this chapter you should:

(a) understand how a government can influence the economy by managing the amounts it spends and the amounts it collects in taxation;

(b) understand how a government can use taxation to promote its policy aims.

NOTES

1 FISCAL POLICY, NATIONAL INCOME AND DEMAND MANAGEMENT

1.1 Introduction

The word 'fisc' means the state treasury or the public purse. Fiscal policy relates to matters concerning the state treasury.

Definition

Fiscal policy is the regulation of the economy through taxation and government expenditure.

Remember that government spending is an injection into the economy, adding to aggregate demand=expenditure=national income, whereas taxes are a withdrawal. A government might intervene in the economy by:

(a) spending more money and financing this expenditure by borrowing;

(b) collecting more in taxes without increasing public spending;

(c) collecting more in taxes in order to increase public spending, and so diverting income from one part of the economy to another.

Demand management, you will remember, is a term used to describe the economic policy of a government when it attempts to influence the economy by changing aggregate demand.

Fiscal policy could be used as an instrument of demand management. Government spending and taxation levels could be used to eliminate an inflationary gap or deflationary gap in the economy. A reduction in taxation would give households a larger income, and so domestic consumption (C) would rise: on the other hand, an increase in taxation would reduce domestic consumption. Extra government spending (G) should create a multiplier effect on national income, although public sector spending might crowd out private sector investment, because of higher rates of interest in the capital markets.

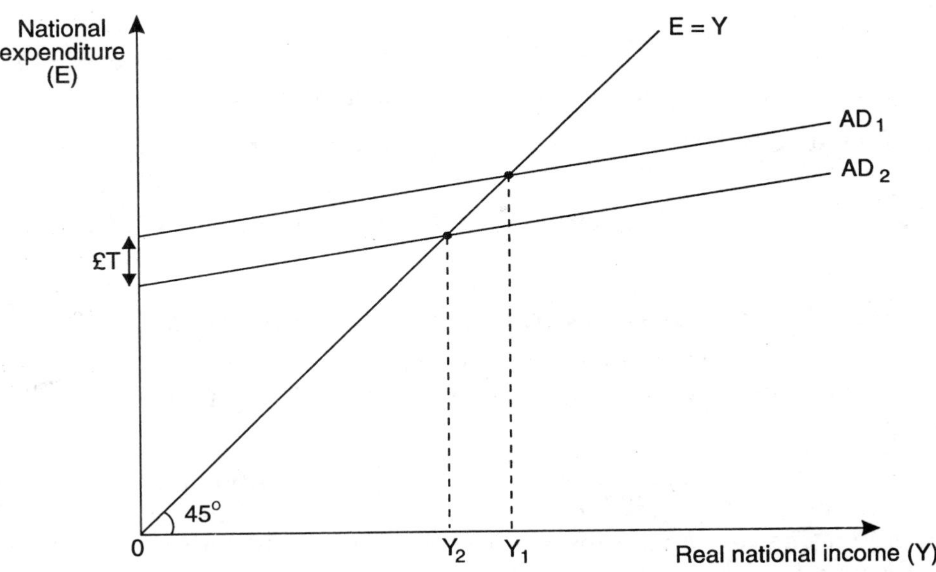

Figure 1 Determination of equilibrium National Income

An increase in taxation by £T, without any matching increase in government expenditure, would reduce the aggregate expenditure in the economy from AD_1 to

NOTES

AD_2 and so the money value of national income would fall from Y_1 to Y_2. This would result in either a fall in real output or it would damp down inflationary pressures.

Similarly, a reduction in taxation without any reduction in government spending would increase the money value of national income. This would either cause real output to increase, or it would give a boost to price rises and inflation.

1.2 Three elements of public finance

Broadly, there are three elements in public finance.

(a) *Expenditure*

Expenditure by the government, at a national and local level, has several purposes (for example, to fund public services such as a health service, or to pay pensions and unemployment benefits).

(b) *Income*

Expenditure must be financed, and the government must have income. Most government income comes from taxation. Other income is obtained from direct charges to users of government services (eg charges to consumers by nationalised industries, and National Health Service charges).

(c) *Borrowing*

To the extent that a government's expenditure exceeds its income, it must borrow to make up the difference. The amount that the government must borrow each year is referred to as the public sector borrowing requirement (PSBR).

1.3 Taxation as a deterrent to economic growth

Activity 1

You may have come across the argument that high rates of income tax stifle economic growth. Certainly the Conservative government made a reduction in income tax rates one of its key objectives. Why do you think high rates of income tax should have such an effect?

Fiscal policy should be formulated within the guidelines that:

(a) taxes should be high enough to allow the government to carry on its functions; but

(b) they should not be set so as to deter private investment and initiative.

1.4 Fiscal policy and macroeconomic objectives

Fiscal policy is concerned with government spending and taxation. Refer back to the discussion of the circular flow of income if you find the following analysis unclear.

(a) If government spending is increased, there will be an increase in the amount of injections, expenditure in the economy will rise and so national income will rise (either in real terms, or in terms of price levels only; ie the increase in national income might be real or inflationary).

(b) If government taxation is increased, there will be an increase in withdrawals from the economy, and expenditure and national income will fall. A government might deliberately raise taxation to take inflationary pressures out of the economy.

Achieving growth in national income without inflation has been a problem afflicting governments for many years. Certainly, government spending and taxation policies can affect economic growth (ie the national income level in real terms), but it can also stimulate further inflation.

Fiscal policy can be used to reduce unemployment and provide jobs. For example, more government spending on capital projects would create jobs in the construction industries; lower employment taxes (such as National Insurance) might make employers more willing to take on extra numbers of employees.

Government spending could, however, create inflationary pressures, and inflation tends to create more unemployment. Fiscal policy must be used with care, even to create new jobs.

1.5 Budget surplus; budget deficit; balanced budget

Suppose that the government wants to stimulate demand in the economy.

(a) *It can increase demand directly by spending more itself* (eg on the health service or education, and by employing more people itself).

  (i) This extra spending could be financed by higher taxes, but this would reduce spending by the private sector of the economy, because the private sector's after-tax income would be lower.

  (ii) The extra government spending could also be financed by extra government borrowing. In the same way as individuals can borrow money for spending, so can a government.

(b) *It can increase demand indirectly by reducing taxation*, which allows firms and individuals more after-tax income to spend (or save).

  (i) Cuts in taxation can be matched by cuts in government spending, in which case total demand in the economy will not be stimulated significantly, if at all.

  (ii) Alternatively, tax cuts can be financed by more government borrowing.

Activity 2

It was often stated by critics of the Conservative government that individuals would be prepared to accept higher rates of tax in order to increase funding for public services; they pointed to the evidence of surveys to support their argument. Other surveys, however, suggest that when people are confronted with a direct choice ('Will you accept a reduction in your income of £5 per week to fund a pay rise for nurses?') they are less keen. Look out for comment on this issue in the press and try to make your own position clear.

Aggregate demand in the economy can be boosted by either more government spending or by tax cuts, financed in each case by a higher public sector borrowing requirement (PSBR). Demand in the economy can also be reduced by cutting government spending or by raising taxes, and using the savings or higher income to cut government borrowing.

Expenditure changes and tax changes are not mutually exclusive options, of course. For example, government may consider a package of measures, possibly including tax increases and reduced government spending, in order to reduce the PSBR.

When a government's income exceeds its expenditure and there is a negative PSBR, ie a public sector debt repayment (PSDR), we say that the government is running a *budget surplus*.

NOTES

When a government's expenditure exceeds its income, so that it must borrow to make up the difference, there is a PSBR and we say that the government is running a *budget deficit.*

When a government's expenditure and income are the same, so that the PSBR is nil, there is a *balanced budget.*

Activity 3

The following table shows budgeted income and expenditure figures prepared by the government of Entropia.

	Income £billion	*Expenditure* £billion
Central government	34	39
Local government	12	27
Nationalised industries	5	7
Other public corporations	1	2

What is the expected PSBR for the year?

1.6 Fiscal policy and the Budget

A government must *plan* what it wants to spend, and so how much it needs to raise in income or by borrowing. It needs to make a plan in order to establish how much taxation there should be, what form the taxes should take and so which sectors of society (firms or households, the rich or the poor etc) the money should come from. This formal planning of fiscal policy is usually done once a year. Since 1993, the annual Budget statement has taken place in November or December and includes the government's plans for both spending and taxation. The Labour government is likely to return the annual budget to March each year.

This annual review of taxation means that a full review of the government's fiscal policy can only be made once a year. In between Budgets, a government must turn to other non-fiscal policy instruments to control the economy, such as influencing interest rate levels.

1.7 The National Debt

Definition

The *National Debt* is the amount of debt owed by the *central* government of a country to its various creditors.

Creditors may be nationals of the country (eg investors in government loan stock) or foreign nationals (perhaps foreign banks or even the International Monetary Fund).

When the National Debt is high, interest repayments will account for a large proportion of central government expenditure. It is important that when a government borrows money, it should be invested or spent in such a way as to make sure that enough income is eventually generated to repay the interest and debt capital. If a government is unable to do this (as in the case of many developing and less developed countries at the moment) it will lose its creditworthiness and find future loans much harder to get.

The ability to repay is probably the major factor in setting an effective limit to the size of a national debt.

The National Debt exists in the form of debt instruments which consist of:

(a) marketable debt (mainly long-term debt, consisting of gilt-edged securities, which are sold to investors and traded on The Stock Exchange); and

(b) non-marketable debt (including National Savings and any non-marketable loans raised by the government).

To service the National Debt, a government must:

(a) pay interest on the debt; and

(b) make capital repayments when they fall due.

However, the problem of making capital repayments can be overcome, if required, by taking out new loans when old loans mature (eg to repay a loan of £100 million, a government can borrow a further £100 million).

If the loan is obtained from the private sector of the country's economy, the National Debt and servicing the debt involve the transfer of funds between different sections of society. When the government borrows, it takes money from one group and spends it on other sections of society. When the government pays interest, it will raise money in taxes from the rest of society and pay this money to its debtors. Once again, there has to be a transfer of the funds.

So the National Debt and servicing the debt involve:

(a) a redistribution of funds within society, through government borrowing and spending, or through taxation to pay debt interest;

(b) borrowing to spend now and only repaying the debt with interest later. In other words, society benefits now, and the payment burden falls on society in later years, perhaps, in some cases, as long as a generation later.

When money is borrowed from abroad, the flow of funds in obtaining the money and in repaying the debt crosses national boundaries, and so there are implications for the balance of payments and the exchange rate of the domestic currency.

1.8 Public expenditure control and the PSBR

The public sector borrowing requirement, or PSBR, is the *annual* excess of spending over income for the entire public sector, not just central government. If the entire public sector had a balanced budget, the PSBR would be nil. When there is an annual excess of income over expenditure, as there was in the UK a few years ago, some of the National Debt can be repaid and there is a Public Sector Debt Repayment (PSDR).

Government spending on both revenue and capital items has to be financed by either:

(a) taxation and other current revenues; or

(b) borrowing.

Keynesian economists argue the need for more government spending in a recession to boost demand in the economy and create jobs. One argument is that it makes sound financial sense to use current revenues from taxation and so on to meet current expenditures and interest payments on debt, but to use borrowing for capital expenditure needs. Since taxation revenue exceeds current spending, the argument concludes that the government should borrow more for the capital spending.

The UK government rejected this argument, and believed that the upward spiral of public expenditure has made the burden of taxation on companies and individuals unbearable.

NOTES

There can be no prospect of bringing the burden of tax back to tolerable levels without firm control over public expenditure growth, by deciding first what can be afforded then setting plans for individual programmes consistent with that decision.

The Chancellor's Autumn Statement, November 1983.

The central government in the UK has also been greatly concerned with local authority spending, and its policies to control the growth of spending have raised a major political storm between government and opposition parties, especially in view of the large number of Labour-controlled councils.

Activity 4

This is an issue that has been widely reported over the last decade. Can you list some of the measures that have been taken by the government to reduce local authority spending?

2 TAXATION POLICY AND ITS EFFECTS

2.1 Introduction

The functions of taxation include the following points.

(a) *To raise revenues for the government*, local authorities and similar bodies (eg the European Community). The revenues are used to provide goods and services that the market economy either does not provide at all (eg defence), or will not provide in sufficient quantities (eg education). They are also used to pay for the upkeep of government administration.

(b) *To discourage certain activities regarded as undesirable.* The imposition of Development Land Tax in the United Kingdom in the mid-70s was partly in response to the well-publicised growth in property speculation.

(c) *To cause certain products to be priced to take into account their social costs.* For example, smoking leads to certain social costs, including the cost of hospital care for those suffering from smoking-related diseases. So the government sees fit to make the price of tobacco reflect these social costs.

(d) *to redistribute wealth.* The higher rates of income tax up to 1979, and capital transfer tax (now replaced by inheritance tax) were designed to transfer wealth from the better off to the less well off through higher social security benefits. Some politicians favour a wealth tax.

(e) *To protect industries from foreign competition.* If the government levies a duty on all imported goods much of the duty will be passed on to the consumer in the form of higher prices, making imported goods more expensive. This has the effect of transferring a certain amount of demand from imported goods to domestically produced goods.

(f) *To provide a stabilising effect on national income.* Taxation reduces the effect of the multiplier, and so can be used to dampen upswings in a trade cycle – ie higher taxation when the economy shows signs of a boom will slow down the growth of money, GNP, and so take some inflationary pressures out of the economy.

Taxation can be used to achieve the same purposes as government expenditure. In addition, it can be used to affect particular sectors of the economy. For example, taxes on wealth, capital and income are potentially effective tools for redistribution of wealth.

2.2 Qualities of a good tax

Adam Smith in his *Wealth of nations* (1776) detailed four features of a good tax system.

(a) Persons should pay according to their ability.

(b) The tax should be certain and easily understood by all concerned.

(c) The payment of tax ideally should be related to how and when people receive and spend their income (eg PAYE is deducted when wages are paid, and VAT is charged when goods are bought).

(d) The cost of collection should be small relative to the yield (by this criterion, the car road tax is an inefficient tax).

Regressive, proportional and progressive taxation are as follows.

(a) *A regressive tax* takes a higher proportion of a poor person's salary than of a rich person's. Television licences and road tax are examples of a regressive tax, since they are the same for people of all wealth classes. A poll tax or community charge is also a regressive tax, because it takes a greater proportion of the income of a poor person than a rich person, even though individual charges can vary from one local authority to another, and in spite of some rebates for the least well-off groups.

(b) *A proportional tax* takes the same proportion of income in tax from all levels of income. Schedule E income tax with a basic tax at 23% is proportional tax, but only within a limited range of income.

(c) *A progressive tax* takes a higher proportion of income in tax as income rises. Income tax as a whole is progressive, since the first part of an individual's income is tax free due to personal allowances and the rate of tax increases in steps from 20p in £1 to 40p in £1 as taxable income rises.

Activity 5

Below are details of three taxation systems, one of which is regressive, one proportional and one progressive. Which is which?

	Income before tax	Income after tax
	£	£
System 1	10,000	8,000
	20,000	15,000
System 2	10,000	7,000
	20,000	14,000
System 3	10,000	9,000
	20,000	19,000

2.3 Advantages of progressive taxation

There are several arguments in favour of progressive taxes.

(a) They are levied according to the ability of individuals to pay. Individuals with a higher income are more able to afford to give up more of their income in tax than low income earners, who need a greater proportion of their earnings for the basic necessities of life. If taxes are to be raised according to the ability of people to pay (which is one of the features of a good tax suggested by Adam Smith) they must include some progressiveness.

(b) Progressive taxes enable a government to redistribute wealth from the rich to the poor in society. It is likely that there will be little redistribution of wealth among the middle-income ranges of society, but there should be some redistribution of wealth from the richest members of society to the poorest. This might be regarded as a matter of social justice but it will also alter the consumption patterns in society. Poorer members will spend their earnings and social security benefits on different types of goods from those that richer people would have bought if the income had remained in their hands.

(c) Indirect taxes (eg taxes on expenditure) tend to be regressive. Progressive taxes are needed to counterbalance regressive taxes in the tax system, and so make the tax system as a whole more fair.

2.4 The disadvantages of progressive taxation

There are some arguments against progressive taxes.

(a) Some would argue that in an affluent society there is less need for progressive taxes than in a poorer society, and there is less need to redistribute wealth from the very wealthy to the fairly well-to-do.

(b) When progressive taxes are harsh, and either tax high income earners at very high rates on marginal income, or tax the wealthy at high rates, it is argued by some that these taxes will discourage initiative.

(c) It is also sometimes argued that individuals and firms suffering from high taxes might try:

(i) to find loopholes so as to *avoid* paying tax (eg non-taxable perks);

(ii) to *evade* taxes, ie withhold information about their income or wealth from the authorities;

(iii) to transfer their wealth to other countries, or establish companies in tax havens where corporate tax rates are low.

But of course some people will try to avoid or evade tax whether it is high or not so high.

2.5 Advantages and disadvantages of a proportional tax

The advantage of a tax which is proportional to income is primarily that of fairness.

The disadvantages of a proportional tax are:

(a) the large administrative system needed to calculate personal tax liabilities on a proportional basis. Income tax, for example, can be a costly tax to collect where individuals (especially self-employed people) require detailed tax assessments;

(b) the tax rules may need to be quite complex in order to be proportional;

(c) it does not contribute towards a redistribution of wealth among the population.

2.6 Advantages and disadvantages of a regressive tax

The main disadvantage of a regressive tax is that it is not fair, because a greater tax burden falls on those least able to afford it.

An advantage of a regressive tax is that it can be relatively easy to administer and to collect. However, a regressive tax could also be expensive to collect. Arguments against a poll tax (in the form of the now abandoned community charge) in the UK were that it is both regressive (and so unfair) and also expensive to administer.

NOTES

2.7 Direct and indirect taxes

Definition

A *direct tax* is paid direct by a person to the Revenue authority. Examples of direct taxes in the UK are income tax, corporation tax, capital gains tax and inheritance tax. A direct tax can be levied on income and profits, or on wealth.

Direct taxes tend to be progressive or proportional taxes. They are also usually unavoidable, which means that they must be paid by everyone.

Definition

An *indirect tax* is collected by the Revenue authority (eg Customs & Excise) from an intermediary (eg a supplier) who then passes on the tax to consumers in the price of goods they sell. Indirect taxes include VAT, excise duty on spirits and beer, and customs duties.

Indirect taxes tend to be regressive (unless they are charged exclusively on luxury items). They are also usually avoidable, which means that people can choose not to pay the tax, by not buying the goods or services on which the tax is levied.

Activity 6

The burden of an indirect tax must either be borne by the producer or passed on by the producer to the customers. If producers feel able to pass on the whole of the burden, what can you deduce about the elasticity of demand for their product?

2.8 Direct taxation: advantages and disadvantages

The main *advantages* of direct taxes on income are that they are fair and just, because they are usually progressive or proportional taxes. They can be levied according to ability to pay. Because of their generally progressive nature they also tend to stabilise the economy, automatically taking more money out of the system during a boom and less during depression. Added to which, because they are more difficult to pass on, they are less inflationary than indirect taxes. Taxpayers also know what their tax liability is.

However, taxes on *income* are often criticised for causing harmful distortions, especially on incentives to work. But as has been pointed out, the research has not come to any definite conclusions on this.

High marginal rates of tax may encourage tax avoidance (ie finding legal loopholes in the tax rules so as to avoid paying tax). In Britain, this led to a growth of making income payments in kind by way of fringe benefits, for example, free medical and life insurance, preferential loans and favourable pension rights. The Conservative government responded to this by bringing an increasing number of fringe benefits into the tax net (for example, the private use of a company car).

A direct tax on *profits* is likely to act as a disincentive to risk-taking and enterprise. The tax will reduce the net return from a new investment and any disincentive effects will be greater when the tax is progressive. Also, a tax on profits will reduce the ability to invest. A considerable part of the finance for new investment comes from retained profits, so any tax on corporate profits will reduce the ability of firms to save. This will limit the sources of funds for investment.

2.9 Indirect taxation: advantages and disadvantages

Indirect taxes are hidden, in the sense that taxpayers are largely unaware of the amount of tax they are paying (eg the tax on beer and spirits). This has considerable advantages from the government's point of view.

Indirect taxes are generally more difficult to evade than direct taxes.

It is sometimes argued that indirect taxes are preferable to direct taxes. This is because they leave the individual with a choice of not paying the tax by not consuming the taxed commodity.

Indirect taxation can be used to encourage or discourage the production or consumption of particular goods and services and so may affect the allocation of resources. For example, the production of goods that produce environmental pollution may be taxed as a means of raising the price in order to reduce demand and output. Similarly, the consumption of cigarettes can be discouraged by high indirect taxation. The consumption of imported goods can be discouraged by high import duties, which add to their price in domestic markets.

Indirect taxation is a flexible instrument of economic policy. The rates of indirect taxes may be changed quickly and easily and can take effect immediately. For example, if the Chancellor wished to boost aggregate demand in the economy he could reduce rates of indirect taxation and this would have a rapid effect on private consumption.

Indirect taxes do, however, have disadvantages.

(a) They can be inflationary. In the UK, a switch from direct tax to indirect tax in the budget of 1979, when VAT rates were increased, resulted in a large increase in the reported rate of inflation. This is, however, largely a one-off effect.

(b) As already stated, indirect taxes tend to be regressive.

(c) Indirect taxes are not impartial in their application in other ways. For example, someone who seeks to relax with a cigarette in a pub is going to be much more heavily hit by indirect taxes than someone who likes walking and reading.

(d) The disincentive effects of indirect taxes are often claimed to be less than those of direct taxes. This is mainly because indirect taxes are not as visible as direct taxes and so are less likely to be taken into account in decision-making.

(e) As we saw in an earlier chapter, firms will maximise their profits at a lower volume of output than if there were no taxes.

2.10 The incidence of taxation

The *incidence* of a tax is the distribution of the tax burden. A tax's *formal* incidence can be distinguished from its *actual* incidence.

(a) In the case of income tax, formal and actual incidence are the same unless workers negotiate a higher post-tax wage, in which case employers bear some of the tax burden. Employers might then raise their product price and pass some of the tax burden on to consumers.

(b) Corporation tax falls formally on profits and so on shareholders. But the tax could be passed on to consumers in the form of a price rise following on a reduction in supply, so that the actual incidence of the tax would fall on the consumers.

(c) According to economic theory, producers will not pass the burden of a profit tax on to consumers. This is because they are already producing at a profit-maximising level of output and the marginal condition MR = MC is not affected by a tax. However, it might be more reasonable to suppose that producers would regard the tax as an additional cost, in which case it would justify a reduction in output and rise in price. The consumers would in this case bear some of the burden.

(d) A general indirect tax on all goods would be borne fully by consumers, since they cannot buy alternative goods which are not taxed. VAT is the closest equivalent to a general indirect tax in Britain. Only necessities are exempt from VAT or zero-rated, eg food, transport, health services – and books!

2.11 Taxation and the redistribution of wealth

Another aspect of taxation is the extent to which it can be used to redistribute wealth, and the consequences this would have for economic activity. Suppose, for example, that a country has no taxation and most national income is earned by a very small and wealthy proportion of the population. The expenditure pattern within the country would probably be:

(a) fairly substantial spending by the wealthy few on luxury goods and specialist services (eg domestic servants);

(b) substantial spending by the poor majority on cheap basic necessities for living, such as simple food and cheap clothing.

Now suppose that a progressive income tax is imposed, which successfully redistributes wealth among the population, so that general income levels rise. The result should be a general rise in living standards, with:

(a) greater demand for some items; and

(b) some switch in demand from cheap goods to better quality, more expensive substitutes.

Chapter roundup

- Fiscal policy seeks to influence the economy by managing the amounts which the government spends and the amounts it collects through taxation. Fiscal policy can be used to manage demand.
- Taxation has effects which a government may wish to create in order to promote its policy aims – for example, a redistribution of income or wealth – as well as providing a means of fine tuning the economy.

Quick quiz

1 Why might taxation be considered a deterrent to economic growth?

2 How might fiscal policy be used by a government to affect national income?

3 List the possible macroeconomic aims of fiscal policy.

4 Define a budget surplus and a budget deficit.

5 How often does a government usually review its fiscal policy?

6 What is the National Debt? What does it consist of?

7 What is the PSBR? What is a PSDR?

8 What are the functions of taxation?

9 What are the qualities of a good tax?

10 Define a regressive tax, a proportional tax and a progressive tax.

11 What are the advantages and disadvantages of a progressive tax?

12 What are the advantages and disadvantages of a regressive tax?

NOTES

Answers to Activities

1 Your answer might include any of the following points.

(a) High tax rates could lead to a reduction in the supply of labour.

(b) They could discourage consumer spending and company investments.

(c) They might encourage tax evasion.

Excessive taxation might deter investment and risk-taking and might curb individuals' initiative and efforts, although the evidence to support this is not conclusive. In the case of taxation of individuals, a counter-argument is that the higher the level of tax on income, the harder an individual will work in order to maintain an adequate level of post-tax income.

3 The expected PSBR is £23 billion. PSBR is the excess of expenditure over income for *all* public sector organisations, including nationalised industries and other public bodies (eg, the BBC in the UK).

4 You might have listed:

(a) rate-capping of over-spending councils;

(b) the abolition of the Greater London Council and the Metropolitan councils in 1986;

(c) the establishment of an independent Audit Commission in 1982. This Commission has the responsibility of providing an independent check on local government finance, and of suggesting ways of improving efficiency and effectiveness, or achieving economies;

(d) encouraging economies through the *privatisation* of certain services hitherto carried out by government workers.

5

	Tax paid on low income	*Tax paid on high income*	*Nature of tax*
System 1	20%	25%	Progressive
System 2	30%	30%	Proportional
System 3	10%	5%	Regressive

6 Demand for the product must presumably be inelastic, at least in the opinion of the producer. Otherwise the producer would fear to pass on the tax burden by increasing prices as this would lead to a fall in demand.

Case Study

This case looks more closely at the principal sources of taxation revenue for the UK central government.

Use both your knowledge of economic theory and material contained in the table to:

(a) distinguish between *direct* and *indirect* taxes; and place *each* of the taxes shown above into one of these two categories;

(b) explain what is meant by a *progressive tax*, and what is meant by a *regressive tax*, giving an example of each from the table;

(c) identify the main changes which have occurred in the structure of UK taxation between 1979 and 1993;

(d) explain how these changes in the taxation system may have influenced incentives and the distribution of income.

NOTES

Case Study (continued)

UK central government taxation revenue:
main tax sources as percentage of total tax income

		1979	1993
		%	%
1	Income taxes	34.1	30.0
2	Social Security taxes (National Insurance contributions)	19.2	20.0
3	Corporation tax	6.8	7.9
4	Value added tax	14.7	22.9
5	Excise duties	15.9	14.3
6	Other expenditure taxes*	7.7	3.7
7	Capital gains tax	0.9	0.6
8	Inheritance tax	0.7	0.6

*includes stamp duty and motor vehicle duties

(Source: National Income Accounts)

Answer to Case Study

(a) Direct taxes are levied on income and profits, or on wealth. The impact (or formal incidence) of a direct tax and its burden (effective incidence) are borne by the same person. The party on whom the tax is levied also has to pay the tax (although it may be argued that in some instances the burden can be passed on elsewhere by compensating wage/salary increase or higher product prices). They cannot be avoided other than by evasion or the assertion of monopoly power. In the table, the examples of direct taxes are income taxes, social security taxes, corporation tax, capital gains tax and inheritance tax.

Indirect taxes are levied on expenditure. Mostly they are collected by the revenue authority, eg Customs & Excise, from an intermediary, eg a supplier of goods or services, who then passes on the tax (or part of it) to consumers in the price of the goods or services. In the table, the examples of indirect taxes are value added tax, excise duties and other expenditure taxes. Motor vehicle duties (part of other expenditure taxes) are normally collected directly from existing vehicle owners. Indirect taxes, to a large extent, are avoidable: other than where a tax is imposed on a basic commodity/service, as with VAT on domestic fuel, people can in theory choose not to pay the tax by not buying the goods or services.

(b) A tax is said to be progressive because it takes proportionately more from those with higher incomes or, possibly, greater amounts of wealth. An example from the table is income tax. Overall it is progressive, as the rate of tax rises in stages according to the level of taxable income.

Corporation tax incorporates an element of progressiveness: companies with taxable profits below or above a certain level are subject to different rates of tax. Capital gains tax also has a progressive element in that the rate of tax is determined by the highest rate of income tax to which that person is subject within a given tax year.

A regressive tax takes a lower proportion of income or wealth, as the level of income or wealth increases. From the table, value added tax and excise duties are forms of regressive tax, since poorer people will pay a higher proportion of their income in these taxes than richer people.

(c) An important feature over the years 1979 to 1993 in the UK was a reduced progressiveness in the system of taxation, put onto a situation of more unevenly distributed pre-tax income. The decline in the progressiveness of taxation was partly the result of a reduction in the highest marginal rates of tax. Also, there was a highly significant switch from direct to indirect taxation: income tax fell from 34.1% to 30.0% of total tax revenue, while VAT rose from 14.7% to 22.9% of total tax revenue during the same period. A fall in the percentage of tax-take of other expenditure taxes only partly offsets this. Within the indirect taxes, VAT now makes a much greater contribution than it did in 1979. This switch of revenue raising from income tax into VAT has further diminished the progressiveness of the tax system as a whole.

(d) Direct taxes, which generally are more progressive, were reduced over the period 1979 to 1993, while indirect taxes as a whole (which tend to be regressive) were increased. It is often claimed, especially by supply-side economists, that lower levels of income tax act as an incentive, because of the resulting increases in disposable income. As a result, people will work harder and this will increase productivity and create more employment. Entrepreneurial risk-taking may be encouraged by the higher after-tax returns. The increased post-tax income will make possible increased saving by both individuals and firms, so making available the funds for increased investment. Real national income consequently will rise, so raising the level of tax revenue.

It can be argued that income-receivers are likely to be well aware of any income tax cut which takes place. They may be less aware of any increases in indirect taxes – especially if they are spread among a range of indirect taxes or are not fully passed on by producers or distributors. If that were to be the case, the incentive effect of reductions in direct taxes could outweigh any incentive effect from increase in indirect taxes. The incentive effect of a reduction in direct taxation is likely to vary between different groups of individuals. Some may work less, so as to maintain the same level of post-tax income, after a decrease in direct taxation. In many cases, however, the pace of work and the number of hours worked, among other things, are determined by factors outside the control of the individual. Various studies suggest that any possible incentive effect of income being increased is often short-lived.

The diminution in the role of direct taxes and the increased importance of indirect taxes has reduced the progressiveness of the tax system and increased the regressive element. As a consequence, lower income groups have been required to take on a greater burden of taxation. In addition, as mentioned earlier, pre-tax incomes have moved in favour of higher income groups. So the distribution of income after taxation has become less equal in the UK.

Further question practice

Now try the following practice questions at the end of this text.

Multiple choice questions **168–179**

Exam style question **17**

Chapter 16

INTERNATIONAL TRADE

Introduction

In the modern economy, production is based on a high degree of specialisation. Within a country individuals specialise, factories specialise and whole regions specialise. Specialisation increases productivity and raises the standard of living. International trade extends the principle of the division of labour and specialisation to countries.

Your objectives

After completing this chapter you should:

(a) understand the theory of comparative advantage and its implications for the development of international trade;

(b) understand the kinds of restrictions which may be applied to the free movement of international trade, and the reasons for and against adopting such measures.

1 ABSOLUTE AND COMPARATIVE ADVANTAGE

1.1 Reasons for international trade

International trade first started with nations exchanging their products for others which they could not produce for themselves. Britain, for example, imports tea and coffee, and exports oil to non-oil producing countries.

International trade arises for a number of reasons.

(a) Different goods require different proportions of factor inputs in their production.

(b) Economic resources are unevenly distributed throughout the world.

(c) The international mobility of resources is extremely limited.

Since it can be difficult to move resources between nations, the goods which embody the resources must move. This is why nations which have more land than labour will concentrate on land intensive commodities such as agricultural products. These will be exchanged for labour-intensive products such as manufactured goods made by countries which have more labour and capital than land. So the main reason for trade is that there are differences in the relative efficiency with which different countries can produce different goods and services.

Economists distinguish the concepts of *comparative advantage* and *absolute advantage*. To explain this distinction we make the following assumptions in what follows.

(a) There are only two countries, country X and country Y.

(b) Only two goods are produced, lorries and wheat.

(c) There are no transport costs and no barriers to trade.

(d) Resources within each country are easily transferred from one industry to another.

1.2 Absolute advantage

A country is said to have an absolute advantage in the production of a good when it is more efficient than another country in the production of that good. This means when it can produce more of a particular good with a given amount of resources than another country. It is a common situation for one country to be more efficient than another in the production of a particular good.

Assuming that country Y produces wheat more efficiently than country X, while country X has an absolute advantage in producing lorries, a simple arithmetical example can illustrate the potential gains from trade. The table below shows the amounts of lorries and wheat that each country can produce, assuming that each country has an equal quantity of resources and devotes half of its resources to lorry production and half to wheat production.

	Lorries	*Wheat (tons)*
Country X	20	100
Country Y	10	150
World total	30	250

The relative or comparative cost of lorry production is lower in country X than country Y, but the situation is reversed in the case of wheat production. Country X has an absolute advantage in lorry production and country Y has an absolute advantage in wheat production.

Greater specialisation will, however, increase total output of both lorries and wheat.

Activity 1

Suppose that each country devotes its entire production resources to the product for which it enjoys an absolute advantage. What will be the total world output of lorries and wheat?

In order to obtain the benefits of specialisation these countries must exchange some part of their individual outputs. It is not possible to specify the exact rate of exchange, but the limits of the exchange rate must be somewhere between the domestic opportunity cost ratios of the two countries. For country X, this is 5 tons of wheat per lorry; for country Y, it is 15 tons of wheat per lorry. One country will not benefit from international trade if the exchange rate is not between these ratios.

1.3 Comparative advantage

When two countries produce the same two goods, as in the example above, and each has an absolute advantage in the production of one good, it is easy to show that specialisation will lead to an increase in their combined output. Specialisation and trade can still be mutually advantageous, however, even if one country has an absolute advantage in the production of *both* goods. This will be the case if each country has a comparative advantage in the production of one good.

Definition

This is summed up in the law of *comparative advantage* (or comparative costs), which states that two countries can gain from trade when each concentrates on the production of that good in which it has greatest comparative advantage. Comparative cost relates to the opportunity costs of producing the goods and not the absolute costs.

The principle of comparative costs can be shown by an arithmetical example. It is now assumed that country X is more efficient in the production of both lorries and wheat. If each country devotes half its resources to each industry the assumed production totals are shown below.

	Lorries	*Wheat (tons)*
Country X	20	200
Country Y	10	150
World total	30	350

In terms of resources used, the costs of production in both industries are lower in country X. If we consider the opportunity costs, however, the picture is rather different. In country X the cost of one lorry is 10 tons of wheat, ie in devoting resources to the production of one lorry in country X there is a sacrifice in terms of 10 tons of wheat. The opportunity cost of one lorry in country Y is 15 tons of wheat. Country X, therefore, has a comparative advantage in the production of lorries.

In country X the opportunity cost of a ton of wheat is $\frac{1}{10}$ of a lorry, while in country Y the opportunity cost is $\frac{1}{15}$ of a lorry. In terms of the output of lorries sacrificed, wheat is cheaper in country Y than in country X. Country Y has a comparative advantage in wheat. If each country specialises completely in the production of the good where it has a comparative advantage, the figures below show that total output of lorries increases, but total output of wheat falls.

	Lorries	*Wheat (tons)*
Country X	40	0
Country Y	0	300
World total	40	300

The world total of lorry production has risen by 10 lorries, but that the world production of wheat has fallen by 50 tons. It is possible to show that the increase in the output of lorries, in value terms, more than offsets the fall in the output of wheat. It is not necessary to do this, however, because by only partially specialising in the more efficient country – country X – it is possible to have more of both commodities (see Activity 2).

Activity 2

Show that the statement above is true by calculating the total world output of lorries and wheat on the assumption that country Y specialises entirely in wheat, while country X devotes 80% of its resources to producing lorries and 20% to producing wheat.

Total output of both goods is greater than that which was obtained when both countries were producing only for domestic consumption. Since the opportunity cost ratios are different in the two countries, beneficial trade is possible. If the opportunity cost ratios were the same in the two countries, the countries would not benefit from specialisation and international trade.

Generalising from this example, we can state the law of comparative advantage.

Each country should export goods in which it has a comparative cost advantage.

In the example above we have assumed that transport costs for international trade are negligible. High transport costs, however, can wipe out the advantages of specialisation and international trade.

1.4 Does the law apply in practice?

The law of comparative advantage does apply in practice, and countries do specialise in the production of certain goods. However, there are certain limitations or restrictions on how it operates.

(a) *Free trade does not always exist.* Some countries take action to protect domestic industries and discourage imports. This means that a country might produce goods in which it does not have a comparative advantage.

(b) *Transport costs can be very high in international trade* so that it is cheaper to produce goods in the home country rather than to import them.

(c) *Countries might produce similar goods, but give them sufficiently unique characteristics to make them competitive in any country of the world.* For example, companies in France, Italy, Spain, Germany and the UK all manufacture cars, but the designs vary so that each country can export its own cars to the other countries. For example, the UK imports Fiats, Volkswagens and Citroens, but exports Rover cars to other EU countries.

Activity 3

In country P, a single unit of production resource will create *either* 6 television sets *or* 750 kg of maize.

In country Q, a single unit of production resource will create *either* 15 television sets *or* 900 kg of maize.

Analyse this situation in terms of the law of comparative advantage assuming that there are no other countries with which P and Q can trade. Will international trade take place and, if it does, who will export what?

2 FREE TRADE AND ITS ADVANTAGES

2.1 The main advantages

The law of comparative advantage states perhaps the major advantage of encouraging international trade. However, there are other advantages to the countries of the world from encouraging international trade. These are as follows.

(a) Some countries have a surplus of raw materials to their needs, and others have a deficit. A country with surplus materials (eg oil) can take advantage of its resources to export them.

A country with a deficit of a raw material must either import the material, or accept restrictions on its economic prosperity and standard of living.

(b) International trade increases competition among suppliers in the world's markets.

Greater competition makes it less likely that a market for a good in a country will be dominated by a monopolist. The greater competition will force firms to be competitive and so will increase the pressures on them to be efficient. It will also perhaps force them to produce goods of a high quality.

(c) International trade creates larger markets for a firm's output, and so some firms can benefit from *economies of scale* by exporting.

Economies of scale improve the efficiency of the use of resources, reduce the output costs and make it more likely that output will be sold to the consumer at lower prices than if international trade did not exist.

(d) There are political advantages to international trade, because the development of trading links provides a foundation for closer political links. An example of the development of political links based on trade is the European Union.

2.2 Free movement of capital

Free trade is associated with the free movement of goods (and services) between countries. Another important aspect of international trade is the free movement of capital.

(a) If a UK company or investor wishes to set up a business in a different country, or to take over a company in another country, how easily can it transfer capital from the UK to the country in question, to pay for the investment?

(b) Similarly, if a Japanese company wishes to invest in the UK, how easily can it transfer funds out of Japan and into the UK to pay for the investment?

Some countries (including the UK in recent years) have allowed a fairly free flow of capital into and out of the country. Other countries have been more cautious, mainly for one of two reasons.

(a) The free inflow of foreign capital will make it easier for foreign companies to take over domestic companies. There is often a belief that certain key industries should be owned by residents of the country. In the UK, for example, there have been restrictions on the total foreign ownership of shares in companies such as British Aerospace and Rolls Royce.

(b) Less developed countries especially, but also more advanced economies, are reluctant to allow the free flow of capital *out* of the country. After all, they need capital to come into the country to develop the domestic economy.

For countries with a large and continuing balance of trade deficit, such as the UK and the USA, it is *essential* that capital should come into the country to finance the deficit. The balance of payments is discussed in detail in the next chapter.

3 FREE TRADE AND PROTECTION

3.1 Introduction

Free trade exists where there is no restriction on imports from other countries or exports to other countries. In practice, however, many barriers to free trade exist because governments wish to protect home industries against foreign competition.

3.2 Protectionist measures

Protection can be applied by a government in several ways.

They include:

(a) tariffs or customs duties;

(b) import quotas;

(c) embargoes;

(d) hidden subsidies for exporters and domestic producers;

(e) import restrictions;

(f) government action to devalue the nation's currency – ie to reduce its foreign exchange value.

3.3 Tariffs or customs duties

Definition

Tariffs or *customs duties* are taxes on imported goods.

The effect of a tariff is to raise the price paid for the imported goods by domestic consumers, while leaving the price paid to foreign producers the same, or even lower. The difference goes to the government.

For example, if goods imported to the UK are bought for £100 per unit, which is paid to the foreign supplier, and a tariff of £20 is imposed, the full cost to the UK buyer will be £120, with £20 going to the government.

NOTES

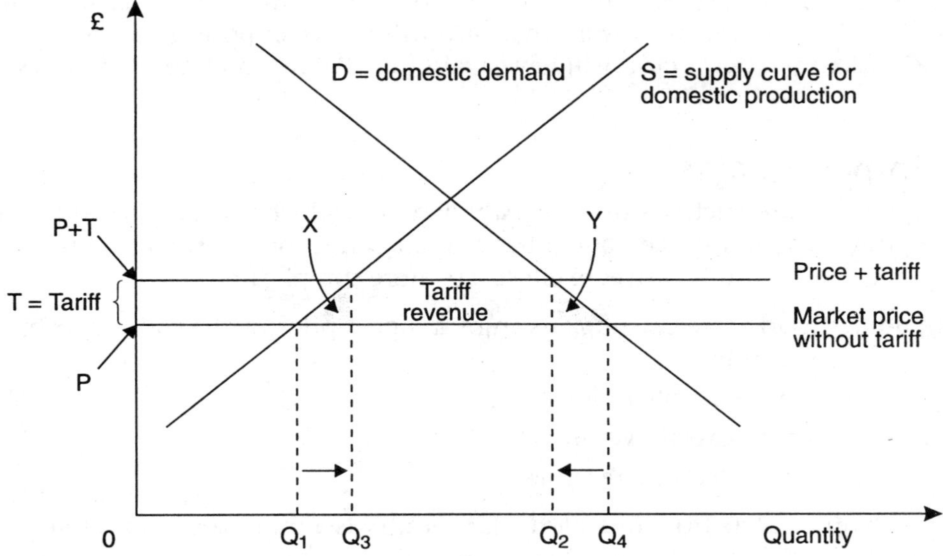

Figure 1 Effects of tariffs on prices and output

In Figure 1 the market purchase price of the good is P. At that price, domestic suppliers are willing to supply Q_1 but consumers are willing to buy Q_4. The difference $Q_1 - Q_4$ is then the amount of imports.

An import tariff will raise the price to the consumer to P + T. The domestic suppliers need not, of course, raise their prices, but at the higher price, consumers demand Q_2.

If the domestic producers were to raise their prices to P + T they would expand their output to Q_3. Imports would fall from $(Q_4 - Q_1)$ to $(Q_2 - Q_3)$.

The end result of imposing the tariff is that:

(a) domestic consumers buy fewer units;

(b) domestic producers supply more to the market;

(c) foreign suppliers provide less to the market;

(d) the government earns some tax revenue.

Activity 4

In the above scenario, what is the total tax revenue earned by the government as a result of imposing the tariff?

In such cases, import duties benefit the domestic producers and the government, but they harm the consumer. The government raises revenue and domestic producers expand their sales, but consumers either pay higher prices if they buy imported goods, or are forced to buy domestic goods. In the latter case there must be some loss of welfare because previously consumers were not buying domestically-produced goods at the world price, P. Now they are forced to because of the higher prices, P + T.

The areas of triangles X and Y represent the net loss to society. Triangle X is the additional amount that is spent by producing the commodity domestically rather than importing it at the world price. Triangle Y is the excess of consumer benefits over social marginal cost which the economy loses by reducing its consumption from Q_4 to Q_2.

Note that the price elasticity of the demand and supply functions may be important in determining by how much a tariff will reduce imports. If demand and supply are price inelastic, a tariff will have a fairly small effect on import volumes.

3.4 Import quotas

Import quotas are restrictions on the *quantity* of a product that is allowed to be imported into the country. The quota has a similar effect on consumer welfare to that of import tariffs, but the overall effects are more complicated.

(a) Both domestic and foreign suppliers enjoy a higher price, while consumers buy less at the higher price.

(b) Domestic producers supply more.

(c) There are fewer imports (in volume).

(d) The government collects no revenue.

An embargo on imports from one particular country is a total ban, ie effectively a zero quota.

3.5 Hidden export subsidies and import restrictions

An enormous range of government subsidies and assistance for exports and deterrents against imports have been practised, such as:

(a) *for exports* – export credit guarantees (ie government-backed insurance against bad debts for overseas sales), financial help (such as government grants to the aircraft or shipbuilding industry) and state assistance via the Foreign Office;

(b) *for imports* – complex import regulations and documentation, or special safety standards demanded from imported goods and so on.

When a government gives grants to its domestic producers, eg regional development grants for new investments in certain areas of the country, or grants to investments in new industries, the effect of these grants is to make unit production costs lower. These give the domestic producer a cost advantage over foreign producers in export markets as well as in domestic markets.

3.6 Government action to devalue or depreciate the currency

If a government allows its currency to fall in value, imports will become more expensive to buy.

Definition

Devaluation is a reduction in the fixed or pegged exchange rate between one currency and other currencies.

This will reduce imports by means of the price mechanism, especially if the demand and supply curves for the products are *elastic*. For example, if the exchange rate between sterling and the US dollar is £1 = $1.60, a good imported from the USA to the UK at a cost of $8,000 would cost the UK buyer £5,000. If the government takes action to reduce interest rates, which has the effect of weakening the value of sterling, the exchange rate might change to £1 = $1.50. The same good costing $8,000 will now cost a UK buyer £5,333, ie £333 more than before. At this higher price, the total UK demand for the US good will probably fall.

The extent of the fall in imports will depend on the price elasticity of demand in the UK for the US good.

3.7 The arguments in favour of protection

The arguments for protection are as follows.

(a) Protectionist measures can be taken against imports of cheap goods that compete with higher-priced domestically-produced goods, and so preserve output and employment in domestic industries.

(b) Measures might be necessary to counter dumping of surplus production by other countries at an uneconomically low price.

(c) Protectionist measures by one country are often taken in retaliation against measures taken by another country that are thought to be unfair.

(d) There is an argument that protectionism is necessary, at least in the short term, to protect a country's *infant industries* that have not yet developed to the size where they can compete in international markets.

(e) Protection might also help a country in the short term to deal with the problems of a declining industry.

(f) Protection is often seen as a means for a country to reduce its balance of trade deficit, by imposing tariffs or quotas on imports.

3.8 The arguments against protection

The arguments against protection are as follows.

(a) Because protectionist measures taken by one country will almost inevitably provoke retaliation by others, protection will reduce the volume of international trade. This means that the benefits of international trade will be reduced.

(b) Because of retaliation by other countries, protectionist measures to reverse a balance of trade deficit are unlikely to succeed. Imports might be reduced, but so too would exports.

(c) It is generally argued that widespread protection will damage the prospects for economic growth among the countries of the world, and protectionist measures ought to be restricted to special cases, which might be discussed and negotiated with other countries.

(d) Protection creates political ill-will among countries of the world, so there are political disadvantages in a policy of protection.

As an alternative to protection, a country can try to stimulate its export competitiveness by making efforts to improve the productivity and lower the costs of domestic industries. This will make them more competitive against foreign producers.

Hidden subsidies and exchange rate devaluation or depreciation are examples of indirect protectionist measures. Other measures, such as funding industrial training schemes and educational policies, might in the longer term result in improvements in domestic productivity.

3.9 The World Trade Organisation (WTO)

The WTO was formed in 1995 as successor to the General Agreement on Tariffs and Trade (GATT). The GATT was originally signed by 23 countries in 1947 as an attempt to promote free trade. The aims of GATT were:

(a) to reduce existing barriers to free trade;

(b) to eliminate discrimination in international trade;

(c) to prevent the growth of protection by getting member countries to consult with others before taking any protectionist measures.

NOTES

Definition

The *most-favoured nation principle* is that when one GATT member country offers a reduction in tariffs to another country, it must offer the same reduction to all other member countries of GATT.

GATT membership reached 128, including many newly industrialising countries.

The GATT talks have taken place over the years in a series of rounds of negotiation.

(a) The 'Kennedy round' of the 1960s was particularly successful and led to tariff cuts of about 30%, bringing the average duty on manufactured goods down to about 10% by 1972.

(b) The 'Tokyo round' of the late 1970s led to further tariff reductions of approximately 30%. Trade between advanced industrialised nations in particular was favoured, with tariff cuts of 38%. The cut was a lower 25% in the case of trade between advanced industrialised and newly industrialised countries.

(c) The talks in the 'Uruguay round', which were concluded in December 1993, represented seven years of work on a very ambitious programme for the liberalisation of world trade.

The December 1993 conclusion of the 'Uruguay round' revised, improved and updated many of the GATT rules originally drafted in the 1940s. It also brought the following changes, some of which are to be phased in over a period of time.

(a) *Industrial tariffs*. Before the 1993 deal, tariffs on manufactured goods averaged 5% in richer countries (down from around 40% in the late 1940s). There is now the prospect of richer countries' tariffs on industrial goods being cut by more than one third. Over 40% of imports of specific types will be duty-free. These changes will bring easier access to world markets and lower prices for consumers.

(b) *Agriculture*. Subsidies and import barriers which distort trade are being cut over the next few years. For example, domestic farm support, including that in Europe and the USA, will be reduced by 20%. These changes should bring better market opportunities for efficient producers, reduced overproduction and lower food prices for consumers in currently protected countries.

(c) *Services*. A framework of rules on basic fair trading principles such as non-discrimination has been established, with further talks on telecommunications and financial services planned. Previously, there were no rules governing international trade in most services.

(d) *Intellectual property*. Agreements were reached on patents, copyright, trademarks, designs and so on. This will facilitate technology transfer and reduce trade in counterfeit goods.

(e) *Textiles and clothing*. The quotas imposed by richer countries since 1974 under the Multi-Fibre Arrangement are to be progressively dismantled over ten years and tariffs are to be reduced. Normal GATT rules will apply at the end of the ten-year period. These changes will allow less developed countries to sell more textiles and clothing abroad and are likely to reduce prices for consumers worldwide.

(f) *Anti-dumping measures*. Clearer rules will make it more difficult for countries to introduce anti-dumping measures, which have often been seen as a disguised form of protectionism.

(g) *Subsidies*. Tighter rules have been introduced on the use of subsidies, with some types of subsidy being prohibited.

(h) *Technical barriers*. Better rules have been introduced to establish international norms for product regulations and standards, which up to now have been fairly extensively used as a disguised form of competition.

(i) *Government procurement.* The coverage of the agreement on government procurement, which had 12 signatories (including the EU) in the 'Tokyo round', has been enlarged to cover more areas.

It has been estimated that the opening up of markets for agricultural and industrial goods following the 1993 GATT accord could add around US $200-300 billion to world income by the year 2002. Some commentators, however, have argued that poorer countries stand to lose. Against this, the GATT secretariat notes that less developed countries will have much lower tariff cuts on their exports than other countries (25% compared with 37%). However, if textiles and clothing, and fish products are removed from the calculation, tariff concessions of the poorest countries average 50% compared with 44% for industrialised nations.

Ratification of the agreement by member governments followed during 1994. The new WTO, which GATT members have now joined, was set up in 1995 as a result of the agreement. GATT itself officially ceased to exist at the end of 1995.

3.10 The European Union and the single European market 1992

The European Union (EU) constitutes a localised free trade agreement among member countries incorporating protectionist measures against other trading nations.

Definition

European Union (EU). Member states are Austria, Belgium, Denmark, Finland, France, Germany, Greece, Ireland, Italy, Luxembourg, the Netherlands, Portugal, Spain, Sweden and the United Kingdom.

The end of 1992 marked the removal of many physical, technical and fiscal barriers among member states, thus creating a large multinational European Single Market (ESM). This objective was expressed in the Single European Act of 1986. In practice, these changes have not occurred 'overnight', and many are still in progress.

Activity 5

The single market and its likely effects have been much discussed in the media. Before reading on, try to jot down any concrete measures you are aware of which have come into force as a result of the single market.

The European single market has various aspects.

(a) European regulations and standards mean that products approved in any one EU country can be freely marketed throughout the Union.

(b) There is a progressive opening up of government and other public body contracts to all EU contractors on an equal basis.

(c) There is to be more competition and efficiency in Europe-wide services in telecommunications and information technology by developing common standards for equipment.

(d) The road haulage market is being liberalised by eliminating bureaucratic red tape; shipping services between member countries are to be provided on equal terms; competition on air routes should increase, resulting in lower fares.

(e) Banks and securities houses authorised in their home country should be free to provide banking and investment services anywhere in the EU. Insurers will have greater freedom to cover risks in other member countries. All restrictions on the movement of capital are being removed.

(f) Protection of ideas will become easier through harmonisation of national laws on patents and trade marks.

(g) Professional qualifications obtained in one country are to be acceptable in all other countries.

Chapter roundup

- World output of goods and services will increase if countries specialise in the production of goods/services in which they have a comparative advantage.
- Just how this total wealth is shared out between countries depends on circumstances. There is a view that poorer, developing countries might be exploited by richer countries and that the total wealth is not distributed fairly. This is one argument for protection and restrictions on free international trade.
- There are various arguments in favour of both protection and free trade, although the balance of opinion favours free trade. Even so, in recent years there has been a growing threat of protection.
  - In the USA, which has had a very large balance of trade deficit, there is a body of opinion which favours protectionist measures against other countries, such as Japan, which supply goods in large volumes to the USA.
  - Free trade unions, such as the EU, threaten to lock out other countries from their free trade union, making it more difficult to export goods to them. Countries such as the USA and Japan, for example, have been concerned that the new rules on trade within the EU could act as protectionist measures against them.

Quick quiz

1 What are the advantages of free trade in international trade?

2 What protectionist measures might be taken?

3 What would be the consequences of imposing an import tariff?

4 Why might action to devalue a currency be a protectionist measure?

5 What are the arguments in favour of protection?

6 What are the arguments against protection?

NOTES

Answers to Activities

1 Total world output will be 40 lorries (produced by country X) and 300 tons of wheat (produced by country Y).

2 World output will be as follows.

	Lorries	*Wheat (tons)*
Country X	32	80
Country Y	0	300
World total	32	380

3 In country P the opportunity cost of making a television set is 125 kg of maize and the opportunity cost of producing 1 kg of maize is $\frac{1}{125}$ television sets.

In country Q the opportunity cost of making a television set is 60 kg of maize and the opportunity cost of producing 1 kg of maize is $\frac{1}{60}$ television sets.

P has a comparative advantage in maize production and will export maize to Q; Q has a comparative advantage in production of television sets and will export television sets to P.

4 The total tax revenue accruing for the government is the volume of imports multiplied by the value of the tariff, in other words:

$$(Q_2 - Q_3) \times T$$

Further question practice

Now try the following practice questions at the end of this text.

Multiple choice questions **180–191**

Exam style question **18**

Chapter 17

THE BALANCE OF PAYMENTS AND EXCHANGE RATES

Introduction

The balance of payments and exchange rates are both important concerns of economic policy. Exchange rates, and changes in exchange rates, are also key concerns of any business which has transactions in foreign currency, and this includes most importers and exporters.

Your objectives

After completing this chapter you should:

(a) understand what is meant by the balance of payments, and be aware of the components in its make-up;

(b) be aware of the effects of surpluses or deficits in the balance of payments;

(c) understand the meaning and the effects of a country's terms of trade;

(d) be aware of the importance of exchange rates and understand how they may be determined.

1 THE BALANCE OF PAYMENTS

1.1 The nature of the balance of payments

Definition

The *balance of payments* is a statistical accounting record of a country's international trade transactions (the purchase and sale of goods and services) and capital transactions (the acquisition and disposal of assets and liabilities) with other countries during a period of time.

Under the current method of presentation of the UK balance of payments statistics the broad classifications of transactions are:

(a) current account transactions. These are sub-divided into transactions in visibles (ie goods) and transactions in invisibles (ie services). The current account is, therefore, the record of a country's trading in exports and imports of goods and services;

(b) changes in the UK's external assets and liabilities.

1.2 The sum of the balance of payments accounts is zero

The sum of the balance of payments accounts must always be zero (ignoring statistical errors in collecting the figures).

This is because every transaction in international trade has a double aspect. In the balance of payments, every plus item should have a matching minus item.

If the balance of payments in principle sums to zero, you may wonder what is meant by a surplus or deficit on the balance of payments. When journalists or economists speak of the balance of payments they are usually referring to the deficit or surplus on the *current account*, or possibly to the surplus or deficit on visibles only. To appreciate these terms, it is helpful to look at balance of payments items in a bit more detail. Below, we use UK statistics to illustrate principles which apply equally to the balance of payments of every other country.

1.3 The UK balance of payments accounts

The UK balance of payments for a recent year is set out in Table 1 below. The components of the table are analysed in greater detail in the next section of this chapter.

NOTES

TABLE 1 UK BALANCE OF PAYMENTS, 1995	£bn
Current account	
Exports	152.3
Imports	(163.9)
Trade in goods balance	(11.6)
Services balance	6.1
Total goods and services balance	(5.5)
Investment income	9.6
Transfers	(7.0)
Current balance	(2.9)
UK external assets and liabilities: net transactions	0.5
Balancing item	2.4
	–

(CSO Pink Book)

2 COMPONENTS OF THE BALANCE OF PAYMENTS

2.1 The current account

We will now consider the components of the balance of payments in more detail, starting with the current account.

2.2 Trade in goods

The trade in goods balance is sometimes referred to as the balance of trade. As can be seen from Table 1, the trade in goods balance is the difference between the value of exported goods from the UK and imported goods to the UK. Trade in goods used to be called 'visible trade'.

Activity 1

Which of the following items would be included in the UK balance of trade statistics?

(a) Spending in the UK by overseas tourists.

(b) Accountancy services performed by firms of UK auditors in Germany?

(c) Timber imported from Scandinavia and re-exported to Spain.

2.3 Other items in the current account

The remaining items in the current account are services, interest, profit and dividends, and transfers. The overall balance on these items used to be called the 'invisibles' balance, and you may still find this term being used. The annual trade in services is invariably in surplus for the UK. The net surplus on financial services is a major reason for this.

Services include transport (by sea and air, both passenger and cargo), tourism, financial (banking, insurance, brokerage, etc) and government services (chiefly due to military and diplomatic presence overseas).

Services have grown in importance in recent years, particularly inward tourism and earnings from financial services.

Investment income consists of items such as:

(a) direct investment earnings. These are the share of profits in overseas branches, overseas subsidiary companies and overseas associated companies. Direct investment earnings might bring income into the country (eg the *profits of UK banks operating overseas*) or cause outflows (profits of overseas firms investing in the UK);

(b) portfolio investment earnings – ie interest and dividends on stocks and shares held in overseas securities by UK residents, or held in UK securities by overseas residents;

(c) interest on borrowing and lending abroad by UK banks.

Transfers include government transfers, such as payments by the UK to the EU budget and foreign aid, and private transfers, such as payments by UK residents to overseas dependants and sums paid by voluntary relief organisations.

2.4 UK external assets and liabilities

Transactions in UK external assets and liabilities record the increases or decreases in:

(a) foreign assets, including foreign currency, that are held by UK residents (including the UK government);

(b) the liabilities of the UK to residents of other countries. These are increases or decreases in UK assets, including sterling, that are held by individuals, firms or governments in other countries.

2.5 Transactions in official reserves

An item under the heading of (transactions in) assets in the balance of payments is 'drawings on or additions to the official reserves'.

The official reserves mainly consist of gold and convertible foreign currencies, held in the government's Exchange Equalisation account with the Bank of England. (Other countries similarly have official reserves, which are kept and managed on behalf of the government by the central bank.) Governments use these reserves to balance the overseas accounts and also to deal in the foreign exchange markets.

In past years, movements on the official reserves were given greater prominence in the UK balance of payments statistics, but other international capital transactions are so large that they now dwarf any changes in official reserves, and so changes in the official reserves are no longer given the same prominence as before. Instead, they are included as just another item in the assets section of the balance of payments account.

Activity 2

If the level of real incomes of the UK population were to rise, would the UK's balance of payments position improve or deteriorate?

3 EQUILIBRIUM, SURPLUSES AND DEFICITS

3.1 Equilibrium in the balance of payments

A balance of payments is *in equilibrium* if, on balance, over a period of years:

(a) the exchange rate remains stable; and

(b) autonomous credits and debits are equal in value (ie the annual trade in goods and services is in overall balance); and

(c) to achieve this situation, the government is not required to introduce measures which:

  (i) create unemployment or higher prices;

  (ii) sacrifice economic growth; or

  (iii) impose trade barriers (eg import tariffs and import quotas).

3.2 Surplus or deficit in the balance of payments

A problem arises for a country's balance of payments when the country has a deficit year after year *on its current account*, although there can be problems too for a country (such as Japan) which enjoys a continual current account *surplus*.

The problems of a *deficit* on the current account are probably the more obvious. When a country is continually in deficit, it is importing more goods and services that it is exporting, and so:

(a) it must either borrow more and more from abroad, to build up external liabilities which match the deficit on current account, eg encourage foreign investors to lend more by purchasing the government's gilt edged securities; or

(b) it must sell more and more of its assets. This has been happening recently in the USA, for example, where a large deficit on the US current account has resulted in large purchases of shares in US companies by foreign firms.

Even so, the demand to buy the country's currency in the foreign exchange markets will be weaker than the supply of the country's currency for sale. As a consequence, there will be pressure on the exchange rate to depreciate in value.

If a country has a *surplus* on its current account year after year, it might invest the surplus abroad or add it to official reserves. The balance of payments position would be strong. There is the problem, however, that if one country which is a major trading nation (eg Japan) has a continuous surplus on its balance of payments current account, other countries must be in continual deficit. These other countries can run down their official reserves, perhaps to nothing, and borrow as much as they can to meet the payments overseas, but eventually, they will run out of money entirely and be unable even to pay their debts.

Political pressure might therefore build up within the importing countries to impose tariffs or import quotas.

It might therefore be argued that a country has a good balance of payments position if, in the long run, it has neither surplus nor deficit on its current account, or at least if, in the long run, its current account deficit is matched by inflows of direct investment (ie long-term) capital.

EXAMPLE: CAUSES AND CONSEQUENCES OF A TRADE DEFICIT

Causes

- Poor exports caused by:
  - a high exchange rate keeping prices of export goods in foreign markets too high;
  - inefficient production, keeping costs of output too high and uncompetitive in foreign markets.
- Excessive imports of consumer goods.
- Imports of raw materials and capital goods by firms, seeking to expand their own output.

Consequences

- The country is importing more goods than it exports, and so the country's general standard of living is being improved.
- The country must import capital from abroad. Foreign investors are only likely to invest:
  - for high interest rates/high profits; and
  - if they still have confidence in the country's economic prospects.
- Unless sufficient foreign investment is forthcoming, there will be pressures on the country's currency to depreciate, because of excess supply over demand for the currency in the foreign exchange markets.

3.3 Practical ways of correcting a current account deficit

The government of a country with a balance of payments deficit will usually be expected to take measures to reduce or get rid of the deficit. A deficit on current account may be corrected by one or more of the following measures:

(a) a depreciation or devaluation of the currency;

(b) direct measures to restrict imports, such as tariffs, import quotas, or exchange control regulations;

(c) domestic deflation to reduce aggregate demand in the domestic economy.

If a country imports raw materials and exports manufactured goods which are made with those materials, the cost of imported raw materials will rise. Therefore producers will have to put up their prices to cover their higher costs. There will be a net fall in export prices, as explained above, but perhaps not by much.

Because the effect of depreciation or devaluation depends on price elasticities of demand in this way, it might be the case that depreciation of the currency on its own would not be enough to correct the balance of payments deficit, unless an extremely large depreciation took place.

3.4 The effects of a fall in the exchange rate

We can now consider what would happen to the UK current account balance if there were a fall in the value of sterling.

(a) The immediate effects will depend on the elasticity of demand for imports. In the short run, demand is likely to be fairly inelastic and so total expenditure on imports will rise.

(b) Exports will be cheaper in overseas markets (in foreign currency), but in the short run UK exporters might be unable to increase their output to meet the higher demand.

(c) Until UK industry adjusts to the change and increases its output of exported goods and home-produced substitutes for imported goods there will be a deterioration in the current account of the balance of payments.

(d) After a time lag, production of exports and import substitutes will rise, so that:

 (i) the volume of exports will rise, thereby increasing the sterling value of exports (regardless of sterling's lower exchange rate);

 (ii) the volume of imports will fall further. This will improve the current account balance.

 The extent of this improvement will depend on the price elasticity of demand for UK exports abroad and the price elasticity of demand for foreign imports in the UK.

(e) The improvement in the balance of payments will have some limit, and the current balance should eventually level off. The effect of the falling exchange rate on the current balance can be shown by a 'J' curve (Figure 1).

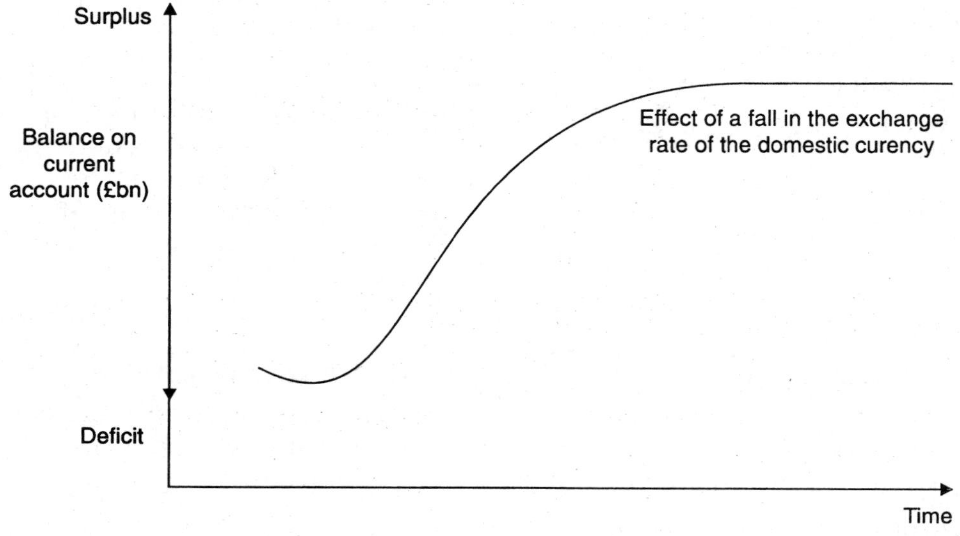

Figure 1 J Curve

3.5 Protectionist measures

Another way of attempting to correct a balance of payments deficit is to take direct protectionist measures to reduce the volume of imports. Protectionist measures were discussed in the previous chapter.

Activity 3

Try to list the various protectionist measures that were discussed in Chapter 16. What are the dangers of imposing protectionist measures?

4 THE TERMS OF TRADE

4.1 Introduction

The balance of trade for any country depends on two things:

(a) the volume of goods exported and imported; and

(b) the relative prices of exports and imports.

Definition

The *terms of trade* are the quantities of domestic goods that a country must give up to obtain a unit of imported goods.

For example, if country X must produce 1.2 units of domestically-produced goods to obtain 1 unit of goods from country Y, the terms of trade could be described as 1.2 units of X goods : 1 unit of Y goods. In other words, the terms of trade are an export : import price ratio, which measures the relative prices of a country's exports against the prices paid for its imports. The terms of trade for a country continually change as export prices and import prices change.

(a) If circumstances change so that X must produce and export 1.5 units of its goods to obtain 1 unit of goods from Y, the terms of trade will have shifted against X and in favour of Y.

(b) If circumstances change so that X must produce and export only 1 unit of its goods to obtain 1 unit of goods from Y, the terms of trade will have shifted in favour of X and against Y.

The ratio of export to import prices (the terms of trade) decides the volume of exports necessary to pay for a given volume of imports. That is to say, the volume of imports that can be bought with the proceeds of a given volume of exports.

Other things being equal, if the price of exports falls relative to that of imports (a fall in the terms of trade) the trade balance will deteriorate, or vice versa.

Note that the trade balance depends not just on the physical volume of exports and imports, but also on the prices at which they are traded.

Activity 4

A country's electronics industry, which is its major export industry, switches from the production of mass low-cost, low-profit margin microchips to the production of more high-powered, high-cost, high profit margin custom-built microchips. Which one of the following effects would you expect to occur?

(a) An improvement in the balance of trade.

(b) A deterioration in the balance of trade.

(c) An improvement in the terms of trade.

(d) A worsening in the terms of trade.

4.2 Measuring the terms of trade and changes in the terms of trade

The terms of trade, are measured as:

$$\frac{\text{unit value of exports}}{\text{unit value of imports}}$$

NOTES

In practice economists are usually concerned, not with a measurable value for the terms of trade, but with a measure of *changes* in the terms of trade, (eg from one year to the next).

Using indices for the average prices of imports and exports, the movement in the terms of trade between 1996 and 1997 would be computed as:

$$\frac{\text{Price of exports 1997/price of exports 1996}}{\text{Price of imports 1997/price of imports 1996}}$$

Change in a country's terms of trade occur because of:

(a) a change in the composition of exports or imports. In the UK two main things (fewer oil exports and manufacturers trading up to higher-price products for export) have improved the UK's terms of trade since 1985;

(b) lower or higher prices of imports/exports (eg the oil price collapse in 1985, which worsened the terms of trade for the UK).

A government has limited powers to influence its country's terms of trade, since it cannot directly influence the composition nor the prices of imports and exports. However, it can affect the terms of trade through a revaluation or devaluation of the currency, which would alter relative import/export prices.

4.3 What does a change in the terms of trade mean?

If a country's terms of trade *worsen*, the unit value of its imports will rise by a bigger percentage than the unit value of its exports. The terms of trade will worsen when the exchange rate of the currency depreciates in value against other currencies.

If a country's terms of trade *improve*, the unit value of its exports will rise by a bigger percentage than the unit value of its imports. The terms of trade will improve when the exchange rate of the country's currency appreciates in value against other currencies.

It would seem logical to assume that improving terms of trade is good for a country and worsening terms of trade are bad. But this is not necessarily the case.

What is the effect of a change in the terms of trade? This should be considered in the context of the country's balance of payments.

4.4 The effect of changes in the terms of trade

If the terms of trade worsen for a country, the country will be unable to afford the same volume of imports, or else its balance of payment position will deteriorate. In contrast, a country with improving terms of trade will be able to afford more imports or will improve its balance of payments.

Changes in the terms of trade affect a country's balance of payments via the price elasticity of demand for the goods traded. If a country's terms of trade improve, so that the price of its exported goods rises relative to the price of its imported goods, there will be a relative fall in the volume of goods exported and a rise in the volume of imports. The size of this fall in exports and increase in imports will depend on the price elasticities of demand for exported goods in foreign markets and imported goods in the country's domestic markets.

Activity 5

From your knowledge of the theory of elasticity of demand, analyse what will happen to the current balance of trade when the terms of trade improve, on the assumptions:

(a) that demand for exported goods and demand for imported goods are both inelastic;

(b) that both demands are *elastic*.

5 EXCHANGE RATES

We have already mentioned exchange rates several times. In simple terms, the concept of an exchange rate is familiar to anyone who has ever taken a day trip across the Channel. But in this section we look at the importance of exchange rates in some detail.

Definition

An *exchange rate* is the rate at which one country's currency can be traded in exchange for another country's currency.

Although it is convenient to refer to the exchange rate for currency – eg the exchange rate for sterling – every traded currency has many exchange rates. There is an exchange rate with every other traded currency on the foreign exchange markets: an exchange rate for sterling with the US dollar, the Canadian dollar, the yen, the deutschmark, the French franc, and so on.

Foreign exchange dealers make their profit by buying currency for less than they pay for it, and so there are really two exchange rates, a selling rate and a buying rate; eg

	Bank's selling rate	*Bank's buying rate*
£/US dollar exchange rate	$1.5020	$1.5080

When exchange rates are quoted in the press, the middle rate between the selling and buying rates would be used. In the example above, the sterling/US dollar exchange rate would be mid-way between $1.5020 and $1.5080, ie $1.5050 to £1.

5.1 Spot rates and forward rates

Broadly speaking, there are two ways in which foreign currency is bought and sold:

(a) *spot* – ie for immediate delivery.

(b) *forward* – ie for delivery at a date in the future.

So, a UK firm might receive US$100,000 from a US customer, and sell it spot to a bank, to receive sterling immediately (in practice three days after the contract is made). If the exchange rate is $1.8000 to £1, the UK firm would receive £55,555.56.

If a firm knows that it is going to receive some foreign currency in the near future, which it will want to sell in exchange for domestic currency, it can make a forward exchange contract with a bank, at an exchange rate that is specified in the contract. Thus, if a firm knows that it is going to receive US$100,000 in three months' time, it can make a forward exchange contract 'now' to sell the US dollars in three months' time at a specified exchange rate. If the 'spot' rate is $1.8000 to £1, the 'forward' rate may be higher or lower than $1.8000 (depending on comparative interest rates in the USA and the UK).

NOTES

Activity 6

Suppose that, when the three month-period is up, the value of the dollar has strengthened against sterling compared with the rate in the forward exchange contract. Will the UK company regret having made a forward exchange contract?

5.2 Factors influencing the exchange rate for a currency

The exchange rate between two currencies – ie the buying and selling rates, both spot and forward – is determined primarily by supply and demand in the foreign exchange markets. Demand comes from individuals, firms and governments who want to buy a currency and supply comes from those who want to sell it.

Supply and demand in turn are influenced by:

(a) the rate of inflation, compared with the rate of inflation in other countries;

(b) interest rates, compared with interest rates in other countries;

(c) the balance of payments;

(d) speculation;

(e) government policy on intervention to influence the exchange rate.

5.3 Purchasing power parity theory

If the rate of inflation is higher in one country than in another country, the value of its currency will tend to weaken against the other country's currency.

Definition

Purchasing power parity theory, which developed in the 1920s, attempted to explain changes in the exchange rate exclusively by the rate of inflation in different countries; it predicts that the exchange value of a foreign currency depends on the relative purchasing power of each currency in its own country.

As a simple example, suppose that there is only one commodity, which costs £110 in the UK and 880 francs in France. The exchange rate would be £1 = 8 francs. If, as a result of inflation, the cost of the commodity in the UK rises to £120, the exchange rate would adjust to:

$$\left(8 \times \frac{110}{120}\right) \times £1 = 7.33 \text{ francs.}$$

If the exchange rate remained at £1 = 8 francs, it would be cheaper to import more of the commodity from France for £110 and the UK would have a balance of trade deficit. This would only be corrected by an alteration in the exchange rate, with the pound weakening against the franc.

Purchasing power parity theory states that an exchange rate varies according to relative price changes, so that

$$\text{'old' exchange rate} \times \frac{\text{price level in country A}}{\text{price level in country B}} = \text{'new' exchange rate}$$

The theory was soon found to be inadequate to explain movements in exchange rates *in the short term*, mainly because it ignores payments between countries (ie demand and supply transactions) and the influence of supply and demand for currency on exchange rates.

NOTES

5.4 Interest rates and the exchange rate

It would seem logical to assume that if one country raises its interest rates, it will become more profitable to invest in that country, and so an increase in (mainly short-term) investment from overseas will push up the exchange rate because of the extra demand for the currency from overseas investors.

This is true, but there is a limit to the amount of investment capital that will flow into a country because of higher interest rates. A major reason for this is that investors may expect a risk premium for investing in a high interest rate currency if they fear that the currency will depreciate in value.

5.5 The balance of payments and the exchange rate

Purchasing power parity theory is more likely to have some validity in the long run, and it is certainly true that the currency of a country which has a much higher rate of inflation than other countries will weaken on the foreign exchange market. In other words, the rate of inflation relative to other countries is certainly a factor which influences the exchange rate.

Although this is obvious, it is not the main influence. This is apparent from the fact that if exchange rates did respond to demand and supply for current account items, then the balance of payments on the current account of all countries would tend towards equilibrium. This is not so, and in practice other factors influence exchange rates more strongly.

5.6 Government intervention

The government can intervene in the foreign exchange markets:

(a) to sell its own domestic currency in exchange for foreign currencies, when it wants to keep down the exchange rate of its domestic currency. The foreign currencies it buys can be added to the official reserves;

(b) to buy its own domestic currency and pay for it with the foreign currencies in its official reserves. It will do this when it wants to keep up the exchange rate when market forces are pushing it down.

The government can also intervene indirectly, by changing domestic interest rates, and so either attract or discourage investors in financial investments in the domestic currency. Purchases and sales of foreign investments create a demand and supply of the currency in the foreign exchange markets, and so changes in domestic interest rates are likely to cause a change in the exchange rate.

Activity 7

Demand for imports in a country is inelastic in response to price changes and demand for the country's exports is also inelastic. The country's government raises interest rates substantially, and interest rates in other countries remain unchanged. What will be the effect of the rise in interest rates on the level of imports and on the level of exports?

---

6 EXCHANGE RATE POLICY OPTIONS

6.1 Exchange rate policies of governments

We shall now go on to consider in more detail the different exchange rate policies which are open to governments. These may be categorised as:

(a) fixed exchange rates;

(b) free floating exchange rates;

(c) margins around a movable peg;

(d) managed floating.

6.2 Fixed exchange rates

A policy of rigidly fixed exchange rates means that the government of every country in the international monetary system must use its official reserves to create an exact match between supply and demand for its currency in the foreign exchange markets, in order to keep the exchange rate unchanged. Using the official reserves will therefore cancel out a surplus or deficit on the current account and non-official capital transactions in their balance of payments. A balance of payments surplus would call for an addition to the official reserves, and a deficit would call for drawings on official reserves.

The official reserves could in theory consist of any foreign currency (or gold) within the fixed exchange rate agreement. The exchange rates of the various currencies in the system might all be fixed against each other. However, for simplicity and convenience, it is more appropriate to fix the exchange rate for every currency against a standard. The standard might be:

(a) gold. If every currency is valued in terms of gold, official reserves would consist mainly, or even entirely, of gold;

(b) a major currency, such as the US dollar;

(c) a basket of major trading currencies. For example, as explained below, the European Currency Unit (ecu) is an international currency based on a basket of currencies of EU countries.

A fixed exchange rate system removes exchange rate uncertainty and so encourages international trade. It also imposes economic disciplines on countries in deficit (or surplus). However, this restricts independence of domestic economic policies. A government might be forced to keep interest rates high or to reduce demand in the domestic economy (eg by raising taxes and so cutting the demand for imports) in order to maintain a currency's exchange rate and avoid a devaluation.

If levels of inflation differ widely in countries subscribing to a fixed exchange rate regime, the regime may not survive for long. The high inflation countries will be forced to devalue in order to keep their exports competitive and to reduce imports.

6.3 Free floating exchange rates

Free floating exchange rates are at the opposite end of the spectrum to rigidly fixed rates. Exchange rates are left to the free play of market forces and there is no official financing at all. There is no need for the government to hold any official reserves, because it will not want to use them.

NOTES

Definition

Floating exchange rates are exchange rates which are allowed to fluctuate according to demand and supply conditions in the foreign exchange market.

Floating exchange rate systems (free floating and managed floating) have been criticised in the past because they allow wide fluctuations in exchange rates. Certainly, in the foreign exchange markets today, there are large fluctuations which are unsettling for international trade. Floating exchange rates are the only option available to governments when other systems break down and fail.

6.4 A movable peg or adjustable peg system

A movable or adjustable peg system is a system of fixed exchange rates, but with a provision for:

(a) the devaluation of a currency, eg when the country has a persistent balance of payments deficit;

(b) the revaluation of a currency, eg when the country has a persistent balance of payments surplus.

6.5 Margins around a movable peg

A movable peg system provides some flexibility. Exchange rates, although fixed, are not rigidly fixed, because adjustments are permitted. Even so, it is still fairly inflexible, because governments only have the choice between a revaluation/devaluation or holding the exchange rate steady. A more flexible system would allow some minor variations in exchange rates. For example, the exchange rate between sterling and the US dollar might be fixed at $2 to £1, but governments might only be required to maintain the exchange rate within a margin of, say, 2% on either side of this rate. If this were the case, the UK government would undertake to keep the exchange rate for sterling between $1.96 and $2.04 to £1. However, if the UK were to run into a fundamental balance of payments disequilibrium, a devaluation (or revaluation) of sterling would occur. Then the UK government would undertake to maintain exchange rates within the required margins of the new exchange rate.

The European exchange rate mechanism (ERM) is an adjustable peg system.

7 EUROPEAN MONETARY CO-OPERATION

7.1 The European Monetary System (EMS)

The European Community opted for a local international agreement on exchange rates, originally known as the `European Snake', but amended in 1979 to the EMS system. In the EMS:

(a) there is a scheme of margins around a central peg for exchange rates between the currencies of the countries in the EMS; but

(b) a policy of managed floating between their currencies and the currencies of countries outside the system.

The exchange rate mechanism (ERM) is the exchange rate agreement of the European monetary system, which was formed on 13 March 1979. The United Kingdom has been a member of the EMS since then, but did not join the exchange rate mechanism of the EMS until October 1990 and left the ERM in 1992.

NOTES

The main features of the EMS are as follows.

(a) It provides for the system of exchange rates for member currencies commonly known as the ERM. Each currency has a central parity rate against the ecu.
(b) The EMS created the new currency, the *European Currency Unit* or *ecu*. An ecu is a unit of currency based on a basket of the currencies of the participating countries. The value of the ecu therefore depends on the weightings given to each individual currency in the basket, and these weightings were based on the relative importance of each currency in European Community trade at the time the ecu was devised.
(c) Within the ERM the exchange rate of the currency of each member country is permitted to vary within a margin of plus or minus a specified percentage against its central parity. Each currency must also keep within the same limit of each other currency within the system.
(d) The exchange rate of each currency is therefore pegged against the ecu and also against every other ERM member currency.
(e) As the ERM is a movable peg system, occasional revaluations or devaluations of the central parity rates can occur, but only as a last resort measure.

7.2 Has the EMS been successful?

The shorter-term aims of consistent economic policies and exchange rate stability have had mixed success.

The successes of the EMS have been:

(a) the relative stability of the value of the ecu against other world currencies, and the slowly developing use of the ecu in international commerce;
(b) member countries coming to accept the need for broadly similar economic policies.

The failures of the EMS have been:

(a) the slowness of progress towards European monetary union;
(b) fairly frequent realignment of currency values, which has occasionally undermined the stability of exchange rates that was being sought;
(c) the fact that the government of an individual member state might refuse to adapt its economic policies to the needs of a stable EMS. For example, in the early years of the presidency of Monsieur Mitterrand, France adopted an independent (but eventually unsuccessful) economic policy.

In August 1993, the ERM virtually collapsed, with the permitted fluctuation bands being widened dramatically (from 24% to 15% for most currencies). It remains to be seen whether the ERM can be revived in a form which will offer much stability in exchange rates.

7.3 European economic and monetary union

One of the aims behind the European Monetary System is European economic and monetary union (EMU). This is a long-standing objective of the EU, reaffirmed in the Single European Act of 1986 and in the Maastricht agreement of 1991.

(a) *Monetary union* can be defined as a single currency area, which would require a monetary policy for the area as a whole.
(b) *Economic union* can be described as an unrestricted common market for trade, with some economic policy co-ordination between different regions in the union.

Although the whole package of measures included in European EMU is not paralleled anywhere else in the world, there have been many international monetary unions. For example, Belgium and Luxembourg are in a monetary union, and the UK and the Republic of Ireland (Eire) were in currency union until the 1970s. There are three main aspects to the European monetary union, should it take place.

(a) A *common currency*. By this, we mean that instead of using sterling in the UK, deutschmarks in Germany and francs in France, a common currency would be used for normal everyday money transactions by everyone in the monetary union.

(b) A *European central bank*. A European central bank would have the role of:

  (i) issuing the common currency;

  (ii) conducting monetary policy on behalf of the central government authorities;

  (iii) acting as lender of last resort to all European banks;

  (iv) managing the exchange rate for the common currency.

(c) A *centralised monetary policy* would apply across all the countries within the union. This would involve the surrender of control over aspects of economic policy and therefore surrender of some political sovereignty by the government of each member state to the central government body of the union.

Advantages of having a single European currency are as follows.

(a) For organisations trading within the single currency area, uncertainty about exchange rate movements would be removed. Business confidence should be improved. There would be no need to hedge against foreign exchange risks. There would also be savings in the transaction costs (bank commission etc) involved in exchanging currencies.

(b) Without transaction costs and the costs of hedging against foreign exchange risks (eg having to arrange forward exchange contracts), trade between countries in the currency area would become easier and the volume of trade should increase.

The disadvantages of a single European currency are a bit more difficult to assess.

The main problem is that each member state's government loses its total control over its domestic monetary policy. In particular, a government cannot use changes in the exchange rate for its currency as a policy weapon to influence the national economy.

Chapter roundup

- The balance of payments accounts consist of a current account and transactions in capital (external assets and liabilities including official financing). The sum of the balances on these accounts must be zero, although in practice there is a balancing figure for measurement errors.
- A surplus or deficit on the balance of payments usually means a surplus or deficit on the current account. It is possible for countries to try to finance a deficit on the current account from a surplus on capital account, temporarily at least. However, to do so, the country must be able to attract finance (eg investment capital) from abroad, and so the country needs to remain 'creditworthy', with investors having confidence in the stability of the exchange rate for the country's currency. (A depreciation in the currency would create a capital loss for foreign investors.)

NOTES

Chapter roundup (*continued*)

- A country can correct a balance of payments deficit by:
  - allowing its currency to depreciate or devalue in foreign exchange value;
  - imposing protectionist measures or exchange control regulations;
  - deflationary economic measures in the domestic economy. These are usually a precondition of any IMF financial assistance to countries in balance of payments difficulties.
- The balance of trade depends not only on the volumes of goods traded, but on the relative prices of exports and imports (ie on the terms of trade).
- Factors influencing the exchange rate are the comparative rates of inflation in different countries, comparative interest rates in different countries, the underlying balance of payments, speculation and government policy on managing or fixing exchange rates.
- The traditional view that exchange rates will depend on the country's balance of trade (more exactly, on its current account surplus or deficit) is still valid. However, capital transactions can influence the exchange rate significantly, especially in the short term.
- Exchange rates basically are set by supply and demand, but governments can intervene to influence them. Two extreme government policies on exchange rates might be fixed or free floating exchange rates.

Quick quiz

1. What is meant by the balance of trade?
2. What is meant by *equilibrium* in the balance of payments?
3. What does the J curve describe?
4. How do deflationary measures help to get rid of a balance of payments deficit?
5. What are the terms of trade? What is the effect of a change in the terms of trade?
6. What are spot and forward exchange rates?
7. What does the theory of purchasing power parity say?
8. How may the government intervene in the foreign exchange markets?
9. What are the advantages and disadvantages of fixed exchange rates?
10. What are the advantages and disadvantages of floating exchange rates?
11. What is the European currency unit?

Answers to Activities

1. Only item (c) would be included. The balance of trade refers to the export and import of *goods*, whereas items (a) and (b) refer to *services*.
2. It would deteriorate. This is because spending in the UK economy would rise and some of the spending would be on imports.
3. You should refer to Chapter 16 to refresh your memory on this.
4. The answer is (c). This is one example of how a country's terms of trade might improve. By switching from low-priced to high-priced products in a major export industry, unit export prices will go up and the terms of trade will improve. The change in the *balance* of trade depends on changes in the volume of exports and imports *as well as changes in export and import prices*.

NOTES

5 (a) If the demand for exported goods is inelastic, the total value of exports will rise if their price goes up.

(b) If the demand for imported goods is inelastic, the total value of imports will fall if their price falls.

Provided that demand for both exports and imports is price-inelastic, an improvement in the terms of trade will result in an improvement in the current balance of trade.

On the other hand if the price elasticity of demand for both exports and imports is elastic, an improvement in the terms of trade will lead to a worsening current balance of trade.

An improvement in the terms of trade might therefore result in a better or a worse balance of payments position. The same applies to a worsening in the terms of trade.

6 No, the opposite. If the forward rate was, for instance, \$1.9 to £1 while the spot rate three months later turns out to be \$2 to £1, the UK company will have benefited from the forward contract. The company will receive \$100,000 ÷ 1.9 = £52,632 (rather than \$100,000 ÷ 2 = £50,000).

7 Higher interest rates should attract more investments from abroad into the country, and so there will be *capital inflows* into the country. The capital inflows should cause an *appreciation in the currency*, because foreign investors must buy the currency to pay for their investments in the country. With an appreciation in the currency, imports become cheaper to buy and exports become more expensive to foreign buyers. With inelastic demand, this means that total spending on imports will fall. The volume of exports will fall, and so total revenue from exports in the exporter's *domestic currency* will fall also. (Total spending by foreign buyers on exports will rise, but only in their own currency.)

Case Study 1

The following data refer to the UK economy and are drawn from HMSO *Economic Trends*.

Year	*Annual rate of growth of GDP*	*Public sector borrowing requirement* (2)	*Balance of payments* (3)
	%	£bn	£bn
1980	– 2.0	+ 11.8	+ 2.6
1981	– 1.1	+ 10.5	+ 6.7
1982	+ 1.7	+ 4.8	+ 4.6
1983	+ 3.7	+ 11.5	+ 3.5
1984	+ 2.0	+ 10.3	+ 1.4
1985	+ 4.0	+ 7.4	+ 2.2
1986	+ 4.0	+ 2.5	– 0.9
1987	+ 4.6	– 1.4	– 5.0
1988	+ 4.9	– 11.9	– 16.5
1989	+ 2.2	– 9.3	– 22.5
1990	+ 0.6	– 2.1	– 18.2
1991	– 2.3	+ 7.7	– 7.6
1992	– 0.5	+ 28.9	– 8.5

(1) + denotes net borrowing, – denotes repayment of previous debt.
(2) + denotes surplus, – denotes deficit.

Case Study 1 (continued)

With reference to this data try to do the following.

(a) Explain what is meant by the following terms and state briefly how they are measured.

(i) Gross domestic product (GDP).

(ii) Public sector borrowing requirement (PSBR).

(iii) Current account of the balance of payments.

(b) Identify and explain the possible relationship between the trend of the PSBR and the rate of growth of GDP.

(c) Identify and explain the possible relationship between the trend of the current account of the balance of payments and the rate of growth of GDP.

Answer to Case Study 1

(a) (i) *Gross domestic product* (GDP) is the term given to the value of output produced within a nation over a given period, normally one year. It includes the value of goods/services produced for export in addition to goods/services produced within the economy for internal use.

Given the basic accounting identity:

Income ≡ Output ≡ Expenditure,

GDP can be measured:

(1) by adding together all of the incomes received from producing the year's output; or

(2) by finding the value of final output, ie applying the added value approach and so avoiding double counting; also including exports but excluding imports; or

(3) by finding the total of expenditures or outlays on goods and services produced by the economy.

Gross means that no allowance has been made for capital consumption or the depreciation of fixed assets.

(ii) The balance between the income and spending of the whole of the public sector is known as the *public sector borrowing requirement* (PSBR). Effectively, it is the amount of funds which the public sector needs to raise each year if its expenditure exceeds its revenue. It includes the borrowing of central government, public corporations and local authorities. In the UK, the major part of the PSBR results from the government running a budget deficit, with central government expenditure exceeding the total of tax revenues. Government outgoings tend to be heavy in the early months of any tax year (for example, because of European Union contributions), whereas government receipts tend to be loaded towards the later months of the tax year. So the weight of government deficit varies throughout the year. The sum of the accumulated PSBR over a period of years adds to the National Debt. If government receipts in any year exceed outgoings, there is a public sector debt repayment (PSDR) and this, of course, serves to reduce the National Debt.

(iii) The *current account of the balance of payments*, being the international trading account of a country, records the trade in goods and services imported and exported, together with other current items, over a given period. The balance in the trade in goods – into and out of the country – is known as the balance of trade. The other items in the current account comprise services, payments/receipts of interest, dividends, profits, and also governmental and private transfer payments (for example, foreign aid payments and money transfers by people living abroad). The overall total of these items of visibles and invisibles will result in either a net surplus or deficit on current account. The relative importance of receipts and payments can vary considerably over a year according to trading patterns and settlement arrangements; quarterly balance of payments deficits or surpluses are not necessarily indicative of the outcome for the year. Also, adjustments to the figures are often necessary well after the year.

(b) The figures show that the rate of growth of the UK's GDP was negative in 1980 and 1981, but then improved (with the exception of 1984), until it reached a peak of 4.9% in 1988. It became negative again in 1991 and 1992 which were years of recession in the UK economy.

The PSBR exceeded £10bn in each year from 1980 to 1984, with the exception of 1982. From 1985 it declined considerably, becoming negative between 1987 and 1990. In this period, with revenues exceeding expenditures, the government was able to make a net debt repayment, so reducing the National Debt. Expenditure again exceeded revenue in 1991, and the PSBR reached the exceptional figure of £28.9bn in 1991.

The figures show an inverse relationship between the growth rate of GDP and the size of the PSBR. High levels of PSBR are associated with low growth rates. If the growth in GDP declines, tax revenues fall while social security payments (for example, to those unemployed) increase. If the economy actually moves into recession, the consequences for the PSBR of this two-way effect may be severe. Efforts to reduce the PSBR, involving cut-backs in public expenditure, may prolong the period of negative growth. Conversely, as the rate of growth of GDP improves, government tax revenue (eg from VAT, income tax and corporation tax) increases while the outgoings on social security payments tend to fall. This upswing in GDP and fall in PSBR may be slowed, as in the period 1992 to 1995, by employers being more wary in taking on additional labour. Generally, however, as growth rates improve PSBR falls.

(c) During the period of negative growth in GDP in 1980 and 1981, the current account of the balance of payments was in surplus. However, during the period of growth in GDP in the mid-1980s, the balance of payments moved into deficit, and became substantial by the end of the decade. As the rate of growth of GDP fell heavily and the economy then moved into recession, so the balance of payments showed improvement with the deficit falling heavily. The figures indicate a direct relationship between growth in GDP and the size of the current account deficit/surplus.

The UK has a noticeable marginal propensity to import, due in part to an underlying lack of competitiveness, as well as to capacity shortages when demand peaks. As the economy picks up and incomes increase, a rise in imports has tended not to be matched by a corresponding increase in exports. Imports rise due to increased UK demand for overseas goods, as well as from increased need for raw materials, components, and capital equipment. There is also some tendency for goods to be diverted from exports to meet the rising consumer demand. As the economy moves into decline, the reverse tends to take place with, in due course, a noticeable fall in imports.

There are some indications that since 1993 there has been an increased movement into exports, as a substitute for the low level of domestic consumer demand. Significant improvements in productivity in UK manufacturing industry have helped to make UK goods more competitive. These factors at least provide the potential for some modification of the relationship indicated by the data.

NOTES

Case Study 2

'Britain's current account deficit soared to its highest level in 2 years last month as the impact of devaluation pushed up the cost of imports to record levels, the Government reported yesterday.

Figures from the Central Statistical Office showed a shortfall of more than £1.5bn in December, more than £300m higher than in November.

The City had been prepared for the trade figures to reflect higher import prices following the 15% fall in the value of the pound in the final quarter of 1992, but was still taken aback to see the import total soar to just under £11bn – more than £200m higher than the previous record.

Dealers were even more alarmed at the volume of imports. These are unaffected by currency movements, but have risen relentlessly, despite the severity of the recession. "Despite the weakness of the economy, import penetration is growing and will continue to grow rapidly once recovery is under way", said Gerard Lyons, chief economist with Japanese-based securities house DKB International.

Over three months to December the current account deficit widened from £2.172bn to £3.706bn, and in 1992 as a whole it rose from £6.323bn to £11.819bn.

Government officials said the small increase in import volume growth was a sign that higher prices were starting to have an effect on demand for overseas goods, while export volumes had yet to feel the benefit of the cheaper pound.'

Adapted from The Guardian, *29 January 1993*

Use this extract to answer the following.

(a) What is meant by 'the current account of the balance of payments'?

(b) What is the state of Britain's current account of the balance of payments?

(c) What happens to the level of imports as the economy recovers from the recession?

(d) Describe the impact of devaluation on the current account of Britain's balance of payments up to December 1992. Why might the impact be different in the longer run?

Answer to Case Study 2

(a) The balance of payments current account for a country measures the expenditures on goods and services flowing between the country and the rest of the world. It is the country's trading account and is divided into the following sections: trade in goods; trade in services; investment income – the flow of interest, profits and dividends; and transfer payments. The current account balance is the sum of the balances on all these items.

(b) The current account is said to be in deficit when total expenditure on imports exceed total receipts from exports. The UK's trade deficit in December 1992 was over £1.5 billion, the highest level for two years, according to the newspaper article quoted. There was an upward trend in the deficit over the year as a whole, over the previous quarter, and compared with the previous month, as shown in the rounded figures below.

	UK current account deficit	
	12/92	*Previously*
	£ billion	*£ billion*
Compared with previous month	1.5	1.2
Over three months	3.7	2.2
Over a full year	11.8	6.3

(c) Total imports expenditure soared to a level of just below £11 billion in December 1992, as the UK economy began to recover from recession. This was the highest level ever recorded, being over £200 million higher than the previous record.

This marked increase in the imports bill can be put down to:

(i) the devaluation of the pound following sterling's suspension from the European exchange rate mechanism in September 1992;

(ii) import penetration – the share of imports as a percentage of gross domestic product – which has continued to grow in spite of the severe economic recession.

It can be expected that import penetration will continue to grow as an economic recovery occurs. As demand rises, so should the demand for imports from consumers, and also from domestic producers who require raw materials and components from overseas to produce at an expanded level of output. If, as in the UK which imports many consumer durables, imports have a high income elasticity of demand, then domestic demand for imports will rise as incomes rise.

Recovery from recession may also encourage a switch to imported goods in cases where limited domestic capacity restricts supply. Supply capacity may be especially limited in industries which have removed plant and machinery from production during the earlier period of recession.

(d) Devaluation of a currency is a reduction in the exchange rate of the currency relative to other currencies. This reduces the price of exports to foreign buyers (ie in foreign currency terms) and increases the price of imports in terms of the domestic currency.

Devaluation should cause switching of expenditure on the part of consumers and firms. Foreign consumers and firms will be encouraged by the new lower prices to switch to UK goods and services. UK consumers and firms will be encouraged to switch from imports to domestically produced substitutes.

In the short term, the UK demand for imports is likely to be inelastic, as previous orders will need to be completed before significant switching of expenditure occurs. However, a price effect will occur relatively quickly and rises in prices of imports did indeed push total expenditure on imports to just under £11 billion for the month of December 1992. On the exports side, foreign consumers and firms will similarly take some time to switch expenditure. In the meantime, lower-priced exports will depress the total value of exports. These factors explain the impact of devaluation on the current account balance up to December 1992.

In the longer term, beneficial effects of the devaluation should begin to have an impact. The expenditure switching referred to above will occur, and gradually production will be adjusted to match the new patterns of demand. According to the Marshall-Lerner condition, if the elasticities of demand for imports and exports add up to greater than 1, the increase in receipts from exports will outweigh the effect on import payments; an improvement in the current account balance will result. The J curve illustrates the combination of deterioration in the current account balance in the short run with improvement in the long run.

Further question practice

Now try the following practice questions at the end of this text.

Multiple choice questions	**192–203**
Exam style question	**19** and **20**

GLOSSARY

Aggregate demand The total of planned expenditure on goods and services in an economy.

Aggregate supply The total supply of goods and services in the economy.

Balance of payments The statistical accounting record of all of a country's external transactions in a given period.

Capital market The market, or group of interrelated markets for investing and raising capital in financial (monetary) form, largely on a long-term basis.

Cartel An association of suppliers for the purpose of co-operating on the fixing of variables, such as price and output levels.

Central bank The institution which has the job of controlling the monetary and banking system, acts as banker to the banks and as lender of last resort.

Commercial banks Institutions conducting general banking business and licensed to make loans and accept deposits on demand, such as those held in cheque accounts.

Comparative advantage The principle that economic agents are best employed in activities which they carry out relatively better than other activities. Applied to international trade, a country will gain from specialising in producing goods in which it has a comparative advantage.

Complements Two goods are complements of each other if changes in the demand for one will have a complementary effect on the demand for the other, eg compact disc players and compact discs; cars and petrol.

Consumption The use of goods and services to satisfy current wants.

Cost-push inflation Inflation resulting from an increase in the costs of production of goods and services, eg through escalating prices of imported raw materials, or from wage increases.

Credit A wide term, broadly referring to the financing of the expenditure of others against future repayment, to enable them to buy goods and services out of future income.

Cross elasticity of demand A measure of the responsiveness of demand for one good to changes in the price of another: the percentage change in the quantity demanded of one good divided by the percentage change in the price of the other good.

Demand The quantity of a good that potential purchasers would buy, or attempt to buy, if the price of the good were at a certain level.

Demand management An approach to economic policy making which seeks to control the level of aggregate demand through fiscal policy and/or monetary policy.

Demand-pull inflation Inflation resulting from a persistent excess of aggregate demand over aggregate supply. Supply reaches a limit on capacity at the full employment level.

Derived demand The demand for a factor of production where this is derived from the demand for the final good that the factor contributes to producing. The demand for labour is, in some cases, identical with the demand for a service itself, as, for example in the case of the hiring of a babysitter.

Diminishing returns The law of diminishing returns (or law of variable production) states that as additional units of a factor of production are employed, while others are held constant, the additional output generated (its marginal physical product) will eventually diminish.

NOTES

Devaluation A reduction in the fixed or pegged exchange rate between one currency and other currencies.

Direct taxation Tax levied directly on individuals or firms, such as income tax, corporation tax and capital gains tax.

Disintermediation The bypassing of financial intermediaries in order to arrange lending and borrowing directly between the ultimate parties to the transaction.

Economic rent Payment received for the services of a factor of production in excess of its transfer earnings or opportunity cost.

Economies of scale Reductions in the average cost of producing a commodity in the long run as the output of the commodity increases.

Elasticity A measure of the responsiveness of the demand for one good to changes in some influential factor (e.g. the goods own price). See cross- and Price elasticity of demand.

Entrepreneur An economic agent who organises the exploitation of factors of production in a firm.

Equi-marginal returns This is the principle that a utility-maximising consumer or household will allocate expenditure so that the marginal utilty gained from the last penny spent on each good is equal for each good that is available.

European Union (EU) Austria, Belgium, Denmark, Finland, France, Germany, Greece, Ireland, Italy, Luxembourg, the Netherlands, Portugal, Spain, Sweden and the United Kingdom.

Exchange rate The price of a currency expressed in terms of another currency

Externalities Positive or negative external effects on third parties resulting from production and consumption activities.

Factors of production The resources or inputs used in production. The main categories of the factors of production are land, labour and capital, with entrepreneurship sometimes treated as a fourth.

Financial intermediary Someone who brings together providers and users of finance, either as broker or as principal (holding money balances of lenders for lending on to borrowers).

Fiscal policy The regulation of the economy through taxation and government expenditure.

Floating exchange rates Exchange rates which are allowed to fluctuate according to demand and supply conditions in the foreign exchange markets.

Gross domestic product (GDP) A measure of the value of the goods and services produced by an economy in a given period.

Gross national product (GNP) Gross domestic product plus the income accruing to domestic residents from investments abroad, less income accruing to foreign residents from investments in the domestic economy.

Indirect taxation Tax on the sale of goods and services, such as value added tax.

Inferior goods Goods for which demand falls as consumers' income rises.

Inflation A sustained rise in the general level of prices.

Interest rate The percentage of a sum lent, which the borrower pays to the lender: in other words, the price of money.

Investment The production or maintenance of the real capital stock (eg machinery, buildings) which will allow the production of goods and services for future consumption.

NOTES

Invisible trade The exporting and importing of services, as distinct from physically visible goods.

Liquidity preference The term used by Keynes for the desire to hold money rather than other forms of wealth, arising from the transactions motive, the speculative motive and the precautionary motive.

Long run The period of time over which all factors of production can be varied.

Macroeconomics The study of the economy as a whole.

Marginal cost The additional cost of producing an additional unit of output.

Marginal efficiency of capital The rate of discount which makes the present value of expected net returns from an investment equal to the capital sum invested.

Marginal productivity theory The theory that the demand for labour is determined by the additional output resulting from the employment of an additional worker.

Marginal utility The additional satisfaction derived from a commodity by an individual from the consumption of one extra unit of the commodity.

Market A situation in which potential buyers and sellers of goods or services come together in order to exchange.

Market failure A situation in which the market mechanism fails to result in economic efficiency and therefore the outcome is sub-optimal.

Merit goods Merit goods are considered to be desirable in themselves, for instance health and education, and the government supplies them for the public benefit.

Microeconomics The study of the behaviour of individual economic units, particularly consumers and firms.

Mixed economy An economy in which both public and private enterprise engage in economic activity. All contemporary economic systems are mixed to some extent.

Monetarism A school of thought in economics which takes the view that instability in the economy is mainly caused by factors within the monetary sector.

Money Something which is generally acceptable in settling debts, or in exchanging for goods.

Money markets The markets for lending and borrowing mainly short-term capital, including the discount market, the interbank market and the commercial paper market.

Money supply The amount or stock of money in an economy.

Monopolistic competition A market structure in which a large number of competing suppliers each sell a differentiated product.

Monopoly A market with only one supplier of a product.

Multiplier The ratio of the change in income to the change in expenditure which caused it.

National Debt The total outstanding debt obligations of central government, comprising both marketable debt (eg securities) and non-marketable debt (eg national savings certificates)

National income A measure of the value of goods and services available to the people in an economy in a given period.

Non-price competition The use of means other than lower prices to try to attract business from competitors. Product differentiation and special offers are examples.

Normal profit The minimum profit which a firm must earn in order to induce it to stay in production. At this level of profit, the opportunity costs of the entrepreneur retaining capital in the business are just covered by total revenue.

Oligopoly A market dominated by a few suppliers.

Opportunity cost The opportunity cost of an action is the value of the alternative action which is forgone by doing it.

Optimum A situation in which the objective of an economic unit is being served in the most effective way possible, given the constraints which apply

Perfect market A perfect market is where there is a large number of buyers and sellers and no individual buyer or seller can influence the market price.

Phillips curve A curve showing a relationship between the level of unemployment and inflation in prices or wages.

Price discrimination The practice of charging different prices for a product to different groups of consumers, or to the same consumer for different units of the product. For price discrimination to succeed, segmentation of the market and prevention of resale between segments must both be possible.

Price elasticity of demand A measure of the responsiveness of demand to changes in price: the percentage change in the quantity of a good demanded, divided by the percentage change in its price.

Price mechanism The way in which prices act as signals which co-ordinate the actions of economic agents in a free market economic system.

Prices and incomes policy A policy which aims to restrain both prices and incomes.

Privatisation Policy to transfer economic activities to private ownership and control, including the sale of shares in previously state owned industries to private individuals and institutions, contracting out of publicly funded services to private companies, and the sale of public housing.

Production possibility curve A curve showing the limits of the quantities of two commodities, or groups of commodities, which may be produced given limited resources.

Productivity Labour productivity can be defined as the output per worker in a given period of time.

Public goods Goods whose benefits cannot be restricted to particular customers. Consumption of public goods is non-rivalous, meaning that consumption by one person does not deprive others of the goods.

Purchasing power parity The theory that, in the long run at least, the equilibrium exchange rate between two currencies is that which equates the domestic purchasing power of each.

Quantity theory of money The theory which holds that changes in the level of prices are mainly caused by changes in the supply of money.

Savings The part of incomes which is not spent on current consumption.

Short run The period of time over which the supply of at least one factor of production is fixed, constraining the productive capacity of a firm. However, the degree of utilisation of variable factors can be changed in the short run.

Social cost The total cost to society of an economic activity. Social costs may diverge from private costs, as in the case of pollution. Taxation policy may aim to reflect social costs so that market prices reflect them.

Substitute A good which can be substituted for another good, or an input which can be substituted for another input

Supernormal profits Profit in excess of the opportunity cost of capital (see Normal profit).

Supply The quantity of a good that existing suppliers would want to produce for the market at a given price.

Supply side economics An approach to economic policy making which advocates measures to improve the supply of goods and services rather than measures to affect aggregate demand.

Tariff A tax on imported goods.

Terms of trade The ratio of export prices to import prices.

Transfer earnings The minimum payment needed to prevent a factor of production from moving to other employment. For example, the transfer earnings of a person who earns £30,000 and whose next best alternative employment is a job paying £25,000, are £25,000.

Transfer payments Payments which are not made in return for goods or services. Student grants and social security payments are examples.

Utility The satisfaction gained by an individual from a particular situation, or from the consumption of goods or services.

Variable costs Costs which vary with the level of output produced by a firm.

Velocity of circulation The average frequency with which money is passed between one economic agent and another.

Visible trade The exporting and importing of physical goods.

MULTIPLE CHOICE QUESTIONS

NOTES

Chapter 1

1 The basic economic problem facing all economies is

A economic growth.

B unemployment.

C inflation.

D scarcity of resources.

A B C D

2 The term 'mixed economy' implies all of the following conditions except which one?

A The allocation of resources is mainly through the price system.

B Producers have an incentive to advertise their products.

C There is some government planning of the use of resources.

D All industries have a mix of small and large companies.

A B C D

3 Which one of the following statements is not true?

A The basic economic problem is the same in planned and free market economies.

B The basic economic problem is one of choice between alternatives.

C Factors of production are limited in supply.

D Choice is necessary because of limited consumer wants.

A B C D

4 When a government wishes to increase its expenditure on education but can do so only at the expense of expenditure elsewhere, this is said to be an example of:

A diminishing marginal utility;

B opportunity cost;

C scale of preferences;

D equi-marginal returns.

A B C D

5

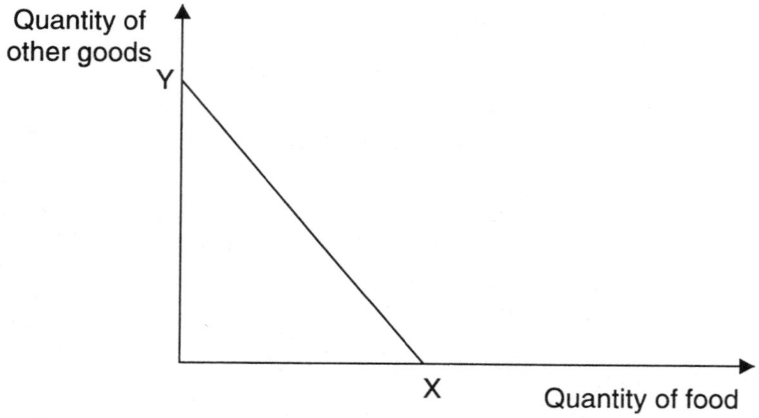

Quantity of other goods

Y

X

Quantity of food

NOTES

The diagram shows the production possibility frontier for the country Begonia. It shows

A the opportunity costs of making food in terms of making other goods;

B diminishing returns to the factors of production making food as more food is produced;

C a fall in demand for food as more of other goods is produced;

D a constant elasticity of supply of food.

A B C D

6 Which of the following would cause the production possibility frontier for an economy to shift outwards?

(1) A reduction in the level of unemployment.

(2) A rise in the rate of investment.

(3) A fall in the price of one factor of production.

(4) A rise in output per worker.

A 1 and 2 only.

B 1, 2 and 3 only.

C 1, 3 and 4 only.

D 2 and 4 only.

A B C D

7 In economics, 'the central economic problem' means:

A consumers do not have as much money as they would wish;

B there will always be a certain level of unemployment;

C resources are not always allocated in an optimum way;

D output is restricted by the limited availability of resources.

A B C D

8 In a free enterprise economy, the price mechanism determines:

(1) the allocation of resources between different industries;

(2) the rewards paid to factors of production;

(3) the types of goods and services produced;

(4) the preferences of consumers.

Which of the above are correct?

A 1 and 3 only.

B 1 and 4 only.

C 1, 2 and 3 only.

D 1, 3 and 4 only.

A B C D

NOTES

9 Which of the following statements is *not* true?

A Profit is the reward to the factor of production called enterprise.

B In the long run, profit will be the same in all firms that are equally efficient.

C Profit is the reward for risk bearing.

D Normal profit is included in average cost.

A B C D

10 Which one of the following statements is *not* true?

A The basic economic problem is the same in planned and free market economies.

B The basic economic problem is one of choice between alternatives.

C Factors of production are limited in supply.

D Choice is necessary because of limited consumer wants.

A B C D

11 There are two commodities, X and Y. The price per unit is £10 for commodity X and £30 for commodity Y. A consumer will achieve equilibrium where

A the ratio of marginal utility to price is three times as great for Y as for X;

B the marginal utility from an extra £1 spent on Y is three times the marginal utility from an extra £1 spent on X;

C the marginal utility from expenditure per unit on Y is three times the marginal utility from expenditure on unit X;

D total utility from expenditure on Y is three times as great as total utility from expenditure on X.

A B C D

NOTES

12 The table below shows the marginal utility for a consumer of units of good X and good Y.

	X	Y
Unit	*Marginal utility*	*Marginal utility*
1st	10	16
2nd	9	14
3rd	8	12
4th	7	10
5th	6	8
6th	5	6
7th	4	4
8th	3	2

The selling price of a unit of X is £10 and the selling price of Y is £20 per unit.

The consumer has £140 to spend on goods X and Y, and will maximise his utility by purchasing:

A 0 units of X and 7 units of Y.

B 2 units of X and 6 units of Y.

C 4 units of X and 5 units of Y.

D 6 units of X and 4 units of Y.

A B C D

Chapter 2

Data for questions 13–16

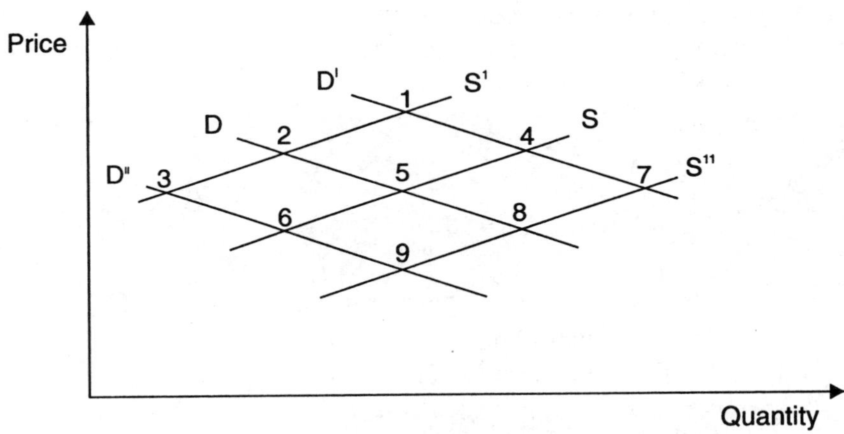

Figure 1

13 In Figure 1, point 5 represents equilibrium. If the government starts to pay a cash subsidy to producers of the commodity, what will the new equilibrium be?

A Point 2

B Point 4

C Point 6

D Point 8

A B C D

NOTES

14 In Figure 1, point 5 represents equilibrium. There is now a fall in the price of another product which is a close substitute for the commodity. What will the new equilibrium be?

A Point 2

B Point 4

C Point 6

D Point 8

A B C D

15 In Figure 1, point 5 represents equilibrium. Two things now happen:

(a) A technical innovation in production equipment reduces the average cost unit of manufacturing the commodity.

(b) The income of households increases in real terms.

What will the new equilibrium price be?

A Point 1

B Point 3

C Point 7

D Point 9

A B C D

16 In Figure 1, point 6 represents equilibrium. The government imposes an indirect tax on the commodity. What will the new equilibrium be?

A Point 3.

B Point 5.

C Unchanged at point 6.

D Point 9.

A B C D

17 Which one of the following would normally cause a rightward shift in the demand curve for a product?

A A fall in the price of a substitute product.

B A reduction in direct taxation on incomes.

C A reduction in price of the product.

D An increase in the price of a complementary product.

A B C D

18 If the price of coffee falls, which one of the following outcomes would be expected to occur?

A A fall in the quantity of coffee demanded.

B A rise in the price of tea.

C A fall in the demand for drinking cups.

D A fall in the demand for tea.

A B C D

NOTES

19 Consider the price and demand for flower vases. The price of cut flowers goes up sharply. Which of the following would you expect to happen?

A The demand curve for flower vases will shift to the left and their price will rise.

B The demand curve for flower vases will shift to the right and their price will rise.

C There will be a movement along the demand curve for flower vases and their price will go down.

D The demand curve for flower vases will shift to the left and their price will go down.

A B C D

20 Consider the price and demand for Channel crossing tickets by ferry. The price of Channel crossings by hovercraft goes up. Which of the following would you expect to happen?

A The demand curve for sea ferry tickets will shift to the left, and their price will go down. More sea ferry tickets will be sold.

B The demand curve for sea ferry tickets will shift to the right, and their price will go up. More sea ferry tickets will be sold.

C The demand curve for sea ferry tickets will shift to the right and their price will go down. More sea ferry tickets will be sold.

D The demand curve for sea ferry tickets will shift to the right and their price will go up. Fewer sea ferry tickets will be sold.

A B C D

21 The summer demand for hotel accommodation in London comes mainly from foreign tourists. Demand for hotel rooms in London in summer could be reduced by a fall in the price or value of which of the following?

Item

1 US dollars.

2 Aeroplane tickets.

3 Sterling.

A Item 1 only.

B Items 1 and 2 only.

C Items 2 and 3 only.

D Item 3 only.

A B C D

NOTES

22 Which of the following changes will cause the demand curve for chocolate to shift to the left?

Change

1 A fall in the price of chocolate.

2 A health campaign which claims that chocolate makes you fat.

3 A rise in the price of chocolate substitutes.

4 A fall in consumers' income.

A Change 1 only.
B Changes 2 and 3 only.
C Changes 2 and 4 only.
D Changes 3 and 4 only.

A B C D

23 Which of the following would cause a reduction in the demand for motor cars?

Item

1 A fall in the price of petrol.

2 A substantial reduction in train fares.

3 A large fall in the cost of motor cycle road tax licences.

A Items 1 and 2.
B Items 1 and 3.
C Items 2 and 3.
D Items 1, 2 and 3.

A B C D

24 As a consequence of a widespread advertising campaign by firms in the industry and an increase in wages to workers in the industry, the price and quantity consumed of a particular product changes. The causes have been:

A A movement along the demand curve and a shift in the supply curve.
B A shift in the demand curve and a shift in the supply curve.
C A movement along the demand curve and a movement along the supply curve.
D A shift in the demand curve and a movement along the supply curve.

A B C D

NOTES

Chapter 3

25 Which of the following statements is true?

1 If the price elasticity of demand is more than 1, a fall in price will result in a fall in total expenditure on the product.

2 The income elasticity of demand will only be zero in the case of inferior goods.

3 The cross-elasticity of demand for complementary goods will always be positive.

A None of them are true.
B Statement 1 only is true.
C Statement 2 only is true.
D Statement 3 only is true.

A B C D

Data for questions 26–7

Price of a good pence	*Demand per week* units	*Supply per week* units
40	200	100
50	150	160
60	100	200

26 When the price rises from 40p to 50p, what is the elasticity of demand?

A 0
B Between 0 and 1
C 1
D Greater than 1

A B C D

27 When the price falls from 60p to 50p, what is the elasticity of supply?

A 0
B Between 0 and 1
C 1
D Greater than 1

A B C D

28 The demand for a product will tend to be inelastic when:

A it has very few close substitutes;
B it is very quickly consumed;
C it tends to be purchased by people on subsistence incomes;
D it has a wide range of different uses.

A B C D

NOTES

29 The graphs of a supply schedule which has a price elasticity of supply equal to 1 will be:

A a rectangular hyperbola;

B any straight line drawn through the origin;

C a straight line drawn through the origin at 45°;

D a vertical line.

A B C D

30 If total receipts of the Dingaling Telephone Company remain unchanged after it has put up its prices, which of the following would describe the price elasticity of demand?

A It is absolutely inelastic.

B It is elastic.

C It has unitary elasticity.

D It is inelastic.

A B C D

31 Yoggipear and Orchard Cow are two rival brands of flavoured yoghurt drinks, which have a cross elasticity of demand of +2. The price of Yoggipear rises from 20 pence to 30 pence per carton. What will be the percentage increase in demand for similar-sized cartons of Orchard Cow?

A 20%

B 25%

C 75%

D 100%

A B C D

32 The cross elasticity of demand between widgets and splodgets is –0.6 and the two goods are complements. The price of splodgets goes up by 10%, and demand for splodgets goes down by 15%. Which of the following will happen, in the short-run time period?

A The equilibrium output and price of widgets will both fall, but we do not know what either of them will now be.

B The demand for widgets will go down by 6%, and the price of widgets will remain unchanged.

C The demand for widgets will go down by 9%, and the price of widgets will remain unchanged.

D The equilibrium output and price of widgets will change, with price above and quantity demanded below where they were before.

A B C D

NOTES

33 Which of the following factors influence the elasticity of supply of a good?

1 The time period over which changes in supply are measured.
2 The marginal cost of producing the good.
3 The range of alternative production opportunities available to suppliers.

A Factors 1 and 2 only.
B Factors 2 and 3 only.
C Factors 1 and 3 only.
D Factors 1, 2 and 3.

A B C D

34 The demand for a product will tend to be elastic when:

A the product has a number of different uses;
B the product is bought mainly by people on subsistence incomes;
C the product has very few close substitutes;
D the product is a non-durable consumer good that is quickly consumed.

A B C D

35 A company sells two products, widgets and fidgets. Widgets have a high price elasticity of demand. Fidgets are relatively price inelastic. The company decides to spend £2 million on an advertising campaign for each product, in order to increase demand. Which of the following statements would be true?

A The supply curve of both products would shift to the right, and for widgets by a greater proportion than for fidgets.
B The advertising campaign would be more successful for fidgets than for widgets.
C The cost of the advertising campaign for fidgets could be covered by raising the price of the product.
D The supply curve of both products would shift to the left, and for widgets by a greater proportionate amount than for fidgets.

A B C D

NOTES

36 Ray Smoter's consumption of petrol varies with his income, as shown by the diagram below.

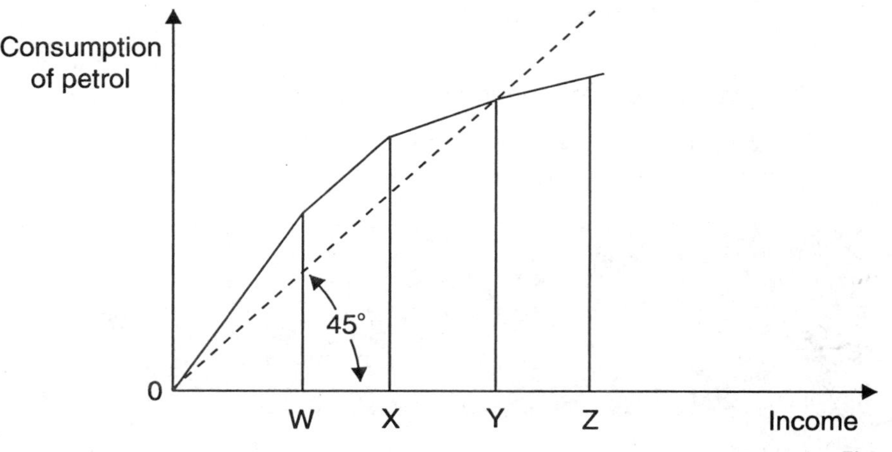

Figure 2

Which of the following statements correctly describes his income elasticity of demand for petrol?

A Less than or equal to unity until his income reaches X and then greater than unity at income levels from X to Z.

B Greater than unity until his income reaches W and then equal to or less than unity at income levels from W to Z.

C Greater than unity until his income reaches X and then less than unity at income levels between X and Z.

D Greater than unity until his income reaches Y and then less than unity at income levels between Y and Z.

A B C D

Chapter 4

37 In a free market economy, the price mechanism

A aids government control;

B allocates resources;

C reduces unfair competition;

D measures national wealth.

A B C D

38 Which of the following statements is not true about the price mechanism?

A Monopoly and other restrictive practices obstruct the smooth reallocation of resources.

B In a private enterprise system, the sovereignty of the consumer is complete.

C Immobility of factors makes the price mechanism less efficient as an allocate device.

D High profits will generally attract resources from less remunerative activities.

A B C D

NOTES

39 Which of the following are imperfections in a market?

1 Consumer brand loyalty to a firm's branded goods, regardless of price.

2 The lack of complete and accurate information for consumers about all goods and services available.

3 The slow response of firms to price changes and the relatively inelastic supply of a good in the short run.

A Items 1 and 2 only.
B Items 2 and 3 only.
C Items 1 and 3 only.
D Items 1, 2 and 3.

A B C D

40 Which of the following are weaknesses of a completely free-enterprise economic system?

1 It only reflects private costs and private benefits.

2 It may lead to serious inequalities in the distribution of income and wealth.

3 It may lead to production inefficiencies and a wastage of resources.

A 1 and 2 only.
B 2 and 3 only.
C 1 and 3 only.
D 1, 2 and 3.

A B C D

41 Muddy Waters Ltd is an industrial company which has altered its production methods so that it has reduced the amount of waste discharged from its factory into the local river. Which of the following is most likely to be reduced?

A Total private costs.
B Social cost.
C External benefit.
D Variable costs.

A B C D

42 The table below shows a market demand schedule and a market supply schedule for beans.

Price per tonne £	*Quantity demanded per month* ('000 tonnes)	*Quantity supplied per month* ('000 tonnes)
280	4,000	9,200
260	5,000	8,800
240	6,400	8,200
220	7,400	7,400
200	8,200	6,600
180	9,000	5,800
160	9,800	4,800

NOTES

What would be the consequences of the introduction by the government of a maximum price for beans of £200 per tonne? Assume that supply quantities can be readily adjusted to any new market conditions.

1 There would be a need for rationing of beans.

2 There would be a 'bean mountain'.

3 There would be a shortage of 1,600,000 tonnes per month.

4 There would be a surplus of 1,600,000 tonnes per month.

5 The price for beans would be unchanged.

A Consequences 1 and 3.

B Consequences 2 and 4.

C Consequence 5 only.

D Consequence 4 only.

A B C D

43 In Ruritania, the government has recently introduced minimum price legislation for agricultural products, whereby the government buys up surplus produce which is not purchased by consumers at the minimum price. The minimum price for most agricultural products is well in excess of the free market price that has been obtained in the markets in recent years.

Which of the following statements is *untrue?*

A The supply of agricultural produce will increase, because more resources will be put into production.

B Demand for agricultural produce will be unaffected, because the government will buy up all surplus food supplies.

C The minimum price legislation will encourage some farmers to be less efficient, and to produce at high unit costs of output.

D There will not be any black market in the sale of agricultural produce at free market prices.

A B C D

NOTES

44 Suppose that, in a certain advanced industrialised country, the government has applied price controls over rents of both public and private rented accommodation for a number of years, and a serious problem of widespread homelessness has built up. Just recently, the rent price controls have been eased. Which of the following consequences should now occur?

1 An increase in homelessness.

2 In the longer term, an increase in new building work.

3 The provision of more rented accommodation.

4 Fewer owner-occupied dwellings.

A Consequences 1 and 2.

B Consequences 2 and 3.

C Consequences 3 and 4.

D Consequences 1 and 4.

A B C D

45 The government of a country is considering how to deal with the problem of production of the agricultural fertiliser filsadrane. The fertiliser is known to pollute land and rivers, but is in demand from farmers. The marginal private costs of production and the marginal social costs of the fertiliser are shown in the diagram below.

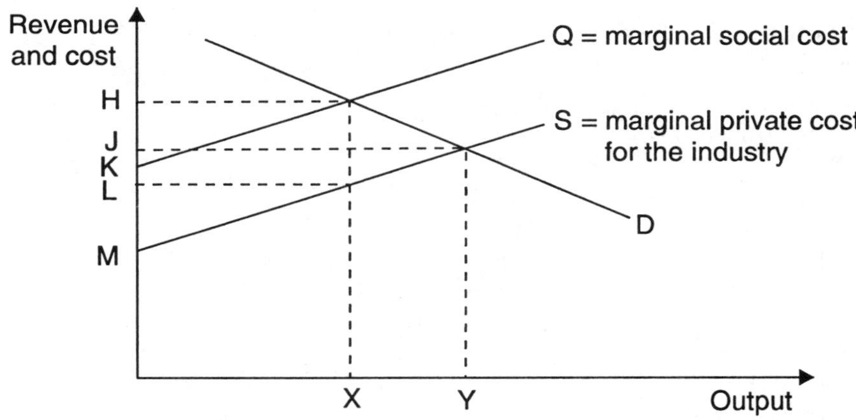

Figure 3

In order to achieve the socially optimum production of filsadrane, the government should

A impose a tax on the fertiliser of HJ per unit;

B impose a tax on the fertiliser of JL per unit;

C impose a tax on the fertiliser of KM per unit;

D grant a subsidy for producing the fertiliser of JL per unit, but impose a production limit of X units.

A B C D

NOTES

Data for questions 46–47

The following are the demand and supply schedules for commodity Z on which the government has just imposed a sales tax of £3 per unit.

Price of Z before tax £	*Demand* ('000s)	*Supply* ('000s)
1	150	120
2	140	140
3	130	160
4	120	180
5	110	200

46 After the imposition of the tax of £3 per unit the new equilibrium price of Z is

A £4

B £5

C £6

D £7

A B C D

47 After the imposition of the tax of £3 per unit, the part of the tax borne by the consumer is

A Nil

B £1

C £2

D £3

A B C D

48 The diagram below represents the market for educational books.

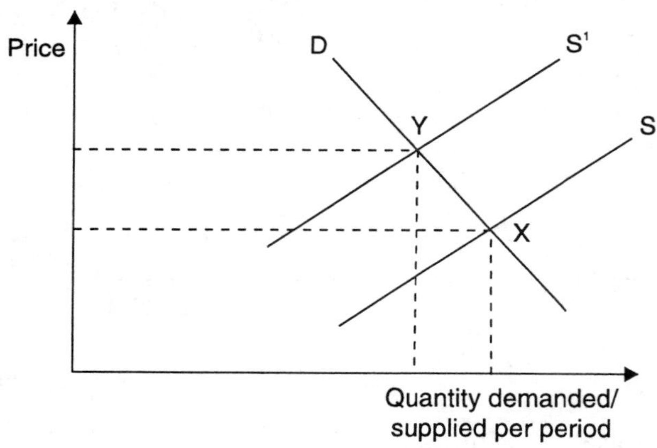

Figure 4

NOTES

Which of the following events most satisfactorily explains the movement of the market equilibrium from X to Y?

A The imposition of an indirect tax on educational books.

B The payment of a subsidy to publishers of educational books.

C The payment of a subsidy to schools purchasing educational books.

D The imposition of a tax on a good that is a close substitute of educational books.

A B C D

Chapter 5

49 When a firm produces one extra unit of output, what is the marginal cost of the unit?

1 The increase in total cost of production.

2 The increase in the variable cost of production.

3 The increase in the average cost of production.

A Definition 1 only.

B Definition 2 only.

C Definition 3 only.

D Definitions 1 and 2 only.

A B C D

50 Which of the following propositions are false?

1 It is possible for the average total cost curve to be falling while the average variable cost curve is rising.

2 It is possible for the average total cost curve to be rising while the average variable cost curve is falling.

3 Marginal fixed costs per unit will fall as output increases.

4 Marginal costs will be equal to marginal variable costs.

A Propositions 1 and 3 are false.

B Propositions 1 and 4 are false.

C Propositions 2 and 3 are false.

D Propositions 2 and 4 are false.

NOTES

51 Locke and Boult Ltd is a firm of security guards which provides nightwatchmen to guard the premises of client firms. One such firm is Chinese Walls plc, which employs a guard from Locke and Boult for its head office building.

Which of the following statements about the cost of the guard are correct?

1 The cost of the guard is a variable cost to Locke and Boult, since the number of guards the firm employs depends on the demand for their services.

2 The cost of the guards is a fixed cost to Chinese Walls plc since the employment of the guard is not related to the volume of the output of the firm.

3 The cost of the guard is a social cost, since the guard protects the premises of Chinese Walls from burglary and fire etc.

A Statements 1 and 2 only are correct.

B Statements 2 and 3 only are correct.

C Statements 1 and 3 only are correct.

D Statements 1, 2 and 3 are correct.

A B C D

52 Are the following statements true or false?

1 Marginal costs are not affected by the behaviour of fixed costs

2 Marginal costs will always exceed average costs when average costs are rising

A Both statements are incorrect.

B Statement 1 is correct. Statement 2 is incorrect.

C Statement 1 is incorrect. Statement 2 is correct.

D Both statements are correct.

A B C D

53 Which one of the following statements is incorrect?

A If the variable cost per unit is constant, a firm would minimise its short-run average cost by producing at maximum capacity.

B All fixed costs will be incurred in the short run, even if the firm were to shut down.

C Average variable cost per unit is another expression for marginal cost.

D When the marginal cost of producing a unit is equal to the marginal revenue from selling it, the firm will make a profit from the unit.

A B C D

NOTES

54 The table below gives data about total costs of production at different levels of output.

Output Units per day	*Total costs* £
0	1,500
1	1,700
2	1,850
3	1,950

What are the average variable cost (AVC) and the marginal cost (MC) of production at an output level of 3 units?

A AVC £150 MC £100

B AVC £150 MC £450

C AVC £650 MC £100

D AVC £650 MC £450

A B C D

55 The law of diminishing marginal returns states that

A as more factors of production are employed, output will rise initially and then fall.

B as more factors of production are employed, output will rise, but at a diminishing rate.

C as more variable factors of production are added to a fixed factor, output will rise at a faster rate initially and then fall.

D as more variable factors of production are added to a fixed factor, output will rise at a decreasing rate after a certain point.

A B C D

56 ATC = Average total cost

AVC = Average variable cost

MC = Marginal cost

Which of the following statements is correct?

A MC will equal ATC when ATC is at its minimum amount, but will not equal AVC and AVC is at its minimum.

B MC will equal AVC when AVC is at its minimum amount, but will not equal ATC when ATC is at its minimum.

C MC will equal ATC when ATC is at its minimum amount and AVC when AVC is at its minimum, which is at the same output level.

D MC will equal ATC when ATC is at its minimum amount and AVC when AVC is at its minimum, but this will occur at different output levels.

A B C D

NOTES

57 The price elasticity of demand for a product = 1

The current selling price per unit is $30

The marginal cost of producing an extra unit would be $25

The average cost of production is currently $22

What would be the effect on total profits of producing and selling one extra unit?

A $5 profit

B $8 profit

C $17 loss

D $25 loss

A B C D

58

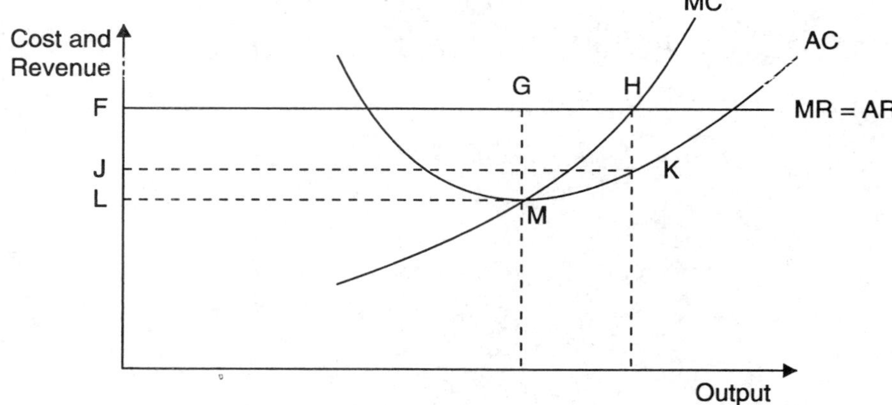

Figure 5

The diagram above shows the cost and revenue curves of Dwindle Ltd. What are the total profits or losses of the company at the output level which maximises profits or minimises losses?

A Losses equal to FHKJ.

B Losses equal to FGML.

C Supernormal profits equal to FHKJ.

D Supernormal profits equal to FGML.

A B C D

59 The Hoppaboard Bus Company has just replaced its original fleet of four buses, each of which had a crew of two, with four new one-man buses. The new buses have the same capacity as the old buses. As a consequence the company has been able to reduce the cost per passenger/mile and run the same service as before. This is because the company has obtained the benefits of

A economies of scale;

B the division of labour;

C higher labour productivity;

D lower maintenance costs.

A B C D

NOTES

60 Suppose that all inputs are increased by 50%, and as a result, total output increases by 30%. This would be an illustration of which of the following?

1 The law of variable proportions.

2 Decreasing returns to scale.

3 A rising long-run average cost curve.

A 1 and 2 only.

B 2 and 3 only.

C 1 and 3 only.

D 2 only.

A B C D

Chapter 6

61

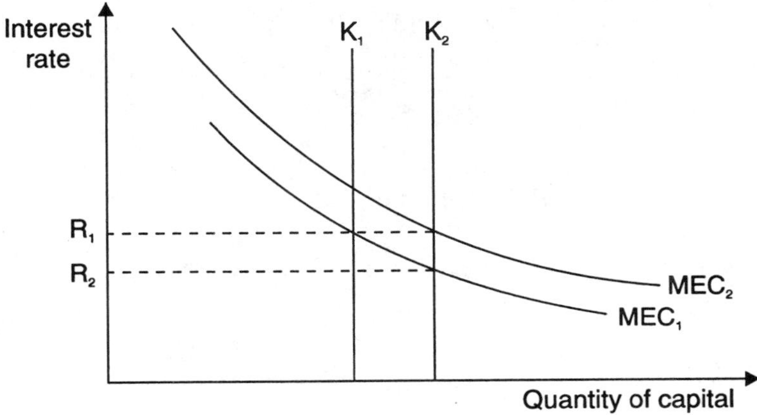

Figure 6

MEC_1 and K_1 represent the current marginal efficiency of capital and existing stock of capital. A rightward shift in the marginal efficiency of capital from MEC_1 to MEC_2 and in the existing stock of capital from K_1 to K_2 could be caused by

A technological innovation;

B more rapid consumption of capital;

C an increase in the willingness of individuals to save;

D a temporary fall in interest rates from R_1 to R_2.

A B C D

62 Plowden Scatter Ltd produces packets of flower seeds. Data about labour productivity and selling prices is as follows.

Number employed	*Number of packets output per week*	*Sales price per packet*
8	4,000	£1.60
9	4,320	£1.50

NOTES

What is the marginal revenue production (MRP) of the ninth employee, and what is the average revenue product (ARP) of nine employees?

A	MRP £80	ARP £720
B	MRP £80	ARP £768
C	MRP £480	ARP £720
D	MRP £480	ARP £768

A B C D

63 All of the following will result in a leftward shift in the supply curve of professional scientists EXCEPT

A a reduction in government spending on science education;

B a fall in the real wage levels of professional scientists;

C an increase in salaries being paid to science graduates in non-scientific jobs in commerce;

D a longer period of pre-qualification training for scientists.

A B C D

64 The output table below refers to the labour productivity of Helen Highwater Ltd, a firm manufacturing bars of scented soap.

Number of workers	*Total product per day (bars of soap)*
4	22
5	32
6	49
7	67
8	85
9	99
10	107
11	114
12	120

Each bar of soap sells for £2 after deducting costs of materials. The firm can have any number of workers at a wage of £16 per day. How many workers should it have in order to maximise profits?

A 6

B 8

C 10

D 12

A B C D

NOTES

65 The mobility of labour can be increased by which of the following items?

1 Improving the frequency of the inter-city passenger train services.

2 Increasing the specialisation of labour.

3 Providing more labour retraining schemes.

A Items 1 and 2 only.

B Items 2 and 3 only.

C Items 1 and 3 only.

D Items 1, 2 and 3.

A B C D

66 The supply of skilled basketweavers is inelastic but not perfectly inelastic. There is an improvement in the productivity of basketweavers. Which of the following would you now expect to happen?

A The number of basketweavers in employment will go down, but their wages will go up.

B The number in employment will be unchanged, and their wages will go up.

C The number in employment will go up, and their wages will go up.

D The number in employment will go up, but their wages will go down.

A B C D

67

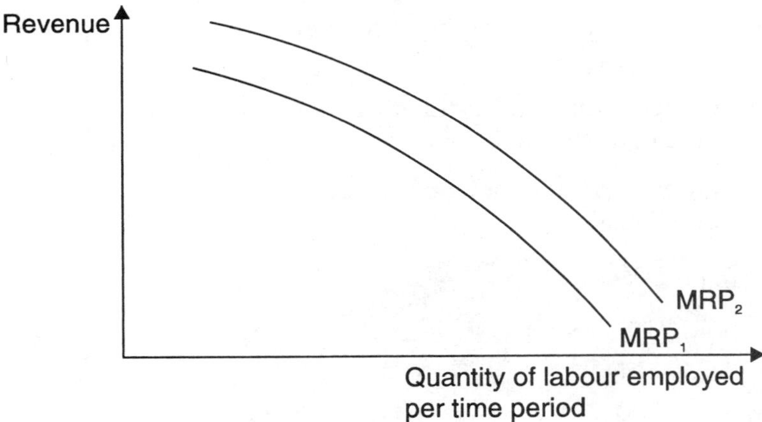

Figure 7

The diagram shows a shift in the value of the marginal revenue product of labour employed by a firm, from MRP_1 to MRP_2. Which of the following factors might help to explain the shift?

1 A rise in the market demand for the firm's product.

2 A rise in the productivity of labour.

3 A fall in the price of labour.

4 A fall in the price of a substitute product.

NOTES

A Factors 1 and 2 only.

B Factors 1, 2 and 3 only.

C Factors 2, 3 and 4 only.

D Factors 1, 2 and 4 only.

A B C D

68 In Monrovia, there are strong trade unions. The National Alliance of Bargemen has successfully negotiated an increase in the wage rate for its members from W_1 to W_2 per week, as shown in the diagram below.

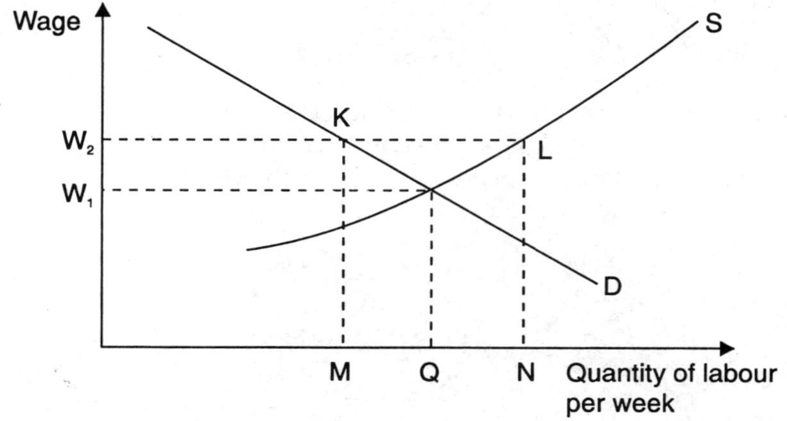

Figure 8

Which of the following will be the effects of the wage rise?

Effect

1 Create an excess supply of labour at the new wage rate W2 equal to QM.

2 Create an excess supply of labour at the new wage rate W2 equal to MN.

3 Create a supply schedule for labour in the industry of W2KLS.

A Effect 1 only will happen.

B Effect 2 only will happen.

C Effects 1 and 3 will happen.

D Effects 2 and 3 will happen.

A B C D

NOTES

69 The National Union of Plasterers is a trade union which operates a closed shop. Members must serve an apprenticeship before becoming qualified plasterers. At the same time that the union raises the apprenticeship period from 2 years to 3 years, there is a fall in demand for new housing, where much of the work of plasterers is done.

The diagram below shows the possible effects of these changes on the original demand curve (DD) and supply curve (SS) for plasterers.

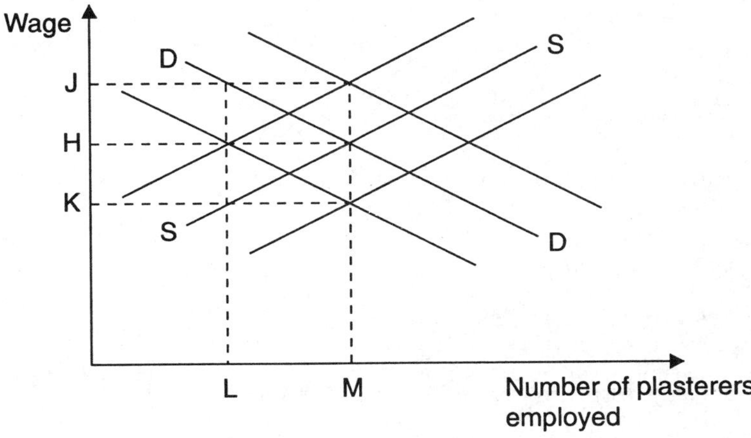

Figure 9

Which of the following is most likely to occur?

A The equilibrium wage will rise to J and the number employed will fall to L.

B The equilibrium wage will remain at H and the number employed will fall to L.

C The equilibrium wage will fall to K and the number employed will remain at M.

D The equilibrium wage will fall to K and the number employed will fall to L.

A B C D

70

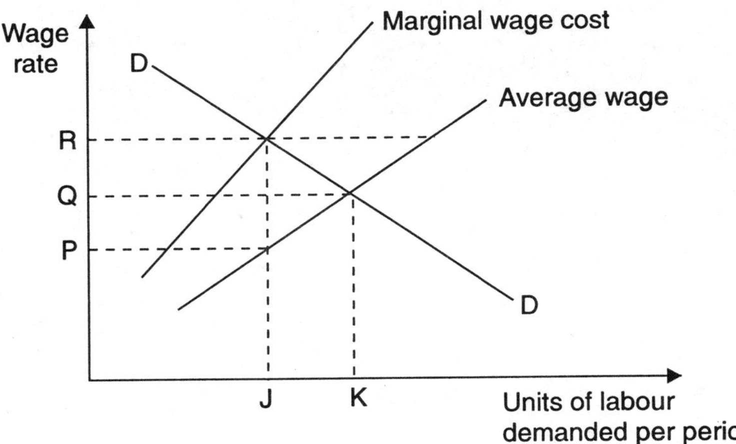

Figure 10

NOTES

The diagram represents a labour market.

Consider two situations.

Situation 1 There are no trade unions, and many small firms employing labour.

Situation 2 There are no trade unions, but the employer is a monopsonist in the market.

What will be the wage level in each situation?

	Situation 1	*Situation 2*
A	Wage P	Wage P
B	Wage P	Wage Q
C	Wage Q	Wage R
D	Wage Q	Wage P

A B C D

71 In the tin mining industry, the demand for tin miners will be less elastic

A the more elastic the demand for tin;

B the lower the proportion of miners' labour costs in the firm's total costs;

C the easier it is to substitute mining equipment for miners' labour;

D the more difficult it is for firms to pass on higher wages costs in a higher price for tin.

A B C D

72 Ira Bull is a farmer who rears horses and cattle. The number of animals he can rear is restricted by his ability to afford animal feed, and he can feed any combination of horses and cows within the following range.

Horses	*Cows*
75	200
100	150

What is the opportunity cost to Ira Bull of rearing one horse?

A 1 cow

B 1½ cows

C 1⅔ cows

D 2 cows

A B C D

NOTES

Chapter 7

73 Complete the following statement.

In conditions of perfect competition, the demand curve for the product of a firm

A is identical to the firm's marginal revenue curve;

B intersects the firm's marginal revenue curve at the point where MC = MR;

C intersects the firm's average cost curve at its lowest point;

D is perfectly inelastic.

A B C D

74 For a profit-maximising firm in conditions of perfect competition, which of the following equations will be true in long run equilibrium?

1 Average Cost = Average Revenue.

2 Marginal cost = Average Revenue.

A Neither equation is correct.

B Equation 1 only is correct.

C Equation 2 only is correct.

D Equations 1 and 2 are both correct.

A B C D

75

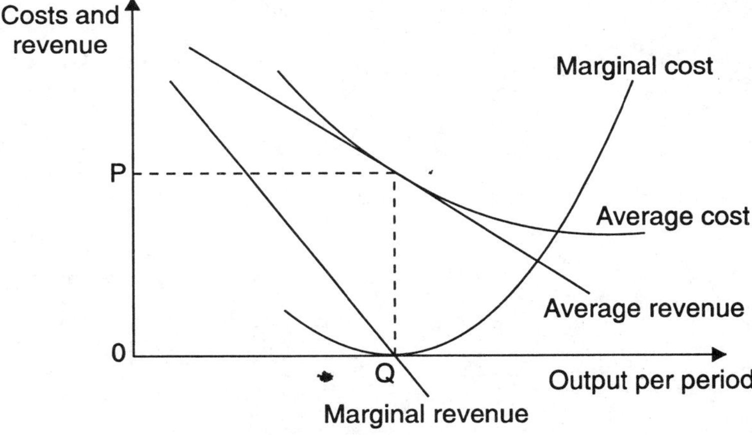

Figure 11

The diagram above shows the cost curves and revenue curves for Hans Tordam Ltd, a firm of tulip growers. Which of the following statements is true?

1 Price P and output Q are the profit-maximising price and output levels for the firm.

2 Price P and output Q are price and output levels at which the firm makes normal profits.

3 Price P and output Q are the revenue-maximising price and output levels.

NOTES

A Statement 1 only is correct.
B Statements 1 and 2 are correct.
C Statements 2 and 3 are correct.
D Statements 1, 2 and 3 are correct.

A B C D

Data for questions 76–78

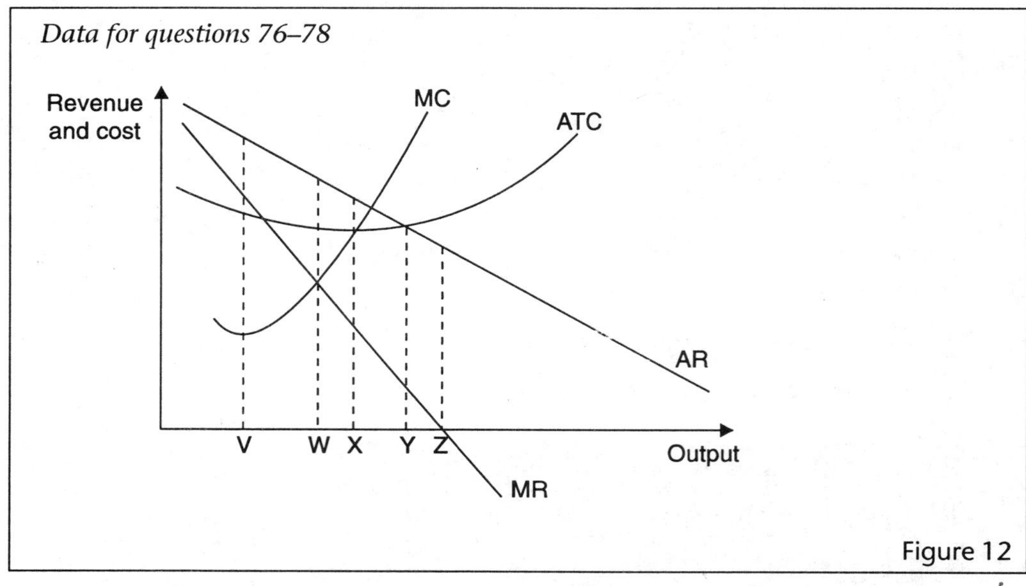

Figure 12

76 At which output level will the firm maximise total revenue?

A Output V
B Output W
C Output Y
D Output Z

A B C D

77 At which output level will the firm be producing the technically optimum output?

A Output V
B Output X
C Output Y
D Output Z

A B C D

78 At which output level will the firm be making only normal profits?

A Output W
B Output X
C Output Y
D Output Z

A B C D

NOTES

79 Toby Hornotterby is a salesman who is paid a sales commission that is a fixed percentage of his firm's total sales revenue. The graph below shows the marginal cost, average revenue and marginal revenue curves of his firm, Amlett Ltd, which produces a single product.

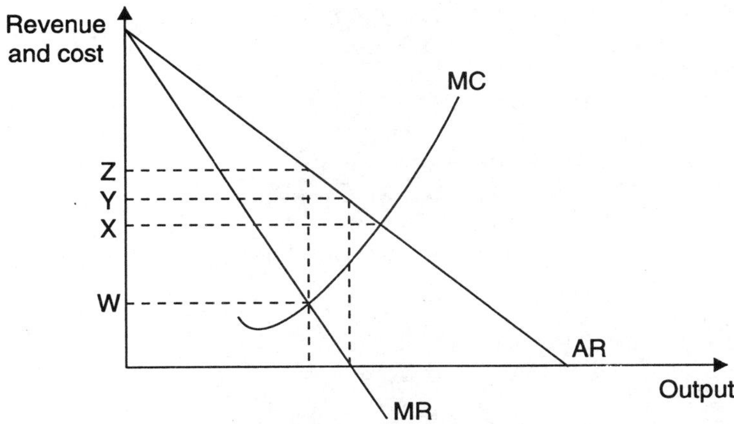

Figure 13

At what price for the product would Toby maximise his sales commission?

A Price W

B Price X

C Price Y

D Price Z

A B C D

80

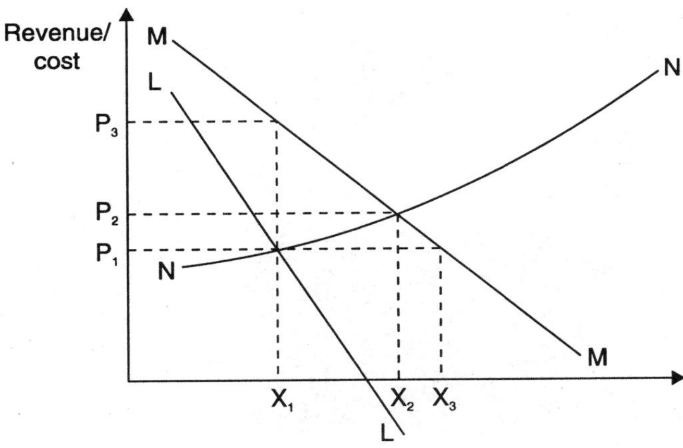

Figure 14

The perfectly competitive industry would

A Produce output X_1 which would sell for P_1.

B Produce output X_1 which would sell for P_3.

C Produce output X_2 which would sell for P_2.

D Produce output X_3 which would sell for P_1.

A B C D

NOTES

81 Which one of the following statements about price discrimination is incorrect?

A Dumping is a form of price discrimination.

B For price discrimination to be possible, the seller must be able to control the supply of the product.

C Price discrimination is only profitable where the elasticity of demand is different in at least two of the markets.

D An example of price discrimination is the sale of first and second class tickets on an aeroplane journey.

A B C D

82 Which one of the following statements about price discrimination is incorrect?

A Charging a different rate for telephone calls according to the time of day is price discrimination.

B Price discrimination might occur for reasons associated with differences in production costs between two or more markets.

C Price discrimination between two markets might be achieved because of transportation costs between the markets.

D Price discrimination can be achieved by separating markets on the basis of geography, age, time or consumers' ignorance.

A B C D

83 Barriers to entry help to protect monopolies. Which of the following items can be effective barriers to entry?

1 Taking over small firms that enter the market.

2 A natural monopoly.

3 A government-awarded franchise.

A Items 1 and 2 only.

B Items 2 and 3 only.

C Items 1 and 3 only.

D Items 1, 2 and 3.

A B C D

NOTES

84 Which one of the following statements is incorrect?

A If the effect of privatisation is to increase competition, the effect might be to reduce or eliminate allocative inefficiency.

B Privatisation means selling off nationalised industries by the government to the private sector.

C The effect of denationalisation could be to make firms more cost-conscious, because they will be under the scrutiny of stock market investors.

D The government might appoint consumer watchdogs to regulate privatised industries.

A B C D

Chapter 8

85 Which of the following are characteristics of monopolistic competition?

1 Freedom of entry into the industry.

2 Homogeneous (ie uniform) products.

3 Advertising.

4 A downward sloping demand curve.

A 1 and 2 only.

B 1 and 4 only.

C 1, 3 and 4 only.

D 2 and 4 only.

A B C D

Data for questions 86–88

Each of the following questions consists of two statements. Select your answer from the following

A Both statements are correct.

B The first statement is correct but the second statement is false.

C The first statement is false but the second statement is correct.

D Both statements are false.

86 *First statement*

If average cost is constant for a firm operating under conditions of imperfect competition, any output will yield maximum profits.

A B C D

Second statement

Where average cost is constant, marginal cost will always equal average cost.

A B C D

NOTES

87 *First statement*

In conditions of *monopolistic competition* firms will eventually reach an equilibrium output which is less than the output level at which average total cost is at a minimum. A B C D

Second statement

In *perfect competition*, at the output level where marginal revenue equals marginal cost, a firm's average variable costs are minimised. A B C D

88 *First statement*

Firms operating under conditions of monopolistic competition will often engage in advertising. A B C D

Second statement

The profits of a firm operating under conditions of monopolistic competition can be increased by a shift of its average revenue curve or a fall in the elasticity of demand for the firm's product. A B C D

89 Which of the following statements best describes long-run equilibrium in a market where there is monopolistic competition?

A Marginal revenue equals average cost.

B There is excess capacity in the industry since firms could reduce average costs by expanding output.

C Firms will earn supernormal profits because price exceeds marginal cost.

D Price equals marginal cost, but does not equal average cost.

A B C D

90 Which of the following explain why a firm in a monopolistically competitive market must be *inefficient?*

1 P > minimum AC.

2 Output is less than that which minimises AC.

3 The AR curve slopes downwards.

4 MC < AC.

A 1 and 2 only.

B 2 and 4 only.

C 1, 2 and 4 only.

D All four.

A B C D

91 The oligopolist is *least* likely to compete through

A advertising;

B improving product quality;

C cutting prices;

D providing incidental services, as an add-on to the basic good.

A B C D

NOTES

92 Which of the following are common features of oligopolistic markets?

1 Advertising.

2 Barriers to entry.

3 Interdependence of decision making.

4 Price stability.

A 1 and 2 only.
B 1, 2 and 3 only.
C 1, 2 and 4 only.
D All of them.

A B C D

93 The purpose of a cartel is to

A rationalise production;
B reduce consumer uncertainty;
C standardise product quality;
D ensure that all producers charge the same price.

A B C D

94 Which of the following would be examples of oligopolists secretly colluding?

1 A dominant firm setting a price for the rest to follow.

2 Reaching agreements on pricing and output at a secret meeting.

3 Allowing increased brand proliferation.

A 1 only.
B 1 and 2 only.
C 2 and 3 only.
D 1, 2 and 3.

A B C D

95 Which of the following events is likely to cause a cartel to dissolve?

1 Barriers to trade are reduced considerably.

2 Consumers prefer to enter into secret price contracts with individual firms in the cartel.

3 The number of firms in the industry falls.

A 1 and 2 only.
B 1 and 3 only.
C 3 only.
D All of them.

A B C D

NOTES

96

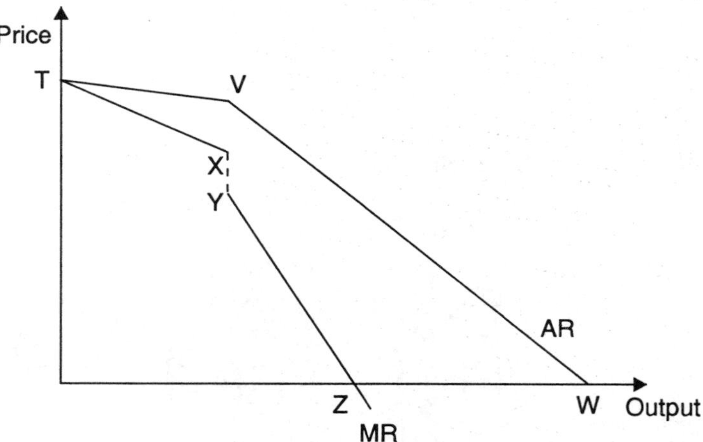

Figure 15

The diagram shows the average revenue curve and marginal revenue curve for an oligopolist firm, Roger Handout Ltd. If Roger Handout Ltd were now to lower the price of its products, its competitors would follow suit and do the same with their product prices. Which of the following is the relevant section of Roger Handout's demand curve to which this situation relates.

A Section TV

B Section VW

C Section TX

D Section YZ

A B C D

Chapter 9

97 The essential requirement of money is that it should always be

1 legal tender;

2 backed by a precious metal;

3 generally acceptable as a means of payment.

A 1, 2 and 3.

B 1 and 2 only.

C 3 only.

D 1 only.

A B C D

98 Which is the best description of the supply of money in an economy?

A Notes and coins issued by the central bank.

B Money created by the commercial banks.

C Coins, notes and bank deposits.

D All items of legal tender.

A B C D

NOTES

Data for questions 99–100

	£ million
Notes and coin in circulation outside the Bank of England	15,000
Notes and coin in the hands of the general public	13,000
Current account balances of UK residents in sterling in British banks	70,000
Deposit account balances of UK residents, in sterling, in British banks	80,000
Deposits of UK residents in foreign currencies in British banks	30,000
Deposits of overseas residents in sterling in British banks	60,000
Private sector building society shares and deposits	108,000
Banks' operational deposits with the Bank of England	1,000

99 Given the data above, what is the amount of M0?

A £13,000 million.

B £14,000 million.

C £15,000 million.

D £16,000 million.

A B C D

100 Given the data above, what is the amount of M4?

A £271,000 million.

B £286,000 million.

C £331,000 million.

D £361,000 million.

A B C D

101 A financial intermediary is best defined as

A an institution which matches lenders' supply of funds with borrowers' demands for funds;

B an institution which operates on the Stock Exchange, matching buyers and sellers of stocks and shares;

C an institution which allows firms to obtain equipment from suppliers by providing leasing or hire purchase finance;

D an institution which acts as a buffer between the Bank of England and the rest of the UK banking system.

A B C D

102 Maturity transformation describes

A the process by which loans get closer to redemption as time passes.;

B the amount payable to redeem a loan or security at its maturity;

C the way in which interest rates vary according to the duration of the loan;

D the process by which short term deposits are re-lent by banks as longer term loans.

A B C D

NOTES

103 Which of the following items will not be found in the assets of a retail bank?

A Overdrafts.

B Bank bills.

C Customers' deposits.

D Loans to the money markets.

A B C D

104 Which of the following is the most liquid asset of a commercial bank?

A Money at call with the discount houses.

B Government Bonds.

C Cash.

D Operational balances with the Bank of England.

A B C D

105 A banking system in a small country consists of just five banks. Each bank has decided to maintain a minimum cash ratio of 10%. Each bank now receives additional cash deposits of £1 million. There will now be a further increase in total bank deposits up to a maximum of

A £500,000.

B £5 million.

C £45 million.

D £50 million.

A B C D

106 A bank's liquidity ratio is

A the ratio of cash to loans;

B the ratio of liquid to illiquid assets;

C the ratio of total assets to total liabilities;

D the ratio of liquid assets to total liabilities.

A B C D

107 Which of the following is an asset to a commercial bank customer?

A The bank's deposits at the Bank of England.

B A current account bank deposit.

C An overdraft.

D Trade bills held by the bank as reserve assets.

A B C D

NOTES

108 Banks are operating a reserve asset ratio of 20%. A customer deposits a cheque for £100, drawn on an account at Bank X, with Bank Y. What would be the maximum increase in deposits by the banking system as a whole?

A 0

B £20

C £100

D £500

A B C D

Chapter 10

109 Which of the following functions does the Bank of England perform?

1 Sole issuer of banknotes in the UK.

2 Banker to the banks.

3 Lender of the last resort to the discount houses.

4 Management of the National Debt.

A 1, 2 and 3.

B 2 and 3 only.

C 1 and 2 only.

D 1 only.

A B C D

110 Which of the following is not regarded as monetary policy?

A Raising the level of taxation.

B Controlling the money supply.

C Rationing credit.

D Using interest rates to influence aggregate demand.

A B C D

111 Base rates in the UK are

A the interest rates at which the Bank of England will trade in eligible bills in the discount markets;

B the rates of interest which commercial banks use for setting many of their other rates;

C the rates of interest at which commercial banks lend to each other in the money markets;

D the rates of interest which commercial banks offer to depositors.

A B C D

112 Which of the following possible actions by the Bank of England is not an example of open-market operations?

A Selling more government bonds but the same amount of Treasury bills.

B Selling less Treasury bills but the same amount of government bonds.

C Selling less bonds and bills.

D Replacing £1m of maturing government bonds with £1m of extra Treasury bills.

A B C D

113 Which of the following is most likely to lead to a fall in the money supply?

A A fall in interest rates.

B Purchases of government securities by the central bank.

C Sales of government securities by the central bank.

D A rise in the amount of cash held by commercial banks.

A B C D

114 Commercial banks maintain a rigid 10% liquidity ratio. The Bank of England buys back £10m of government bonds on the open market. How much will the eventual change in the level of bank advances be?

A £10m.

B £90m.

C £100m.

D £1m.

A B C D

115 Which of the following are the likely consequences of a fall in interest rates?

1 A rise in the demand for consumer credit.

2 A fall in investment.

3 A fall in government expenditure.

4 A rise in the demand for housing.

A 1 and 2 only.

B 1, 2 and 3 only.

C 1, 3 and 4 only.

D 2, 3 and 4 only.

A B C D

116 The Bank of England decides to engineer a rise in interest rates. The banks have excess liquidity. What should it do?

A Buy more bills.

B Buy fewer bills.

C Sell more bills.

D Sell fewer bills.

A B C D

117 Which of the following does not engage in the buying and selling of shares in other companies?

A Investment trusts.

B Stock exchanges.

C Insurance companies.

D Pension funds.

A B C D

118 Which of the following is not a function of stock exchanges?

A Providing a market in existing securities.

B Directly funding the start-up costs of new companies.

C Acting as a market for government securities.

D Advertising the prices of stocks and shares.

A B C D

119 Finance houses tend to specialise in:

A granting loans for house purchase;

B providing hire purchase finance for consumer durables;

C providing savings facilities;

D providing overdraft facilities.

A B C D

Chapter 11

120 If there is a reduction in government spending, there will not necessarily be a fall in national income if there is an increase in:

1 exports;

2 taxation;

3 investments.

A 1 and/or 2.

B 1 and/or 3.

C 2 and/or 3.

D Any or all of 1, 2 and 3.

A B C D

NOTES

121 Which of the following items is most likely to increase the circular flow of income?

A Increased taxation.

B Increased spending on imports.

C Lower government spending.

D Reductions in personal savings.

A B C D

122 Which of the following would not give the value of the UK's Gross national product?

A Gross national expenditure minus exports.

B Gross domestic product plus net property income from abroad.

C Total factor incomes earned by UK residents.

D Net national income plus depreciation.

A B C D

123 Net national product at factor cost
+ Capital consumption
+ Indirect taxes on expenditure
– Subsidies
equals

A Gross national product at market prices.

B Gross national product at factor cost.

C Gross domestic product at market prices.

D Gross domestic product at factor cost.

A B C D

Data for questions 125–128

	£million
Consumers' expenditure	2,500
General government final consumption	800
Gross domestic fixed capital formation	750
Value of physical increase in stocks and work in progress	0
Exports of goods and services	1,200
Imports of goods and services	1,000
Taxes on expenditure (indirect taxes)	650
Subsidies	100
Net property income from abroad	40
Capital consumption (depreciation)	450

124 Gross national product at factor cost in this economy is

A £3,700 million.

B £3,740 million.

C £4,290 million.

D £4,840 million.

A B C D

NOTES

125 Gross national product at market prices in this economy is

A £4,050 million.
B £4,090 million.
C £4,250 million.
D £4,290 million.

A B C D

126 Gross domestic product at market prices in this economy is

A £3,740 million.
B £3,850 million.
C £4,050 million.
D £4,250 million.

A B C D

127 National income at factor cost in this economy is

A £3,290 million.
B £3,740 million.
C £3,800 million.
D £3,840 million.

A B C D

128 Which one of the following items is not included in the calculation of gross national product at factor cost?

A The cost of building new government offices.
B Value added tax on business services.
C Dividends received from shares in a company abroad.
D Imputed rent of owner-occupied houses.

A B C D

129 An individual earns £30,000 in a year. Of this £8,000 is tax free. The rate of income tax is 25p in the £1. The individual's personal disposable income for the year is

A £22,000.
B £22,500.
C £24,500.
D £30,000.

A B C D

130 The following data relates to national income statistics in Muvovia, which are compiled in the same way as in the UK.

	1995 Actual prices £ million	1996 Actual prices £ million
Consumers' expenditure	200,000	225,000
General government final consumption	70,000	74,000
Gross domestic fixed capital formation	54,000	60,000
Imports	92,000	99,000
Exports	93,000	94,000
Taxes on expenditure	52,000	50,000
Subsidies	8,000	10,000

The general rate of inflation in Muvovia between 1995 and 1996 was 10%. The real change in gross domestic product at market prices between 1995 and 1996, in percentage terms, was

A a fall of about 1%;

B a rise of about 1%;

C a rise of about 2%;

D a rise of about 2½%.

A B C D

131 Which one of the following statements is correct?

A Two countries with the same total national income will have roughly the same living standards.

B Services provided free to the public, such as police work and state education, are valued at opportunity cost in the national income statistics.

C Official statistics might over-estimate the national income for a country with a strong unofficial economy.

D Gross national product figures are often used in preference to net national product figures because of difficulty in calculating capital consumption.

A B C D

Chapter 12

132 An inflationary gap in the economy could be closed by an increase in the

A supply of money;

B government's budget surplus;

C average propensity to consume;

D country's export surplus.

A B C D

NOTES

133 Which of the following may cause an increase in national income?

A A fall in investment.

B A rise in exports.

C An increase in saving.

D A fall in consumer spending.

A B C D

134 Which of the following investments creates an injection into the circular flow of income?

A An increase by a firm in its stocks of finished goods, prior to a marketing campaign.

B The purchase by a pension fund of shares in a newly-privatised company.

C The purchase of a second-hand piece of farming machinery with their savings by a farming co-operative group.

D The takeover of one company by another company.

A B C D

135 The marginal propensity to consume measures

A the relationship between changes in consumption and changes in consumer utility;

B the proportion of household incomes spent on consumer goods;

C the proportion of total national income spent on consumer goods;

D the relationship between changes in consumption and changes in income.

A B C D

136

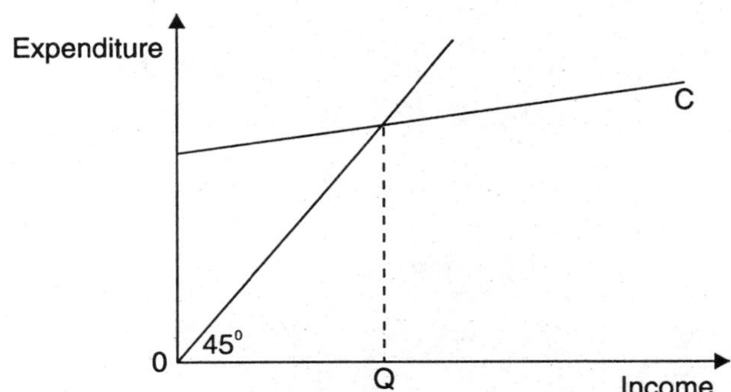

Figure 16

The diagram shows the consumption function for a nation's economy. The marginal propensity to consume is:

A constant at all levels of income.

B positive at income levels below Q and negative at income levels above Q.

C greater than the average propensity to consume at income levels below Q and less than the average propensity to consume at income levels above Q.

D greater than the average propensity to consume at all income levels.

A B C D

137 APC = Average propensity to consume

MPS = Marginal propensity to save

In a country with a very low income per head of the population:

A APC will be low and MPS will be low;

B APC will be low and MPS will be high;

C APC will be high and MPS will be low;

D APC will be high and MPS will be high.

A B C D

138 Which of the following responses is correct?

A fall in the rate of interest may directly result in

1 a switch to more capital-intensive methods of production;

2 a decline in the marginal efficiency of capital;

3 higher levels of investment.

A Responses 1 and 2 are correct.

B Responses 1 and 3 are correct.

C Responses 2 and 3 are correct.

D Responses 1, 2 and 3 are correct.

A B C D

139 The effect of the multiplier on national income will be small

A when there is high unemployment in the economy;

B when the marginal propensity to save is low;

C because of a deflationary gap;

D because of leakages from the circular flow in addition to savings.

A B C D

NOTES

140 The multiplier effect of government investment is likely to be greater where

A there is excess production capacity in the private sector of industry;

B there is a high marginal propensity to consume;

C the increased spending is financed by higher taxation;

D there is a high level of stocks in firms.

A B C D

141 In a closed economy with no government sector, the consumption function is thought to be

C = £30,000 + 0.4Y

Investment is £30,000 per year.

Which of the following statements is correct?

A Equilibrium income is £80,000
Value of the multiplier = 1.67.

B Equilibrium income is £80,000
Value of the multiplier = 2.50.

C Equilibrium income is £100,000
Value of the multiplier = 1.67.

D Equilibrium income is £100,000
Value of the multiplier = 2.50.

A B C D

142 In an open economy, the marginal propensity to consume domestically-produced goods is 0.25 at all levels of income. If exports increase by £100 million, and there are no other charges, national income will increase by

A £25 million.

B £100 million.

C £125 million.

D £133 million (approx).

A B C D

143 *Statement 1*

An increase in saving will *always* act to the benefit of a country

Statement 2

The paradox of thrift suggests that an attempt to increase the amount saved out of a given level of national income will result in a fall in national income.

A Statement 1 is correct.
Statement 2 is correct.

B Statement 1 is correct.
Statement 2 is incorrect.

C Statement 1 is incorrect.
Statement 2 is correct.

D Statement 1 is incorrect.
Statement 2 is incorrect.

A B C D

NOTES

Chapter 13

144 Structural unemployment is best defined as unemployment caused by

A defects in the industrial and commercial structure;

B a long term decline in a particular industry;

C a mismatch between available jobs and the unemployed;

D a switch from labour-intensive to capital-intensive production methods.

A B C D

145 Which of the following reasons for unemployment would be classified as frictional?

1 Unemployment resulting from the decline of the textile industry and expansion of the microcomputer industry.

2 Individuals between jobs.

3 Those who are unemployable because of a mental or physical handicap.

4 Unemployment resulting from the slow adjustment of aggregate demand.

A Reason 1 only.

B Reasons 1 and 2 only.

C Reasons 2 and 3 only.

D Reasons 3 and 4 only.

A B C D

146 The short-run Phillips curve is likely to

A have a negative slope;

B have a positive slope;

C be horizontal;

D be vertical.

A B C D

147 Which of the following factors may have contributed to a rise in the natural rate of unemployment in the UK since the 1970s?

1 A decline in world trade.

2 The recession in British manufacturing industry.

3 An increase in the participation rate of married women.

4 Technical progress.

A 1, 2, 3 and 4.

B 2, 3 and 4 only.

C 1, 2 and 3 only.

D 3 and 4 only.

A B C D

NOTES

148 Which of the following measures has not been recommended by Friedman and like-minded monetarist economists as a means of reducing the natural rate of unemployment to a lower level?

A Measures to stimulate consumer demand for more goods.

B Schemes to retrain workers in new job skills.

C Measures to cut trade union power.

D Restructuring the income tax system.

A B C D

149 Weightings in the retail price index for country T for the year 19X2 were as follows.

Food	317
Drink	63
Transport and vehicles	82
Utilities and fuel (water, gas etc)	75
Clothing	116
Housing	109

From this, we can conclude that

A people placed less value on transport than on housing;

B people ate more by volume than they drank;

C spending on food has risen faster than spending on any other category;

D people spent a greater proportion of their income on clothing than they did on utilities and fuel.

A B C D

150

Commodity	*Price in base year*	*Price in year 19X1*	*Weights*
P	£2.0	£2.6	5
Q	£0.5	£0.7	4
R	£4.0	£4.6	1
			10

From the above table, what is the price index for the basket of commodities P, Q and R in 19X1?

A 104.4

B 121.5

C 127.5

D 132.5

A B C D

151 If a retail price index changed from 250 to 260 over a period of 12 months, this would indicate that

A the standard of living has fallen;

B wages will need to rise by 4% if incomes are to keep pace with price rises;

C the pattern of consumer expenditure has probably changed during the year;

D the value of money has fallen.

A B C D

NOTES

152 The Keynesian view of inflation is associated with which of the following concepts?

A Rational expectations of inflation.

B Supply side economics.

C The natural rate of unemployment.

D The inflationary gap.

A B C D

153 Which of the following factors might cause cost-push inflation?

1 Higher wage levels in domestic industries.

2 Higher consumer spending.

3 Higher import prices.

A Factor 1 only.

B Factors 1 and 2 only.

C Factors 1 and 3 only.

D Factors 2 and 3 only.

A B C D

154 Which of the following measures can help to tackle the problem of cost-push inflation?

1 Higher direct taxation.

2 Wage increases being linked to productivity improvements.

3 Higher interest rates.

4 A revaluation of the currency.

A Measures 1, 2 and 3 only.

B Measures 1, 2 and 4 only.

C Measures 2, 3 and 4 only.

D Measures 2 and 4 only.

A B C D

155 Which of the following measures would be most consistent with the views of Friedman and other monetarist economists, for reducing the rate of inflation or unemployment?

A The government should impose an incomes policy to keep inflation down.

B The government can achieve lower unemployment, but only by accepting high levels of inflation.

C The government should control the money supply so as to keep output in the economy at a full employment level.

D Lower unemployment can be achieved without higher inflation if the government reduces welfare benefits for the unemployed.

A B C D

NOTES

Chapter 14

156 The relationship between money supply and prices can be expressed in the quantity theory of money identity as follows.

A M/V = P/T
B MV = PT
C MP = VT
D MT = VP

A B C D

157 For the quantity theory of money equation MV = PT to explain short-run price behaviour, it is necessary that

A P varies inversely with M;
B interest rates remain unchanged;
C changes in V in the short run are predictable;
D T remains unchanged.

A B C D

158 Supporters of the quantity theory of money argue that

1 the velocity of circulation (V) is more or less constant;
2 the quantity of transactions (T) is given;
3 that the amount of money (M) is independent of V, T and P (the price level);
4 there should be no growth in the money supply.

A 1, 2, 3 and 4.
B 1, 2 and 3 only.
C 2, 3 and 4 only.
D 1, 3 and 4 only.

A B C D

159 Controlling the PSBR can be difficult because of

1 the political desirability of cutting taxes;
2 the political desirability of increasing government expenditure;
3 the effects of automatic stabilisers in an economic recovery;
4 an ageing population.

A 1, 2 and 4.
B 1, 2 and 3.
C 1, 2, 3 and 4.
D 2, 3 and 4.

A B C D

NOTES

160 Which of the following will not reduce the demand for real money balances?

A An increase in the opportunity cost of holding money.

B An increase in the interest paid on risky assets.

C An increase in optimism about the future.

D An increase in uncertainty regarding future transactions.

A B C D

161 According to Keynes, which one of the following is very sensitive to changes in interest rates?

A The money supply.

B The speculative demand for money.

C The precautionary demand for money.

D The transactions demand for money.

A B C D

162 Which of the following will not result in an increase in the transactions demand for money?

A An increase in the standard rate of income tax.

B An increase in VAT.

C An increase in the level of income.

D A general rise in the price of goods and services.

A B C D

163 Which of the following actions by the government would be most likely to increase aggregate monetary demand?

A Reductions in subsidies on food, offset by a reduction in taxation.

B A rise in the Bank of England's short-term interest rate (for open market operations).

C Increased value added tax on a wide range of goods.

D Insisting that public corporations should break even.

A B C D

164 Other things remaining the same, according to Keynes, an increase in the money supply will tend to reduce

A interest rates;

B liquidity preference;

C the volume of bank overdrafts;

D prices and incomes.

A B C D

NOTES

165

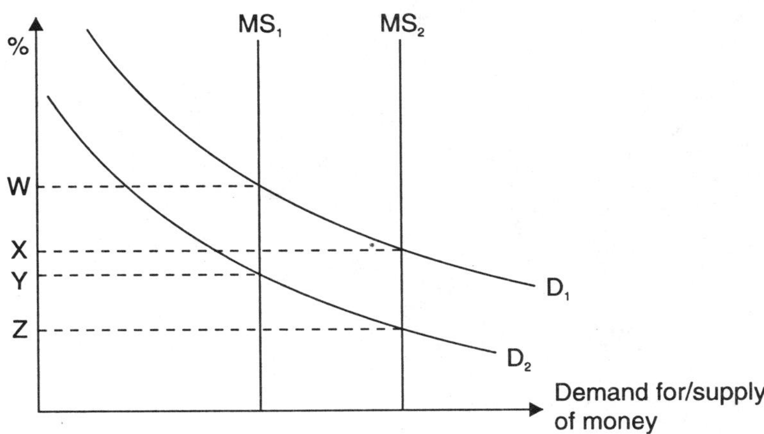

Figure 17

There is an increase in the demand for money. The interest rate, according to Keynes's analysis, will change

A from W to Y;

B from Z to X;

C from Y to X;

D from Z to W.

A B C D

166 If the real rate of interest is 3% pa and the expected rate of inflation is 6% pa, the nominal interest rate will be approximately

A ½%

B 2%

C 3%

D 9%

A B C D

167 Monetarist analysis is based on the concept of a portfolio of assets and suggest that

A in a recession individuals use up their savings rather than reducing their consumption;

B individuals hold wealth in a variety of forms, the balance depending on the relative profitability and liquidity of different assets;

C individuals divide their wealth equally between money and financial assets irrespective of the rate of interest;

D individuals with stocks and shares keep a broadly balanced portfolio of equities to spread risk.

A B C D

NOTES

Chapter 15

168 Which one of the following is an item of fiscal policy? Measures by the government

- A to set a national minimum wage;
- B to support the exchange rate for the country's currency;
- C to control growth in the money supply;
- D to alter rates of taxation.

A B C D

169 Which one of the following fiscal measures would be least likely to create inflationary pressures, either directly or as a secondary effect?

- A An increase in the standard rate of value added tax.
- B An increase in the excise duties on tobacco products.
- C A decision to tax social security benefits to the sick and unemployed.
- D An increase in personal allowances against income tax.

A B C D

170 The government of a country wishes to achieve a balanced budget every year. All of the following would therefore be likely to result in an increase in taxation, *except*

- A a training policy aimed at reducing the numbers of long-term unemployed;
- B an increase in the birth rate and reduction in the death rate;
- C a balance of payments deficit;
- D an extension of the minimum school-leaving age from 16 years to 18 years.

A B C D

171 If a government wished to increase consumer spending, it could increase rates of

- A income tax;
- B corporation tax;
- C import duties;
- D social security payments.

A B C D

NOTES

172 The Budget will have a neutral effect on the country's macroeconomic activity when

A the multiplier effect of government spending and revenue cancel each other out;

B the government achieves a balanced budget with total expenditure equalling total revenue;

C any increase in government spending is equalled by an increase in government revenue;

D the distribution of the tax burden remains the same as in the previous year.

A B C D

173 Which of the following will not be the immediate purpose of a tax measure by the government?

A To discourage an activity regarded as socially undesirable.

B To influence interest rates up or down.

C To protect a domestic industry from foreign competition.

D To price certain products so as to take into account their social cost.

A B C D

174 Which of the following government aims might be achieved by means of fiscal policy?

1 A redistribution of income between firms and households.

2 A reduction in aggregate monetary demand.

3 A change in the pattern of consumer demand.

A Objectives 1 and 2 only.

B Objectives 1 and 3 only.

C Objectives 2 and 3 only.

D Objectives 1, 2 and 3.

A B C D

175 Howard earns £8,000 per year and pays £1,000 in income tax. Hugh earns £16,000 per year and pays £2,500 in income tax. Hymie earns £24,000 per year and pays £5,500 in income tax. The income tax system is

A regressive;

B flat rate;

C proportional.

D progressive.

A B C D

NOTES

176 The government of a certain country decides to introduce a poll tax, which will involve a flat rate levy of £200 on every adult member of the population. This new tax could be described as

A regressive;

B proportional;

C progressive;

D *ad valorem*.

A B C D

177 If a reduction in the taxes on alcoholic drinks resulted in a less even distribution of wealth in society, with a greater proportion of wealth in the hands of the rich sections of society, we could conclude that, *on average*

A people with low incomes spend more on alcoholic drinks than people with high incomes;

B people with low incomes spend less on alcoholic drinks than people with high incomes;

C people with low incomes spend a bigger proportion of their income on alcoholic drinks than people with high incomes;

D people with low incomes spend a lower proportion of their income on alcoholic drinks than people with high incomes.

A B C D

178 What are the likely consequences of a large increase in the rate of value added tax (assuming government does not increase its spending)?

1 A deterioration in the balance of payments.

2 An increase in the retail price index.

3 Higher unemployment.

A Consequences 1 and 2 only.

B Consequences 1 and 3 only.

C Consequences 2 and 3 only.

D Consequence 2 only.

A B C D

179 The total yield from an indirect tax on a good is likely to be greatest when

A demand is inelastic, supply is elastic;

B demand is inelastic, supply is inelastic;

C demand is elastic, supply is elastic;

D demand is elastic, supply is inelastic.

A B C D

NOTES

Chapter 16

180 Assume that two small countries, X and Y, produce two commodities, P and Q, and that there are no transport costs. One unit of resource in Country X produces 4 units of P or 8 units of Q. One unit of resource in Country Y produces 1 unit of P or 3 units of Q.

Which one of the following statements is true?

A Country X has an absolute advantage over Country Y in producing P and Q, and so will not trade.

B Country X does not have an absolute advantage over Country Y in producing P and Q.

C Country Y has a comparative advantage over Country Y in producing Q.

D Country X has a comparative advantage over Country Y in producing P and Q.

A B C D

181 According to the law of comparative advantage, the consequences of protectionism in international trade are that protectionist measures will prevent

A each country of the world from maximising its economic wealth;

B each country of the world from maximising the value of its exports;

C the countries of the world from maximising their total output with their economic resources;

D each country of the world from achieving equilibrium in its balance of payments.

A B C D

182 The table below shows the production capability of one unit of resource in each of two countries, in terms of producing cars and rice.

	Cars		*Rice*
Bandia	3	or	45 tonnes
Sparta	10	or	60 tonnes

Assume that there are no transport costs, and that opportunity costs are constant for all levels of output. The law of comparative advance would predict that

A Bandia will export rice and Sparta will export cars.

B Sparta will export rice and Bandia will export cars.

C Sparta will export both rice and cars.

D Sparta will export cars and there will be no trade in rice between the countries.

A B C D

NOTES

183

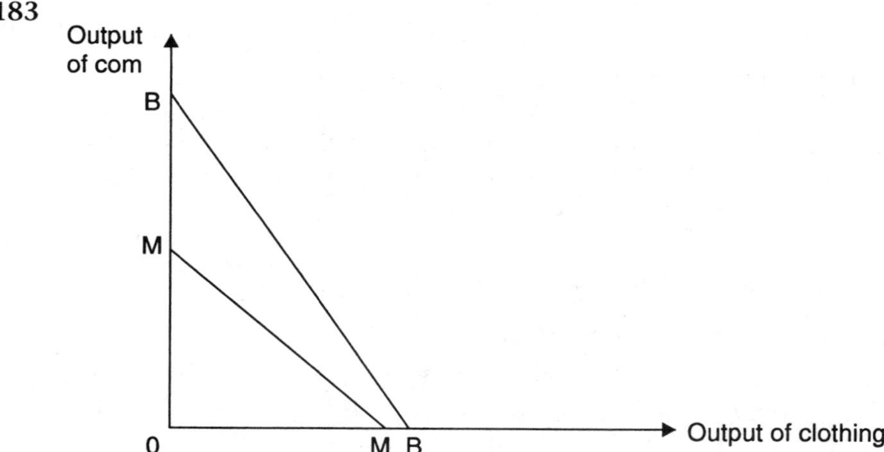

Figure 18

In the diagram, MM and BB represent production possibility boundaries of two countries, Mula and Burra respectively. Each country produces just two goods, corn and clothing. From the diagram, it can be seen that

A Mula has a comparative advantage in the production of clothing.

B Burra has an absolute advantage in the production of both corn and clothing.

C in the absence of international trade, Burra has a higher national income per head of the population than Mula.

D Burra has a comparative advantage in the production of clothing.

Data for questions 184–185

The diagram below shows the tariffs for a country whose government maintains the exchange rate at E.

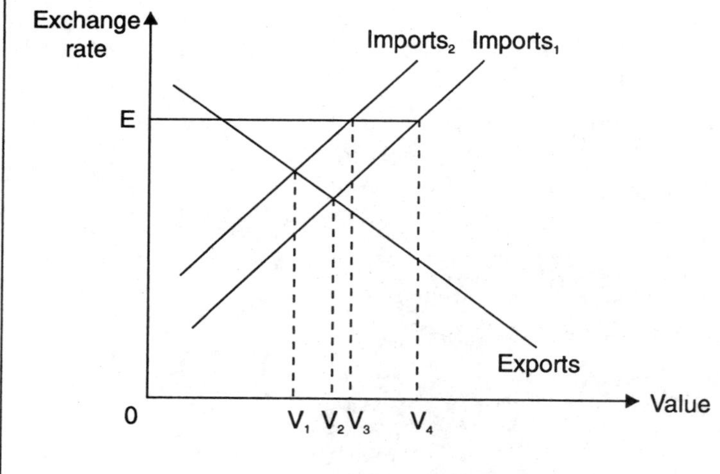

Figure 19

NOTES

184 The value of imports prior to the imposition of tariffs is

A V_1

B V_2

C V_3

D V_4

A B C D

185 If, instead of imposing the tariffs and ignoring capital movements, the exchange rate had been allowed to find its own level, the value of imports would be

A V_1

B V_2

C V_3

D V_4

A B C D

Data for questions 186–188

The diagram below shows the domestic demand of a country for butter (DD). HS represents domestic supply, and WS is supply from other countries of the world, which is infinite at price OR.

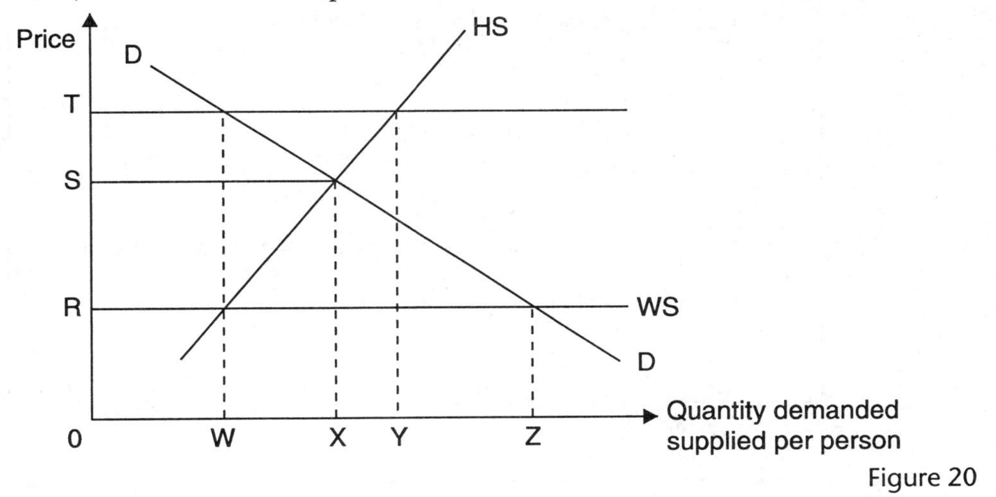

Figure 20

If the country has free trade in butter, it consumes OZ of which OW is produced domestically and WZ is imported.

186 Other things being the same, if the government were to pay a subsidy of RT to its domestic butter producers for each unit of butter they supplied, the level of domestic production of butter would become

A OW;

B OX;

C OY;

D OZ.

A B C D

NOTES

187 If the government pays a subsidy of RT to domestic producers for each unit they supply, the level of domestic consumption will be

A OW;
B OX;
C OY;
D OZ.

A B C D

188 If, instead of paying a subsidy to domestic butter producers, the government imposed a tariff of TR per unit on butter imports, the level of domestic production would be

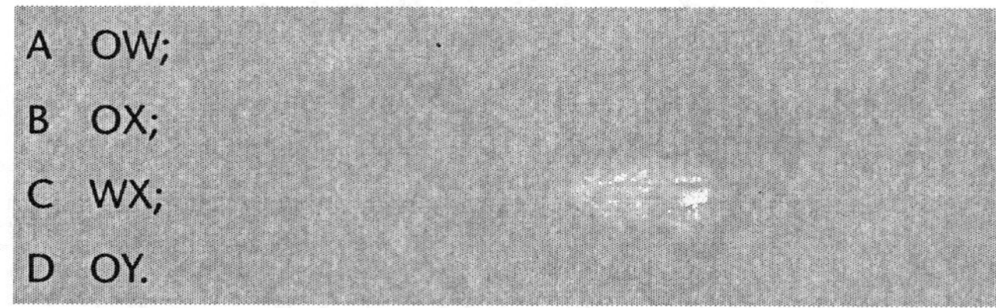

A OW;
B OX;
C WX;
D OY.

A B C D

Data for questions 189–190

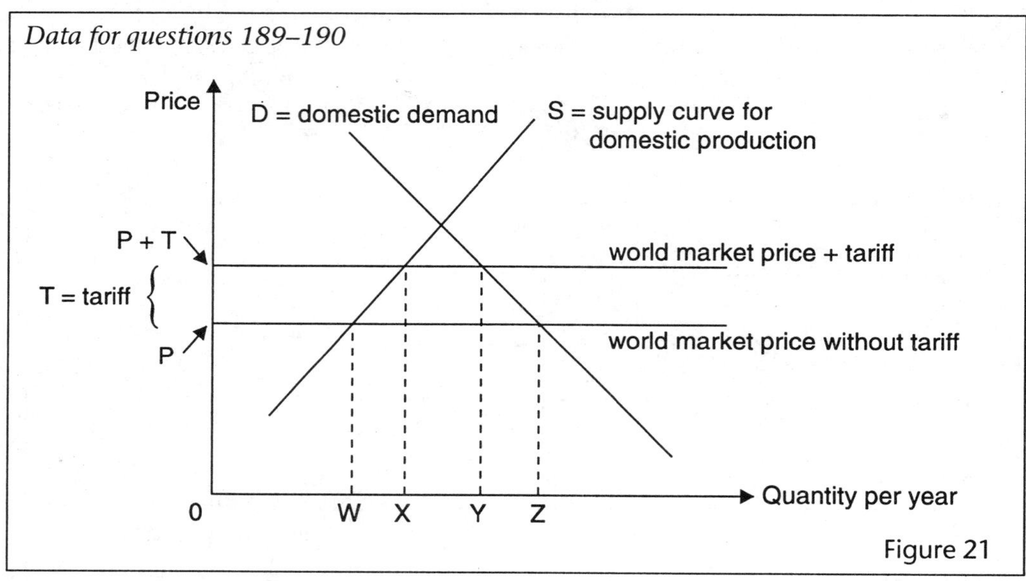

Figure 21

The diagram shows the demand curve (D) in the country Alsatz for a certain product. A supply curve for domestic production of the product is S. The product is available in unlimited quantities on the world markets at price P. Domestic producers are able to supply as much of the domestic market demand as it is economically worthwhile for them to do. The government of Alsatz, worried about high imports and wishing to protect domestic firms, imposes a tariff of T per unit on imports from the world market.

189 Before the imposition of the tariff the quantity of imports of the product would have been

A OW;
B OX;
C OZ;
D WZ.

A B C D

NOTES

190 After the imposition of the import tariff, the government's tax revenue from the tariff per year will be

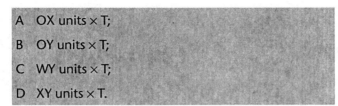

A OX units × T;

B OY units × T;

C WY units × T;

D XY units × T.

A B C D

191

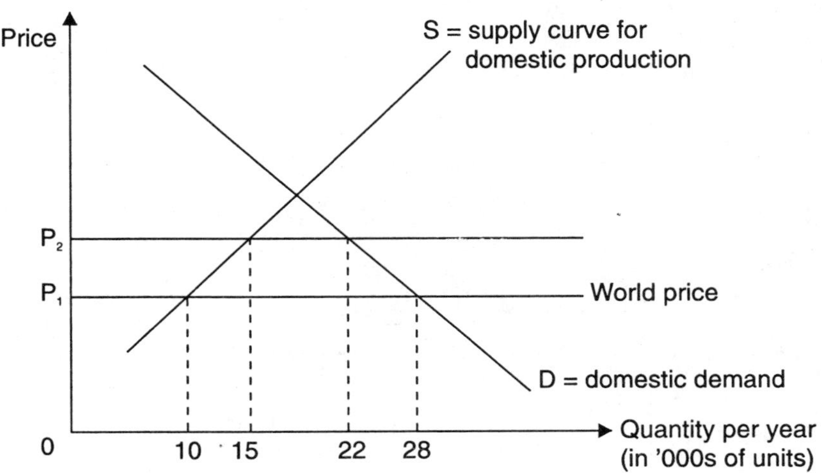

Figure 22

The diagram above shows the demand curve (D) for a certain production in the country Brashia. The supply curve for domestic producers of the country is shown as S. The product is available in unlimited quantities on the world markets at price P_1. However, in order to protect its domestic firms, the government of Brashia imposes an import quota of 9,000 units of the product per year. Due to supply restrictions, the price of the product in the country goes up to P_2.

Imports of the product per year to Bashia will now be

A 5,000 units;

B 6,000 units;

C 7,000 units;

D 9,000 units.

A B C D

NOTES

Chapter 17

Data for questions 192–194

	£'000 million
Trade in goods balance	+18
Trade in services balance	+6
Investment income	+3
Transfers	–2
Investment abroad	27
Investment in the country from abroad	12
Lending by domestic banks etc abroad	30
Borrowing by residents etc from abroad	25
Official reserves (additions to: –, drawings on: +)	–2
Balancing item	–3

192 The current balance was, in £'000 millions

A 18

B 20

C 22

D 25

A B C D

193 Transactions in external assets totalled, in £'000 millions,

A –42

B –44

C –57

D –59

A B C D

194 Transactions in external liabilities totalled, in £'000 millions,

A 37

B 39

C 52

D 57

A B C D

195 Which of the following financial transactions will have an adverse effect on the UK's balance of payments, at least in the short run?

1 Increased tourism abroad by UK residents.

2 Increased private export of investment capital abroad.

3 The payment of a cash grant to a developing country by the UK government.

A Item 1 only.

B Items 1 and 2 only.

C Items 1 and 3 only.

D Items 2 and 3 only.

A B C D

NOTES

196 Suppose that the exchange rate for the German deutschmark against the US dollar is DM2 = $1, and the sterling-US dollar exchange rate is $1.50 = £1. If the US dollar appreciates in value against the deutschmark but the sterling-US dollar rate remains stable, then other things being equal

A UK goods will become more expensive in Germany but will not change price in the USA.

B UK and US goods will both become cheaper in Germany.

C US goods will become cheaper in both the UK and Germany.

D US goods will become cheaper in Germany and more expensive in the UK.

A B C D

197 From a given base year, a country's export prices rise by 8% and import prices rise by 20%. During this period, the terms of trade will have

A risen from 100 to 111.1;

B risen from 100 to 112;

C fallen from 100 to 90;

D fallen from 100 to 88.

A B C D

198 Inflation in a country's economy has led to a deterioration in the balance of payments. Which of the following reasons might explain this?

1 The terms of trade have worsened due to the higher export prices.

2 Higher domestic prices have made imported goods more attractive.

3 Excess demand in domestic markets has reduced the volume of goods available for export.

A Reasons 1 and 2 only.

B Reasons 1 and 3 only.

C Reason 2 only.

D Reasons 2 and 3 only.

A B C D

NOTES

199 The government of a certain country embarks on a policy of reflating the economy. At the same time, it uses its control over interest rates to maintain the stability of the exchange rate for the country's currency. For which of the following reasons might the country's balance of payments go into deficit in the short term?

1 Manufacturers divert goods that would otherwise be exported into domestic markets.

2 Foreign investors, attracted by the economic relation, invest money in the country.

3 Economic expansion raises aggregate demand in the economy, so that demand for imports rises.

A Reasons 1 and 2 only.
B Reasons 1 and 3 only.
C Reasons 2 and 3 only.
D Reason 3 only.

A B C D

200 Suppose that the US dollar – £ sterling exchange rate is initially \$1.50 = £1. During the subsequent period of time, inflation in the USA is 2% and in the UK it is 12%. If the only movement in the exchange rate during this period could be explained by purchasing power parity theory, the exchange rate at the end of the time period would be

A \$1.3500 = £1
B \$1.3660 = £1
C \$1.6470 = £1
D \$1.6500 = £1

A B C D

201 When interest rates in the UK are higher than interest rates in the USA

A the US dollar will be sold at a discount against sterling in the forward exchange market, and the forward rate for the dollar will be higher than the spot rate;

B the US dollar will be sold at a discount against sterling in the forward exchange market, and the forward rate for the dollar will be lower than the spot rate;

C the US dollar will be sold at a premium against sterling in the forward exchange market, and the forward rate for the dollar will be higher than the spot rate;

D the US dollar will be sold at a premium against sterling in the forward exchange market and the forward rate for the dollar will be lower than the spot rate.

A B C D

NOTES

202 A country's currency is allowed to fluctuate in value against other currencies, except that from time to time its government will raise or lower rates and will use its official reserves to push exchange rates up or down. Such a system of exchange rates for the currency is known as

A free floating;

B dirty floating;

C adjustable peg;

D margins around a moveable peg.

A B C D

203 Devaluation of the currency will

A improve the terms of trade and *not* increase the cost of living;

B improve the terms of trade but increase the cost of living;

C worsen the terms of trade but *not* increase the cost of living;

D worsen the terms of trade and increase the cost of living.

A B C D

NOTES

EXAM STYLE QUESTIONS

NOTES

Chapter 1

1

(a) Define 'opportunity cost'.

(b) Illustrate with examples the practical importance of this concept with reference to the individual, the firm and the state.

Chapter 2

2

(a) Sharp frosts in Brazil in the summer of 1994 sent coffee prices soaring to an eight year high as fears were raised that the 1995/96 coffee harvest would be damaged. Brazil accounts for a quarter of world coffee production. Other major producers in Africa and central America were frost free.

What is the likely short-run and long-run effect of the Brazilian frost on coffee growers in Africa?

(b) Explain the likely effect of the frost on the demand for tea.

(c) What would be the economic effect of world wide publicity in 1995 which claimed that the caffeine in coffee was a potential health risk?

Chapter 3

3

Explain what is meant by the term 'price elasticity of demand' for a product.

What factors determine the price elasticity of demand for a product?

Chapter 4

4

(a) What are the differences between private costs and benefits and social costs and benefits?

(b) Illustrate your answer to (a) using as an example either a road building scheme, or a new factory.

Chapter 5

5

(a) Explain briefly the distinction between the short run and the long run in the economic theory of the firm.

(b) Explain how firms are subject to:

(i) economies of scale;

(ii) diseconomies of scale.

Chapter 6

6

The formulation of a European Social Charter has once again raised the idea of a legal minimum wage for member states. A number of European Union governments are resisting the implementation of such legislation on the grounds that it would product a significant increase in unemployment.

In your role as economic advisor, explain why some governments' members have come to this conclusion and explain the economic arguments for a legal minimum wage.

Chapter 7

7

(a) Compare the equilibrium output and price of firms under conditions of perfect competition and monopoly.

(b) Explain why consumers may not always suffer if a competitive industry becomes monopolised.

Chapter 8

8

(a) Using examples, explain the main features of a market characterised by oligopoly.

(b) Explain the kinked demand curve model of price stability in oligopoly markets.

Chapter 9

9

(a) What is money and what function does it serve?

(b) What is the importance of the distinction between narrow and broad money?

10

(a) Describe the functions of financial intermediaries.

(b) Discuss the importance of these functions to the business sector of a modern economy.

Chapter 10

11

(a) Explain the role of the central bank in a mixed economy.

(b) What would be the advantages and disadvantages of the central bank being completely independent of the government?

Chapter 12

13

(a) Why is the level of business investment important in the economy?

(b) How might governments encourage a higher level of business investment?

Chapter 13

14

(a) Explain carefully what is meant by the term 'natural rate of unemployment'.

(b) How could a government reduce the natural rate of unemployment?

15

(a) What is inflation and how is it caused?

(b) What are the costs of inflation to the economy?

Chapter 14

16

Compare and contrast the Keynesian and monetarist approaches to the demand for money. What are the implications of the two different approaches for government economic policy?

Chapter 15

17

A government wants to increase tax revenue from the personal sector to meet increased public expenditure. Discuss the relative merits of:

(a) income tax; and

(b) expenditure taxes to raise the revenue.

Chapter 16

18

(a) Describe the main reasons why international trade occurs.

(b) Describe the potential benefits of international trade to a business.

Chapter 17

19

(a) Explain what is meant by the *terms of trade* and describe *two* processes that would lead to a change in a country's terms of trade.

(b) Explain the effect on a country's balance of trade of a fall in its terms of trade.

20

Discuss the relative advantages of fixed versus floating exchange rates for:

(a) a country as a whole; and

(b) individual business based there.

ANSWERS TO MULTIPLE CHOICE QUESTIONS

NOTES

Chapter 1

1 The basic economic problem is one of scarce resources and economics is the study of how those resources are or should be used. The answer is D.

2 The answer is D.

3 The answer is D.

4 The answer is B.

5 A production possibility curve or frontier shows how much output can be produced with available resources. Since a graph is two-dimensional, it must be limited to just two goods, or to good X and all other goods. Begonia can produce X units of food or Y units of other goods, or any combination of food and other goods on the production possibility frontier. By producing more food, the country must produce fewer other goods, and vice versa, and so the line XY shows the opportunity costs of making one good (food) in terms of making other goods. The answer is A.

6 The answer is D.

7 The answer is D.

8 The answer is C.

9 The answer is B.

10 The answer is B.

11 Consumers' equilibrium is reached where

$$\frac{Mx}{Px} = \frac{My}{Py}$$

Mx = marginal utility from spending on an extra unit of X
Px = the price of X
My = marginal utility from spending on an extra unit of Y
Py = the price of Y

The answer is C.

12

	Marginal utility per £1 spent	
Unit	*X*	*Y*
1st	1.0	0.8
2nd	0.9	0.7
3rd	0.8	0.6
4th	0.7	0.5
5th	0.6	0.4
6th	0.5	0.3
7th	0.4	0.2
8th	0.3	0.1

Taking units of X and Y in order of marginal utility per £1 until the £140 is used up, we reach a utility-maximising combination of 6 units of X and 4 units of Y, where the marginal utility per £1 spent is the same for both products.

The answer is D.

NOTES

Chapter 2

13 The effect of a cash subsidy is to shift the supply curve to the right. Producers are willing to supply bigger quantities at the same market price, because they will get a cash subsidy from the government in addition to the market price. The new supply curve goes through points 7, 8 and 9, and so the new equilibrium, given no change in demand, is at point 8. The answer is D.

14 The effect of a fall in the price of a substitute product will be to increase demand for this substitute, and so reduce demand for the commodity in the question. The demand curve will shift to the left, to the line going through points 3, 6 and 9. The new equilibrium will be at point 6. The answer is C.

15 The effect of the fall in average unit costs of production will be to shift the supply curve to the right. Suppliers will be willing to supply bigger quantities at any given market price.

The effect of the increase in household income will increase the demand for all normal goods at any given price, and so assuming that the commodity is a normal good, the demand curve will shift to the right. The new equilibrium will be at point 7. The answer is C.

16 This is the reverse of the situation in question 1, because the effect of an indirect tax is to reduce the income net of tax for suppliers at any given market price. The new supply curve will go through points 1, 2 and 3. Since the demand curve is unchanged, going through points 3, 6 and 9, the new equilibrium is at point 3. The answer is A.

17 A reduction in income tax will increase real household income, and so demand for normal products will shift to the right – ie quantity demanded will be greater at any given price. Items A and D will cause a leftward shift in the demand curve. Item C would cause a movement to the right along the demand curve. The answer is B.

18 Coffee and tea are substitute products. So a fall in the price of coffee will result in higher demand for coffee and lower demand for its substitute product, tea. The price of tea might therefore fall. Demand for drinking cups is probably insufficiently related to the consumption of coffee to make them a complementary product to coffee. Even so, lower coffee prices would be likely to raise the demand for drinking cups rather than reduce it. The answer is D.

19 It is assumed that cut flowers and flower vases are complementary goods. The rise in price of cut flowers will have an adverse effect on demand for flower vases, and the demand curve for flower vases will shift to the left. Given no change in supply conditions for vases, the new equilibrium price for vases will be lower. The answer is D.

20 Sea ferry tickets and hovercraft tickets for Channel crossings are presumably substitute goods. An increase in the price of hovercraft tickets will cause a shift to the right (increase in demand) for sea ferry tickets. Given no change in supply conditions, the consequence will be an increase in the number of sea ferry tickets sold, at a higher price than before. The answer is B.

21 A fall in the price of *sterling* would make London hotels cheaper for foreign tourists. A fall in the price of aeroplane tickets would make London cheaper to visit for foreign tourists. Events 2 and 3 would lead to a *rise* in demand for hotel rooms. In contrast, a fall in the value of the US dollar would make the UK more expensive to visit for US tourists and tourists from other countries where

NOTES

the US dollar is widely used, and demand for hotel rooms in London would fall. The answer is A.

22 A demand curve shifts to the left when demand for the good at any given price level is less than before. Changes 2 and 4 both have this effect, although change 4 applies to normal goods, *not* to inferior goods. Change 1 causes a movement along the existing demand curve. Change 3 causes a shift to the *right* of the demand curve. The answer is C.

23 It is assumed that petrol is a complement of motor cars, and so a fall in petrol prices should *increase* the demand for cars. Trains and motor cycles are presumably substitutes to cars, and so reduction in their costs (train fares and the cost of maintaining a motor cycle on the road) should result in a fall in demand for cars. The answer is C.

24 Advertising should have the effect of shifting the demand curve for a good to the right, assuming that the purpose of the advertising campaign is to stimulate demand. Advertising might also cause some shift to the right in the supply curve, if marginal costs of supply are increased as a consequence of the advertising expenditures. Higher labour costs will shift the supply curve to the left, on the assumption that labour costs are marginal costs. The answer is B.

Chapter 3

25 *Statement 1* is incorrect. When demand is price elastic, a fall in price will *increase* total spending on the good. *Statement 2* is incorrect, because when household income rises, demand for an inferior good will fall: income elasticity of demand will be negative, not zero. *Statement 3* is incorrect. If goods A and B are complements, a rise in the price of B will cause a fall in the demand for A, and so cross elasticity of demand is negative. The answer is A.

26
$$\frac{\text{Change in q}}{\text{Change in p}} \times \frac{(p_1 + p_2)}{(q_1 + q_2)}$$

$$\frac{\text{50 units}}{\text{10p}} \times \frac{(40p + 50p)}{(\text{200 units} + \text{150 units})} = \frac{50}{10} \times \frac{90}{350} = 9/7 = 1.3$$

The answer is D.

27
$$\frac{\text{40 units}}{\text{10p}} \times \frac{(50p + 60p)}{(\text{160 units} + \text{200 units})} = \frac{40}{10} \times \frac{110}{360} = 11/0 = 1.2$$

The answer is D.

28 Statement A is correct: demand will tend to be elastic when the product has a large number of close substitutes. The rate of consumption and the variety of uses for a product could be irrelevant to *elasticity*. However, a high rate of demand/consumption might suggest consumer goods, which tend to have elastic demand. Statement C is incorrect. If a product is bought by people on subsistence incomes, a rise in its price is unlikely to result in higher total spending on the product (ie demand will *not* be inelastic) and if demand switches to cheaper substitutes, which is likely, demand for the product will be price elastic. Products with a wide range of uses tend to have a variety of substitutes (eg butter) and so demand is quite likely to be elastic. The answer is A.

29 Statement A is only true of a *demand* curve. Statement D refers to inelastic supply (elasticity = 0). The answer is B.

30 When price elasticity of demand = 1, any change in price will be matched by a change in demand quantity, so that total *revenue* (P × Q) would remain unchanged. The answer is C.

31
$$\frac{\text{\% change in demand for Orchard Cow}}{\text{\% change in price of Yoggipear}} = +2$$

Let % change in demand for Orchard Cow be X.

% change in price of Yoggipear is (10p ÷ 20p × 100%) = 50%.

$$\frac{X}{50\%} = +2. \; X = 100\%.$$

The answer is D.

32 Widgets and splodgets are complements. When the price of splodgets goes up by 10%, demand for widgets will go *down* by (× 0.6) 6% at that price. The demand curve for widgets has shifted to the left, and a new equilibrium price and output quantity will be established, at a lower output and price. However, since we do not know what the supply curve for widgets is, we cannot say what the new equilibrium price will be. The answer is A.

33 All three factors influence elasticity of supply. Supply is usually more elastic in the longer term than the short term, in response to price changes, because in the short term, more resources are fixed and committed to producing the good. The supply curve for a good is the sum of the *marginal cost curves* of all firms in the industry, and the slope of the curve – ie elasticity – will therefore be dependent on marginal cost. Supply is also more elastic when producers have more readily-available production opportunities to which they can switch their resources. The answer is D.

34 A rise in the price of a good bought by people on subsistence incomes is likely to make them switch their buying to other (substitute) products, and so demand for the good will tend to be elastic. A fall in the price of the product will have a reverse effect, making consumers demand significantly more of the product since it is now relatively cheaper than before, compared to the price of substitutes. The answer is B.

35 Oddly enough advertising (a form of non-price competition) is more likely to be successful for products which allow price elasticity of demand – ie for products whose demand is influenced by factors other than price. Statements A and D are incorrect because the supply curves of the products will be unaffected. Statement C is not necessarily correct because the higher total profits (and revenue) from the higher price will not necessarily cover the costs of the advertising. The answer is B.

36 The 45° angle shows how consumption of petrol would rise with income when income elasticity of demand = 1 (unity). When the graph line is steeper than this (between 0 and W) income elasticity is > 1. When the graph line is at the same 45° angle (between W and X, when the consumption line is parallel to

NOTES

the 45° line), income elasticity = 1. When the graph line is less steep (above X), income elasticity is < 1. The answer is B.

Chapter 4

37 In a free market economy, it is the interaction of supply and demand through the price mechanism that determines what should be produced and who should get it. The answer is B.

38 The consumer is king only when there are perfect markets and perfect competition. With monopoly, monopolistic competition, oligopoly and imperfect markets the price mechanism still operates, but firms have some influence and the sovereignty of the consumer is not complete. The answer is B.

39 Brand loyalty can make consumers pay more for a good, without getting any greater total satisfaction from consuming it. Lack of information to customers will result in bad purchasing decisions. The slowness of the price mechanism in creating a response in supply or demand to price changes is a further market imperfection. The answer is D.

40 The need to limit or avoid these weaknesses is the chief argument in favour of some government involvement in the allocation of economic resources – ie in favour of a mixed economy or even a command economy. The answer is D.

41 Social cost is the sum of the private cost to a firm *plus* the external cost to society as a whole. Here, social cost is the sum of production costs (private costs) plus the cost of pollution (external cost). The firm's private costs might have been increased by the measures to reduce pollution, but the external costs will have fallen, so that total social costs should have fallen too. The answer is B.

42 Before the maximum price regulations were introduced, the equilibrium price was £220, with 7,400,000 tonnes demanded and supplied each month. With a maximum price of £200, demand will be 8,200,000 tonnes per month and supply only 6,600,000 tonnes per month. With demand exceeding supply, there will be a bean shortage and a need for rationing – since prices cannot be raised to eliminate the excess demand. The answer is A.

43

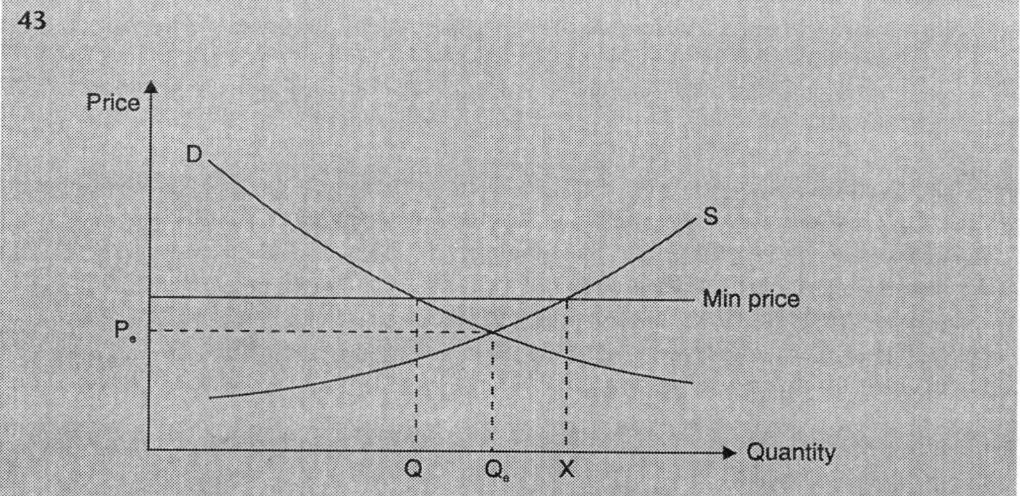

Statement B is incorrect because demand will fall for Q_e to Q, although the government *will* have to buy up the surplus production, which is (X – Q) in the diagram above. *Statement A* is correct, since supply will increase from Q_e to X.

Statement C is correct, because farmers can still make profits even when they incur higher costs – this is likely to create some production inefficiencies. Statement D is correct – although the negative statement might have confused you. Black markets are associated with maximum price legislation, not minimum prices. The answer is B.

44 When rent controls are eased, the effect is similar to raising or removing minimum prices in the rented housing market. We should expect higher rents, more supply of housing and a closing of the gap between demand for rented housing and supply of rented accommodation. Changes 2 and 3 should therefore occur. The reverse of change 1 should happen, and homelessness should decrease. Given widespread homelessness, it is unlikely that the easing of rent controls will have any effect on demand for owner-occupied dwellings. The answer is B.

45 A tax equal to the vertical distance between the marginal social cost and the marginal private cost of production would shift the supply curve to Q, establishing a free market price of H and output of X. This is where demand equals the marginal social cost of production, which is the socially optimum production level. The answer is C.

46 The price to suppliers will now be £3 less than the price paid by customers, and so the new equilibrium price is where demand and supply are equal in amount, with the price to customers £3 more than the price for suppliers. This occurs at a with-tax price of £4. The answer is A.

47 Continuing the analysis, the old pre-tax equilibrium price is £2, with demand and supply of 140,000 units. Since the price with tax will be £4, customers will bear £(4 – 2) = £2 of the tax. The answer is C.

48 The supply curve shifts to the left, from S to S_1. Item A causes this to happen. Item B causes the supply curve to shift to the *right* and items C and D cause shifts in the *demand curve*. The answer is A.

Chapter 5

49 A numerical example might help to explain this. Suppose that a firm has made 100 units of output, and produces an extra unit, to make 101 in total. The costs might be as follows.

	Cost of 100 units	*Cost of 101 units*
	£	£
Total variable cost	200	202
Total fixed cost	100	100
Total cost	300	302
Average cost	£3.00	£2.99

The marginal cost is £2, which is the increase in the total variable cost and also the increase in the total cost, since fixed costs are the same at both volumes of output. The answer is D.

NOTES

50 Proposition 3 is false: it is *average* fixed costs per unit (AFC) that fall as output increases. Marginal fixed costs = 0. Since AFC falls, any fall in average variable cost (AVC) must mean a falling average total cost (ATC) since AVC + AFC = ATC. Proposition 2 must therefore be false. The answer is C.

51 To the extent that the guard protects society against crime, his costs are a social benefit rather than a social cost. Statements 1 and 2 are correct, however, for the reasons explained in each statement. The answer is A.

52 Fixed costs are unchanged in the short run, and the behaviour of marginal costs is not affected by fixed costs. When AC is rising, since AFC is falling, MC *must* always be higher than AC. The answer is D.

53 The variable cost per unit is sometimes used as another way of explaining marginal cost, but only in the sense that we mean the variable cost of the next unit produced. Since the MC per unit varies with output (according to the law of diminishing returns) the *average* variable cost for all units produced will not be the same as the marginal cost of the next unit. The other statements are correct: Statement A is true because average fixed costs per unit decline continuously as output increases. Statement D is correct because MC includes normal profit as a cost. The answer is C.

54 Total variable costs = £(1,950 – 1,500) = £450, and so AVC = £450 ÷ 3 = £150. MC = £1,950 – £1,850 = £100. The answer is A.

55 As more variable factors of production are added so a fixed factor output will at first rise more than proportionately but eventually will increase less than proportionately. The answer is D.

56

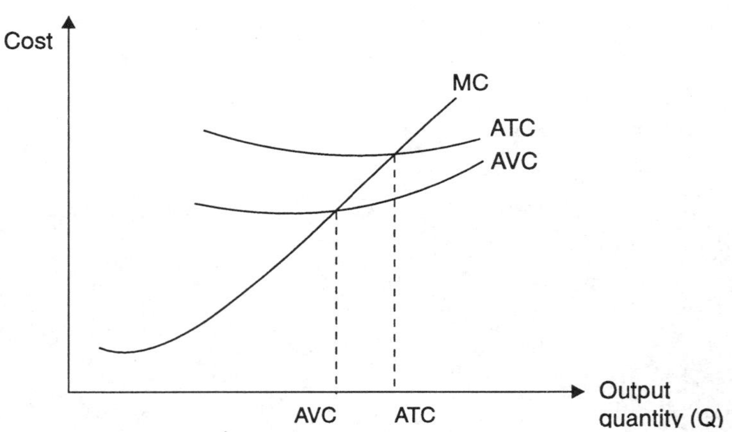

The answer is D.

57 Since elasticity of demand = 1, the total revenue from selling an extra unit would remain unchanged (the quantity sold would fall) and MR = 0. Since MC = \$25, there would be an incremental loss of \$25. The answer is D.

58 Profits are maximised where MC = MR, which is here at point H. (AR – AC) = supernormal profit per unit = FJ = HK. Output = FH = JK. So supernormal profits are given by the area FHKJ. The answer is C.

59 The company is running the same services as before, and so is not expanding its output and economies of scale are not achieved here. The lower costs per passenger mile will be the result in a reduction in the work force from eight to just four and so there will be greater productivity. The answer is C.

60 The law of variable proportions is another name for the law of diminishing returns, which refers to the short run when at least one factor of production is fixed. Since *all* inputs are increased by 50% we must be looking at the long-run average cost curve and, in this example, at decreasing returns to scale, since the percentage increase in inputs exceeds the percentage increase in outputs. The answer is B.

Chapter 6

61 The MEC curve represents the return that can be obtained from extra amounts of capital invested, and so is a demand curve for capital. A rightward shift in the MEC curve indicates that more investment opportunities are available which offer a high return. This is what should happen when there is technological innovation (item A) and at interest rate R_1, demand for capital would be K_2. If capital is consumed more quickly, it will make lower returns and the MEC curve will shift to the *left* (item B). The willingness of individuals to save (item C) affects the *supply* of capital, but not demand and the MEC. A fall in interest rates (item D) would result in a movement along MEC_1 to quantity of capital K_2, but would not cause a shift in the curve to MEC_2. The correct answer is A.

62

Employees	*Total output*	*Price per packet* £	*Total revenue* £	*Average output*
8	4,000	1.60	6,400	
9	4,320	1.50	6,480	480 packets

MRP = £(6,480 – £6,400) = £80
ARP = 480 × £1.50 = £720
The correct answer is A.

63

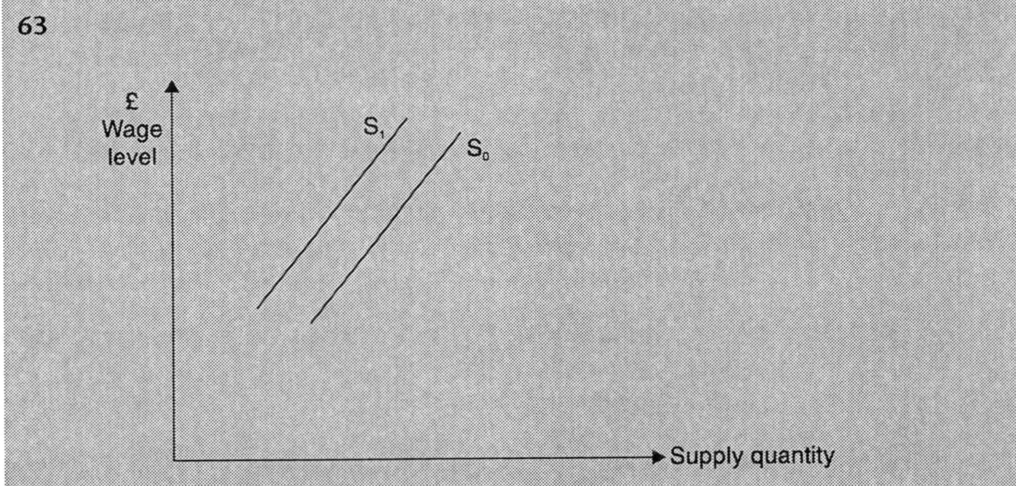

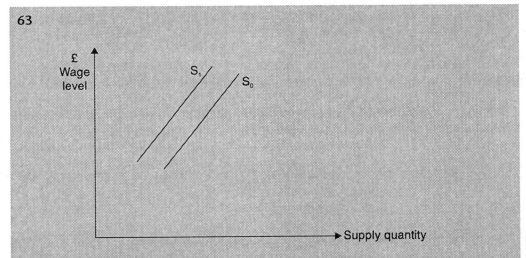

You must distinguish between factors which cause a *shift* in the supply curve, from S_0 to S_1 (so that at *any* given wage level, fewer people will offer themselves for the work) and a *movement along* the supply curve (so that fewer people will offer themselves for work if the wages offered are reduced). Item B, an increase in wages below the rate of increase in the cost of living, is a reduction in wages which will cause a movement along the supply curve. Items A, C and D will alter conditions so that there *is* a leftward shift in the supply of scientists. The correct answer is B.

NOTES

64

Employees	Sales value of total product £	Marginal product £	Marginal cost £
4	44	–	–
5	64	+20	+16
6	98	+34	+16
7	134	+36	+16
8	170	+36	+16
9	198	+28	+16
10	214	+16	+16 *
11	228	+14	+16
12	240	+12	+16

*Profits are increased up to the point where the MRP of labour exceeds the MC of labour, and are maximised where MRP = MC, which is at an employment level of 10. The correct answer is C.

65 Labour immobility describes the reluctance or inability of labour to switch from areas and industries where there is unemployment to areas and industries where there is a demand for workers. There can be reluctance of workers to move to another geographical area to find work, but an improved railway system (item 1) might provide a solution to some of the problem (eg getting managers living in the north of England to take up jobs in London). *Occupational* immobility of labour can be overcome by retraining schemes (item 3) to train workers with out-of-date skills to learn skills for which there is a demand from employers.

Greater specialisation of labour (item 2) might result in greater labour productivity, but this has no bearing on the mobility of labour. The correct answer is C.

66

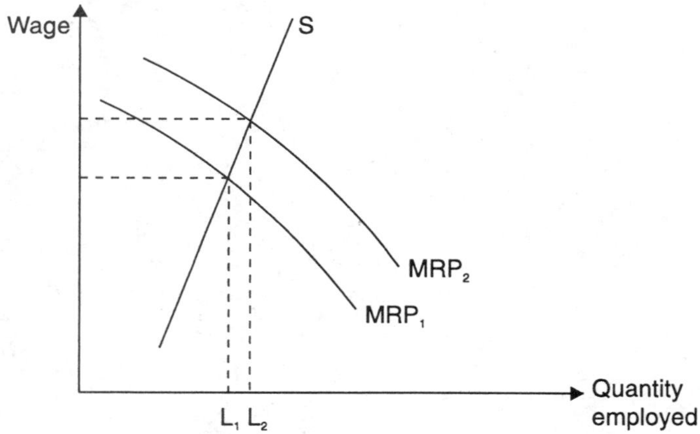

The diagram shows that a shift in the MRP of labour due to productivity improvements, from MRP_1 to MRP_2, will result in a relatively small increase in employment numbers from L_1 to L_2 and a relatively large increase in wages from W_1 to W_2. The correct answer is C.

67 The revenue-earning power of labour can be improved by higher prices for the firm's product or by greater productivity. Lower costs for labour (factor 3) represent a shift in the supply curve for labour, not the MRP curve. A fall in the price of a substitute product (factor 4) will cause a *fall* in the demand and a shift to the left or downwards in the MRP curve. The correct answer is A.

68 The new supply curve, given a minimum wage of W_2, will be W_2KLS, and the new employment level will be M. However, the supply of labour wanting to work at that wage level will be N, leaving an excess supply in the industry of MN. The correct answer is D.

69 The change in the apprenticeship rules will shift the supply curve for plasterers to the left, since the union controls supply through its closed shop. The demand for plasterers will shift to the left as demand falls. The new equilibrium is at wage H and employment level L. The correct answer is B.

70 When there are many firms competing for workers, the supply curve is the average wage curve. In effect, each firm must pay the average wage for the industry to attract workers, and so in Situation 1 wages are where supply and demand intersect at wage Q and employment K. When there is a single buyer or monopsonist employer, as in Situation 2, the supply curve for labour becomes the marginal cost curve for labour. The firm will not employ more labour if its marginal cost exceeds its marginal revenue product (the demand curve). Wages will therefore be where MC = MRP (demand) at employment level J and wage P. The correct answer is D.

71 If wages account for a *higher* proportion of total costs, the demand for labour is likely to be *more* elastic, since a rise in labour costs would have a bigger effect on costs of production. The correct answer is B.

72 Ira Bull can raise between 75 and 100 horses, but for each extra horse that he raises, he must reduce the number of cows he rears by 2. The opportunity cost is calculated as

$$\frac{(200 - 150 \text{ cows})}{(100 - 75 \text{ horses})} = \frac{50}{25} = 2$$

The correct answer is D.

Chapter 7

73 In conditions of perfect competition, the firm can sell whatever output it produces at the market price. The demand curve is the marginal revenue curve, as well as the average revenue curve (ie price curve).

The demand curve is therefore perfectly elastic, rather than perfectly inelastic, as suggested by Statement D. The answer is A.

74 At profit-maximising equilibrium, MR = AR = AC = MC and so MC = MR, AC = AR, MR and AR and MC = AR. The answer is D.

75

1 Profit is maximised at price P and output Q, because this is where MC = MR.

2 At this price/output level, average cost equals average revenue. Normal profit is included in cost, and so the firm is making normal profits only, but no supernormal profits.

3 Total revenue is maximised because this is the price/output level where MR = 0.

The answer is D.

76 Sales revenue is maximised when MR = 0. The answer is D.

77 The technically optimum output level is where average total costs are minimised. The answer is B.

78 Normal profits only will be earned at the output level where price equals average cost (AR = ATC). The answer is C.

79 Toby earns a fixed percentage commission, and so his total commission will be maximised at the price which maximises total sales revenue. As long as marginal revenue (MR) is above 0, the firm's total revenue will be increasing as it sells more output. Sales revenue will be maximised at the point where MR drops to 0, just before it starts to become negative. This is at Price Y. (Amlett Ltd would maximise *profits*, as distinct from sales revenue, where MC = MR, which is when the price is Z and MR = MC = W.) The answer is C.

80 Line MM is the demand curve and NN is the supply curve. In perfect competition, these are in equilibrium where they intersect, at price P_2 and output X_2. Note that a monopoly firm would produce at the output level where MC (the supply curve NN) equals MR (line LL), which is output X_1, when the price would be P_3. The answer is C.

81 First and second class tickets are not an example of price discrimination, because even though they are tickets for the same aeroplane journey, they are different products – eg in terms of service and travel comfort – rather than the same product being sold at two or more different prices. All the other statements are true, with B and C being key conditions for price discrimination to be achievable. The answer is D.

82 Statement A is correct because it is an example of the same product being sold at two or more different prices, according to the time of day. Statement D is true: the same good or service may be sold at different prices in different geographical areas, to people of different ages (eg half price for children), on the basis of time (eg see Statement A) or because consumers in one market are ignorant of lower prices in another market. Statement C is correct, because price discrimination for a good in two geographical markets can only be sustained if it is too expensive for a customer to buy goods in the low-price market, incur transport costs to ship them to the higher-price market, and sell them at a competitive price in that market. Statement B is incorrect, because production costs should not have any influence on price discrimination, only on a firm's output levels. The answer is B.

83 There are other barriers to entry too, such as patent laws and high costs of entering the market. A natural monopoly (Item 2) can be extended to economies of scale generally, because new entrants into a market will need to achieve a scale of output where they too can achieve economies of scale to be cost-competitive.

84 Privatisation *could* mean selling off nationalised industries, but it can also refer to deregulation of industries to allow private firms to compete with state-run business (eg private bus companies) and contracting out work previously done by government employees to private firms (eg refuse collection).

Statement C is correct, and refers to the influence of stock market competition on newly-privatised monopolies. Statement D is correct: an example in the UK is the regulatory body Oftel for BT (formerly British Telecom). The answer is B.

NOTES

Chapter 8

85 A feature that characterises monopolistic competition from perfect competition or monopoly, for example, is that the products produced by firms are *not* homogeneous. Thus, characteristic 2 does not apply. The answer is C.

86 Even if AC is constant, and so AC = MC, profits are maximised at one particular output level where MC = MR, as shown in the diagram below. The first statement is therefore false.

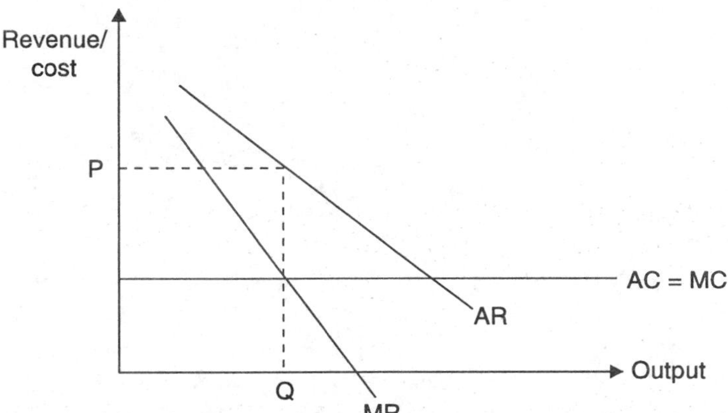

However, the second statement is correct, as the diagram also shows, because since AC is constant, each additional unit produced (MC) must cost the same amount. The answer is C.

87 In monopolistic competition, a firm's equilibrium is where MR = MC, and this is at an output level below minimum AC. For a firm earning no supernormal profits, the equilibrium situation is illustrated in Figure 1 below. The second statement is false because although average *total* cost is minimised, average *variable* costs are not at a minimum and diminishing returns already apply. Figure 2 tries to show this.

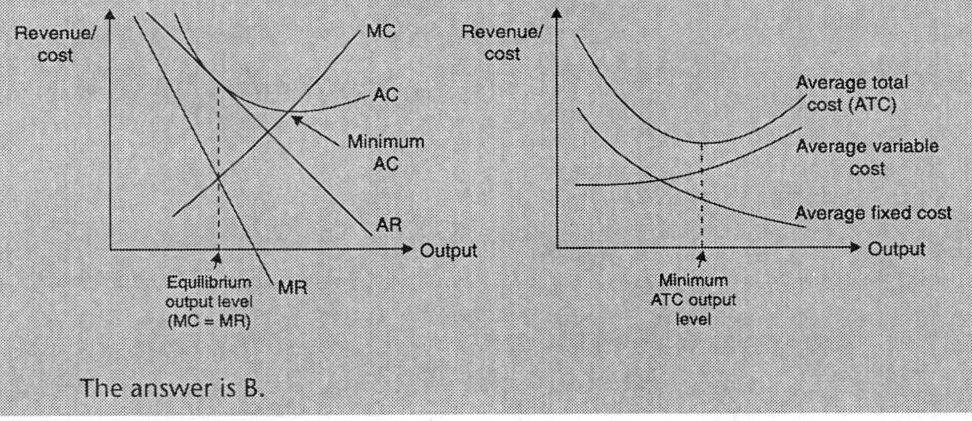

The answer is B.

88 The second statement in fact *explains* why the first statement is correct. Firms in monopolistic competition will often use advertising to try to shift their demand curve to the right, or to make demand for their product more price-inelastic (enabling them to earn bigger profits by raising prices). The answer is A.

NOTES

89

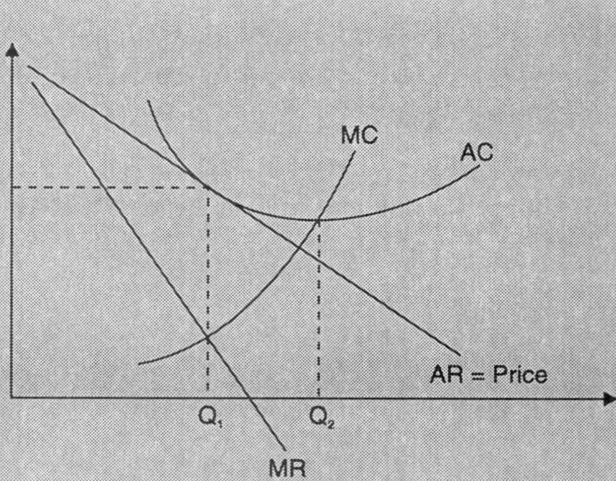

For long-run equilibrium in monopolistic competition, MR = MC and AR = AC, but it is *wrong* to say that MR = AC (Statement A or that AR = MC (Statement D). Since AR = AC, the firm does *not* earn any supernormal profits (Statement C). Statement B is correct because at the profit-maximising output Q_1, average cost is not at a minimum. AC is minimised at output Q_2, which is higher. Since firms could produce more output at a lower AC, we would say that there is excess capacity in the industry. The answer is B.

90 The answer is D.

91 Oligopoly is usually characterised by price stability, as illustrated by the so-called kinked oligopoly demand curve. Oligopolists are unlikely to cut prices, and are more likely to resort to *non-price competition* such as advertising and sales promotion (Item A), innovation and technical differences (Item B) and incidental services (Item D). The answer is C.

92 The answer is D.

93 The answer is D.

94 Colluding oligopolists prefer to reduce the amount of product differentiation, as this makes it easier for them to behave like a monopolist. So permitting variations of the product to proliferate will tend to weaken the strength of the cartel. The answer is B.

95 Barriers to trade make it more likely for new entrants who are not part of the cartel to enter the industry and set their own prices and output. With contract pricing, it becomes possible for firms to hide the price and output agreements reached with their customer. This makes it harder for the rest of the cartel to hold to the collective agreements. The fewer the number of firms in the cartel, the easier it will be to monitor and enforce the cartel agreement. The answer is A.

96 The demand curve is TVW (the AR curve). The demand curve has a kink at V, and is more inelastic at price levels below and output levels above this point. When demand is inelastic, this is because a move to lower price will be matched by a similar move by competitors, so that the increase in demand from the reduction in price will be relatively low. The answer is B.

NOTES

Chapter 9

97 Money should always be generally acceptable as a means of payment. The correct answer is C.

98 Coins, notes and bank deposits are all relatively liquid assets which could be converted into spending on goods and services. The correct answer is C.

99

	£ million
Notes and coin in circulation outside the Bank of England	15,000
Banks' operational deposits with the Bank of England (ie the banks' own bank accounts)	1,000
M0 =	16,000

The correct answer is D.

100 Notes and coins in circulation outside the Bank of England include £2,000 million held as till money by the banks themselves.

	£ million
Notes and coin in the hands of the general public	13,000
Current account balances of UK residents, in sterling	70,000
Deposit accounts in sterling of UK residents with British banks	80,000
Private sector building society shares and deposits	108,000
M4 =	271,000

Note. M4 excludes foreign currency deposits of UK residents with British banks. M4 also excludes sterling deposits of overseas residents with British banks. It is worth adding that M4 also excludes sterling deposits of UK residents with non-British banks, whatever these might be – data would be impracticable to collect. The correct answer is A.

101 Financial intermediation is the process of taking deposits from customers and re-lending to borrowers (at a higher rate of interest). Item B could refer to a firm of market makers. Item C refers to a leasing company or finance house. Item D refers to a discount house. The correct answer is A.

102 Maturity transformation is a feature of the role of financial intermediaries, such as building societies and banks. Item B describes redemption value. Item C is sometimes described as a yield curve. The correct answer is D.

103 Customers' deposits are *liabilities* of a bank, not assets. The assets of a typical retail bank include notes and coin (till money), and near-liquid assets such as deposits with money market institutions (eg inter-bank loans), bills of exchange and certificates of deposit (CDs). Most of the assets of a retail bank are their loans and overdrafts to customers. (Operational assets such as buildings and equipment are very small in value compared to a bank's financial assets.) The correct answer is C.

104 Cash is the most liquid asset of all. The correct answer is C.

105 If the banks maintained a 10% cash ratio, the credit multiplier for any initial increase in cash deposits would be 1/10% = times 10.

Maximum increase in bank deposits = £1 million × 5 banks × 10 (credit multiplier)
= £50 million

However, this £50 million includes the initial deposits of £5 million, and so the *further* increase in total bank deposits is £50 million – £5 million = £45 million. The correct answer is C.

106 A bank's liquidity ratio is the ratio of its liquid assets to total liabilities. The correct answer is D.

107 A current account deposit is an asset to a bank's customer and a liability for the bank. The correct answer is B.

108 The deposit creation at Bank Y would be offset by deposit destruction at Bank X. The correct answer is A.

Chapter 10

109 The Bank of England is the sole issuer of banknotes in England and Wales. Scottish clearing banks also issue notes. The correct answer is B.

110 Items B, C and D are all examples of monetary policy. Raising the level of taxation is an example of fiscal policy. The correct answer is A.

111 Item C refers to the London InterBank Offered Rate or LIBOR. Item A refers to the money market dealing rates of the Bank of England, which the Bank can use to signal to the banking system its wish for a change in LIBOR and base rates etc. Item D refers to deposit rates. The correct answer is B.

112 Item D is an example of funding, items A, B and C are all examples of open-market operations. The correct answer is D.

113 Government securities purchased from the central bank will be paid for by cheques drawn on accounts held at the commercial banks. The balances on these accounts will fall, reducing the money supply. The correct answer is C.

114 The result of the Bank of England's open market operations will be to expand the liquidity base by £10m, enabling banks to create an additional £90m worth of advances. The money multiplier is 10 and the total increase in the money supply would be £100m. The correct answer is B.

115 A fall in interest rates would increase investment. The correct answer is C.

116 Selling more bills will force the price of bills down and the rate of discount up. The correct answer is C.

117 The Stock Exchange is an organised capital market where shares are traded. The correct answer is B.

118 Stock exchanges do not directly fund the start-up costs of new companies. The correct answer is B.

119 Finance houses specialise in providing hire purchase facilities for consumer durables. The correct answer is B.

NOTES

Chapter 11

120 To avoid a fall in national income, given Y = C + I + G + (X – M), a fall in G must be offset by an increase in C, I (item 3) or X (item 1). The correct answer is B.

121 The first three items represent *withdrawals* from the circular flow of national income, and so would reduce the circular flow. The answer is D.

122 The expenditure approach to calculating GNP would have to subtract imports and add exports. The answer is B.

123 Net national product at factor cost plus capital consumption equals gross national product at factor cost. By adding back taxes on expenditure and subtracting subsidies, we then get from GNP at factor cost to GNP at market prices.

124 – 127

		£m	
	Consumers' expenditure	2,500	
	General government final consumption	800	
	Gross domestic fixed capital formation	750	
	Total domestic expenditure	4,050	
	Exports	1,200	
	Imports	(1,000)	(D)
(Question 126)	GDP at market prices	4,250	
	Net property income from abroad	40	
(Question 125)	GNP at market prices	4,290	(D)
	GDP at market prices (see above)	4,250	
	Factor cost adjustment		
	Taxes on expenditure	(650)	
	Subsidies	100	
	GDP at factor cost	3,700	
	Net property income from abroad	40	
(Question 124)	GNP at factor cost	3,740	(B)
	Capital consumption	(450)	
(Question 127)	National income at factor cost	3,290	(A)

128 GNP at factor cost is calculated by removing taxes on expenditure, such as sales tax or value added tax. The answer is B.

129 Personal disposable income consists of salaries and other income minus *direct* taxes such as income tax. Here, the income tax is 25% of (30,000 – 8,000) = £5,500, leaving personal disposable income of £30,000 – £5,500 = £24,500. The answer is C.

130

	1990	*1991*
	£ million	£ million
Consumers' expenditure	200,000	225,000
Government expenditure	70,000	74,000
Fixed capital formation	54,000	60,000
	324,000	359,000
Exports	93,000	94,000
Imports	(92,000)	(99,000)
GDP at market prices	325,000	354,000

Increase (354 – 325) = £29,000 million

% increase in money terms $= \frac{29,000}{325,000} \times 100\% = 8.9\%$

% change in real terms, with 10% inflation, is a fall of about 1%.
The answer is A.

131 Capital consumption represents an estimated cost based on *current prices* for the gradual using up of the nation's productive fixed assets. It is difficult to estimate accurately. Statement A is incorrect, largely because inter-country comparisons of living standards would be based on national income per *head* rather than total national income. Statement B is incorrect because services provided free such as policing are included in the statistics at actual cost. Statement C is incorrect because when there is a strong unofficial economy, with economic activity not reported to the government to avoid taxation etc, official statistics will *underestimate* national income. The answer is D.

Chapter 12

132 An inflationary gap exists when there is full employment, and aggregate demand exceeds the ability of the economy to produce output, and so prices rise. An inflationary gap is closed by increasing the physical output capacity of the economy, or by reducing aggregate demand. Item B does this, because a bigger surplus of taxation income over government spending reduces aggregate demand. The answer is B.

133 Since Y = C + I + G (X – M), a fall in C or I would reduce national income, but a rise in exports X would increase national income. Savings are a withdrawal from the circular flow and so would reduce national income, unless they could be diverted into higher investment. The answer is B.

134 Stock-building is an investment, because it involves incurring expenditures now for some benefit in the future. Although the purchase of shares (item B), second hand machinery (item C) or an already-existing company (item D) are all investments for the individuals or organisations concerned, they are merely the transfer of ownership of already-existing assets; there is no creation of new fixed asset capital investment or stocks. From the point of view of the national economy as a whole, these do not count as investment and do not provide an injection into the circular flow. The answer is A.

NOTES

135 This can be written as

$$MPC = \frac{\Delta C}{\Delta Y}$$

where C is consumption, Y is income and Δ means 'small change in'. The answer is D.

136 The consumption function is a straight line and so has the formula C = a + bY, where a is a fixed amount of spending, Y is the size of income and b, a constant value, is the marginal propensity to consume. Because of the fixed minimum consumption, the average propensity to consumer will be *higher* than the MPC at lower income levels, and so statements C and D in the question must be incorrect. The consumption function is always upward sloping, implying that more income (Y) implies more consumption, and so statement B must be incorrect. The answer is A.

137 In a country with a low standard of living, people will spend a very high proportion of their income, and of any extra income they might get on essential goods for consumption, such as food and clothing. APC will therefore be high, and since MPC will be high too, MPS must be low (MPC + MPS = 1). The answer is C.

138 A fall in the rate of interest will make capital investments worthwhile, with a yield equalling or exceeding the rate of interest. This was not the case at higher interest rates. One consequence of cheaper capital could be a switch from labour-intensive to more capital-intensive methods of production (Response 1). However, the marginal efficiency of capital, which is (conceptually) the rate of *return* obtainable from investments, ranked in order from best to worst, is unaffected. The answer is B.

139 The marginal propensity to import (m) and the marginal rate of taxation (t) help to reduce the size of the multiplier, in addition to the marginal propensity to save (s). So, any leakages from the circular flow will have an effect on the multiplier. The answer is D.

140 The government investment multiplier will work through to private sector investment (through the government multiplier effect). Excess production capacity in industry (item A) and a high level of stocks (item D), however, will avoid the need for *new* investment by industry. A higher rate of marginal taxation (implied by item C) will reduce the multiplier. A high marginal propensity to consume (item B) helps to keep the multiplier high. The answer is B.

141 In equilibrium,

$$\begin{aligned} Y &= C + I \\ Y &= (30{,}000 + 0.4Y) + 30{,}000 \\ 0.6Y &= 60{,}000 \\ Y &= 100{,}000 \\ mpc &= 0.4 \end{aligned}$$

$$\text{Multiplier} = \frac{1}{(1 - 0.4)} = \frac{1}{0.6} = 1.67$$

The answer is C.

NOTES

142 Increase in national income (in £millions) $= 100 \times \frac{1}{(1-0.25)}$

$$= \frac{100}{0.75} = 133.3$$

The answer is D.

143 Saving is good for the economy when it leads to greater investment, but higher savings without matching higher investment can lead to a fall in national income, as suggested by the so-called paradox of thrift. Thus statement 1 is not *always* true (and therefore incorrect). The answer is C.

Chapter 13

144 Structural unemployment is caused by a mismatch between available jobs and the unemployed. This could be caused by a geographical mismatch (eg jobs available in London and unemployed people in Liverpool) or by a mismatch of skills (eg unemployed labourers, job vacancies for skilled workers in electronics). Items B and D could be causes of structural unemployment, but do not fully describe it. The correct answer is C.

145 Reason 1 refers to structural unemployment while reason 4 is the result of insufficient aggregate demand (cyclical unemployment). The unemployable tend to be classified as frictionally unemployed. The correct answer is C.

146 The short-run Phillips curve has a negative slope implying that there is a trade-off between the rate of inflation and the level of unemployment. The correct answer is A.

147 Factor 1 is a demand-side effect which would contribute to demand-deficient (or cyclical) unemployment rather than the natural rate. To the extent that technical progress results in structural unemployment, it would add to the natural rate as would factors 2 and 3. The correct answer is B.

148 Friedman argued that stimulating demand will only have a temporary effect on unemployment, and that demand-led expansion of the economy would soon become inflationary (with no increase in real output). He argued in favour of supply side measures to reduce the natural rate of unemployment. Retraining schemes (item B) should reduce structural unemployment. Cutting trade union power (item C) was seen as a way of reducing unemployment. Lower income taxes (item D) and lower benefits for the unemployed would make individuals more willing to work and less willing to remain unemployed. The correct answer is A.

149 Weightings of an item in a retail price index try to allow for the *quantities* of a commodity that are consumed so that

Price × Weighting = Weighted value

It is the weighted value (weighting multiplied by price) that should show how much of their total income people have spent on each category. Since the weightings themselves are estimates of volume consumed, the correct answer is B.

NOTES

150

	Price £	Base year Weight	Total £	Price £	19X1 Weight	Total £
P	2.0	5	10.0	2.6	5	13.0
Q	0.5	4	2.0	0.7	4	2.8
R	4.0	1	4.0	4.6	1	4.6
			16.0			20.4

$$\text{Index in 19X1} = \frac{20.4}{16} \times 100 \text{ (base year)} = 127.5$$

The correct answer is C.

151 The RPI attempts to measure the cost of living and the rate of inflation. If the index goes up, prices have gone up, there has been some inflation, and so the value of money has fallen. The *standard* of living might have gone up or down, depending on changes in incomes, but the RPI does not measure this (national income per capita is a better measure for item A). The RPI has gone up by 4%, but the increase in wages needed to keep pace with this will depend on other factors too, such as income tax rates. So item B is not correct. Item C is incorrect, because to analyse changes in the RPI, we assume that consumption patterns have remained much the same. The correct answer is D.

152 Keynes' analysis of inflation considered the situation where aggregate demand exceeded the ability of the economy to produce real output to meet the demand, resulting in demand-pull inflation and an inflationary gap.

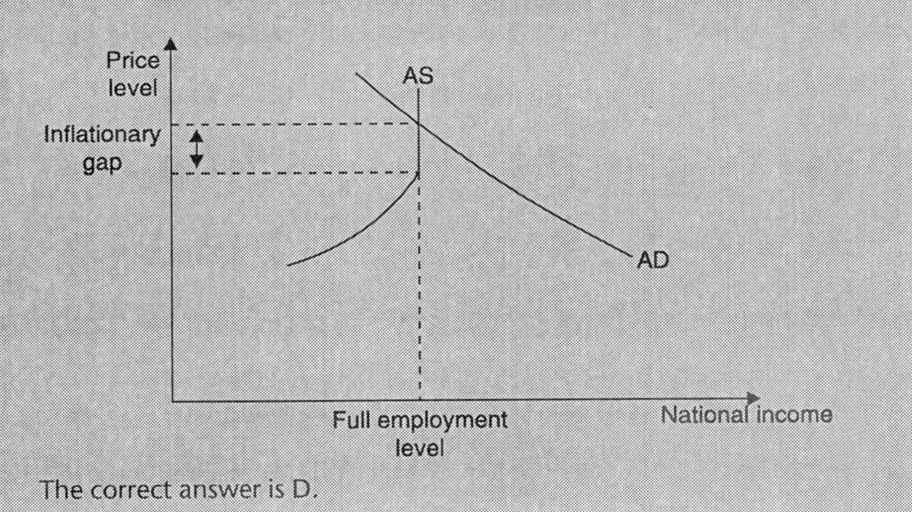

The correct answer is D.

153 Higher wages result in higher output costs per unit (unless labour productivity improves to compensate for the higher wages). This leads to firms having to raise their prices and so to cost-push inflation. Higher import prices, whether raw materials for industry, capital goods for industry or consumer goods, lead to import-cost-push inflation. Factor 2 is a cause of demand-pull inflation. The correct answer is C.

NOTES

154 Cost-push inflation is inflation caused by higher unit costs of production being passed through into higher prices. If wage increases are linked to productivity improvements (measure 2), unit labour costs of production will be kept down. A revaluation of the currency (measure 4) will make imported goods and raw materials cheaper to buy. Higher direct taxation (eg higher income tax) and higher interest rates would be intended to dampen *demand* in the economy, and would be measures for dealing with demand-pull inflation. The correct answer is D.

155 The monetarists argue that *inflation* should be brought under control by keeping the growth in the money supply under control. They also argue that lower unemployment is achievable without higher inflation (which would normally happen, with the Phillips curve effect) by reducing the natural rate of unemployment or non-accelerating inflation rate of unemployment (NAIRU). This can be done by supply side measures, such as reducing incentives for individuals to be unemployed (eg cutting welfare benefits), and reducing income tax rates to give individuals a bigger incentive to work more to earn more money. The correct answer is D.

Chapter 14

156 The quantity theory of money identity states that MV = PT. The correct answer is B.

157 T has to be unchanged for the equation MV = PT to be a predictor of price behaviour. Any increase in M, given no change in V in the short run, would result in a matching percentage increase in prices P. The correct answer is D.

158 If the economy is growing then quantity theorists would argue that a matching growth in the money supply is necessary to avoid deflation. The correct answer is B.

159 Automatic stabilisers will ensure that tax revenues rise and government expenditures fall in an economic recovery, exerting a downward influence on the PSBR. The correct answer is A.

160 Items A, B and C will all tend to reduce the demand for real money balances (item C reducing the precautionary demand for money). An increase in uncertainty concerning future transactions would tend to increase the precautionary demand for real money balances. The correct answer is D.

161 According to Keynes the money supply could be fixed by the authorities. The demand for money depends on three motives (transactions, precautionary and speculative) but it is the speculative demand for money that is sensitive to changes in interest rates, and this explains the liquidity preference schedule. The correct answer is B.

162 An increase in the standard rate of income tax will reduce the transactions demand for money. The correct answer is A.

163 Higher value added tax, which is a sales tax, will make goods more expensive to buy. Consumers will need more money to pay for them, and so their transactions demand for money will rise. The correct answer is C.

164 Lower interest rates should be a consequence of an increase in the money supply, with a movement along the liquidity preference curve rather than a shift in the liquidity preference curve (item B). The correct answer is A.

NOTES

According to Keynes, changes in the money supply act on interest rates, and do not have a direct effect on expenditure in the economy; however, any effect on expenditure, and so on prices and incomes, would tend to *raise* rather than reduce prices. The correct answer is A.

165 An increase in the demand for money refers to a shift in liquidity preference from D_2 to D_1. Given a fixed money supply (Keynes's analysis) the interest rate must therefore increase. The only solution which shows an increase in interest rates given a fixed money supply is from Z to X (money supply = MS_2). The correct answer is B.

166 Nominal rate of interest = Real rate of interest + Rate of inflation (approx) = 3% + 6% = 9%. The correct answer is D.

167 Portfolio balance theory argues that individuals hold their wealth in various forms ranging from money and financial assets to physical assets such as housing. The correct answer is B.

Chapter 15

168 Fiscal policy is concerned with the government's tax income, expenditure and borrowing (to make up the difference between income and expenditure). The answer is D.

169 An increase in VAT rates (item A) and an increase in tax on tobacco (item B) will add directly to the cost of living. Higher personal allowances (item D) will increase consumers' disposable income, which would be inflationary if the economy is operating at or near full capacity already. Taxing welfare benefits would reduce the disposable income of the targeted consumers, and so would not be inflationary. (The political or moral correctness of such a decision is a different matter!) The answer is C.

170 If the government seeks to balance its budget, tax revenue and expenditure must be equal, with a PSBR = 0. Only developments which increase government spending will therefore cause a need for increased tax revenue. Since items A, B and D will all call for higher government spending – on the funding of training programmes, spending on the health service and state (old age) pensions, or state education – we can identify item C as the correct answer by process of elimination. A balance of trade deficit does not have to be financed by the government. The answer is C.

171 Higher taxation will tend to reduce consumer spending. Higher import tariffs might result in greater consumer expenditure on imports inclusive of tariffs, but the volume and the net-of-tariff value of imports purchased will fall. Higher social security payments will give consumers more cash to spend (assuming that it does not have to raise taxes to pay for the increases). The answer is D.

172 The multiplier effect of extra government spending might be different from the demultiplier effect of extra taxation. For example, if the multiplier effect of government spending is 3 and the demultiplier effect of extra taxation is 2, a Budget which plans to raise and spend £1,000 million will have the effect of *increasing* spending in the economy by £1,000 million (+ £3,000 million – £2,000 million). This is why options B and C are incorrect. In contrast, raising £750 million and spending just £500 million, in the same situation would have a neutral effect on economy activity, since (£500m × 3 – £750 × 2) = 0. The answer is A.

NOTES

173 The main purpose of taxation will be to raise revenue for the government. Other aims might be to redistribute wealth or affect demand in the economy. Of the aims listed in the question, A, C and D could all be the purpose of a tax. In the UK, for example, there used to be a tax on development land, to discourage price speculation (item A). Taxes on imported goods can help to protect domestic industries (item C). Some goods such as tobacco and alcoholic drinks can be taxed highly to try to reflect their social cost (item D). Changes in rates of tax do not have a direct influence on interest rates, which can be influenced by a government's *monetary* policies. The answer is B.

174 Objective 1 could be achieved by raising (or lowering) taxes on firms and lowering (or raising) taxes on households. Objective 2 could be achieved by raising taxation in order to reduce consumers' disposable income and so to reduce aggregate expenditure in the economy: these consequences should lead to a fall in the demand for money. Objective 3 can be achieved either by taxing income or by means of selective indirect taxes on certain goods. The answer is D.

175 A progressive tax is one in which individuals on higher incomes pay a greater proportion of their income in tax. Hugh earns twice as much as Howard but pays 2½ times as much income tax. Hymie earns 1½ times as much as Hugh but pays over twice as much in income tax. The answer is D.

176 A flat-rate poll tax, with no concession for the lower-paid, would take a higher proportion of the income of lower-income earners than of higher-income earners. Taxes that have this effect are regressive taxes. Television licences and road tax for cars are other examples. The answer is A.

177 A reduction in taxes on alcoholic drinks will leave all consumers of alcohol with more income. A less even distribution of wealth in society means that richer people will now be relatively better off than before, which means that they have obtained a bigger benefit from the tax cuts. The conclusion points to either answer B or answer D. The benefit has to be *relative*, since the distribution of wealth refers to relative (proportionate) wealth, and so answer D must be correct, rather than answer B.

178 Higher rates of value added tax will feed through directly to higher prices and an increase in the RPI (consequence 2). It is likely that the volume of goods purchased will fall, because of the higher prices, and with the fall in demand, there will be a cut-back in industrial output and so higher unemployment (consequence 3). The balance of payments will *not* be adversely affected, since exports will not be subject to VAT, and the effect on imports of higher *domestic* taxes will be to reduce import demand and so *improve* the balance of payments. The answer is C.

179 The total yield from an indirect tax is likely to be greatest when (a) demand for the good is relatively unaffected by the addition of a tax on to the price and (b) supply is relatively unaffected, even though suppliers will be receiving the price net of the tax. The answer is B.

NOTES

Chapter 16

180 Country X has an *absolute* advantage over Country Y in making P and Q, because 1 unit of resource in Country X will make more of either P or Q than one unit of resource in Country Y. However, international trade should still take place because of *comparative* advantage in producing P and Q.

The opportunity costs of producing a unit of P is ($\frac{4}{8}$) = $\frac{1}{2}$ unit of Q in Country X and only $\frac{1}{3}$ unit of Q in Country Y.

Similarly, the opportunity cost of producing a unit of Q is 2 units of P in Country X and 3 units of P in Country Y.

Country X has a comparative advantage in producing P and Country Y has a comparative advantage in the production of Q. International trade should be beneficial for both countries, with Country X exporting P and Country Y exporting Q.

The answer is C.

181 A conclusion from the law of comparative advantage is that if free trade is allowed, countries will specialise in the production of goods and services in which they have a comparative advantage over other countries. As a result, the world's economic resources will be put to their most productive uses, and total output will be maximised. It does not follow that each country of the world will maximise its own national income or economic wealth (statement A), because the distribution of the wealth between the individual countries in the world could be uneven, with some countries earning much more than others from their output and their exports. The answer is C.

182 To Bandia, the opportunity cost of making rice is $\frac{1}{15}$ car and the opportunity cost of making a car is 15 tonnes of rice.

To Sparta, the opportunity cost of making rice is higher than in Bandia, because it is $\frac{1}{6}$ car. The opportunity cost of making a car is less, because it is just 6 tonnes of rice.

Since Bandia has a comparative advantage over Sparta in making rice and Sparta has a comparative advantage over Bandia in making cars, international trade will occur, with Bandia exporting rice and Sparta exporting cars. The answer is A.

183 A production possibility boundary shows the possible combinations of two goods that a country can produce with its resources. The slope of the line for each country indicates the opportunity cost of producing corn in terms of lost production of clothing, and the opportunity cost of producing clothing in terms of lost production of corn. In Burra, the opportunity cost of producing corn is a lot less than it is in Mula. (If it were the *same* in both countries, the slopes of the production possibility boundaries would be parallel to each other.) This means that Burra has a comparative advantage in the production of corn. By the same analysis, we can conclude that Mula has a comparative advantage in the production of clothing.

Statement B cannot be proved or disproved. *Absolute* advantage cannot be ascertained from the diagram. Burra might be a country with *many more resources* than Mula, and absolute advantage refers to the production capabilities of each country *per unit of resource.*

NOTES

Statement C cannot be proved or disproved either, because although Burra can produce more output in total than Mula, its national income per head of population depends on *population size*, for which we do not have any information. The answer is A.

184 The supply curve for imports without tariffs is Imports_1 and the supply curve for imports with tariffs added on is Imports_2.

The value of imports before the imposition of the tariffs at exchange rate E is where the curve Imports_1 intersects the line for E, which is where imports equal V_4.

The imposition of the tariffs, at exchange rate E, would reduce imports to V_3. The answer is D.

185 If there are no import tariffs, and the exchange rate is allowed to find its own level, equilibrium between exports and imports would be achieved at level V_2 (balance of trade deficit/surplus = 0) and at a much lower exchange rate than E. This is on the assumption, of course, that capital outflows and capital inflows are also in balance. The answer is B.

186 A subsidy shifts the supply curve downwards (to the right) and producers of butter will receive RT more than the market price. At output OY, domestic producers would need a price of OT, which is higher than the world price by the amount of the subsidy RT. At output levels above OY, domestic producers cannot compete with the world price OR, in spite of the subsidy. Demand and supply will be in equilibrium at price OR and quantity OZ. Of this, OY will be produced domestically and YZ imported. The answer is C.

187 See the comments for question 187 above. The answer is D.

188 With a tariff of RT on imports, the supply curve for butter in the country's market becomes the domestic supply curve HS up to output level OY and price OT. At output levels above OY, the supply curve becomes the world supply curve, at price OT (inclusive of tariff).

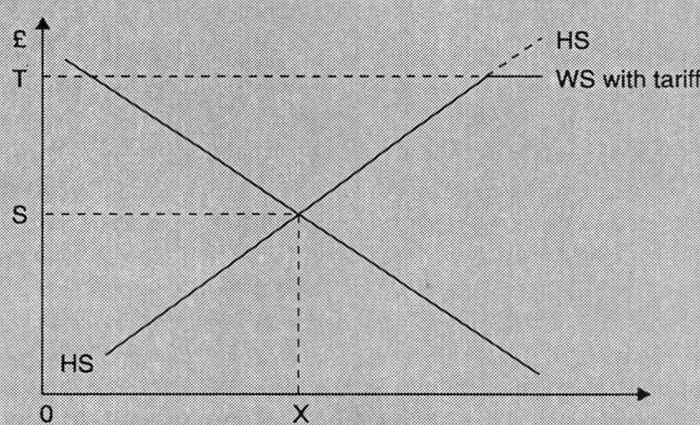

Demand and supply are in equilibrium at output OX, all produced domestically, and price OS. The answer is B.

189 Before the tariff is imposed, the quantity bought and sold in the Alsatz market will be OZ, which is where the demand curve D intersects the supply curve (= world market price without tariff). Of the total demand OZ, domestic suppliers will produce up to the level where their supply curve reaches the world market price level, and so they will produce OW. Since domestic firms supply OW out of OZ units, imports must be the differences, which is WZ. The answer is D.

190 With the imposition of the tariff, the quantity bought and sold in the Alsatz market will fall to OY, which is where the demand curve D intersects the new supply curve (= world market price plus tariff). Of this total demand OY, domestic suppliers will produce up to the level where their supply curve reaches world market price plus tariff, which is quantity OX. Since domestic firms will now produce more (OX) and domestic demand has fallen to OY, imports will fall to XY. Only imports are charged the tariff, and so the government's tax income will be XY × T. The answer is D.

191 At a price of P_2, demand per year will be 22,000 units. At this price, domestic suppliers will be willing to supply 15,000 units, and so only 7,000 units of the product would have to be imported. The answer is C.

Chapter 17

192 The current balance is the trade balances plus investment income and transfers, and 18 + 6 + 3 – 2 = 25. The answer is D.

193 & 194

The balance of payments for 19X2 will be

	£'000 million	£'000 million
Current balance		+ 25
Transactions in external assets		
Investment abroad	–27	
Lending abroad	–30	
Additions to official reserves	–2	
(Question 194)		–59
Transactions in external liabilities		
Investment from abroad	12	
Borrowing from abroad	25	
(Question 195)		37
Balance item		–3
		–25

Question 193 – the answer is D.

Question 194 – the answer is A.

195 The balance of payments is said to be in deficit when there is a deficit on the combined currant account balances. Capital movements are not included, and so item 2 is irrelevant. The trade in services balance includes services such as *tourism* (item 1); British tourism abroad creates an outflow and has an adverse effect on the balance of payments. *Transfers* are an item of invisible trade which includes such items as payments by the UK government to the European Union and international organisations such as the United Nations, and cash grants to developing countries (item 3). The answer is C.

NOTES

196 When the US dollar depreciates against the deutschmark (DM), but maintains its value against sterling, it follows that sterling will depreciate against the DM too. When sterling and the US dollar depreciate in value, UK and US goods become cheaper for Germany to buy. The relative prices of UK and US goods will remain the same as before, and so US goods will not change in price in the UK (and UK goods will not change in price in the USA). The answer is B.

197

	Unit value of exports	*Unit value of imports*		*Terms of trade*
Base year	100 ÷	100 ×	100 =	100
Current level	108 ÷	120 ×	100 =	90

The answer is C.

198 *Reason 1*. With domestic inflation, export prices will go up. Total exports in value might go up or down, depending on the price elasticity of demand for exports. However, higher export prices would improve the terms of trade, not weaken them.

Reason 2. High prices for domestically produced goods will increase demand for (substitute) imported goods, and so add to total imports.

Reason 3. If inflation is caused by excess demand in domestic markets, firms will produce goods for their domestic market, and not have the output capacity to export as well. We might say that output has been diverted from export markets to domestic markets, so that total exports will fall in value.

The answer is D.

199 'Balance of payments' in the question refers to balance of payments on current account. Capital movements (Reason 2) do *not* have a short-term effect on the balance of payments, although in the longer term, there will be outflows of interest and dividend payments to the foreign investors.

When an economy is reflated, the government will take steps to increase aggregate demand. Some of this extra demand will be satisfied by imported goods (Reason 3) and some by domestically-produced goods. Unless industry has sufficient spare capacity to meet the extra domestic demand and also to carry on producing for the same volume of exports as before, the growth in domestic demand will result in some switch by firms from selling to export markets to selling to domestic markets (Reason 1). The answer is B.

200 Purchasing power parity theory predicts that changes in exchange rates between two currencies are attributable to the different rates of price inflation in each country.

$$\text{New exchange rate} = \text{old exchange rate} \times \frac{1 + \text{inflation rate in currency's country}}{1 + \text{inflation rate in other country}}$$

The inflation rate is a proportion, and so 10% = 0.10 etc.

Therefore we have a new US dollar/pound sterling exchange rate of

$$\$1.50 \times \left(\frac{1.02}{1.12}\right) = \$1.3660.$$

The dollar has strengthened in value against sterling because the rate of inflation has been lower in the USA than in the UK. The answer is B.

201 The interest rate differential between two countries/currencies is the reason for the difference between the spot exchange rate (rate for buy or selling now) and the forward rate; a rate that can be arranged now by means of a *forward exchange contract* for buying or selling at an arranged time in the future.

When interest rates are lower in Country X than Country Y, the currency of Country X will be quoted forward at a *premium* against the currency of Country Y. A premium is *deducted* from the spot rate to arrive at the forward rate.

If US dollar interest rates are lower than sterling interest rates, and supposing that the spot rate is \$1.5000 = £1 and the 3 month forward premium is 1½ cents, the US dollar-sterling exchange rate in a 3 month forward exchange contract would be \$1.50000 – \$0.0150 = \$1.4850 to £1.

The answer is D.

202 Such a system is not free floating because there is government intervention. Equally there is no peg around which exchange rate movements are limited. The answer is B.

203 Devaluation of the currency will make imports more expensive. The price of exports should not be directly affected by the devaluation, and so the terms of trade (unit value of exports ÷ unit value of imports) will worsen. Higher costs of imports will add to the cost of living. The answer is D.

NOTES

ANSWERS TO EXAM STYLE QUESTIONS

NOTES

Chapter 1

1

(a) The cost of an item measured in terms of the alternatives foregone is its opportunity cost. The concept of opportunity cost arises because resources are scarce. In choosing which goods to produce from scarce resources, society is forced to do without those goods which might otherwise be produced. In choosing what to produce the next best alternative foregone or sacrificed is referred to as the opportunity cost of what is produced.

(b) Individuals have a limited amount of buying power, which is set by the income they receive. This income restricts the range of goods and services they are able to consume and so they are forced to choose between alternatives. In choosing to buy a textbook, for example, a student may do without a meal in a restaurant. The meal is therefore the opportunity cost of the textbook. For another individual the decision to choose to buy a new compact disc player may involve the sacrifice of a foreign holiday. Their income is such that they can have one or the other but not both. So the foreign holiday, as the next best alternative to buying a compact disc player, represents the opportunity cost of the compact disc player.

A limited income is the main kind of resource constraint the individual faces and makes it necessary to choose between alternatives. Time, however, is also a scarce resource for the individual. If a student decides to spend an evening at home revising for an economics exam, for example, the opportunity cost of such revision may be the time not spent revising for an accountancy exam.

At the level of the firm the concept of opportunity cost may be illustrated with reference to the diagram below, which shows a production possibility curve. We assume that the firm only produces two goods, X and Y.

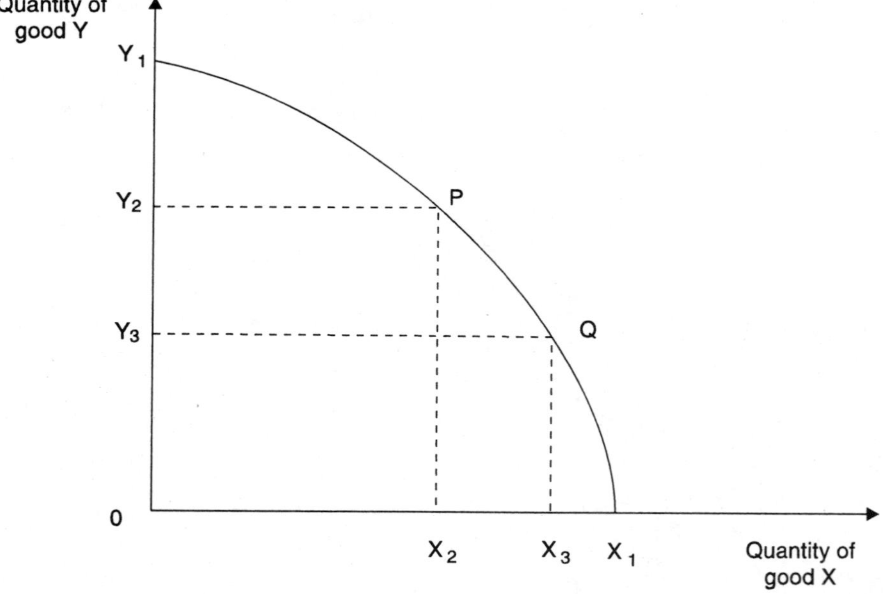

The production possibility curve shows the maximum output the firm can produce when all of its resources, in the form of labour, capital, land and raw material inputs are being fully used. Given the resources available to the firm it may decide to produce either Y_1 units of good Y (for example washing machines), or X_1 units of good X (for example refrigerators), or some combination of the two, shown by points along the production possibility curve.

If the firm decides to produce X_1 refrigerators and no washing machines the opportunity cost of producing X_1 refrigerators is Y_1 washing machines. In other words, Y_1 washing machines represents the forgone output of the firm's decision to manufacture X_1 refrigerators.

If the firm is currently producing at point P on the production possibility curve, producing Y_2 units of Y and X_2 units of X and after that moves to point Q, production of Y will fall to Y_3, while the production of X will increase to X_3. In order that the firm may increase the output of X from X_2 to X_3 it is necessary to reduce the output of Y from Y_2 to Y_3. This means the opportunity cost of increasing the output of X from X_2 to X_3 is $(Y_2 - Y_3)$ of Y.

The firm may wish to move from point P on the production possibility curve to point Q because it observes a change in demand for its products: a demand for more refrigerators but fewer washing machines. The firm therefore redeploys its resources, switching labour, plant and machinery from the production of washing machines to the production of refrigerators. The most serious concern of the firm, however, will be the opportunity cost of forgone output where the firm could profitably sell more of both of its products. In deciding to increase the output of product X the opportunity cost to the firm will be the profit forgone on that output of product Y that it is unable to supply to consumers.

The firm must calculate where the greatest returns are to be obtained – in producing more of good X or more of good Y. In devoting resources to the increased production of good X the firm must realise that it is sacrificing the profit opportunities that are available in producing good Y. This choice is forced on the firm because of the limited resources it has available. The firm will be unable to increase output of both goods because it has limited ability to raise the necessary finance to engage more factors of production. So the firm has to choose which product to supply more of and, at the same time, which product to supply less of. The opportunity cost of the increased output for good X is therefore the profit sacrificed on the reduction in output of good Y.

The concept of opportunity cost applies to the state when it decides between alternative spending programmes. The state's ability to finance its spending programmes is limited to the sum obtained from taxation and the extent of its ability to borrow. However, there are many competing claims to this source of finance. The government may, for example, be considering the construction of a major new hospital building programme, or a major programme of new road building and motorway repairs. If the decision is taken to undertake the new hospital building programme the resources devoted to this cannot also be used in the road building programme. In this case we may say that the opportunity cost of the additional hospital construction is the road building which is forgone. The ministers responsible must balance the cost of these programmes against the social benefits to be gained. On the basis of this information the government may be able to make a decision as to which programme to support. In some circumstances, however, decisions will be based on government priorities.

The concept of opportunity cost also applies to the state, in that state expenditure financed by taxation implies a reduction in private expenditure. This is because, after taxation, individuals are left with less disposable income with which to buy consumer goods. For society as a whole, therefore, an increased level of state spending involves a sacrifice of private goods and services which individuals will be unable to consume. The Chancellor of the Exchequer recognised this problem when he stated in the Autumn Financial Statement of 1986 that 'A pound cannot be used twice. A pound used in higher public expenditure is a pound not available for reductions in taxation.' In other words the opportunity cost of a pound's worth of public expenditure is a pound's worth of private expenditure taxpayers must go without

NOTES

Chapter 2

2

> **Tutorial note**
>
> (a) If the demand for coffee is price inelastic, any noticeable rise in the world price of coffee might have only a minor effect on the demand for coffee. If so, African producers could more easily take advantage of the situation. The long-run effect on African producers would depend on complex world-wide supply factors.
>
> (b) Any switch into demand for tea will depend on the extent of substitution effects.
>
> (c) Any scare effect of the publicised risk could be short lived and so have limited implications. If, however, there is a major long-term effect on the demand for coffee this would have wider consequences, possibly extending well outside the coffee industry.

(a) Over the shorter term, the increased prices of coffee in world markets would benefit African producers. There would be a diminished supply of coffee available. At the same time, if the demand for coffee is price inelastic, while there is a relative shortage of coffee, prices would continue to remain high. So African producers would be able to market their coffee more easily and at the higher world price. In Figure 1, the fall in the supply of coffee is shown by the leftward shift of the supply curve from S_1 to S_2. Consequently, the sustained demand for coffee pushes the price up from P_1 to P_2.

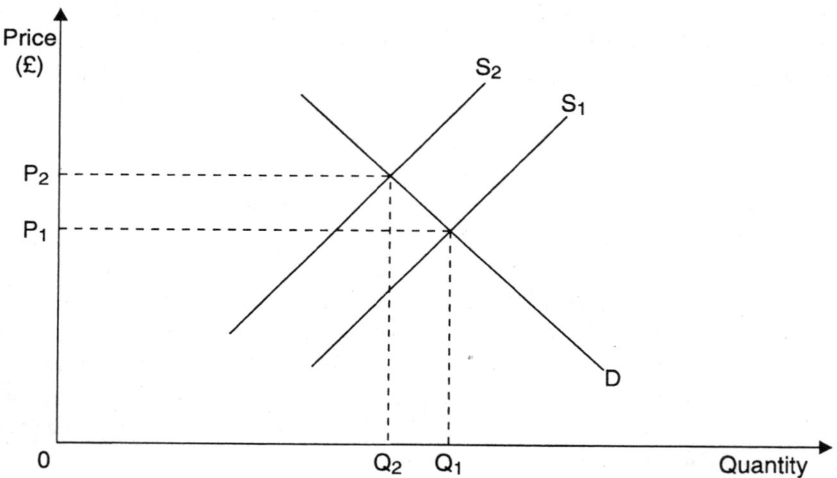

Figure 1

Over the longer term, this would be likely to encourage African growers to extend existing coffee plantations. It would also possibly encourage new plantations to be opened up by existing producers, or by entrepreneurs newly entering the African coffee market. This would depend, though, on their long-term view of the world coffee market and the likelihood of the higher prices being maintained. It might take several years to develop successfully a coffee plantation as a marketing entity. In the meantime the rate of return on invested funds is likely to be low. It is also possible that the costs of raw coffee production might rise anyway in the shorter term, for example with the increasing demand for coffee plants. Also, price movements on world commodity markets are often exaggerated – at least to begin with- in relation to the underlying conditions. There is evidence, for instance, that coffee dealers at the time underestimated the ability of Brazilian producers to make good their ravaged plantations to some extent. Potential investors into additional coffee production would need to assess likely future world prices and the alternative avenues of investment available outside coffee supply.

All of this analysis rests, of course, on the assumption that African coffee is regarded as a complete substitute for Brazilian coffee. If, for instance, African coffee was regarded as somewhat inferior in quality to Brazilian coffee, this would reduce the chance of African producers being able to take full advantage of the rise in world prices.

(b) Tea is probably the closest substitute for coffee. This means that with the rise in coffee prices there is likely to be some switch of demand into increased purchase of tea, as consumers maximise their utility. The effect on the demand for tea will depend on (i) the income effect, and (ii) the substitution effect of the rise in coffee prices.

The income effect will depend on the proportion of people's income spent on coffee. The larger the proportion, the more likely that they will feel they have to cut back their consumption of coffee, as the price rises. The substitution effect will depend on what acceptable alternatives are available and to what extent they are regarded as close substitutes. If people are willing to drink (more) tea instead of coffee, there will be a switch of demand from coffee into tea. There could also be some switch into alternative drinks, for example fruit juices.

(c) A world-wide publicity campaign on the health risks of caffeine would reduce the demand for caffeinated coffee. An early switch of demand into decaffeinated coffee, the closest substitutes, would be likely. This would tend to depress the price of caffeinated coffee and raise the price of decaffeinated coffee. As mentioned in (b), there is likely also to be some switch of demand into alternative drinks. In Figure 2, the health scare results in a shift in the demand curve for caffeinated coffee from D_1 to D_2, with a consequent fall in price from P_1 to P_2.

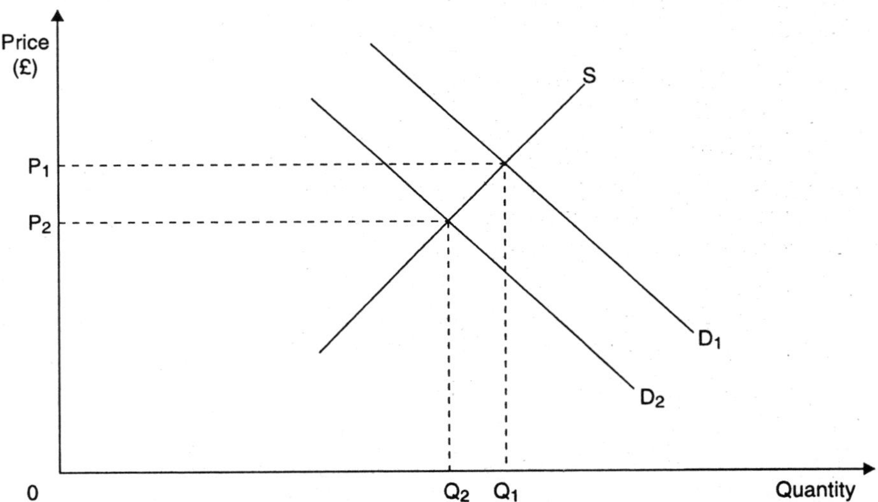

Figure 2

The health scare could be quite short-lived, with demand for coffee (and substitutes) going back to the pre-scare position. If, on the other hand, the effects were relatively permanent, the consequences could be widespread. The coffee industry would need to contract, or at any rate that part of it geared to the supply of caffeinated coffee, while substitute drinks industries would expand to meet the increased demand. There could, of course, be much wider employment effects.

Chapter 3

3

> **Tutorial note**
>
> Diagrams can help to explain price elasticity of demand: these need to be clear and linked, by numerical examples, with the context of the answer.
>
> Do not forget that price elasticity of demand is the ratio of the percentage change in quantity to the percentage change in price; the ratio of absolute changes is simply the slope of the demand curve. Demand is more elastic in the long run.
>
> In stating the determining factors, be careful not to over-emphasise the necessity/luxury point. Substitutability and the proportion of income involved are much more important.
>
> Note that the natural rate of unemployment is a situation where the labour market is in equilibrium, in the sense that all those willing and capable of working at the existing wage rate can get jobs. It does not mean that no one is unemployed, but that such unemployment as exists could be regarded as voluntary.

Price elasticity of demand (PED) measures the extent of change in demand for a product/service in response to a change in its price. It is concerned with movements along a given demand curve: the conditions of demand, other than price, remain unchanged. This is shown by:

$$\text{PED} = \frac{\text{Percentage change in quantity demanded}}{\text{Percentage change in price}} = \frac{(\Delta/Q) \times 100}{(\Delta/P) \times 100}$$

Demand is elastic (PED > 1) when, for instance, a cut in price results in a bigger percentage expansion in demand. So, in diagram (a), a cut in price from £12 to £6 (50% reduction) leads to an expansion in demand from 100 to 300 (200% expansion).

$$\text{PED} = \frac{200\%}{50\%} = 4.0$$

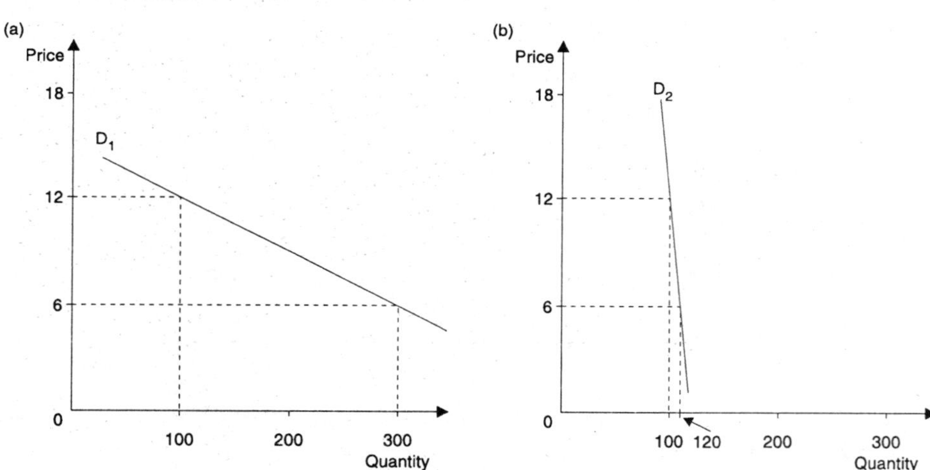

Demand is inelastic (PED < 1) when a cut in price results in a smaller percentage expansion in demand. So, in diagram (b), a cut in price from £12 to £6 (50% reduction) leads to an expansion in demand from 100 to 120 units (20% expansion).

$$\text{PED} = \frac{20\%}{50\%} = 0.4$$

(PED will be negative for all normal demand curves, so it is usual to omit the use of + and – signs.)

PED has revenue effects. In diagram (a), the price fall results in an increase in revenue, while in (b), the reduction in price results in a fall in revenue. Demand is unitary when a percentage fall in price brings about an equal expansion of demand, so leaving revenue unchanged.

Price elasticity can, of course, apply also to price rises. What has been stated so far merely operates in reverse. Therefore, if price is increased and revenue falls, demand is elastic.

To sum up:

Price	*Revenue*	*Demand*
Decrease	Rises	Elastic
Increase	Falls	Elastic
Decrease	Falls	Inelastic
Increase	Rises	Inelastic

The key factor determining PED is substitution. Food as a whole has a highly inelastic demand, as there is no real substitute for it. However, between different foods much substitution is possible.

Whether a good is a necessity is relevant up to a point. For the basic essentials of living, demand tends to be inelastic (often very much so). Even if the price rises we will still attempt to buy them (though perhaps in smaller quantities or with lower quality). On the other hand, the demand for some luxury goods, eg diamonds, is markedly inelastic: the absence of substitutes is far more the determining factor.

Those items which represent only a minor part of income are likely to have inelastic demand. A large percentage increase in the price of such products would probably make little difference to demand, whereas the reverse is true of major budgetary items.

Some goods are bought as a matter of habit, eg cigarettes. Price changes may need to be substantial to make any difference to demand, and so demand will be relatively inelastic.

The durability or potential life of a product will also be a determining factor. If the price of durable products rises we can, if necessary, defer their replacement; whereas expendable products must be replaced. Therefore demand for durable products will tend to be price elastic.

The structure of the market supply may be a significant factor. In an oligopoly situation, above a certain point (x) a price increase by one firm is unlikely to be matched by competitors, so making demand price elastic. Below point x, price reduction by one firm is likely to be followed by similar reductions by competitors, so making demand price inelastic.

Some products have a complex composite demand. So, the different categories of demand for petrol – commercial use, commuter use, leisure time travel – may have different demand elasticities. At the same time, ownership of a car involves heavy sunk costs other than on petrol: awareness of this may make consumers either more or less responsive to changes in the price of petrol.

Time will also be important. Over the shorter period, purchasers may be constrained by existing contracts or even by habit. Over the longer term, buying can adjust more easily to price changes, so increasing the elasticity of demand.

Chapter 4

4

> **Tutorial note**
>
> In our suggested solution, we use the example of a road building scheme for part (b). In the case of a new factory, pollution and other environmental effects not charged directly to the factory owner form part of the social costs.

(a) Producers and consumers in a market make their output and consumption decisions for their own private benefit. The private benefit of a decision is a measure of the benefit obtained from it directly by the supplier or consumer. Against the private benefit the economic agent will weigh the private cost of the decision: for the firm, the private costs represent the costs to it of the resources used in production.

The distinction between social costs and benefits and private costs and benefits is essentially a matter of the people on whom they have an impact. While private costs and benefits affect those who undertake the activities which give rise to them, social costs and benefits have an impact on people in general, whether or not they themselves undertake the activities.

More broadly stated, social cost measures the cost to society as a whole of an economic activity. Set against that is the social benefit: the positive effect on society as a whole.

For many activities, there is a difference between the private costs and benefits of the activity and its social costs and benefits. This difference is sometimes called a spillover effect. Where third parties outside the particular market involved are affected in this way, the consequence of the activity which impacts upon them is called an externality. The existence of externalities means effects (for example, pollution) occurring for which there is no market.

(b) A decision by government to build a road provides an example where spillover costs and benefits are very likely to occur. Various benefits and costs are likely to arise from such a project, depending on the nature of the project and whether a toll is to be charged to road users.

A new road will probably mean shorter journey times and possible less fuel consumption for motorists and freight traffic, allowing private individuals more time for other activities such as leisure, and reducing firms' transport costs. These benefits for each road user may be set against their private cost in using the road if a toll is charged.

Spillover effects reflecting social costs and benefits of the project are likely to have an impact on groups other than road users.

(a) Negative effects could be increased traffic noise and a deterioration in air quality for any residents living near the new road. If the new road leads to people travelling more rather than less because journeys are now more convenient, the increased road use will have a wider effect, adding to the total amount of pollution in the environment overall.

(b) Positive externalities may include reduced noise and cleaner air for residents in other areas if the new road now bypasses their area.

(c) Shops, offices and filling stations close to the new road may also benefit from increased trade when the new road is built.

(d) The new road may be safer than alternative routes which it replaces, so that both local residents and road users have the benefit of reduced risk of road traffic accidents.

The government will want to take account of the social costs and social benefits of the project in full before deciding whether to build the road. Included in costs, of course, will be the resource costs in constructing the road. The task of cost-benefit analysis will be easier if all costs and benefits are quantified in financial terms, although it can be difficult for spillover effects such as increased road safety, for which no market exists. There may be a quantifiable effect on house values of those whose residential environment is affected by the new road, although the effect may be difficult to predict in advance of the project.

Chapter 5

5

> **Tutorial note**
>
> In looking at the question of economies and diseconomies of scale, it is important, as in this solution, to distinguish between the short-term and the long-term position. Remember that these terms are not indicative of time periods, as such.
>
> It is important to show that scale can apply at operational level, eg at factory level, as well as in respect of the firm as a whole.

(a) In the short run, at least one factor of production is in fixed supply; costs of this fixed factor are therefore fixed costs. The remaining factors can be varied. In Figure 1, production volume up to OZ yields diminishing unit costs, as fixed costs are spread more widely. Production beyond point Z means that the combination of resources is becoming less effective so that, for example, supervision of the workforce may be more difficult. From O to Z, increasing returns are experienced; beyond Z, there are diminishing returns. But those returns are within the scale set by the (one or more) fixed factor. So, in the short run, existing capacity constrains any effort at reducing unit costs.

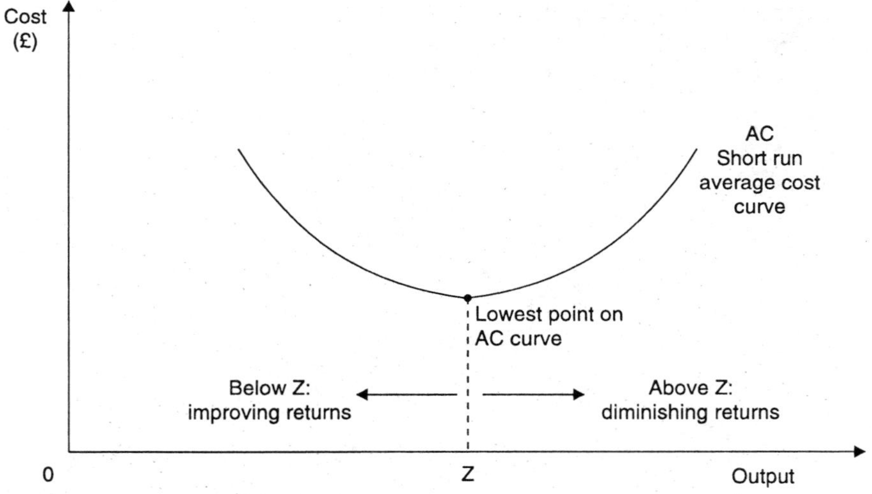

Figure 1

In the long run, all factors are variable making possible a wide range of factor combinations. Capital in the form of different size factories or different cost/size machines may be combined with different sizes of the labour force. True economies of scale – derived from changing the scale of operations – can now be obtained.

(b) (i) Economies of scale may arise for a variety of reasons.

(1) Technical economies may occur: a machine 1½ times the size of the existing one might enable production to be doubled. Capital equipment may be available only in certain sizes (or prices). By utilising more fully the capacity of a machine, unit costs will fall. The same

NOTES

principle can apply across a whole range of resource inputs, eg in the employment of a qualified accountant. A manager will need to be paid his or her salary whether production is low or high. The cost of a market research project is not likely to be twice as much if the size of the firm doubles. A related aspect concerns the problem of combining resources in different ways to provide, more or less effectively, different levels of output. Only certain combinations may be possible technically or operationally.

(2) Much production is carried out as the result of a breaking down of the production process into component parts so that work becomes specialised. This has led to much division of labour, each worker carrying out perhaps standardised and repetitive operations. In turn, much of this routine work has become automated. The machines carrying out these operations are themselves specialised; yet the work does not have to be intricately divided into standard activities in order for specialisation to yield scale economies. The setting up of units (or departments), each specialising in a range of ancillary activities (eg marketing, finance) is also an example of specialisation, providing possible economies of scale.

(3) Economies of scale may come from growth in the size of the firm as distinct from expansion in operational terms. This would be likely to yield economies of scale in general management, finance and possibly also in marketing. So the cost of the finance function per unit of output for the larger firm can be less than that for the smaller firm.

(ii) The ultimate increase in the costs of the firm is illustrated by Figure 2, in which each SRAC curve expresses the short-run situation. Unit costs can be reduced by moving onto a potentially higher volume SRAC curve. Each could, for instance, represent the costs of operating a certain size of factory. By $SRAC_5$ all possible scale accuracies have been achieved and the long-run effects of diminishing returns have set in. The SRAC curves are tangential to the long-run average cost (LRAC) curve of the firm.

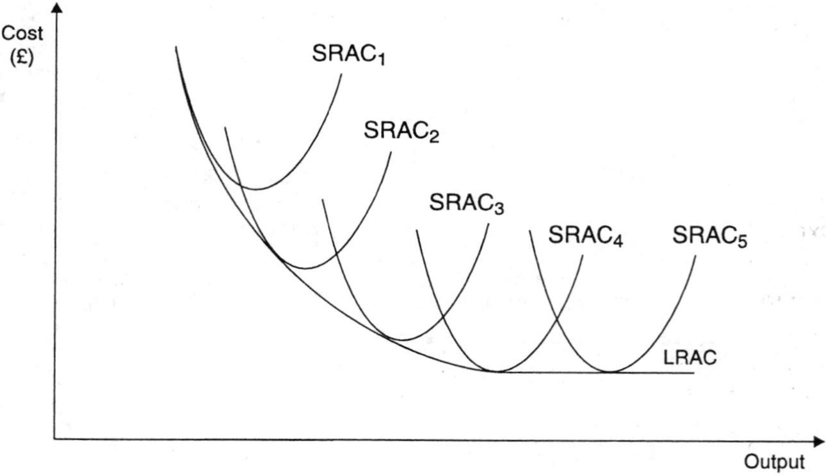

Figure 2

Unit costs do not continue to fall indefinitely and diseconomies of scale may set in. Specialisation among the workforce may be taken to the point at which work becomes meaningless, as employees are isolated from the end-result of their efforts. Control of larger groups of workers becomes more difficult and increased absenteeism, as well as industrial strife, ensue. Diminished motivation could be leading to a fall in the quality of output and a higher level of rejects of items produced. Larger machines may be more prone to breakdown. Systems breakdowns may be experienced as work

NOTES

becomes bigger in scale and procedures more complex. Computer malfunctioning is a common problem, often the direct result of attempts to operate at a much larger scale.

Management of the firm could become more difficult as the firm grows in size. Communication problems may be experienced and overall control can be more difficult. Raising sales volume may require a more intensive marketing effort and unit costs of promotion and selling may start to rise.

If the firm is large enough within its particular industry, as the firm grows, *external* diseconomies of scale could be experienced. This could be, for example from the rising cost of recruiting, training and employing specialists, or because of rising prices for specially made bought-in components.

This does not mean that in each case there is a finite limit to the scale of operations or the manageable size of the firm. Developments in technology or in control techniques might, at some later stage, make possible a larger scale of economic activity. However, within existing technology and control capability, continued increase in the scale of activity will lead eventually to increasing costs.

Chapter 6

6

> **Tutorial note**
> Whatever the political arguments about a legal minimum wage, this question requires you to put forward the theoretical economic arguments for and against such a policy.

A legal minimum wage level is usually set by governments to protect low-paid workers, who are often young school-leavers, from being exploited by employers. It is said that otherwise they will be paid unacceptably low wages and may never be given training opportunities that would enable them to move into superior better-paid jobs. In recent years, some economists (often referred to as supply siders because they advocate micro-economic measures affecting the supply conditions in the economy) have argued that minimum legal wage legislation should be resisted. Such economists argue that a legal minimum wage not only fails to benefit the type of worker it is designed to help, but it also harms the economy in general. This argument can be illustrated using Figure 1.

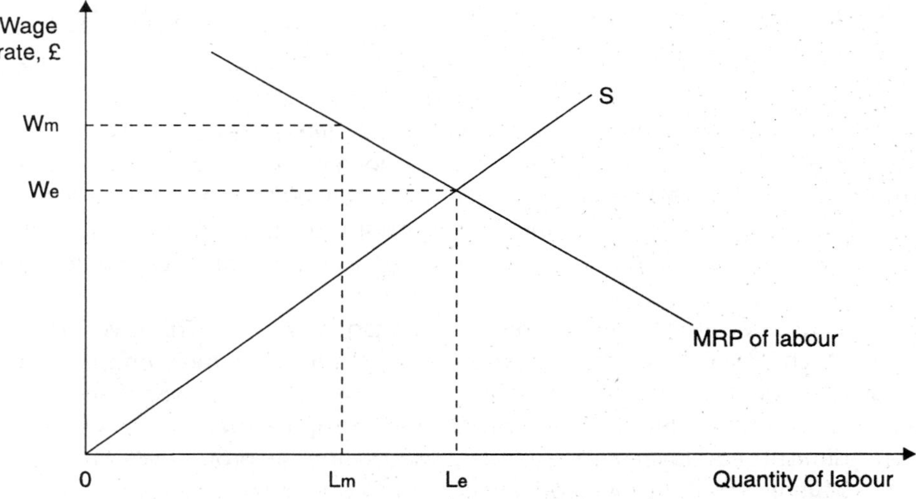

Figure 1

NOTES

The demand of labour is given by the marginal revenue product (MRP). The free market in this case sets the equilibrium wage level at W_e and creates employment for L_e workers. A legally imposed minimum wage level above the equilibrium market-clearing wage level, such as W_m reduces the total employment of the protected labour while providing a higher level of wages for those lucky enough to be in jobs. The critics of this policy point out that:

(a) $(L_e - L_m)$ amount of labour which is willing to work and can get jobs at the freely determined market wage level is denied that opportunity if there is a legal minimum wage;

(b) society as a whole loses the production of the now unemployed labour, $(L_e - L_m)$, due to the higher imposed wage level; and

(c) in a free labour market, workers' earnings reflect their productivity. The imposition of a higher controlled wage level results in bad distribution of the economy's resources; some workers are paid more than their productivity warrants, while others are made to be unemployed. It could also lead to general inflation if applied to a large segment of the working population.

It needs to be realised that, in their purest form, these arguments rest on certain assumptions about the labour markets: that they are perfectly competitive in supply as well as in demand; and that they are static. In practice, labour is often purchased under conditions of monopsony, for example where there is a single employer or a combination of a few large employers who can dominate the wage setting process in a particular industry or in a particular geographical area by their actions. Under conditions of monopsony, wage rates can be increased within certain limits without causing unemployment or reductions in output.

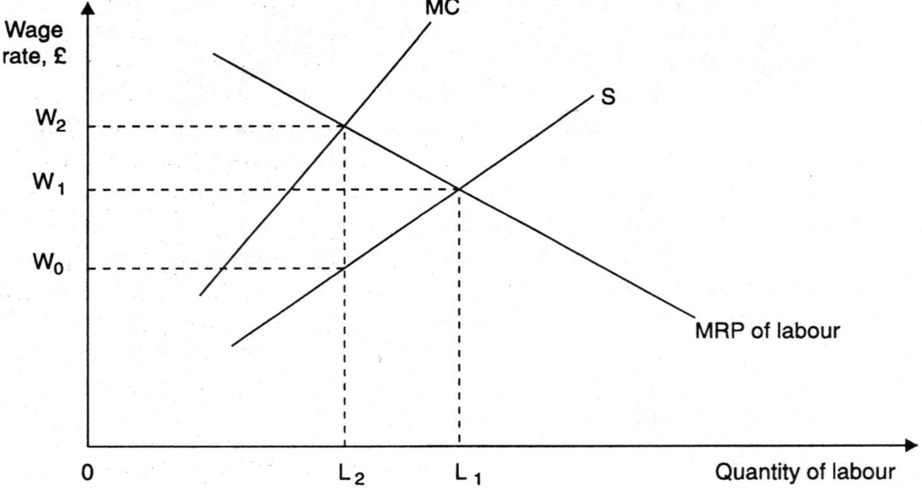

Figure 2

Figure 2 helps to show this. Under competitive conditions the outcomes in the market are a wage level of W_1 and employment of L_1. However, when labour is purchased by a monopsonist, that is a single employer, the supply curve is not the curve S. This is because to attract more labour the monopsonist must pay a higher wage rate, not just to newly attracted labour, but also to the previously employed workers. So the marginal cost of an additional worker is his or her wage rate plus the increase in the wages paid to every one of the previously engaged workers. This gives us the MC curve, which is above the supply curve of labour. Left to itself, the monopsony market conditions would result in the employment of L_2 workers at the wage rate of W_0 (the point where MC = MRP, which is what profit maximising firms will aim for). The monopsonistic employer is now making super-normal profits. We know that L_1 workers can be employed at wage rate W_1 under competitive conditions, for example when normal profits are earned.Therefore, any legally fixed wage rate between W_1 and W_2 can result in a higher level of wages and greater employment.

NOTES

So, under monopsony conditions, a legal minimum wage level could be of benefit to the workers concerned as well as to society as a whole. Additionally, higher wages for this special category of worker could:

(a) give their employers the incentive to use labour efficiently and to provide it with skills through training;

(b) motivate such workers to work harder or improve their productivity through voluntary efforts (such as attending evening classes); and

(c) remove at least some people from the group that constitutes the poor in a society.

Chapter 7

7

> **Tutorial note**
>
> This question tests your basic theoretical understanding (part a), as well as your analytical abilities (part b). Clearly, part (a) requires illustrative diagrams to be drawn.

(a) A firm will maximise its profits when the price and output combination is such that the marginal revenue of an additional unit of output is equal to the marginal cost of producing it.

Perfect competition is an idealised model of a market structure characterised by the following conditions.

- (i) There are numerous buyers and sellers.
- (ii) The sellers are firms making a homogeneous product.
- (iii) There is free entry and exit of firms into and out of the market
- (iv) Economic agents (consumers and firms) have perfect information.

The individual firm in perfect competition must accept and cannot influence the ruling market price in the industry. If it raised its price above this level, it would sell none of its output. As a result, the demand curve faced by the firm is a horizontal line, which will be the same as the marginal revenue curve. Figure 1 illustrates the equilibrium output of Q_1 and the equilibrium price of P_1; since MR = MC at this point, profits of the firm are maximised.

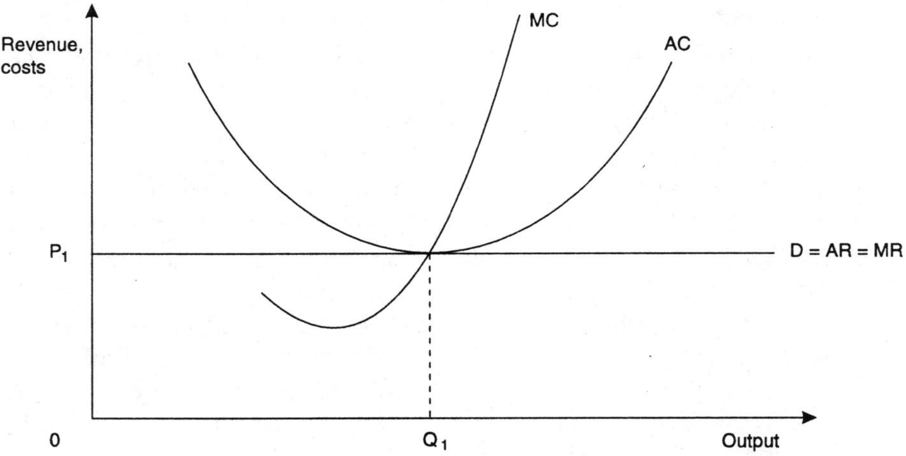

Figure 1 Perfect competition

Because firms are free to enter or to leave the market, firms in perfect competition will not make supernormal profits in the long run. New firms will start up production, expanding supply and collectively bringing down the

NOTES

market price until there are no longer supernormal profits to be earned. At this point, firms are producing at the minimum point of their long-run average cost curves, as illustrated in Figure 1.

A market dominated by a single firm is called a *monopoly*. The monopolist can choose to set price at different levels and, as a price-maker, faces a downward sloping demand (average revenue) curve.

Because there are barriers to the entry of new firms to the industry, supernormal profits are not competed away by other firms. The long-run equilibrium price and output of a monopoly firm is illustrated in Figure 2.

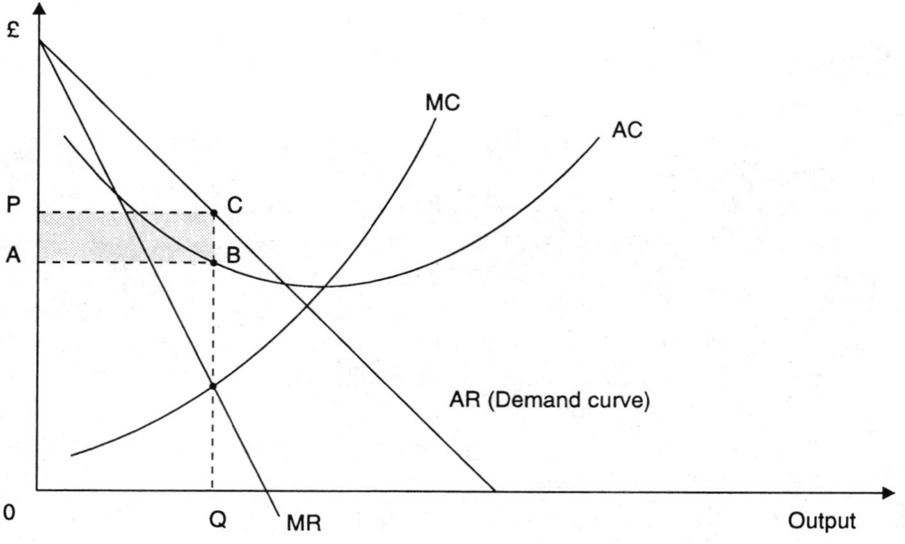

Figure 2 Monopoly

The profit maximising position for the firm is still where MC = MR. This occurs at output Q in Figure 2, where the price paid by consumers is P. In this equilibrium position, the monopolist is ensuring supernormal profits represented by the area of the rectangle PABC, which is the output quantity multiplied by the difference between average revenue (price) and total average costs (AC).

If demand for the firm's product is relatively inelastic, then the demand curve is more steeply downward sloping and the position of the monopolist is further removed from that of perfect competition: the monopolist is then more able to earn supernormal profits than if demand is more elastic.

Unlike the firm in perfect competition, the monopolist illustrated by Figure 2 is not producing at the lowest point of his average cost curve. This indicates a bad allocation of resources in the case of the monopolist, since the firm is not operating as efficiently as it could. Additionally, the earning of supernormal profits by the monopolist could be viewed as a bad distribution of income compared with perfect competition, when all firms only earn normal profits.

(b) The larger size of monopoly firms compared with smaller firms in competition with one another means that monopolists may be able to take advantage of economies of scale. For example, there are considerable economies in operating a single domestic gas supply network compared with a number of networks competing in the same areas. Monopolist firms may be able to spread fixed costs over larger amounts of output. They may also gain from economies in bulk buying of inputs and in marketing and distribution costs.

Monopoly firms may be in a stronger position to finance research and development activities, enabling them to make technological advances which will lower unit costs of production. They may also be able to develop new products to meet consumers' needs.

The presence of economies of scale could reduce monopolists' production costs below that of firms in a competitive market. Equilibrium will then be at a point further down the monopolist's downward sloping demand curve than it would be without the scale economies. The resulting profit maximising position will be at a lower price and higher output level than in the competitive market.

If a competitive industry were to become monopolised, consumers' interests might also be served by some form of regulation of the industry. Some monopolistic companies in the UK are subject to price regulation, such as BT, the telecommunications operator. Such regulation may enable scale economies to be achieved while preventing consumers from suffering from the full effects of monopolistic pricing policies.

Chapter 8

8

> **Tutorial note**
>
> We can make a distinction between collusive and competitive oligopoly. The former, where not forbidden, is more likely where products are homogeneous and there is common interest between the firms. The latter is likely to be characterised by product differentiation, non-price competition and variability of market conduct. Barriers to entry and interdependence will be common to all oligopolies. The interdependence (greater where the products are homogeneous) in turn constrains market behaviour.
>
> The kinked demand curve model illustrates oligopoly price stability. The marginal cost curve could be positioned at different points on the vertical section of the demand curve without bringing about price changes. The model is not intended, however, to imply a complete absence of price changes in the oligopoly market.
>
> You should emphasise the features of uncertainty and interdependence in oligopoly markets and show how this affects business behaviour, especially in relation to pricing policy and product differentiation.

(a) An oligopolistic market is made up of, or dominated by, a small number of large businesses. With only a few firms in an industry, each member firm is influencing or influenced by each of the other member firms. Uncertainty is introduced into decision-making because firms cannot be sure how other firms will react. This can encourage price stability, as firms will be wary of the eventual consequences of starting a price war.

Oligopoly market behaviour will be conditioned by the type of oligopoly which exists.

(i) *Perfect or homogeneous oligopoly*. Here, the products are essentially identical. This exists in the markets for basic products such as chemicals, steel and cement, where prices will tend to a common level.

(ii) *Imperfect or differentiated oligopoly*. Here, differences between the products allow for some difference in prices between the firms. Examples of differentiated oligopoly are in the motor vehicle, pharmaceutical, newspaper, consumer electrical appliance and detergent markets. In the shorter term, each firm may be able to attract customer loyalty because of product advantages. In the longer term, cross elasticity of demand will be higher between the products of the member firms, and awareness of this constrains market conduct.

Barriers to entry often exist, arising from the minimum efficient scale of activity (reflecting capital costs for setting up), a high break-even point, as well as from well established and effective branding of goods. Any new entrant is likely to be an already well-established firm which has decided to diversify its markets, and so brings with it developed business and marketing skills. Oligopoly firms tend to be mature organisations, often with business interests in more than one industry. This makes possible product cross-subsidisation and leads to the stability of oligopolies in leaner periods.

The firms compete to some extent on price but also through non-price means, for example by emphasis on product quality, product innovation, sales promotions and incentives to dealers. The aim of each firm is to promote customer loyalty and to retain market share. There are many possible variables of oligopoly behaviour, so creating an uncertain environment for each firm. There is therefore no straightforward, inclusive model of oligopoly practice.

There are two basic models of oligopoly market practice.

(i) *Collusive oligopoly*. The firms co-operate and behave as one, in effect as a monopolist. This may be a formal cartel with a common policy on prices and market shares, the objective being joint profit maximisation. Alternatively, they might operate a cartel *de facto*, achieving the aims of a formal cartel by informal, implicit means. Restrictive practices legislation in the UK is intended to prevent the operation of formal or informal cartels.

(ii) *Competitive oligopoly*. Each firm aims to maximise its own profits. While there will be some price competition, the main emphasis will be on product differentiation.

(b) The kinked demand curve model explains the price stability that is characteristic of oligopolistic markets. The model combines two demand curves for the firm.

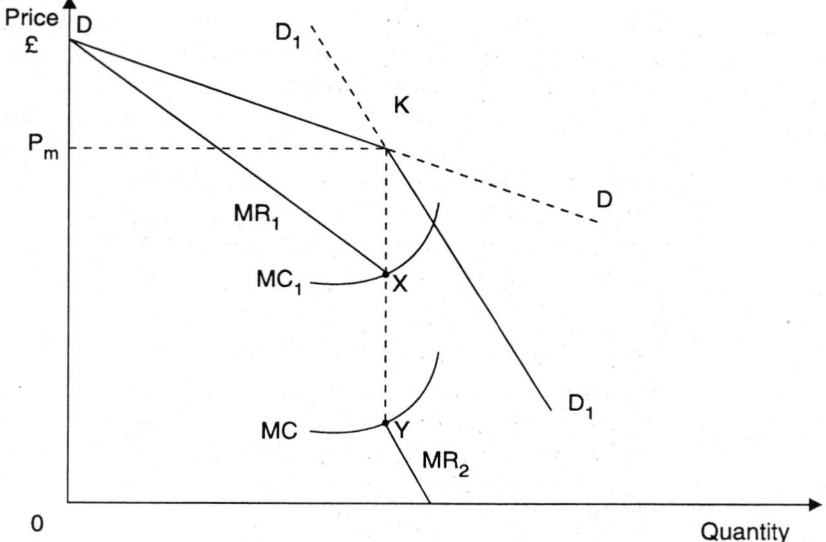

(i) A more elastic demand curve, DD in the diagram, represents demand for the firm's products on the basis that it alone changes price: its competitors keep prices unchanged at P_m, the market price. Accordingly, the firm loses (or gains) market share as it raises (or lowers) its price.

(ii) On a less elastic curve, D_1D_1, price changes by the firm are followed by its competitors. The result is that sales volume is little changed.

It is assumed that if the firm raises its price, this is unlikely to be followed by its rivals. Therefore the firm loses sales to its competitors. If the oligopolist were to reduce its price, this would be followed by competitors seeking to maintain market share. So the relevant parts of the demand curves are DK and KD_1: the firm has a kinked demand curve DKD_1. Each of the demand curves has its own related marginal revenue curve, MR_1 and MR_2 respectively. The marginal revenue curve relevant to the kinked demand curve shows a break, which is dependent upon the difference in demand elasticities at P_m of the two demand curves. The greater the difference in elasticity, the greater will be the break.

The diagram also shows the marginal cost curve passing through the break in the kinked demand curve. If costs increase, from MC to MC_1, the equilibrium price and output combination remains unchanged, with profits being maximised at the output level where MC = MR.

The kinked demand curve model explains oligopoly price stability, even in certain conditions of rising costs. There will, however, be exceptions to this stability. After a period of prolonged recession in the industry concerned, price cutting may be necessary to off-load dated stocks. Where committed fixed costs are high, cost cutting is more likely in order to raise revenue. Conversely, where total demand for the industry's product is growing strongly, it is quite likely that price will be raised, at first by the price leader. Similarly, in prolonged periods of inflation, with strong customer demand, upward price adjustments will be made at intervals.

Chapter 9

9

(a) Earlier forms of money were typically in the form of commodities which have intrinsic value. A form of commodity money used in relatively recent times is gold. More often nowadays, money takes forms which do not themselves have value, for example banknotes. Money is best defined in terms of what it does, and we therefore need to look at the functions of money.

Money has four basic functions:

(i) as a medium of exchange;

(ii) as a unit of account;

(iii) as a standard of deferred payment;

(iv) as a store of value.

As a medium of exchange, money provides perhaps its most useful function, since without it we would be reduced to the level of bartering our goods and services for those produced by other people.

Money's function as a unit of account follows from its use as a medium of exchange. Money is used to measure the value of different goods and services and to present those values in a common medium so that the relative values of those different goods and services can be compared.

The function of money as a standard of deferred payment permits transactions to be spread over a period of time while maintaining the eventual outcome at a fixed value. This is subject, of course, to changes in the value of money (which is discussed further below). For example, for goods which take a long time to produce, the transaction value can be fixed in money when the order for the goods is placed. Money can change hands before the delivery of the goods (payments in advance) or sometime after the delivery (credit payments).

Money is only one of the many stores of value. Investments in property, works of art and company shares, for example, are all stores of value. Money is perhaps the most flexible store of value since it can be easily turned into another form of value at any time. It is therefore described as the most liquid store of value.

(b) A narrow concept of the money stock, as the term implies, is one which defines money more narrowly or stringently. To be included within the definition of money, a financial asset must be:

(i) a means of payment for transactions; and

(ii) a liquid store of wealth.

Narrow measures stress money's function as a means of exchange.

In the UK, the most narrow definition of the money stock is M0, the monetary base, which consists of notes and coin in circulation, including banks' till money and their operational deposits with the Bank of England. M0 is a very narrow definition of the money stock because it comprises the means of immediate payment and the most liquid store of wealth.

The concept of broad money, as its name implies, is one which includes more elements than narrow money. In particular, as well as current account balances, broad money includes items such as savings accounts:

(i) which are not generally a means of making payment for transactions; and

(ii) which are a less liquid store of wealth than items which would be classified as narrow money.

Broad money therefore includes what might be called quasi-money, and stresses money's function as a store of value with a reasonable degree of liquidity.

In the UK, M4 is the most important definition of broad money because it is used in monitoring monetary conditions in the economy. M4 is a broad definition of money, consisting of:

(i) notes and coin in circulation with the private sector;

(ii) the private sector's sterling deposits at UK banks and building societies.

Financial assets come in varying degrees of liquidity and usability as a means of payment. As the existence of different definitions of narrow money and broad money shows, it is not possible to specify precisely what the two concepts mean.

In the UK, monitoring ranges are set for both M0 and M4 to indicate what adjustments are required in the setting of monetary policy. In circumstances where a government wishes to control the money supply, different narrow and broad measures provide possible targets. However, in recent years it has become accepted that accurate monetary control through interest rates is impossible, particularly for broad money, while financial innovations such as the offering of interest rates on sight deposits are occurring.

10

(a) *Financial intermediaries* are organisations which channel funds from institutions and individuals who have a financial surplus to institutions and individuals which wish to borrow funds. In this way they intermediate between lenders and borrowers, earning their profits from the difference in the rate of interest paid to depositors and the rate of interest charged to borrowers.

The main financial intermediaries in the UK economy are:

(i) the banks

(ii) the building societies

(iii) other institutions, including insurance companies, pension funds, unit trust companies and investment trust companies.

Disintermediation describes the bypassing of financial intermediaries so that borrowers and lenders deal directly with each other, with the possible consequence that costs can be saved. Companies increasingly take advantage of such opportunities, although when the proposed transaction is to be with an unrelated company, a bank will still usually be involved in arranging the deal.

(b) The most obvious role of financial intermediation is in providing ways of linking lenders of money with potential borrowers. Lenders do not need to find an individual borrower, but can deposit their money with a bank, building society, investment trust company or other financial intermediary.

This role in linking lenders and borrowers has the important consequence that the intermediary is able to package the amounts lent by savers into the amounts which borrowers require. For example, many building society accounts containing deposits of relatively small sums may be used to finance the smaller number of relatively large sums which mortgage borrowers require.

The intermediation process leads to risk reduction by the pooling of the risks of lending money to borrowers among the various lenders who deposit money with the intermediary. Risk reduction is also effected by unit trust companies through the spreading of investments across a variety of stocks and shares in a way which enables a small investor to take advantage of the effects of portfolio diversification, which are normally only easily available to the larger investor.

The role of the financial intermediary provides what is called maturity transformation. That is, the intermediary bridges the gap between the desire of many lenders for liquidity and the need of most borrowers for loans over longer periods. The intermediary does this by providing investors with financial instruments which are liquid enough for investors' needs and by providing funds to borrowers on a long-term basis.

The banks represent what is called the primary money market, and remain the major financial intermediaries in the UK. The clearing banks dominate the retail banking market. The sector also includes other commercial banks, and the Bank of England, the central bank which acts as an intermediary in government lending and borrowing.

The building societies intermediate between savers and borrowers in the housing market, but in recent years have become increasingly important providers of more general banking services. They are also involved in other operations, such as estate agency.

Other institutions generally perform specific intermediation roles in particular markets or sectors. Pension funds and unit trusts act as vehicles for investment, as do the insurance companies, along with the various other services such companies provide.

The existence of financial intermediaries offering a wide range of products to potential lenders may serve to encourage savings and investment. This may improve the prospects of economic growth in the economy in general, and will assist the general functioning of economic activity. If the intermediaries do not perform this role effectively, the economy may suffer. For example, commercial banks in the UK have been criticised for their unwillingness to provide long-term investment funds to British industry in recent years.

Chapter 10

11

Tutorial note

Arguments for and against central bank independence must bear in mind the need for monetary policy – the central bank's concern – to be consistent with wider economic policy. The overall system needs to ensure accord between monetary and fiscal policy.

(a) A central bank typically has as its main function the regulation of money and credit in an economy. The range of functions carried out by central banks varies considerably, but many of them are not necessary functions of a central bank and could be carried out by other organisations. Bank notes could be issued by another government department or by privately owned banks, as they are in Scotland and some other countries. Nevertheless, there are many activities common among central banks. The functions of the Bank of England, the central bank of the UK, will be outlined by way of illustration.

The Bank of England ('the Bank') is banker to the government. Virtually all government revenue, whether from taxation or borrowing, is paid into the Exchequer Account held at the Bank. This account is then drawn upon to pay the various government expenses. The Bank also maintains the National Loans Fund out of which loans are made to local authorities and other public bodies.

In periods when central government expenditure exceeds revenue, the Bank makes ways and means advances to the government to cover longer-term budget deficits, and the bank arranges the issue of securities such as Treasury Bills (typically for 3-month periods) and gilts (usually for periods of several years). This in turn involves administering the National Debt: issuing securities, periodically paying interest to the holders of securities, and repaying loans on maturity dates.

The Bank is also responsible for the control (printing, issue and withdrawal) of bank notes.

The Bank is responsible for managing the UK's gold and foreign currency reserves. In this capacity, on behalf of the Treasury, it manages the Exchange Equalisation Account. The Bank uses the foreign currency holdings in this account to intervene in the foreign exchange markets to influence the value of sterling against other currencies.

The Bank is banker to the banking/financial system. All banks and licensed deposit takers have to hold operational deposits at the Bank upon which they can draw as necessary. Through these balances, differences are settled by daily clearing between the various banks.

In its relationship with the banks, the Bank is able to implement government monetary policy. It uses open-market operations, involving the sale and purchase of government securities. This helps determine the liquidity of the banks, which affects their power to make loans and advances. The Bank can also influence banks and other licensed deposit takers to restrict lending or to favour certain business categories (eg exporters).

The central bank is used in mixed economies for implementing, and in some cases, developing monetary policy. It may use direct interventionist methods which are often discriminatory in effect. For instance, it may place ceilings on the level of bank lending, require the placing of special deposits by commercial banks at the central bank, or may arrange more favourable borrowing terms for exporters. For some years, the Bank of England has tended to move away from such direct means and, at the the government's request, has depended very much upon interest rate policy. It has the role of setting interest rates at a rate compatible with the government's inflation target. The mechanism for achieving this is the sale and purchase of government securities. If wishing to reduce liquidity and the demand for money, the Bank will raise interest rates by restricting the supply of securities. It will then ease any shortage of funds by lending – as 'lender of last resort' – to institutions at higher interest rates.

Many central banks, to varying extents, also have a role as supervisor of the country's banking system. Broadly, this is concerned not only with financial stability, but also with the reputation of the country's banking system.

(b) *Advantages*

Full or a high measure of independence for central banks is argued for on the grounds that this can prevent the worst monetary excesses, in some cases resulting in hyperinflation. The highly independent Bundesbank owes its origins to the economic (and political) experiences of Germany in the 1920s. High levels of existing public expenditure commitments combined with electoral pressures (and other factors) build in strong underlying inflationary pressures. An independent central bank is seen as an essential counterweight to the potentially reckless decisions of politicians. As well as avoiding the worst excesses, a strong central bank is regarded as vital for the shorter-term stability of domestic prices and the currency, and so is important to overseas trade. Any government wishing to reduce an already high rate of inflation will, however, have to listen carefully to the advice of its central bank if it is to have any real success.

All of this does not mean that the central bank does or should set the main objectives of government economic policy. This is still the province of the government; it might set a target for inflation and the central bank would then develop monetary policy accordingly.

Disadvantages

Arguments against independence for the central bank are that it is an unelected body and so does not have the open responsibility of politicians. This, however, is only partly true. The largely independent Federal Reserve Bank of the USA is very conscious of its public profile and wishes to maintain its professional reputation. Danger in this respect is minimised by the formal publication of decisions and recommendations of the central bank.

It is also argued that in practice the central bank would be setting the parameters of monetary policy and effectively removing it from government control. Further, it is claimed that central bank views on monetary policy could be in conflict with other economic objectives of the government. A central bank may, for instance, be concerned mainly with achieving a low level of inflation while the government is concerned also with economic growth and reducing the numbers of those unemployed. If monetary policy is followed slavishly, the result could be prolonged recession and heavy under-utilisation of resources.

Conclusions

The case for and against independence rests largely on what in practice 'independence' actually means. Formal independence could be much diminished by the way in which the appointment and re-appointment of top bank officials is made, or through failure to publish the bank's recommendations. Monetary policy must be co-ordinated with other aspects of macroeconomic policy. Failure to do this could mean, for instance, that inflation targets are being undermined by inappropriate or ill-timed tax cuts. The existence of an independent central bank can only go some way towards ensuring effective economic management.

Chapter 11

12

(a) National income can be defined as gross national product (GNP) at factor cost less depreciation. The gross national product is a calculation of the overall level of activity in an economy, taking into account the following components:

Total consumption by households	(C)
Total expenditure on investment	(I)
Total government expenditure	(G)
Exports	(X)
Imports	(M)
Income from property abroad	

This can be summarised in the following equation (ignoring income from property abroad):

$$GNP = C + I + G + (X - M)$$

To gain a true picture of economic activity, we must consider only net investment, ie investment in new capital goods less an allowance for old capital goods that are wearing out (which can be considered as disinvestment). As a result the aggregate depreciation in the economy is deducted from GNP to give national income.

Three sets of statistics can be used to calculate GNP. Firstly, it is calculated by measuring the total *expenditure* in the economy by households, firms and the government. This figure is adjusted to take into account imports and exports: exports are merely expenditure in the economy by foreign consumers, and imports can best be considered as negative exports. Income from property abroad refers to rewards paid by foreigners to domestic households for the use of domestic factors of production. Expenditure-based GNP measures what the

NOTES

spending agents in the economy have paid out for the goods and services they have consumed. Consequently, since goods and services are sold to spending agents gross of indirect taxes, expenditure-based GNP will include an indirect tax element. To make expenditure-based GNP comparable to other methods of GNP calculation, the figures have to be adjusted to remove the indirect tax element (and also, conversely, any element of subsidy). With-tax GNP is known as GNP at market prices, and GNP net of tax as GNP at factor cost (ie GNP adjusted to represent that portion of expenditure received by firms).

Secondly, GNP is calculated by measuring the total income received by households and firms. Since all expenditure in an economy which is not used to pay for imports must be received by participants in that economy, income-based GNP should have the same value as expenditure-based GNP. There is no need to adjust income-based GNP for indirect taxes and subsidies since the government will already have collected its indirect taxes from expenditure before it is received by households and firms as income. Imports can be completely ignored since income cannot naturally include money paid out to foreign countries (and expenditure-based GNP takes imports out of consideration by deducting them from exports).

Thirdly, GNP is calculated by measuring the output from firms in the economy. Since expenditure in the economy, less any amounts spent on imports and to pay indirect taxes, must be paid to firms in exchange for goods, we would expect the total amounts of goods sold to be equal to expenditure-based GNP. However, it must be taken into account that the latter also includes income from property abroad.

(b) The three approaches for calculating GNP generally do not produce the same results in practice, and can only be reconciled by introducting residual errors. There are a number of difficulties in collecting the statistical information, as follows.

(i) Some of the definitions are arbitrary, for example:

(1) production only includes goods and services paid for and not work done by individuals for their own benefit; and imputed or notional value is usually given to such work;

(2) goods which have a serviceable life of several years are included in national income at their full value in the year in which they were bought, although in fact they will render services over a number of years;

(3) government services which are not paid for (eg the police) are included in national income at cost.

(ii) Much of the raw data are anyway incomplete and inaccurate; income-based GNP, for example, is compiled partially from tax returns; other data is based on estimates.

(iii) There is a serious danger of double-counting: if a firm buys vegetables from a farmer to produce soup, both the output of the vegetables by the farmer and the output of the vegetables by the firm in the form of soup will be included in output-based GNP.

(iv) Although transfer payments (ie the transfer of income from one person to another, for instance from a taxpayer to a person getting social security) do not affect national income, net transfer payments from abroad increase the total size of a nation's income and they should be calculated.

(v) National income includes a rise in the value of stocks; since this does not reflect real income, it should not be included.

NOTES

Chapter 12

13

> **Tutorial note**
>
> Part (a) looks at the importance of investment as a component of aggregate demand and its effect on the productive potential and therefore the growth rate of the economy. Our suggested solution uses a production possibility curve as illustration here. Alternative illustrations of the multiplier effect could be used. In part (b), we consider the various methods the government might use to influence the level of business investment, concentrating in particular on the level of interest rates and business confidence in the economy.

(a) Investment represents one of the main injections into the circular flow of income. Investment, whether undertaken by the government or by private businesses, is one of the key components of aggregate demand and any change in its level will have a multiple effect on the level of national income.

In addition, investment is important in determing the long-term growth rate of an economy. It can be seen as current consumption forgone in order to achieve a higher rate of growth and a higher level of consumption in the future. This is because investment increases the productive potential of the economy, increasing the capital to produce and therefore to consume. This may be illustrated using a production possibility curve as below.

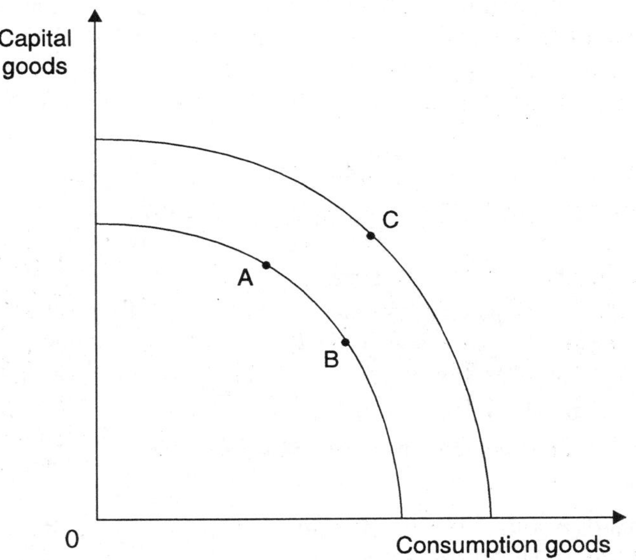

An economy choosing to produce at a point such as B will have a higher current level of consumption, but a lower growth rate, than an economy choosing to produce at point A. The higher level of investment at A will enable the economy to achieve an outward movement of the entire curve and so consume a higher level of both capital and consumer goods in future, such as at C.

Investment is important in raising the economy's productive potential. not only by increasing the size of the capital stock, but also by accelerating the rate of technical progress. This is because any new investment will tend to incorporate the most recent technological developments. New technology tends to reduce the costs of production and consumers will benefit, not only from any cost savings which are passed on in the form of lower prices, but also from any new or improved products which become available as a result.

(b) There are a number of ways in which the government might seek to encourage a higher level of business investment. One of the first options it might consider is to control interest rates. The rate of interest is often a major factor in determining the level of business investment, which will only be undertaken if the expected return from the investment exceeds the anticipated cost of financing it. The rate of interest represents the cost of funds: the lower the interest rate, the more new investments will be considered worthwhile.

Although the government may attempt to stimulate investment by reducing the rate of interest, it may be unsuccessful where the level of business confidence is low. If the economic outlook is poor or uncertain, firms are unlikely to be willing to undertake new or additional investment as they cannot be confident of enough demand for the output the investment will generate. For this reason the government will attempt to encourage business confidence, for example by announcing a credible economic policy for sustained growth. The ability of the government to meet its policy targets will also have a major influence on business expectations. Consequently, its success in stabilising the economy, controlling inflation and so on will be an important factor in determining business behaviour.

The government can provide direct encouragement to businesses, for example by offering investment grants or by providing tax incentives. In practice, the widespread use of grants and generous capital allowances does not appear to have had a significant effect on the overall volume of investment. However, the incentives offered to businesses to invest in particular areas as part of the government's regional policy has had some success in influencing location decisions.

The government might also try to encourage investment indirectly by influencing the volume of consumption. Policies to keep the level of consumer spending down would mean higher levels of saving; this may encourage higher levels of investment through the increased availability of funds.

Chapter 13

14

> **Tutorial note**
>
> The natural rate of unemployment is a situation where the labour market is in equilibrium in the sense that all those willing and capable of working at the existing wage rate can get jobs. It does not mean that no one is unemployed, but that such unemployment as there is could be seen as voluntary.
>
> Answers relating the natural rate of unemployment to the intersection of the Phillips curve and the unemployment axis are also acceptable.

(a) The economist Phillips noted a relationship between the rate of inflation and the rate of unemployment. The higher the first, the lower the second, and vice versa.

However, Phillips' hypothesis has been challenged because it did not hold up in the UK during the late 1960s and early 1970s when rising inflation was accompanied by rising unemployment. It was argued that inflationary expectations and the natural rate of unemployment conspired to oppose the theory.

Looked at using the diagram below, it was suggested that if the rate of unemployment was 5%, an attempt to reduce it to, say, 3% would lead to inflation as suggested by Phillips' theory. The attempt results in a move along PC_1 to 3% unemployment and 3% inflation. However, this inflation then becomes the norm and workers demand higher wages to compensate. Employers then realise that their higher sales prices are being devalued by paying higher wages and, overall, the unemployment rate rises to 5% again, but at a 3% inflation rate.

NOTES

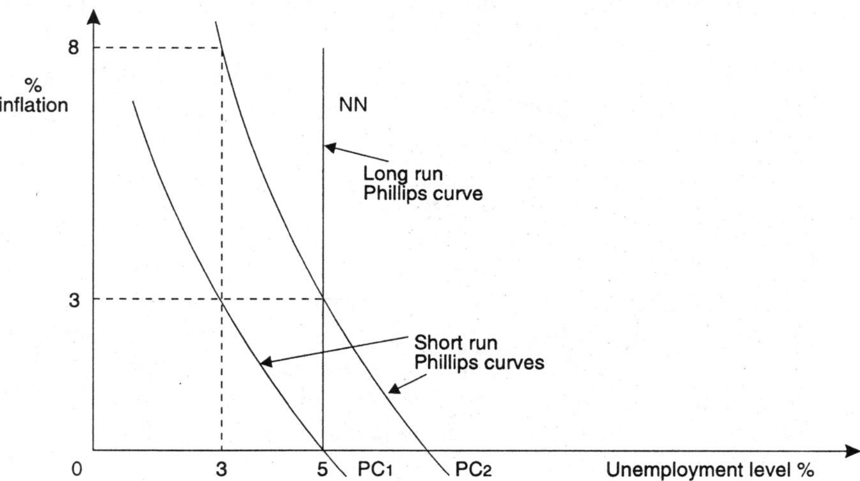

In essence a new curve, PC_2, has been created by the inflationary expectations. The natural rate of unemployment is therefore the rate at which there is no further pressure on inflation to increase.

(b) Any attempt to reduce unemployment below the level of the natural rate by increases in aggregate demand will only fuel inflation further. Short-term movements along the existing curve will simply result in new curves with ever higher inflationary expectations and no longer-term benefit to the rate of unemployment.

Therefore, it seems that macroeconomic demand side policies can have little or no impact on the natural level of unemployment. Specific policies have to be thought up to make work more attractive to the unemployed and to make workers more attractive to prospective employers if the natural rate of unemployment is to be reduced.

As for the unemployed, such policies could be both carrot and stick types of policy. For example, carrots might include improving communications about job opportunities and giving financial assistance for relocation to areas which are relatively short of labour. Sticks might include a reduction in unemployment benefits which would alter the balance between income when out of work and income when in work, making finding a job more important and attractive. A reduction in the rate of personal income tax would also improve work incentives.

Supply side measures can be used to increase the flexibility of the labour market. For employers, training and other skills programmes would make labour more employable. Also, specific subsidies could be given to employers to increase numbers employed. In the UK this policy has been used to try to reduce unemployment in certain areas of the country.

15

Tutorial note

Inflation is a situation of rising prices. One cause may well be too much money chasing too few goods, but that is not the definition of inflation.

(a) Inflation can be defined as a rise in the overall price level of goods and services. Normally, the rise would have to continue over a sustained period before it would be described as inflation.

A one-off rise in the price level would not generally be regarded as inflation. For example, raising taxes is considered to be a deflationary act on the part of government. However, the immediate impact of an increase in indirect taxes is to increase prices. In practice, inflation is measured by means of price indices which would include the effect of indirect taxes. Therefore, it can be seen that the practical view of inflation has moved away slightly from the pure economic one.

Economic theorists would generally recognise three potential causes of inflation, although there is much debate as to whether the third cause listed below is a genuine one. The three causes are:

(i) demand-pull;

(ii) cost-push;

(iii) an increase in the money supply.

Demand-pull inflation occurs when demand exceeds supply, leading to a rise in prices in an attempt to restore equilibrium. Examples of things which might lead to demand-pull inflation are excessive government spending and expectations of further inflation. The latter could induce people to buy goods early in order to get them at a lower price; this creates the already anticipated price rises.

Cost-push inflation occurs when the cost of production of goods and services rises, regardless of their relative supply. The prices of goods and services are pushed up as companies try to maintain their profit margins. Examples of cost-push demand are an increase in wages, possibly caused by the relative power of workers and unions compared with employers, and increases in raw material costs such as the rise in oil prices in the 1970s.

Finally, monetarists would argue that inflation is caused by increases in the money supply on the basis of the equation MV = PT. If T, the number of transactions, and V, the velocity of money in circulation are constant, the effect of an increase in M, the supply of money, is to increase P, the price level.

(b) Inflation can be costly to a country in terms of its balance of payments when its inflation is at a higher level than that of its international competitors. Its products become less competitive and its exports decline. Also, higher prices in the home market attract imports.

Inflation can also lead to a redistribution of wealth. For example, those people with fixed incomes, such as many pensioners, find the relative value of their income declining in terms of the goods that it will buy. Inflation can lead to an unplanned redistribution of income in several ways.

First, employees in a strong negotiating position are able to increase their wages to counteract the adverse effects of inflation. In general, you might think that those with economic power would tend to gain more than the weak during times of inflation than at other times.

Secondly, creditors gain at the expense of debtors. Since the value of money effectively falls during times of inflation, the real value of a debt becomes less over time.

The value of assets which increase in value in line with or above the general rate of inflation becomes greater. For example, in the UK there has been a tendency for people to put a substantial proportion of their savings into property because houses have usually risen in value faster than the general level of inflation. This redistribution into property is arguably not promising if the country's productive capacity is to be retained or increased. At any rate, the housing slump of the 90s made it a less attractive proposition.

Inflation erodes the value of money and therefore makes it more difficult for it to act as a store of wealth and a medium of exchange. At the extreme, during times of hyperinflation such as in Germany in the early 1920s and South American countries in the 1980s, money can become so useless that people resort generally to barter.

In general, it is not inflation itself which is the problem. It is the fact that the inflation is unexpected which causes the most difficulty. If inflation were known in advance, then people could, in theory at least, compensate for it.

Also, differing rates of inflation between different countries or different sectors cause problems, especially of redistribution. If all areas had the same rate of inflation, many of the problems would disappear.

Chapter 14

16

The Keynesian approach to the demand for money is outlined in his theory of liquidity preference. The theory states that money in the form of cash holdings (liquid funds) is demanded by the individual for two main reasons. The first reason is transactionary; that is, for the purposes of undertaking day-to-day purchasing transactions. Keynes argues that the quantity of money required for such purposes is relatively stable in the short run, but does depend on price expectations. Where the individuals believe prices are likely to rise in the near future, their transactionary demand for money will rise to facilitate stocking up on items due to rise in price. In other words, in inflationary times the transactionary demand for money is higher than during a time of stable prices.

The second reason given for holding money is a precautionary one, whereby a stock of liquid funds will be held to guard against future uncertainties in income flows and expenses. Generally speaking, in a stable economy, the demand for money for such purposes is minimal.

Keynes further argues that all money not held in liquid form is invested in bonds which yield returns in the form of interest. Individuals, therefore, in opting to hold liquid funds must forego the potential interest their money could earn if invested. In consequence, the liquidity preference or demand curve for money is downward sloping, as shown in Figure 1.

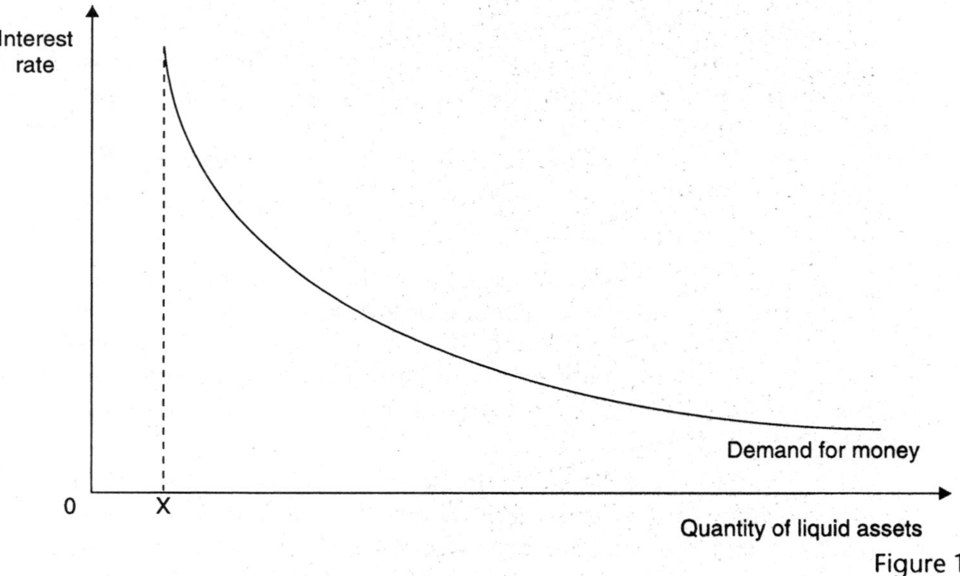

Figure 1

Although the diagram shows that, as a general rule, higher interest rates are associated with a lower demand for money, a certain minimal quantity of money (X) is required for daily purposes, and even if interest rates rise further, the demand for money will be unchanged. In other words, at a certain level of interest rate the liquidity preference curve becomes vertical. The policy implications of the Keynesian approach are that changes in the supply of money will affect the circular flow of income and therefore national income only indirectly, via the interest rate. This implication arises because of Keynes' assumption that the money supply is fixed by government at any particular time, and changes in the supply will lead to changes in interest rates. This only indirectly affects the demand for money and therefore goods and services, as can be seen clearly in Figure 2.

NOTES

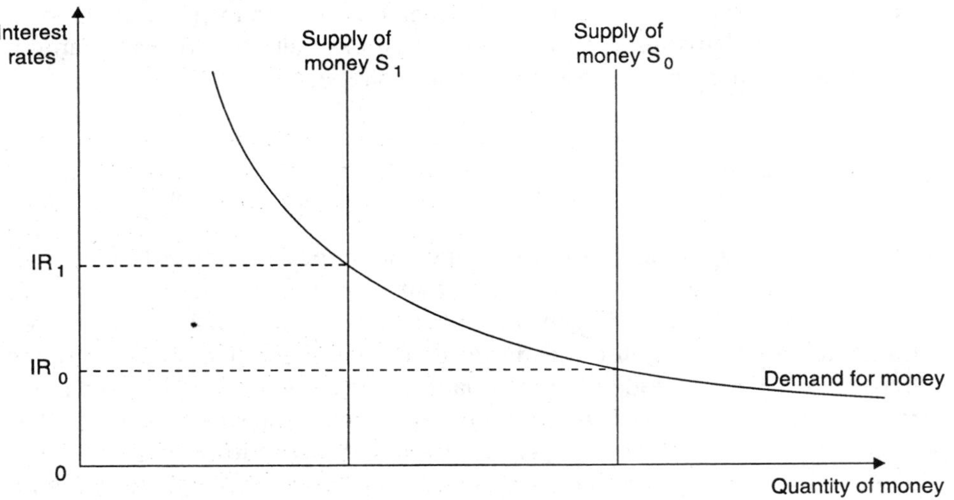

Figure 2

Chapter 15

17

Tutorial note

The limiting phrase 'from the personal sector' needs to be borne in mind. The question essentially involves the respective merits and weaknesses of income taxes and expenditure taxes for raising additional revenue.

You should note that while income taxes can easily be made progressive, taxes on general expenditure (eg VAT) tend to be regressive. The question also gives the opportunity to discuss the disincentive effects of taxes on work effort, and the incentive to save under expenditure taxes. When answering the question you need not discuss forms of public expenditure.

Generally, the choice of tax should agree with the principles of ideal taxation, that is it should be reasonably fair, to minimise distortion of trade and impairment to the functioning of the economy, and be efficient as a means of raising revenue. At the same time, the tax should raise, or contribute to raising, the level of revenue needed to implement public policy. Income tax and expenditure taxes each have their merits and drawbacks in this area.

(a) As a progressive means of taxation, income tax is considered to be relatively fair and equitable, as it is levied according to the ability to pay. However, since the reduction of the top rate of tax to 40% in the UK it is now only mildly progressive, but it can redistribute income, if that is the aim. The more it is effective as a means of redistribution, the more effect there will be on consumption patterns. There may, for instance, be a transfer of funds from those with a relatively high MPS to those with a distinctly high MPC.

Income tax tends to act as a stabiliser in the economy, with more money being taken out of the system in a boom, and less in a recession. Taxpayers generally are aware of their tax liability for the forthcoming financial year and can plan accordingly.

On the whole it is probably less inflationary than indirect taxes. In a situation of relatively weak labour markets it is difficult for worker groups to pass on the burden of higher income tax through wage increases. At the same time, indirect taxes may well result in a rise in the RPI, which is the trigger for inflationary adjustments in the system.

Against this, there is likely to a high level of awareness by individuals of their tax burden, which is enhanced by the political emphasis placed on income tax rates. Income tax can be a disincentive to work, especially for those entering a relatively low tax threshold or at marginal points eg moving from 25% to 40% liability. The income tax burden could affect geographic and occupational labour mobility. There may not be enough inducement for people to undergo expensive training programmes to improve their skills. If the tax rate is high compared to overseas countries, it may result in emigration of skilled and professional workers.

Income tax tends to have high collection costs, especially higher rate tax assessments. Taxpayer self-assessments are intended to contain such costs.

As a method of raising tax, income tax is rather inflexible, especially in the time it takes to implement any changes. The ability to adjust allowances and introduce new allowances makes the system more flexible.

The high level of awareness of burden means that there is a strong incentive to look for avoidance schemes, ie the establishment of legal loopholes to reduce total revenue. Also, very high tax rates may encourage tax evasion, ie the non-reporting of legally taxable income.

(b) Expenditure taxes may take the form of VAT, excise duties on beer and spirits, and import duties.

A major merit is that by raising revenue through taxing expenditure rather than income, the individual is left with the choice as to how income should be spent. This is particularly the case when taxes on expenditure focus mainly on non-essentials.

There tends to be a low level of awareness of the amount of tax which is actually being paid – certainly in comparison to income tax.

Expenditure taxes can be used to encourage or discourage the production and consumption of certain goods or services, eg the high rate of tax on cigarettes.

Although there is some evasion, for example of VAT payments by firms, on the whole the level of evasion is low.

Expenditure taxes can be used as a flexible policy instrument, so that rates of tax can be changed at short notice.

However, such taxes generally are regressive, being a greater burden on low-income earners than on high-income earners. This will be the more so if taxes are imposed on basic commodities. The regressive feature could, of course, be designed deliberately as an offset to a progressive system of income tax.

The revenue taken out is subject to the variability of spending. If demand is price-inelastic, this will be less so; if price elastic, more so.

Inevitably, there will be some impact on trade and the workings of the free market, depending on how differential the taxes are. The more general the expenditure taxes, the more impartial the effect. Certain taxes are, in fact, highly selective, eg beer is heavily taxed, while books and newspapers are exempt. The incidence of a tax will often be shared, that is part of the tax will be borne by the seller; this is dependent on the seller's bargaining power.

Chapter 16

18

> **Tutorial note**
>
> The prime justification of international trade is comparative advantage. This benefits the greater number through more efficient use and distribution of resources, though there will be individual losers.

(a) International trade started because of the diversity of conditions between different countries. It enabled countries to obtain resources/goods which they were unable to produce for themselves, because of climate, resource differences, or because they lacked the skills or know-how. It also enabled them to obtain goods from abroad more cheaply than they could be produced at home. International trade depends not only on this absolute advantage but, more importantly, on comparative advantage.

Within a medical research organisation the leading research scientist also might happen to be the organisation's best computer operator. Obviously the research scientist's comparative advantage is greater in research and so he or she should concentrate on that. This enables him or her to provide a relatively rarer capability and so increases the value of the organisation. Someone else should be employed as a computer operator. Applying this principle at the international level, countries should specialise in what they are relatively best at, rather than what they are absolutely best at. Earlier in this century, the USA, with its almost complete self-sufficiency in natural resources, could produce most products more cheaply than all other countries. Yet it was to its overall benefit to import a range of goods and to concentrate its efforts on those products in which its relative advantage was greatest.

Comparative cost relates to the opportunity cost of producing goods; expressed in alternative terms, each country should specialise in the supply of goods and services in which it has the lowest opportunity cost ratio. The countries so operating will all benefit and total output will be higher than otherwise would be the case. Maximum mutual benefit will occur when the rate of exchange of one good for another lies between the respective opportunity cost ratios of any two trading countries.

Comparative advantage and the process of international trade work to the advantage of the greater number, so there may be some individual losers. Agricultural workers might become unemployed as a country switches trading emphasis and resources into economically more advantageous industrial products. In the longer run, the greater number of people are likely to benefit from the change of trading emphasis, given the existing opportunity cost ratio.

It could be that, as one country specialises in the production of A, economies of scale reduce the cost of a unit of A. This would mean improved efficiency in the use of resources, so reducing output costs and making possible lower selling prices.

Given the high minimum efficient scale in many industries, closed domestic markets would result in much supply being in the hands of monopolists. International trade stimulates competition, leading to improved operating efficiency, innovation in the means of production and supply, and perhaps also better quality of output.

For the potential benefits of international trade to be realised, there must also be a free movement of investment funds between nations, with funds being attracted to those activities which offer the greatest return.

Constraints on economic activity arising from resource mis-match between countries can also be overcome by international trade. A country with resource shortages, eg of certain raw materials, might be obliged to suffer limitations on industrial activity, unless it can make good the deficit from abroad. Countries in surplus in those resources can export them to countries in need.

Consumers benefit from world trade. There is a resulting increase in the choice of different goods, as well as increased diversity available within each product group. There can be greater innovation in product design. Furthermore, any cost reductions resulting from specialisation should benefit the consumer.

(b) The potential benefits to business from international trade come from the opportunities available to those operating in world markets, as well as from the increased competition. Any restrictions on trade may not permit the movement into a country of certain goods, but may permit the setting up of subsidiaries by foreign-owned companies in order to manufacture and market within the host country. The removal of trade (and financing) restrictions enable companies to make more rational decisions about how they will develop and operate throughout the world.

For domestic producers, the existence of competition from abroad can be an advantage. It can help to keep home suppliers on their toes and make them use more efficient methods and adopt innovatory ideas for products and means of production and supply.

The availability of world markets can enable a firm, already the leader of its industry in the home market, to expand abroad and so exploit economies of scale. It is then more likely to expand in its core activities, in which its strengths are greatest, rather than attempt to diversify into more peripheral activities, in which it may have noticeable weaknesses.

Domestic producers will also be freer in seeking out optimal means of fulfilling resource needs. A wider range of suppliers will be available, and they will need to compete with each other on price, quality and reliability of supply. New ideas on product and component design and development are more likely to be produced. In a closed economy some input needs might not be met, or might be supplied at excessively high prices.

Input costs should fall as world trade increases, while export possibilities make expansion of sales easier. The resulting economies of scale and improved efficiency should result in lower (real) selling prices. This in turn provides the basis for further expansion. In addition, if world trade is supported by the free movement of investment funds, it will enable firms to raise funds where the cost is most favourable. In this way constraints upon business expansion are lessened or removed.

Chapter 17

19

Tutorial note

In (a), the terms of trade are affected by movements in the relative prices of exports and imports. A further factor is a change in the composition of exports or imports. In relation to part (b), the key point is the change in the relative elasticities of demand for exports and imports.

(a) The terms of trade indicate the rate at which a country's exports are exchanged for its imports, ie the volume of other countries' products which a nation can obtain in exchange for a given volume of its own products. It may be measured against any other particular country or in terms of all other countries (in the aggregate) with which it trades.

If country A must produce 1.3 units of goods to obtain 1 unit of goods from country B, then the terms of trade are 1.3 units of A goods: 1 unit of B goods.

If the ratio changes so that 1.4 of A's goods are exchanged for 1 of B's goods for example, the terms of trade for A have deteriorated.

This, however, is only in terms of the volume of goods exchanged. Exchange also involves prices. Basically, the terms of trade are measured as:

$$\frac{\text{Unit value of exports}}{\text{Unit value of imports}}$$

In practice, the terms of trade are measured as the ratio of an index of export prices to an index of import prices – multiplied by 100. The indices are based on a sophisticated system of weighting for the relative importance of the various goods entering into import and export trade.

So, for a particular point in time, the terms of trade can be calculated as:

$$\frac{\text{Index of export prices}}{\text{Index of import prices}} \times 100$$

Movement in the terms of trade, for instance between 1996 and 1997, would be calculated as:

$$\frac{\text{Price of exports 1997/Price of exports 1996}}{\text{Price of imports 1997/Price of imports 1996}}$$

Changes in a country's terms of trade arise from changes in prices of imports and exports, as well as changes in the composition of exports and imports.

A rise in a country's terms of trade could result from:

(i) export prices rising while import prices fall;

(ii) export prices rising by more than import prices rise; or

(iii) export prices falling by less than import prices fall.

A rise in export prices relative to import prices could be the result of the exchange rate strengthening. Overseas buyers will then have to use more of their currency to buy UK goods. This could arise from an increased volume of demand for British goods which is forcing up the price of sterling. It could be that there is speculation in favour of sterling. Alternatively, it could be that the authorities are following a high exchange rate policy and are using the reserves and higher interest rates, if necessary, to support the domestic currency.

An alternative price effect could be through a rise in the price of imported commodities. The result would be to depress the terms of trade.

Over a period of time there could be a change in the composition of exports, so that more higher-value goods and less low-value goods are being exported. Alternatively, country A could have become more self-sufficient in high-grade, high-price products so that the average price of imports has fallen.

(b) The effect on a country's balance of trade of a fall in its terms of trade would depend on the price elasticity of demand of the goods traded.

A fall in the terms of trade indicates that import prices have risen relative to export prices. Alternatively the country's exchange rate could have depreciated.

With the fall in the terms of trade the country has become more competitive in world markets. On the face of it, this would result in a rise in the volume of exports and a fall in the volume of imports. The effect on values would depend on respective price elasticities of demand. If the demand for imported goods is price elastic, the volume and value of imports will fall. If the demand for imports is price inelastic, as with raw materials and a wide range of foodstuffs, the volume of demand may fall little if at all and the value of imports will rise. If export demand is price elastic, both the volume and value of exports will rise. If export demand is price inelastic, the total value of exports will fall.

The overall effect on the balance of trade will depend on this respective price elasticity of demand for exports and imports. On the basis that the sum of these elasticities is greater than unity, a fall in the terms of trade will result in an improvement in the balance of trade.

20

> **Tutorial note**
>
> The words 'relative advantages' have been interpreted as referring to points both for and against. Exchange rates and their adjustment are sometimes considered as the solution to all economic ills. Highly interventionist policies on exchange rates have their own danger: the exchange rate has a particular function to perform in the economic system. Unless an exchange rate system, either fixed or floating, is supported by sound and effectively applied economic policy, it is doomed to failure.

(a) Fixed exchange rates operate through an official exchange rate set by the authorities. Dealing rates are allowed to move a given percentage on either side of that rate. If the actual rate moves to a point nearing the outer limit, official intervention takes place, ie by use of exchange reserves or by a joint support arrangement between the central banks of different countries. In this way there will be some movement from day to day in the actual exchange rate. It is intended that at intervals the official rate will be adjusted to fit in with changed economic circumstances.

A floating exchange rate means that in theory the rate will find its own level according to the laws of supply and demand. Exchange rates then serve as the balancing mechanism for the complete spectrum of internationally traded goods, services and capital movements. Speculative money flows – moving between centres, seeking out the most attractive (short-term) return – are now of greater significance in determining (shorter-term) exchange rates than transactions in goods and services. In practice, there will be official intervention to avoid the more extreme day-to-day movements in the currency, without necessarily attempting to keep it within a certain range.

A fixed exchange rate lessens uncertainty about the exchange rate and so encourages overseas trade. In certain respects it also imposes discipline on those countries with trade deficits, since at some stage deflationary measures will have to be taken to restore equilibrium on the balance of payments. Therefore, the government might need to raise interest rates or take action to reduce domestic demand (hoping thereby to cut the demand for imports as well as to reduce inflationary pressures). The alternative would be a forced devaluation of the currency.

A fixed exchange rate might operate well if the official rate has been set close to purchasing power parity. This truly reflects relative economic performance (differing levels of economic efficiency and of inflation), but can soon be out of alignment. With an over-valued currency, once the market exchange rate begins to move towards the outer limit, speculation may become intense. Considerable official reserves are necessary to support a currency and even these may not be enough given the volume of speculation that can take place through the movement of massive capital flows. For political reasons, governments often delay taking corrective action and when they do it may not be sufficiently effective. If the currency is under-valued, this can result in excessive domestic expansion and investment which is not justified in the longer term. When it is necessary to readjust a falsely valued currency, the economic consequences can be severe; devaluation might need to be accompanied by strong domestic deflationary measures. In the past, countries with fixed exchange rates have often delayed for too long the adjustment of the official exchange rate, so increasing the severity of the deflationary measures.

So far as exchange rates are a true reflection of relative economic efficiency, the continuous adjustment of the exchange rate (floating) permits an economy to adapt according to current international pressures. So, in theory, the country should be able to avoid periodic traumatic readjustment and the government has more freedom to follow domestic economic policies, eg for growth or high employment. It will also have less need for official reserves. Floating exchange rates may help to insulate a country against inflation abroad. Higher prices of imported goods may be offset by a rise in the exchange rate, but a country on a fixed exchange rate would import inflation.

The argument against a floating exchange rate is that there will be greater day-to-day fluctuation in the exchange rate, which will cause much uncertainty. Whether this is so would depend greatly on the economic policies followed.

The readjustment process does not always work that well. It depends very much on elasticity of demand for imports and exports as well as on elasticity of supply. If domestic inflation is not controlled, the competitive advantage from a depreciating currency will be lost and the currency will merely fall further. The situation could continue to deteriorate, with rising import prices, higher wages and higher domestic prices. Allowing a currency to float is no substitute for sound domestic economic policies.

Overall, the function of an exchange rate is to facilitate trade and exchange by representing current relative exchange values. Periodic readjustment of fixed exchange rates was intended to overcome their disadvantage in this respect, but governments mostly failed to take the necessary action in time. There is also the problem of setting the rate at a relative level. The growth of vast capital flows has made it more difficult to sustain fixed rates once they come under real pressure. The skilfully managed float, sliding to find its own level, has much to commend it, but this also needs appropriate government policies.

(b) The advantages for individual businesses of a fixed exchange rate are:

(i) certainty and stability: business people can enter into contracts with more certainty, sure of the effects in international exchange terms, and without the need to hedge the risks, for example by forward exchange transactions. Therefore business transactions will be facilitated;

(ii) so far as the official exchange rate is set at an appropriate level and sound economic policies are followed, for a while business may benefit from a relatively stable economic environment.

If, nevertheless, eventually there has to be a devaluation of the currency, the effects on the firm can be considerable. For a while, the fixed exchange rate will to some extent have insulated the firm from international pressures, eg an artificially high exchange rate might have benefited a firm whose main business is importing. Any severe deflationary measure by the government could be highly de-stabilising for trade.

In a system of freely floating exchange rates, fairly continuous adjustment would mean that the exporting/importing firm would be currently and continuously in direct relationship with movements in international markets. The amount of fluctuation in the currency would depend a great deal on how effectively the national economy is managed. However, there would be periods of change, affecting even the normally stable currencies. As already mentioned, business may be able to protect itself against this, at a cost, by entering into forward transactions where the exchange rate is known in advance.

INDEX

F

G

H

I

K

L

M

ORDER FORM

To order your BUSINESS BASICS books, ring our credit card hotline on 0181-740 2211. Alternatively, send this page to our Freepost address or fax it to us on 0181-740 1184.

To: BPP Publishing Ltd, FREEPOST, London W12 8BR **Tel: 0181-740 2211**
Fax: 0181-740 1184

Forenames (Mr / Ms): ____________________

Surname: ____________________

Address: ____________________

Post code: __________ Date of exam (month/year): __________

Please send me the following books:

	Price	*Quantity*	*Total*
Accounting	£13.95	....	....
Human Resource Management	£13.95	....	....
Law	£13.95	....	....
Organisational Behaviour	£13.95	....	....
Economics	£13.95	....	....
Information Technology	£13.95	....	....
Marketing	£13.95	....	....
Quantitative Methods	£13.95	....	....

Please include postage:

UK: £3.00 for first plus £2.00 for each extra	....	....
Europe (inc ROI): £5.00 for first plus £4.00 for each extra	....	....
Rest of the World: £8.00 for first plus £6.00 for each extra	....	....
	Total	

I enclose a cheque for £ ______ or charge to Access/Visa/Switch

Card number | | | | | | | | | | | | | | | | | | | |

Start date (Switch only) __________ Expiry date __________

Issue number (Switch only) __________

Signature ____________________

REVIEW FORM

Name:

College:

We would be grateful to receive any comments you may have on this book. You may like to use the headings below as guidelines. Tear out this page and send it to our Freepost address: **BPP Publishing Ltd, FREEPOST, London W12 8BR.**

Topic coverage

Objectives, activities with solutions, chapter roundups and quizzes

Glossary

Multiple choice and exam style questions

Student-friendliness

Errors (please specify and refer to a page number)

Other